THE AHHIYAWA TEXTS

Society of Biblical Literature

Writings from the Ancient World

Theodore J. Lewis, General Editor

Associate Editors

Edward Bleiberg
Billie Jean Collins
Daniel Fleming
Martti Nissinen
William Schniedewind
Mark S. Smith
Terry Wilfong

Number 28
The Ahhiyawa Texts

The Ahhiyawa Texts

by

Gary Beckman
Trevor Bryce
Eric Cline

Society of Biblical Literature
Atlanta

THE AHHIYAWA TEXTS

Library of Congress Cataloging-in-Publication Data

Beckman, Gary M.
The Ahhiyawa texts / by Gary M. Beckman, Trevor Bryce, Eric H. Cline.
p. cm. — (Society of biblical literature ; no. 28)
Includes bibliographical references and index.
ISBN 978-1-58983-268-8 (paper binding : alk. paper)
1. Hittite language—Texts. 2. Hittites—History. 3. Achaeans—History. I. Bryce, Trevor, 1940- II. Cline, Eric H. III. Title.
P945.A3B43 2011
891′.998—dc23

2011042792

Printed in the United States of America on acid-free, recycled paper conforming to ANSI/NISO Z39.48-1992 (R1997) and ISO 9706:1994 standards for paper permanence.

Contents

ABBREVIATIONS

AA	*Archäologischer Anzeiger*
AfO	*Archiv für Orientforschung*
AnSt	*Anatolian Studies*
AoF	*Altorientalische Forschungen*
ArOr	*Archiv Orientální*
BiOr	*Bibliotheca Orientalis*
BSA	*Annual of the British School at Athens*
CRAIBL	*Comptes rendus de l'Académie des Inscriptions et Belles-lettres (Paris)*
JEOL	*Jaarbericht van het Vooraziatisch-egyptisch Genootschap Ex Oriente Lux*
MAOG	*Mitteilungen der Altorientalischen Gesellschaft*
MDOG	*Mitteilungen der Deutschen Orient-Gesellschaft*
OJA	*Oxford Journal of Archaeology*
OLZ	*Orientalistische Literaturzeitung*
Or	*Orientalia*
OrAnt	*Oriens Antiquus*
PAPS	*Proceedings of the American Philosophical Society*
SMEA	*Studi Micenei ed Egeo-Anatolici*
TUAT	*Texte aus der Umwelt des Alten Testaments*
UF	*Ugarit-Forschungen*
WAW	Writings from the Ancient World
ZA	*Zeitschrift für Assyriologie und vorderasiatsiche Archäologie*

Explanation of Signs and Symbols

Single brackets [ ] enclose restorations.

Angle brackets < > enclose words or signs omitted by the original scribe.

Double angle brackets << >> enclose words or signs added in error by the original scribe.

Parentheses ( ) enclose additions in the English translation.

A row of dots ... indicates gaps in the text or untranslatable words.

^{er} indicates an erasure.

Asterisk indicates a reading supported by examination of a photograph correcting published copy.

List of Illustrations

Series Editor's Foreword

Writings from the Ancient World is designed to provide up-to-date, readable English translations of writings recovered from the ancient Near East.

The series is intended to serve the interests of general readers, students, and educators who wish to explore the ancient Near Eastern roots of Western civilization or to compare these earliest written expressions of human thought and activity with writings from other parts of the world. It should also be useful to scholars in the humanities or social sciences who need clear, reliable translations of ancient Near Eastern materials for comparative purposes. Specialists in particular areas of the ancient Near East who need access to texts in the scripts and languages of other areas will also find these translations helpful. Given the wide range of materials translated in the series, different volumes will appeal to different interests. However, these translations make available to all readers of English the world's earliest traditions as well as valuable sources of information on daily life, history, religion, and the like in the preclassical world.

The translators of the various volumes in this series are specialists in the particular languages and have based their work on the original sources and the most recent research. In their translations they attempt to convey as much as possible of the original texts in fluent, current English. In the introductions, notes, glossaries, maps, and chronological tables, they aim to provide the essential information for an appreciation of these ancient documents.

The ancient Near East reached from Egypt to Iran and, for the purposes of our volumes, ranged in time from the invention of writing (by 3000 B.C.E.) to the conquests of Alexander the Great (ca. 330 B.C.E.). The cultures represented within these limits include especially Egyptian, Sumerian, Babylonian, Assyrian, Hittite, Ugaritic, Aramean, Phoenician, and Israelite. It is hoped that Writings from the Ancient World will eventually produce translations from most of the many different genres attested in these cultures: letters (official and private), myths, diplomatic documents, hymns, law collections, monumental inscriptions, tales, and administrative records, to mention but a few.

Significant funding was made available by the Society of Biblical Literature for the preparation of this volume. In addition, those involved in preparing this volume have received financial and clerical assistance from their respective institutions. Were it not for these expressions of confidence in our work, the arduous tasks of preparation, translation, editing, and publication could not have been accomplished or even undertaken. It is the hope of all who have worked with the Writings from the Ancient World series that our translations will open up new horizons and deepen the humanity of all who read these volumes.

Theodore J. Lewis
The Johns Hopkins University

Preface

This project began in snowy Montreal, during the final dinner held at the workshop on *Mycenaeans and Anatolians in the Late Bronze Age: The Ahhiyawa Question*, organized by Annette Teffeteller at Concordia University in January 2006. We (the three co-authors of this volume) were providentially seated together at the dinner. By the end of the meal, the plan for this volume had been hatched, for in the course of our conversation about the Ahhiyawa texts, the problem of asking American undergraduate students to study these documents had come to the fore. The editions, translations, and discussions of these various texts have been published in a variety of languages, including German, French, Italian, and English. Moreover, they have been published in a multitude of different books and articles scattered across the academic landscape, many in journals not readily available at small college or university libraries. Not since Ferdinand Sommer's book *Die Aḫḫijavā-Urkunden*, published in 1932 and written in German, has any serious attempt been made to collect all of the texts and republish them together in a single place (although see the abbreviated catalogue in Cline 1994: 121–25). We decided that it was time to do something about the situation and to present the texts as a corpus and in one language, with a fresh transliteration and translation of the texts, as well as commentary on each one. We do so in order to make them accessible to graduate students and undergraduates alike, in addition to professional scholars active in related fields, such as Classics and/or Near Eastern archaeology.

After much deliberation, we decided to present the texts following the standard order as set forth by Laroche (1971) in his *Catalogue des Textes Hittites* (CTH), rather than attempting to present them chronologically, since the dating of so many of them is still problematic. For those unfamiliar with the CTH system, we note that the numbering is arranged as follows:

Historical Texts (CTH 1–220)
Administrative Texts (CTH 221–290)
Legal Texts (CTH 291–298)
Lexical Texts (CTH 299–309)

Literary Texts (CTH 310–320)
Mythological Texts (CTH 321–370)
Hymns and Prayers (CTH 371–389)
Ritual Texts (CTH 390–500)
Cult Inventory Texts (CTH 501–530)
Omen and Oracle Texts (CTH 531–582)
Vows (CTH 583–590)
Festival Texts (CTH 591–724)
Texts in Other Languages (CTH 725–830)
Texts of Unknown Type (CTH 831–833)

Of the Ahhiyawa texts presented here, nos. 1–26 have long been known and therefore have CTH numbers. The final texts (nos. 27A–B and 28) are fairly recent discoveries and do not have CTH numbers. In order to create a definitive corpus for these texts, we have now given each of them a new number as well, in the same manner that J. A. Knudtzon long ago numbered the so-called Amarna Letters. Thus, each now has a number within the series AhT 1–28 (not AT, because this is already the siglum for the Alalakh texts).

The translations follow the style of the WAW series; that is, with little or no grammatical commentary and as little use of brackets as possible. Gary Beckman was responsible for these translations, as well as for the transliterations of the texts and the brief introductions to each. Trevor Bryce was responsible for the commentary following each text, which puts each into a larger historical and interpretive framework. Eric Cline was responsible for this preface, the introduction, and the epilogue, as well as for overseeing the project as a whole and shepherding it through the publication process. We are grateful to Dr. Geoff Tully for drawing the maps and to Ted Lewis and Billie Jean Collins for their support and assistance throughout, as well as their patience.

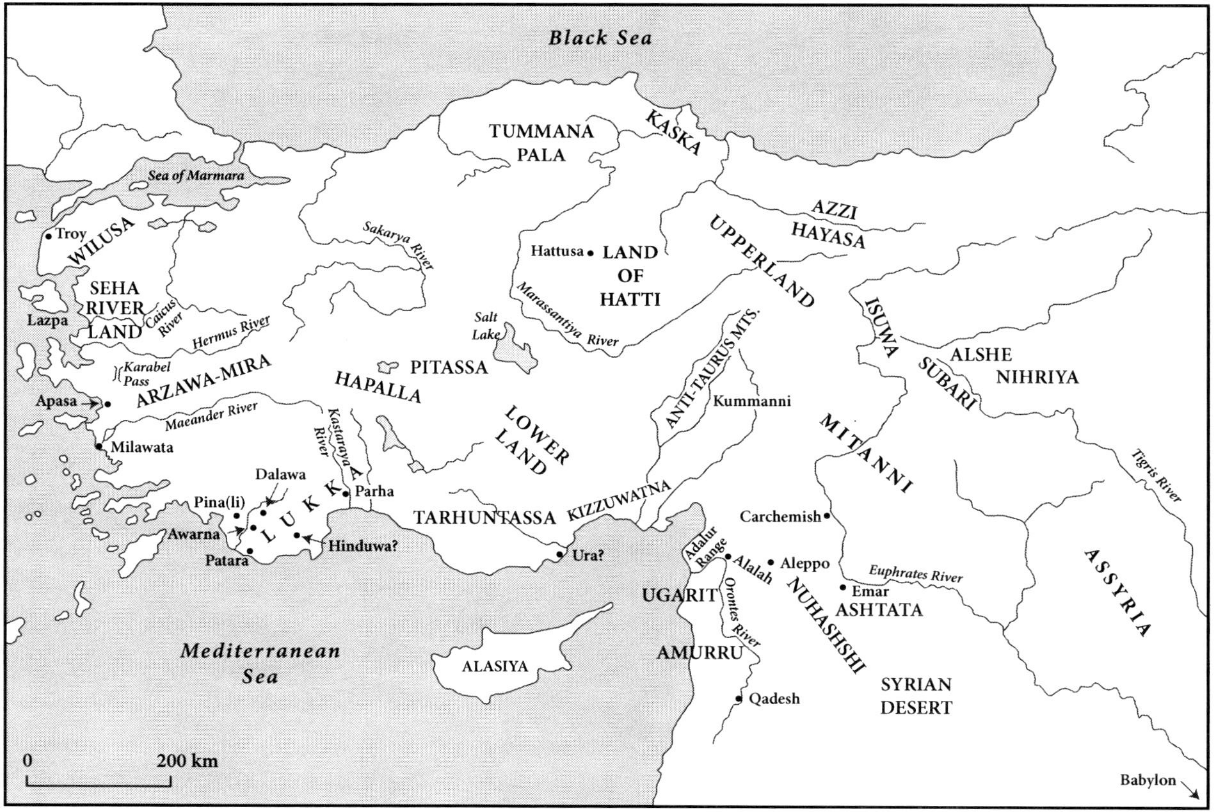

Late Bronze Age Anatolia, northern Syria, and northern Mesopotamia.

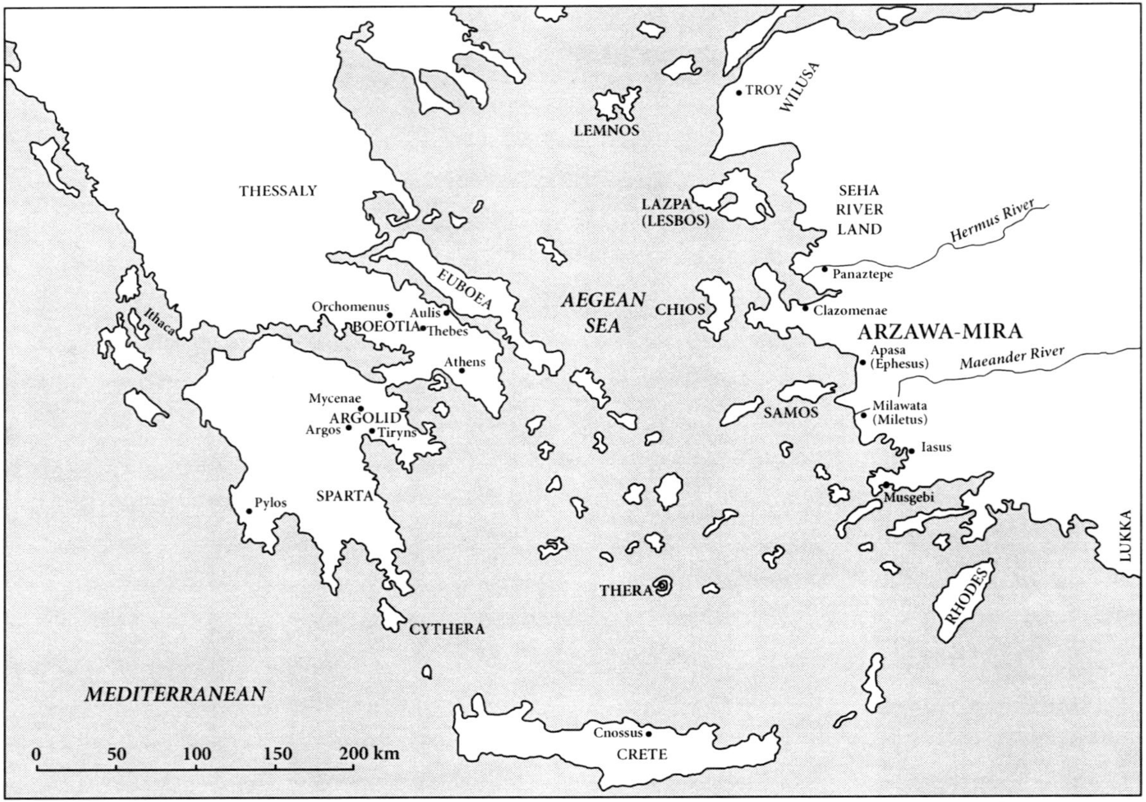

Late Bronze Age Greece and western Anatolia.

Introduction: The Ahhiyawa Problem

The Ahhiyawa Problem—or Ahhiyawa Question, as it is sometimes called—still remains unsolved and unanswered almost a century after it was first introduced. Simply stated, the question asks whether the term "Ahhiyawa" (and the earlier version "Ahhiya"), as found in nearly thirty Hittite texts from the time of Tudhaliya I/II and Arnuwanda I in the late-fifteenth–early-fourteenth century B.C.E. to that of Tudhaliya IV and Suppiluliuma II in the thirteenth century B.C.E., was a reference to the Bronze Age Mycenaeans. If so, was it meant to be a reference to all of the Mycenaeans on mainland Greece and elsewhere? Or, since we know that the Mycenaeans were split up into what were essentially a series of small city-states, was it a reference only to those in a specific region or locality, such as the Peloponnese (e.g., Mycenae), Boeotia (e.g., Thebes), Rhodes, or western Anatolia? Could the meaning have changed over time, as Hittite relations with these foreigners evolved over the centuries? Furthermore, if it was not a reference to the Mycenaeans, then to what—and to whom—did it refer? The discussion is more than merely an academic one because the texts, at least indirectly, may shed light on various aspects of the Trojan War, or at least on the kernels of truth that seem to underlie the story as told to us by Homer.

The origins of the Ahhiyawa Question, and the ensuing debate, go back to 1924, when the Swiss scholar Emil Forrer gave a lecture in Berlin and then published two articles on the topic, in the German periodicals *MDOG* and *OLZ* (1924a, 1924b; see now Beckman forthcoming). Based on his readings of approximately twenty-five texts among the thousands that had been found in the archives of the Hittite capital city Hattusa during the German excavations that had begun at the site in 1906 under the direction of Hugo Winckler, Forrer tentatively linked Ahhiyawa to the Mycenaeans of the Bronze Age Greek mainland, that is, the Achaeans. He also made connections between specific individuals and place names mentioned in the Ahhiyawa texts and those from Greek legends about the Trojan War. These included identifying Lazpa in the Ahhiyawa texts as the island of Lesbos; Taruisa as the city of Troy; Attarissiya and Tawagalawa as the legendary Greek heroes Atreus and Eteokles; and so on.

Forrer was not the first to suggest such possibilities, for Luckenbill—back in 1911—had already suggested a link between Alaksandu in the Ahhiyawa texts and Alexander/Paris, legendary prince of Troy (Luckenbill 1911; see now Beckman forthcoming), a connection which Forrer repeated and endorsed. However, Forrer's articles were the most systematic and thorough studies presented up to that point.

Forrer's suggestions were met with a variety of reactions, ranging from acceptance to disbelief. Reservations were raised almost immediately by a number of scholars, including Kretschmer in 1924 (see also 1935, 1936), who equated Wilusa in the Hittite texts with (W)Ilios/Troy of Greek legend rather than with Elaiusa in Cilicia as per Forrer, and Hrozný in 1929, who linked Milawata in the texts with the city of Miletus in western Anatolia, rather than with the lesser known location of Milyas, as per Forrer (Beckman forthcoming). Forrer presented his thoughts on more relevant texts in 1926 and, following attacks on his work by Friedrich (1927) and Götze (1927a-c), still more texts in 1929 (1929a–b; for the full historiographic discussion, see Beckman forthcoming). Additional relevant texts, or editions of texts, were also studied by Götze in 1928 and 1933 (**AhT 1A–B** and **AhT 3**: the Annals of Mursili II and the Madduwatta text, respectively), as well as by Güterbock in 1936 (**AhT 14**: a possible letter concerning Urhi-Teshshup) and Szemerényi in 1945 (**AhT 2**: the treaty between Tudhaliya IV and Shaushga-muwa of Amurru).

The most vocal of his opponents was Ferdinand Sommer, who in 1932 published a comprehensive volume in German entitled *Die Aḫḫijavā-Urkunden* (i.e., *The Ahhiyawa Documents*), containing translations of all of the texts in question that were available at that time, with his interpretations, including previously unpublished editions of additional Ahhiyawa texts: a letter from a king of Ahhiyawa sent to a Hittite king, perhaps Muwattalli II (**AhT 6**); a letter sent by a Hittite official to a Hittite king, perhaps Hattusili III (**AhT 8**); an edict of Tudhaliya IV (**AhT 11**); a prayer of Mursili II/Muwattalli II/Urhi-Teshshup (**AhT 12**); two letters (**AhT 9–10**); a memorandum (**AhT 13**); a boundary list (**AhT 18**); and two oracle reports (**AhT 20–21**). In his book, Sommer disagreed with nearly all of Forrer's suggestions, and argued that Ahhiyawa was simply an Anatolian state (cf. Bryce 1989a: 297).

As Denys Page records in the first of his Sather Lectures presented at the University of California, Berkeley in 1957–58 (Page 1959), Fritz Schachermeyr summarized the situation in 1935, in his volume *Hethiter und Achäer*. Soon thereafter, Sommer continued his attack, publishing a 128-page article entitled "Aḫḫijawā und kein Ende?" in the journal *Indogermanische Forschungen* in 1937. Since then, the pendulum has swung back and forth, as George Huxley (1960), Gerd Steiner (1964), and others weighed in on the debate (see, e.g., bibliography in Page 1959 and, more recently, in Bryce 1989b), even as additional texts were added to the corpus (e.g., Houwink ten Cate 1983/84; Košak 1982), important joins were made to existing pieces (e.g., Hoffner 1982), and additional learned and knowledgeable voices joined or continued the discussion (e.g., Güterbock 1983, 1984, 1986; Bryce 1989a, 1989b; Steiner 1989, 2007). The most recent survey of the current state of affairs was published by Fischer in 2010, to mixed reviews (see, e.g., Kelder 2010a).

At the moment, as has been stated elsewhere (Cline 1994: 69; 1996: 145), if the Mycenaeans can be equated with the Ahhiyawans (Ahhiyawa = Achaia = Achaeans = Mycenaeans), then there is substantial textual evidence for contact between the Hittites and the Mycenaeans throughout the course of the Late Bronze Age, in a variety of contexts ranging from hostile to peaceful and back again, as will be discussed in the Epilogue below. If, however, the Mycenaeans are not the Ahhiyawans, then they are never mentioned by the Hittites. This, though, seems unlikely, for Ahhiyawa must, essentially by default, be a reference to the Mycenaeans. Otherwise, we would have, on the one hand, an important Late Bronze Age culture not mentioned elsewhere in the Hittite texts (the Mycenaeans) and, on the other hand, an important textually attested Late Bronze Age "state" without archaeological remains (Ahhiyawa).

Unfortunately, particularly in regard to the relationship between the Hittites and Ahhiyawa over time, the precise date of many of the Ahhiyawa texts is unclear. Some can be assigned to a specific period within an individual king's reign, but others only to a king's reign, and still others only to a particular century at best. Bearing these limitations in mind, we might still attempt to order the texts chronologically, as seen in Table 1. Note that the order of the texts is almost certainly subject to change somewhat, especially for those dated only to a particular century. However, the date and order of the most important texts, including the Indictment of Madduwatta, the Annals of Mursili II, the so-called Tawagalawa and Milawata Letters, as well as others, are fairly firmly established now. If Ahhiyawa is equated with the Mycenaeans, as seems likely, these texts can be used to discuss in detail the relations between the Hittites and the Mycenaeans over the course of the Late Bronze Age, as will be done below, after the presentation of the texts themselves.

We are also left with the question of which Mycenaeans were being referred to by the Hittites when they were using the term "Ahhiyawa," for the Mycenaean world was large and not always unified during the centuries of the Late Bronze Age. Previous scholars have attempted to place Ahhiyawa in Rhodes, Thrace, Cilicia, northwest Anatolia, and elsewhere in the Mediterranean region (see maps and references in Niemeier 1998 as well as references in Cline 1994: 69). However, Hawkins, in his 1998 article, while noting that Ahhiyawa is located "'across the sea', and reached at or via the islands," also showed conclusively that there is no room on the Anatolian mainland for Ahhiyawa (Hawkins 1998:

esp. 30–31). In the same year, Niemeier persuasively and logically eliminated all of the other suggested possibilities except for mainland Greece (see previously Bryce 1989b: 3–6; also Mountjoy 1998; Hope Simpson 2003; and now Kelder 2004–2005, 2005, 2010b; contra Steiner 2007, who remains almost the lone voice of dissent).

It now seems most reasonable to identify Ahhiyawa primarily with the Greek mainland, although in some contexts the term "Ahhiyawa" may have had broader connotations, perhaps covering all regions that were settled by Mycenaeans or came under Mycenaean control (see, e.g., Bryce 2011: 10). Furthermore, if Ahhiyawa is primarily on the Greek mainland, and is to be equated with one of the known Mycenaean kingdoms, it seems most likely that it should be identified with Mycenae, as has been suggested by a number of scholars, most recently Kelder (2010b: 93–99), in part because of Mycenae's clear international connections during the Late Bronze Age, including imports found at the site itself (Cline 1994). Arguments for an identification with Boeotian Thebes (Latacz 2004) are not convincing and can be readily dismissed (cf. Kelder 2010b: 88–93).

Kelder, though, has recently suggested that Ahhiyawa was much larger than anyone has supposed to date. He sees it as a "Great Kingdom," ruled from Mycenae, and equates it with essentially the entire Mycenaean world, including "the (larger part of the) Peloponnese, the Thebaid, various islands in the Aegean and Miletus on the Anatolian west coast, with Mycenae as its capital" (Kelder 2010b: 120, cf. also a similar statement on p. viii). Although he is quite correct that "Archaeologically speaking, the Greek mainland in the Late Bronze is remarkably uniform" (Kelder 2010b: 118), and that "the cultural uniformity, the uniformity of the palatial administrations, and the ability to embark on large-scale projects ... allow for some sort of an overarching authority" (Kelder 2010b: 119), it is difficult to see how this entire region could truly have been ruled by a single king. Kelder himself pointed out in earlier articles (and repeats in his recent book) that the existence of a "larger Mycenaean state" ruled by a single *wanax* is not supported by the Linear B texts (Kelder 2005b: 135–38; 2008: 74; 2010b: 20, 119).

However, several years earlier, Kelder (2005, 2006) had proposed a slightly different suggestion, which he also mentions in passing in his book (2010b: 44) and which seems much more compelling. He cited a portion of the Indictment of Madduwatta (**AhT 3**), wherein Beckman (1999: 153) had suggested reconstructing the text to read "100 [chariots and ... infantry] of Attarissiya [drew up]" (Kelder 2005a: 155; 2005b: 139, 144; 2010b: 24; see also Steiner 2007: 597 and, several decades earlier, Güterbock 1983: 138). Attarissiya, as known from this text, is almost certainly to be equated with the unnamed "enemy ruler of Ahhiya," referred to in the oracle text **AhT 22** (§25). Ahhiya is an early, and older, form of the name Ahhiyawa; these two texts are the earliest of all the

Ahhiyawa texts, with one dating to the time of Tudhaliya I/II and the other from just afterward but describing events from his reign.

An updated, but similar, translation from the Indictment of Madduwatta is given in the pages below and can be repeated here, with the bellicose context made clear:

> §12 (obv. 60–65) But [later] Attarissiya, the ruler of Ahhiya, came and was plotting to kill *you*, Madduwatta. But when the father of My Majesty heard, he dispatched Kisnapili, infantry, and chariotry in battle against Attarissiya. And you, Madduwatta, again did not resist Attarissiya, but yielded before him. Then Kisnapili proceeded to rush [...] to you from Hatti. Kisnapili went in battle against Attarissiya. 100 [chariots and ... thousand infantry] of Attarissiya [drew up for battle]. And they fought. One officer of Attarissiya was killed, and one officer of ours, Zidanza, was killed. Then Attarissiya turned [away(?)] from Madduwatta, and he went off to his own land. And they installed Madduwatta in his place once more.

Based upon that reconstruction, that is, that Attarissiya of Ahhiya (Ahhiyawa) may have fielded as many as one hundred chariots, in addition to infantry, Kelder suggested that "the military capacity of Ahhiyawa as indicated in the Hittite texts, as well as certain political and geographical characteristics, point towards a larger entity in the Aegean than anything that is attested in Linear B texts" (Kelder 2005a: 159; see also now comments in Kelder 2010b: 34). He further stated that Ahhiyawa "must have had the military capacity at least three times the size of that of the Kingdom of Pylos. It has already been established that there is no indication in the Linear B texts of such an entity in the Mycenaean world; any evidence for it therefore must be sought elsewhere" (Kelder 2005: 159). He concluded that "the only plausible explanation ... is that Ahhiyawa was more than one of the Mycenaean palatial states" (Kelder 2005a: 158), that is, that "Ahhiyawa must have been a conglomerate of several of these kingdoms" (Kelder 2010b: 44).

While not confirmed by any means, one wonders whether Kelder might have been on to something with this suggestion, despite the fact that he seems to abandon it by the end of his own book. It is quite possible that the entity known as Ahhiyawa to the Hittites (and Tanaja to the Egyptians) may have been larger than any one Mycenaean palatial kingdom and could well have been a unified force comprised of several of them. We need only look at the Mycenaean forces mustered by Agamemnon for the Trojan War, as listed in the Catalogue of Ships in Book II of the *Iliad*, to see that the Mycenaeans were reportedly capable of creating such an entity. Although the *Iliad* was, of course, not written until the eighth century B.C.E. and cannot be used as historical evidence in general, the Catalogue of Ships in specific is regarded by scholars as an authentic piece reflecting Bronze Age realities. If so, someone like Agamemnon (or his real-life equivalent), who is described as "King of Kings" in the *Iliad*, could easily have been regarded by the Hittites as a Great King, despite the existence of other minor kings from the same general area. The beauty of this suggestion is that one is not forced to part ways with the evidence of the Linear B tablets for multiple small Mycenaean kingdoms (as one must do in following Kelder's later argument for a "Greater Mycenae"). The obvious analogy would be to the political conglomeration known to the Hittites as Assuwa, which the Hittites themselves indicate was a confederation of twenty-two smaller cities and states in northwest Anatolia during the later-fifteenth century B.C.E. (KUB 23.11; see discussion in Cline 1996: 141–42).

So, is it possible that Ahhiyawa was similarly a confederation of Mycenaean kingdoms, rather than one single kingdom? Such a suggestion may resolve many of the lingering questions about Ahhiyawa, including the problem of why there was a single "Great King" recognized by the Hittites, when we know that there were multiple Mycenaean kings ruling at the same time. If so, we might perhaps draw a parallel and see Ahhiyawa as a very early version of the Delian League (which itself morphed into the Athenian Empire), with members contributing money, men, and ships to a common cause such as overseas trade or warfare. Mee (1998: 143) suggested something very similar more than a decade ago, when he wrote: "My proposal for the location of Ahhiyawa is based on Thucydides who saw the Thalassocracy of Minos as a forerunner of the Athenian Empire. Could Ahhiyawa also have been a maritime confederacy which was led by one of the mainland Mycenaean states, such as Mycenae?" The answer, it seems, is yes; such would have been quite possible, and plausible.

At the very least, perhaps we can say that the Ahhiyawa Problem/Question has been solved and answered after all, for there is now little doubt that Ahhiyawa was a reference by the Hittites to some or all of the Bronze Age Mycenaean world. It seems that Forrer was largely correct after all.

TABLE 1. THE AHHIYAWA TEXTS IN ROUGH CHRONOLOGICAL ORDER.

1. AhT 22 (CTH 571.2). Oracle report. Late-fifteenth–early-fourteenth century B.C.E. Reign of Tudhaliya I/II.
2. AhT 3 (CTH 147). Indictment of Madduwatta. Early-fourteenth century B.C.E. Reign of Arnuwanda I.
3. AhT 1A (CTH 61.I). Ten-Year Annals of Mursili II, years 3–4. Late-fourteenth century B.C.E.
4. AhT 1B (CTH 61.II). Extensive Annals of Mursili II, years 3–4. Late-fourteenth–early-thirteenth century B.C.E.
5. AhT 20 (CTH 570.1). Oracle report. Late-fourteenth–early-thirteenth century B.C.E. Mursili II.
6. AhT 12 (CTH 214.12.A). Prayer of Mursili II/Muwattalli II/Urhi-Teshshup(?). Late-fourteenth–mid-thirteenth century B.C.E.
7. AhT 9 (CTH 209.16). Letter from a king of Hatti(?) (perhaps Mursili II or Hattusili III) to a king of Ahhiyawa(?). Mid-fourteenth–thirteenth century B.C.E.
8. AhT 7 (CTH 191). Letter from Manapa-Tarhunta of the Seha River Land to a king of Hatti (probably Muwattalli II). Early-thirteenth century B.C.E.
9. AhT 6 (CTH 183). Letter from a king of Ahhiyawa to a king of Hatti (probably Muwattalli II). Early- to mid-thirteenth century B.C.E.
10. AhT 4 (CTH 181). Letter from a king of Hatti (probably Hattusili III) to a king of Ahhiyawa—the "Tawagalawa Letter." Mid-thirteenth century B.C.E.
11. AhT 8 (CTH 209.12). Letter from a Hittite official to a king of Hatti (Hattusili III?). Mid-thirteenth century B.C.E.
12. AhT 15 (CTH 214.12.D). Letter from a king of Hatti (Hattusili III?) to another Great King. Thirteenth century B.C.E.
13. AhT 26 (CTH 590). Votive prayer of Puduhepa(?) (wife of Hattusili III). Mid-thirteenth century B.C.E.
14. AhT 18 (CTH 214.16). "Boundary" list(?). Mid- to late-thirteenth century B.C.E. Reign of Hattusili III or Tudhaliya IV(?)
15. AhT 14 (CTH 214.12.C). Extract from a letter(?) from a king of Hatti(?) (Tudhaliya IV?) concerning Urhi-Teshshup. Mid- to late-thirteenth century B.C.E.
16. AhT 11 (CTH 211.4). Offenses of the Seha River Land (royal edict of Tudhaliya IV?). Late-thirteenth century B.C.E.
17. AhT 5 (CTH 182). Letter from a king of Hatti (probably Tudhaliya IV) to a western Anatolian ruler (Tarkasnawa, king of Mira?)—the "Milawata Letter." Late-thirteenth century B.C.E.

18. AhT 2 (CTH 105). Treaty between Tudhaliya IV and Shaushga-muwa, king of Amurru. Late-thirteenth century B.C.E.
19. AhT 27A and B (RS 94.2530, 94.2523). Letters, respectively, from Suppiluliuma II and Penti-Sharruma, a Hittite official, to Ammurapi, king of Ugarit. Late-thirteenth century B.C.E.
20. AhT 28 (Tekoğlu and Lemaire 2000). Inscription of Warika, king of (Ah)Hiyawa. Mid- to late-eighth century B.C.E.

UNASSIGNABLE TEXTS

21. AhT 10 (CTH 209.17). Letter. Thirteenth century B.C.E.
22. AhT 13 (CTH 214.12.B). Memorandum(?). Thirteenth century B.C.E.
23. AhT 16 (CTH 214.12.E). Fragment. Late-thirteenth century B.C.E.
24. AhT 17 (CTH 214.12.F). Fragment. Late-thirteenth century B.C.E.
25. AhT 19 (CTH 243.6). Inventory. Thirteenth century B.C.E.
26. AhT 21 (CTH 570.2). Oracle report. Thirteenth century B.C.E.
27. AhT 23 (CTH 572.1). Oracle report. Late-thirteenth century B.C.E.
28. AhT 24 (CTH 572.2). Oracle report. Thirteenth century B.C.E.
29. AhT 25 (CTH 581*). Letter. Thirteenth century B.C.E.

TABLE 2. CHRONOLOGY OF HITTITE NEW KINGDOM RULERS.[1]

Tudhaliya I/II[2]	late-fifteenth–mid-fourteenth century B.C.E.
Arnuwanda I	
Hattusili II?	
Tudhaliya III	
Suppiluliuma I	ca. 1350–1322 B.C.E.
Arnuwanda II	ca. 1322–1321 B.C.E.
Mursili II	ca. 1321–1295 B.C.E.
Muwattalli II	ca. 1295–1272 B.C.E.
Urhi-Teshshup (Mursili III)	ca. 1272–1267 B.C.E.
Hattusili III	ca. 1267–1237 B.C.E.
Tudhaliya IV	ca. 1237–1209 B.C.E.
Arnuwanda III	ca. 1209–1207 B.C.E.
Suppiluliuma II	ca. 1207–? B.C.E.

1. The following is but one of several Hittite chronologies that have been proposed by scholars, but is the one that is followed in this volume.
2. It is uncertain whether there were one or two early New Kingdom rulers of this name; the scholarly convention, therefore, is to use "I/II."

Texts

AHT 1A–1B

ANNALS OF MURSILI II, YEARS 3–4 (CTH 61)

The ascent to the Hittite throne of Mursili II as an untried youth sparked rebellion among many of the vassals recently subjugated by his late father Suppiluliuma I. It took Mursili a decade to pacify all of his Anatolian and north Syrian realm, and in celebration he memorialized his travails in a composition known to scholars as his Ten Year Annals. Further historiographic efforts of this king, undoubtedly in cooperation with the directors of the scribal school in the capital, resulted in the production of a more comprehensive text, the so-called Extensive Annals, that carried forward the year-by-year description of his deeds into the latter part of his reign. This longer work not only continues the earlier Ten Year Annals, but revises the accounts of years one through ten to provide much greater detail. Presented here are the portions of both sets of Annals covering the third and fourth years of Mursili's rule, during which period he was primarily active in the west of Anatolia, conquering and dismembering the rival kingdom of Arzawa.

AHT 1A

TEN-YEAR ANNALS (CTH 61.I)

A. KBo 3.4 + KUB 23.125
B. KBo 16.1 + KUB 31.137 + KBo 16.2 (+) KBo 44.239 (+) KBo 44.2
C. KUB 19.38 (+) KUB 14.21

B ii

§12 ———

29. MU-*an-ni-m*[*a … pa*]-⸢*a*⸣-*un nu-za* ^{m}*A*[*r-nu-wa-an-da-aš*]
30. ŠEŠ-*YA an*[-*da … nu-mu* ÉRIN.MEŠ ^{UR}(^{U}*Ḫu-u-wa-a*)*r-ša-na-aš-ša*]
31. *Ù* ÉRIN[!].MEŠ ^{URU}[*Šu-ru-da*[?] *pí-ra-an ar-ḫa pár-še-er*]
32. *na-at-kán I-N*[*A* KUR ^{URU}*Ar-za-u-wa an-da ú-e-er*]
33. *nu A-NA* ^{m}*Uḫ*[-*ḫa*-LÚ ^{LÚ}*ṬE*$_4$-*MA u-i-ya-nu-un*]
34. *nu-uš-ši ḫa-a*[*t-ra-a-nu-un am-me-el-wa-ták-kán ku-u-e-eš*]
35. *an-tu-u-uḫ-ša-aš* [ÉRIN.MEŠ ^{URU}*At-ta-a-ri-im-ma*]
36. ÉRIN.MEŠ ^{URU}*Ḫu-wa-a*[*r-ša-na-aš-ša Ù* ÉRIN.MEŠ ^{URU}*Šu-ru-da*]

§12 (B ii 29–41) In the following year I went [to …] My brother [Arnuwanda had …] The troops of the towns of Huwarsanassa and [Suruda(?) fled] before me, [and entered the land of Arzawa]. Then I [sent a messenger] to Uhhaziti, writing to him: "[Give back to me those] men—[the troops of the towns of Attarimma], Huwarsanassa, [and Suruda—who] have come to you." But Uhhaziti [wrote back to me as follows: "I will] not [give anyone back] to you." [And] when [he … to me], with force, […] his subjects […]

37. *an-da ú-e-er* [*nu-wa-ra-aš-mu* EGIR-*pa pa-i*]
38. ^{m}*Uḫ-ḫa*-LÚ-*iš-ma-m*[*u* EGIR-*pa ki-iš-ša-an ḫa-at-ra-a-it*]
39. ⸢*Ú*⸣-*UL-wa-at-ta k*[*u-in-ki* EGIR-*pa pí-iḫ-ḫi nu-wa-ra-aš-mu-kán*]
40. [*ma-aḫ*]-*ḫa-an* GÉŠPU-*z*[*a* …]
41. [o o o] ⸢ARAD.MEŠ-*ŠU*⸣ […]

(*gap of about 10 lines*)

§13'

51'. […] x [… *nu-mu*]
52'. [*I-NA* ^{URU}*Ti-ik-ku-u*]*k-ku-wa* ⸢EGIR-*an*⸣ *za-aḫ-ḫi-y*[*a ti-ya-at*]
53'. [*na-an* ^{d}UTU^{ŠI} *za-a*]*ḫ-ḫi-ya-nu-un nu-mu* ^{d}UTU ^{URU}[*A-ri-in-na*]
54'. [GAŠAN-*YA* ^{d}U NIR.GÁ]L EN-*YA* ^{d}*Me-ez-zu-ul-la-aš* [DINGIR.MEŠ-*ya*]
55'. [*ḫu-u-ma-an-te*]-*eš pí-ra-an ḫu-i-e-er nu-za* ^{LÚ}[KÚR]
56'. [*tar-aḫ-ḫu-un*] *na-an-kán ku-e-nu-un nu* ^{URU}*Ti-i*[*k-ku-uk-ku-wa-an*]
57'. [URU-*an ar-ḫa*] *wa-ar-nu-nu-un* KUR ^{URU}*Da-aš-ma*[-*ḫa-an*]
58'. [KUR-*e ar-ḫa*] ⸢*wa-ar-nu-nu-un*⸣

---

§14'

59'. [o o o o o o o o -*i*]*t-ta-ka-*⸢*at-ta-ša*⸣[…]
60'. *ḫ*[*u*?- …] x x x *wa-*⸢*al-ḫu*⸣-*u*[*n*]
61'. *na-an* […]
62'. *nam-ma* […]-*un*
63'. *nu* ^{URU}x[…]
64'. *nu-mu-k*[*án*? …]-*a-an*
65'. ⸢LÚ⸣ […]

(*gap*)

A ii

§15'

1. *nam-ma* [*pa-ra*]-⸢*a I-NA*⸣ ^{URU}*Iš-ḫu-pí-it-ta pa-a-un nu* ^{URU}⸢*Pal-ḫu-iš-ša*⸣[-*an*]
2. GUL-*un nu-mu-uš-ša-an I-NA* ^{URU}*Pal-ḫu-iš-ša* EGIR-*an*[3] ⸢$^{LÚ!}$KÚR⸣ $^{<URU>}$[*Pé*]-*eš*$^{!}$-*ḫu-ru-*⸢*uš*⸣
3. MÈ-*ya ti*^{er}-*ya-*⸢*at*⸣ *na-an*$^{!}$ ⸢*za*⸣-*aḫ-ḫi-ya-nu-un nu-mu* ^{d}UTU ^{URU}*A-ri-in-na* GAŠAN-*YA*
4. ^{d}U NIR.GÁL *BE-LÍ-YA* ^{d}*Me-ez-zu-ul-la-aš* DINGIR.MEŠ-*ya ḫu-u-ma-an-te-eš pí-ra-an ḫu-i-e-er*

3. Trace following in copy probably to be ignored.

§13' (B ii 51'–58') [He met me] in battle behind the town [of Tikkukkuwa, and] I fought [with them]. The Sun-Goddess [of the city of Arinna, My Lady, the Powerful Storm-God], My Lord, Mezzulla, [and all the gods] ran before me, so that [I defeated the enemy] and destroyed them. I burned [down the town of Tikkukkuwa] and the territory of the town of Dasmaha.

§14' (B ii 59'–65') *Too fragmentary for translation*

(gap)

§15' (A ii 1–6) Furthermore, I went forth to the town of Ishupitta and attacked the town of Palhuissa. Behind Palhuissa the enemy of the town of Peshuru met me in battle, and I fought with them. The Sun-Goddess of Arinna, My Lady, the Powerful Storm-God, My Lord, Mezzulla, and all the gods ran before me, so that I destroyed the Peshurian enemy behind Palhuissa and in addition burned down the town.

5. *nu-kán* ^{LÚ}KÚR *Pí*^{er}*-iš-ḫu-ru-un I-NA* ^{URU}*Pal-ḫu-iš-ša* EGIR*-an* ⸢*ku*⸣*-e-nu-un*
6. *nam-ma* URU*-an ar-ḫa wa-ar-nu-nu-un*

---

§16’

7. *nam-ma* ^{URU}*Pal-ḫu*[4]*-iš-ša-az* EGIR*-pa I-NA* ^{URU}⸢KÙ⸣.BABBAR*-ti ú-wa-*⸢*nu*⸣*-<<nu>>-un*
8. *nu-za* ÉRIN.MEŠ ANŠE.KUR.RA.MEŠ *ni-ni-in-ku-un nam-ma a-pé-e-da-ni* MU*-ti I-NA* ⸢KUR⸣ [5]*Ar-za-u-wa*
9. *i-ya-an-ni-ya-nu-un-pát A-NA* ^{m}*U-uḫ-ḫa*-LÚ*-ma* ^{LÚ}*ṬE*$_4$*-MA u-i-ya-nu-un*
10. *nu-uš-ši ḫa-at-ra-a-nu-un* ARAD.MEŠ*-YA-wa-at-ták-kán ku-i-e-eš an-da ú-e-er*
11. *nu-wa-ra-aš-ta* EGIR*-pa ku-it ú-e-wa-ak-ki-nu-un*[6] *nu-wa-ra-aš-mu* <<EGIR*-pa*>>
12. EGIR*-pa Ú-UL pa-iš-ta*[7] *nu-wa-mu-za* DUMU*-la-an ḫal-zi-eš-še-eš-ta*[8]
13. *nu-wa-mu-za te-ep-nu-uš-ki-it ki*$^{!}$*-nu-un-wa e-ḫu nu-wa za-aḫ-ḫi*$^{er\rightarrow}$*-ya-u-wa-aš-ta-ti*$^{\leftarrow er}$
14. *nu-wa-an-na-aš* ^{d}U *BE-LÍ-YA DI-NAM*[9] *ḫa-an-na-a-ú*

---

§17’

15. *ma-aḫ-ḫa-an i-ya-aḫ-ḫa-at nu* GIM^{er}*-an*[10] *I-NA* $^{\text{ḪUR.SAG}}$*La-wa-ša a-ar-ḫu-un*
16. *nu-za* ^{d}U NIR.GÁL EN*-YA pa-ra-a ḫa-an-da-an-da-a-tar*[11] *te-ek-ku-uš-ša-nu-ut*[12]
17. *nu* ⸢^{GIŠ}⸣*kal-mi-ša-na-an ši-ya-a-it nu* ^{GIŠ}⸢*kal*⸣*-mi-ša-na-an*[13] *am-me-el* KARAŠ.ḪI.A*-YA*
18. *uš-*⸢*ki*⸣*-it* KUR ^{URU}*Ar-za-u-wa-ya-an uš-ki-it nu* ^{GIŠ}*kal-mi-ša-na-aš*[14] *pa-it*
19. *nu* KUR ^{URU}*Ar-za-u-wa* GUL*-aḫ-ta ŠA* ^{m}*U-uḫ-ḫa*-LÚ*-ya* ^{URU}*A-pa-a-ša-an* URU*-an* GUL*-aḫ-ta*

---

4. B iii 3’ inserts *-u-*.
5. B iii 5’ inserts ^{URU}.
6. B iii 9’: *ú-e-ki-iš-ki-nu-un.*
7. B iii 10’: *pé-eš-ta.*
8. B iii 11’: *ḫal-zi-iš-ši-iš-ta.*
9. B iii 14’: [DI*-ša*]*r*.
10. B iii 15’: *ma-aḫ-ḫa-an.*
11. B iii 17’: *ḫa-an-da-a-an-da-tar.*
12. B iii 17’: *te-ek-ku-nu*$^{!}$*-uš-š*[*a-*.
13. B iii 18’: *-š*]*a-an ši-ya-it nu* ^{GIŠ}*kal-mi-iš-n*[*a-*.
14. B iii 20’: *-e*]*š-na-aš.*

§16' (A ii 7–14) Then from Palhuissa I came back to Hattusa and mobilized infantry and chariotry. Further, in that same year I marched to Arzawa. I sent a messenger to Uhha-ziti, writing to him: "Because I asked you for my subjects back—those who had come to you—and you did not give them back to me, and kept calling me a child and belittling me—come now, let us do battle, and the Storm-God, My Lord, shall judge our case!"

§17' (A ii 15–32) When I had set out and arrived at Mt. Lawasa, the Storm-God, My Lord, made manifest his providence. He launched a lightning bolt, and my army saw the lightning bolt, as did the land of Arzawa. The lightning bolt traveled and struck the land of Arzawa, (in particular) Apasa, the city of Uhha-ziti. Uhha-ziti fell on his knees and became ill, and being ill, he did not come against me in battle again. Rather, he dispatched his son Piyama-Kurunta against me, together with infantry and chariotry. He met me in battle at the Astarpa River, and I, My Majesty, fought with him. The Sun-Goddess of Arinna, My Lady, the Powerful Storm-God, My Lord, Mezzulla, and all the gods ran before me, so that I defeated Piyama-Kurunta, son of Uhha-ziti, together with his infantry and chariotry, and destroyed them. I pursued him and crossed the territory of Arzawa and entered Apasa, city of Uhha-ziti. Uhha-ziti did not offer me resistance but ran away from me. He went across the sea to the islands and remained there.

20. ^{m}*U-uḫ-ḫa*-LÚ-⸢*na*⸣[15] *gi-nu-uš-šu-uš a-še-eš-ta na-aš ir-ma-li-ya-at-ta-at*[16]

21. *nu ma-aḫ-ḫa-an* ^{m}*U-uḫ-ḫa*-LÚ-*iš* GIG-*at*[17] *na-aš-mu nam-ma za-aḫ-ḫi-ya*

22. *me-na-aḫ-ḫa-an-da Ú-UL ú-it nu-mu-kán* ^{erasure} <m>SUM-*ma*-^{d}LAMMA-*an* DUMU-*ŠU*

23. *QA-DU* ÉRIN.MEŠ ANŠE.KUR.RA.MEŠ *me-na-aḫ-ḫa-an-da pa-ra-a ne-eš-ta*[18]

24. *na-aš-mu I-NA* ^{ÍD}*A-aš-tar-pa I-NA* ^{URU}*Wa-al-ma-a* MÈ-*ya*[19] *ti-ya-at*

25. *na-an* ^{d}UTU^{ŠI} *za-aḫ-ḫi-ya-nu-un nu-mu* ^{d}UTU ^{URU}*A-ri-in-na* GAŠAN-*YA*

26. ^{d}U NIR.GÁL *BE-LÍ-YA*[20] ^{d}⸢*Me*⸣-*ez-zu*$^{!}$-*ul-la-aš* DINGIR.MEŠ-*ya ḫu-u-ma-an-te-eš pí-ra-an ḫu*[21]*-i-e-er*

27. *nu-za* ^{m}SUM-*ma*-^{d}LAMMA-*an* ⸢DUMU ^{m}*U*[22]*-uḫ-ḫa*⸣-LÚ *QA-DU* ÉRIN.MEŠ-*ŠU* ANŠE.KUR.RA.MEŠ-*ŠU tar-aḫ-ḫu-un*

28. ⸢*na*⸣-*an-kán ku-e-nu-un* ⸢*nam*⸣-*ma*-⸢*an* EGIR⸣-*an-pát AṢ-BAT nu-kán I-NA* KUR ^{URU}*Ar-za-u-wa*

29. [*pár*]-*ra-an-da pa-a-un nu I-NA* ^{URU}*A-pa-a-ša A-NA* URU^{LIM}

30. *ŠA* ^{m}*U-uḫ-ḫa*-LÚ *an-da-an pa-a-un nu-mu* ^{m}*Uḫ-ḫa*-LÚ-*iš Ú-UL ma-az-za-aš-ta*

31. *na-aš-mu-kán* ⸗*ḫu-u-wa-iš na-aš-kán a-ru-ni pár-ra-an-da*

32. *gur-ša-u-wa-na-an-za pa-it na-aš-kán a-pí-ya an-da e-eš-ta*

---

§18'

33. KUR ^{URU}*Ar-za-u-wa-ma-kán ḫu-u-ma-an pár-aš-ta nu ku-i-e-eš* NAM.RA *I-NA* $^{ḪUR.SAG}$*A-ri-in-na-an-da*

34. *pa-a-ir nu-za-kán* $^{ḪUR.SAG}$*A-ri-in-na-an-da-an e-ep-pir ku-i-e-eš-ma* NAM.RA.ḪI.A

35. *pa-ra-a I-NA* ^{URU}*Pu-ú*[23]*-ra-an-da pa-a-ir nu-za-kán* <<*nu-za-kán*>> ^{URU}*Pu-ra-an-da-an e-ep-pir*

36. *ku-i-e-eš*[24]*-ma-kán* NAM.RA.MEŠ *a-ru-ni pár-ra-an-da IT-TI* ^{m}*Uḫ*[25]*-ḫa*-LÚ *pa-a-ir*[26]

---

15. B iii 22': ^{m}*Uḫ-ḫa*[-LÚ]-*na-ma*.
16. B iii 23' adds -*pát*.
17. B iii 24': *ir-ma-li-ya-at-ta-at*.
18. B iii 27': *na-a-iš-ta*.
19. B iii 28': *za-aḫ-ḫi-ya*.
20. B iii 30': EN-*YA*.
21. B iii 31' inserts -*u*-.
22. B iii 32' omits.
23. B iii 42' omits.
24. B iii 43': *ku-iš*-.
25. B iii 44': ^{m}*U-uḫ*-.
26. B iii 44': *pa-it*.

§18’ (A ii 33–45) All the land of Arzawa fled: some of the people went to Mt. Arinnanda and dug in on Mt. Arinnanda; some of the people went to the town of Puranda and ensconced themselves in Puranda; and some of the people went across the sea with Uhha-ziti. Then I, My Majesty, went after the people to Mt. Arinnanda, and fought with (those at) Mr. Arinnanda. The Sun-Goddess of Arinna, My Lady, the Powerful Storm-God, My Lord, Mezzulla, and all the gods ran before me, so that I defeated (those at) Mt. Arinnanda. The captives whom I, My Majesty, brought to the royal establishment numbered 15,500. The captives whom the noblemen of Hattusa and the infantry and chariotry brought back were without number. I dispatched the captives to Hattusa, and they were led away.

37. ⸢*nu*⸣ ^{d}UTU^{ŠI} *I-NA* $^{ḪUR.SAG}$*A-ri*^{er}*-in-na-an-da A-NA* NAM.RA[27] EGIR-*an-da pa-a-un*

38. *nu* $^{ḪUR.SAG}$*A-ri-in-na-an-da-an za-aḫ-ḫi-ya-nu-un nu-mu* ^{d}UTU ^{URU}TÚL-*na* GAŠAN-*YA* ^{erasure}

39. ^{d}U NIR.GÁL *BE-LÍ-YA*[28] ^{d}*Me-ez-zu-ul-la-aš* DINGIR.MEŠ-*ya ḫu-u-ma-an-te-eš pí-ra-an*

40. *ḫu*$^{!}$*-u*$^{!}$*-i-e-er* ^{erasure} *nu-za* $^{ḪUR.SAG}$*A-ri-in-na-an-da-an tar-aḫ-ḫu-un*

41. *nu-za* ^{d}UTU^{ŠI} *ku-in* NAM.RA *I-NA* É.LUGAL *ú-wa-te-nu-un*

42. ⸢*na*⸣*-aš* 1 SIG_7 5 *LI-IM* 5 *ME* NAM.RA ⸢*e*⸣*-eš-ta* ^{URU}KÙ.BABBAR[29]*-aš-ma-za* EN.MEŠ ÉRIN.MEŠ ANŠE.KUR.RA.MEŠ-*ya*

43. *ku-in* NAM.RA.MEŠ *ú-wa-te-et nu-uš-ša-an kap-pu-u-wa-u-wa-ar*[30]

44. NU.GÁL *e-eš-ta nam-ma-kán* NAM.RA.MEŠ ^{URU}KÙ.BABBAR-*ši pa-ra-a*

45. *ne-eḫ-ḫu-un na-an ar-ḫa ú-wa-te-er*

---

§19'

46. *nu*^{er}*-za ma-aḫ-ḫa-an* $^{ḪUR.SAG}$*A-ri-in-na-an-da-an tar-aḫ-ḫu-un*

47. *nam-ma* EGIR-*pa I-NA* ^{ÍD}*A-aš-tar-pa ú-wa-nu-un nu-za* BÀD.KARAŠ

48. *I-NA* ^{ÍD}*Aš-tar-pa wa-aḫ-nu-nu-un nu-za* EZEN MU^{TI} *a-pí-ya i-ya-nu-un*

49. *nu ki-i I-NA* MU.1.KAM ^{erasure} *i-ya-nu-un*

---

§20'

50. ⸢*ma-aḫ*⸣*-ḫa-an-ma ḫa-me-eš-ḫa-an-za ki-ša-at nu* ^{m}*U-uḫ-ḫa*-LÚ-*iš ku-it* ⸢GIG-*at*⸣

51. *na*[*-aš-ká*]*n a-ru-ni an-da e-eš-ta* DUMU.MEŠ-*ŠU*<<*-NU*>>*-ya-aš-ši kat-ta-an e-šir*

52. ⸢*nu-kán*⸣ ^{m}*U-uḫ-ḫa*-LÚ-*iš a-ru-ni an-da* BA.ÚŠ DUMU.MEŠ-*ŠU*-<<*NU*>>*-ma-za ar-ḫa*

53. ⸢*šar*⸣*-ra-an-da-at nu-kán* 1*-aš* ŠÀ A.AB.BA-*pát e-eš-ta* 1*-aš-ma-kán*

54. ^{m}⸢*Ta-pa-la-zu*⸣*-na-ú-li-iš a-ru-na-az ar-ḫa ú-it nu-kán* KUR ^{URU}*Ar-za-u-wa ku-it ḫu-u-ma-an*

55. x [o o o o] ⸢*I-NA* ^{URU}⸣*Pu-ra-an-da ša-ra-a pa-a-an e-eš-ta*

56. *nu-*[*ká*(*n* ^{m}*Ta-pa-l*)]*a-*⸢*zu*⸣*-na-wa-liš*[31] *I-NA* ^{URU}*Pu-ra-an-da ša-ra-a pa-it*

---

27. B iii 45' adds MEŠ.
28. B iii 47': EN-*YA*.
29. B iii 51': ^{URU}*Ḫa-at-t*[*u-*.
30. B iii 53' adds *-pát*.
31. B iv 5': *-ú-li-iš*.

§19' (A ii 46–49) When I had conquered Mt. Arinnanda, I came back once more to the Astarpa River. I pitched camp at the Astarpa River and celebrated the annual festival there. This I accomplished in one year.

§20' (A ii 50–56) When spring arrived, because Uhha-ziti was still ill, he remained in the midst of the sea. His sons were with him, and Uhha-ziti died in the midst of the sea. Then his sons parted company: one remained right there in the midst of the sea, while the other, Tapalazunawali, came out from the sea. Because all of Arzawa had gone up to Puranda [...], Tapalazunawali went up to Puranda (too).

§21'

57. [(*ma-aḫ-ḫa-an-ma-za-kán* EZEN MU)]^{TI} *kar-ap-pu-un nu I-NA* ^{URU}*Pu-ra-an-da* MÈ-*ya*[32] *pa-a-un*

58. [(*nu-kán*)] ^{m}*Ta-p*[(*a-la*)-*zu-na-w*]*a-liš IŠ-TU* ÉRIN.MEŠ ANŠE.KUR.RA.MEŠ ^{URU}*Pu-ra-an-*⸢*da*⸣[33]*-za kat-ta ú-*⸢*it*⸣

59. [*na-aš-m*]*u za-aḫ-ḫi-ya me-*⸢*na-aḫ-ḫa-an-da*⸣ *ú-it na-aš-mu-kán A-NA* A.ŠÀ A.GÀR-*ŠU*

60. [(*an-da*)] MÈ-*ya*[34] *ti-ya-at na-an* ^{d}UTU^{ŠI} MÈ-*ya-nu-nu-un*

61. [(*nu-mu* ^{d})]UTU ^{URU}*A-ri-in-na* GA[ŠAN-*YA*] ⸢^{d}⸣U NIR.GÁL *BE-LÍ-YA*

62. [(^{d}*Me-ez-zu-u*)]*l-la-aš* DINGIR.MEŠ-*ya ḫu*[*-u-ma-an-t*]*e-eš pí-ra-an ḫu-u-i-e-er*[35] *nu-za* ^{m}*Da-pa-la-zu-na-ú-wa-li-in*[36]

63. [o o o (*QA-DU*)] ÉRIN.MEŠ-*ŠU*[37] ANŠE.KUR.RA.MEŠ-*ŠU*[38] ⸢*tar*⸣*-aḫ-ḫu-un na-an-kán ku-e-nu-un*

64. [(*nam-ma-an* EGIR)]-*an AṢ-BAT nu pa-a-un* ^{URU}*Pu-ra-an-da-an an-*⸢*da*⸣ *wa-aḫ-nu-nu-un*

65. [*na-an-kán an-da*] *ḫa-at-ke-eš-nu-nu-un nu-uš-ši-kán ú-i-d*[(*a-a*)-*a*]*r ar-ḫa da-aḫ-ḫu-un*

---

§22'

66. [(*nu-kán ma-aḫ-ḫa-an* ^{URU})*P*]*u-ra-an-da-an an-da ḫa-at-ke-eš-nu-nu-un*

67. [(*nu-kán* ^{m}*Ta-pa-la-z*)*u-n*]*a-ú-liš ku-iš* DUMU ^{m}*U-uḫ-ḫa*-LÚ *I-NA* ^{URU}*Pu-ra-an-da še-er e-eš-ta*

68. [(*na-aš na-aḫ-šar-ri*)-*ya-a*]*t-ta-at na-aš-kán* ^{URU}*Pu-ra-an-da-za* GE_6-*az kat-ta ḫu-wa-iš*

69. [*nam-ma-za* DUMU.MEŠ-*ŠU* (NA)]M.RA.MEŠ-*ya ša-ra-am-na-az pí-ra-an ḫu-u-i-nu-ut*

70. [(*na-an-kán* ^{URU}*Pu-r*)*a-an-da-z*]*a kat-ta pí-e-ḫu-te-et*

---

§23'

71. [*ma-a*(*ḫ-ḫa-an-ma* ^{d})UTU^{ŠI} *iš-t*]*a-ma-aš-šu-un* $^{m!}$*Da*[39]*-pa-la-zu-*⸢*na*⸣*-ú-*⸢*liš-wa*⸣*-kán*

---

32. B iv 8': *za-aḫ-ḫi-y*[*a*].
33. B iv 10': *-ta-*.
34. B iv 12': *za-aḫ*[-.
35. Preverb and verb written above line.
36. B iv 15': ^{m}*Ta-pa-la-zu-na-u*[-.
37. B iv 16' omits.
38. B iv 16' omits.
39. B iv 28': ⸢^{m}*Ta*⸣-.

§21' (A ii 57–65) When I had finished with the annual festival, I went in battle to Puranda, and Tapalazunawali came down from Puranda, together with (his) infantry and chariotry. He came against me in battle, and he met me in battle on his own ground. I, My Majesty, fought with him. The Sun-Goddess of Arinna, [My] Lady, the Powerful Storm-God, My Lord, Mezzulla, and all the gods ran before me, so that I defeated Tapalazunawali, together with his infantry and his chariotry, and I destroyed them. I pursued him and proceeded to invest Puranda. I bottled [it up] and cut off its water.

§22' (A ii 66–70) When I had bottled up Puranda, then Tapalazunawali, son of Uhha-ziti, who was up in Puranda, took fright and fled by night down from Puranda. [In addition], he took charge of [his children] and the populace with their provisions and led them down from Puranda.

§23' (A ii 71–78) When I, [My Majesty], heard that Tapalazunawali [had fled by night], taking charge of his wife, children, and populace, together with their provisions, and leading them down, then I, [My Majesty], sent [infantry] and chariotry after him. They hounded Tapalazunawali on the road and captured his wife, children, and populace, and [brought] them back. Tapalazunawali alone escaped. The infantry and chariotry themselves kept the populace whom [they had hounded] on the road.

72. [GE$_6$-*az kat-ta* (*ḫu-u-wa-a-iš* DAM-*SÚ-y*)]*a-wa-za* DUMU.MEŠ-*ŠU* NAM.RA.MEŠ-*ya*
73. [(*ša-ra-a-am-na-za pí-ra-an ḫ*)]*u-i-nu-ut nu-wa-ra-an-kán kat-ta pé-e-ḫu-te-et*
74. [(*nu-uš-ši*) ^{d}UTU^{ŠI} ÉRIN.MEŠ (ANŠE.KUR.R)]A.MEŠ EGIR-*an-da u-i-ya-nu-un*
75. [*na-a*(*t* ^{m}*Ta-pa-la-zu-na-ú-li-i*)]*n* KASKAL-*ši* EGIR-*an-da ta-ma-aš-*⸢*šir*⸣
76. [(*nu-uš-ši-kán* DAM-*SÚ* DUMU.MEŠ-*Š*)*U* NA]M.RA.MEŠ-*ya ar-ḫa da-a-ir na-an* EGIR-*pa*
77. [(*ú-w*)*a-te-er* (^{m}*Ta-pa-la-zu-na-ú-li-iš-ma-ká*)]*n*$^!$ 1-*aš* SAG.DU-*aš iš*$^!$-*pár-za-aš-ta*
78. [(NAM.RA-*ma-kán ku-in* KASKAL-*ši t*)*a-ma-aš-šir n*]*a-an-za-an* ÉRIN.MEŠ-*pát* ANŠE.KUR.MEŠ *da-a-aš*

---

§24’

79. [(*m*)*a-aḫ-ḫa-an-ma-k*(*án ú-wa-nu-un*) *I*(-*NA* U)D.N.KA(M ^{UR})^{U}*Pu-r*]*a-an-da-an an-da ḫa-at-k*[*e-e*]*š-nu-*⸢*nu*⸣*-un*
80. [… *za-aḫ-ḫi-ya-nu*]*-un* ^{erasure} <<*ḫu-i-e-er*>>
81. [*nu-mu* ^{d}UTU ^{URU}*A-ri-in-na* GAŠAN-*YA* ^{d}U NIR.GÁL EN-*Y*]*A* ^{d}*Me-ez-zu-ul-la*[-*aš*]
82. [DINGIR.MEŠ-*ya ḫu-u-ma-an-te-eš pí-ra-an ḫu-u-i-e-er nu-z*]*a* ^{URU}*Pu-ra-an-da-a*[*n tar-a*]*ḫ-ḫu-un*
83. [*nu-za ku-in* NAM.RA *I-NA* É.LUGAL *ú-wa-te-nu-un n*]*a-aš* 1 SIG$_7$ 6 *LI*[-*IM* N] *ME* ⸢NAM⸣.RA
84. [*e-eš-ta* ^{URU}KÙ.BABBAR-*aš-ma-za* EN.MEŠ ÉRIN.MEŠ ANŠE.KUR.RA.MEŠ]-*ya ku-i*[*n* NAM].RA GUD UDU
85. [*ú-wa-te-et nu-uš-ša-an kap-pu-u-wa-u-wa-ar* NU.GÁL *e-e*]*š-t*[*a*]
86. [*na-an-kán* ^{URU}KÙ.BABBAR-*ši pa-ra-a ne-eḫ-ḫu-un na-an ar-ḫa*] ⸢*ú-wa*⸣-*te*$^!$-*er*

A iii

§25’

1. […]
2. […]
3. [… *a-ru-ni*] ⸢*an-da*⸣ [*e-e*]*š-ta*
4. [… ^{m}SUM-*ma*-^{d}LAMM]A-⸢*aš*⸣[-*ma* D]UMU ^{m}*U-uḫ-*⸢*ḫa*⸣-LÚ
5. [… *n*]*a-aš-k*[*án a*]-*ru-na-az*
6. [*ar-ḫa pa-it na-aš* … *I*]*T-TI* LU[GAL KU]R ***Aḫ-ḫi-ya-wa-a***
7. [*an-da ú-it nu-uš-ši*$^?$ ^{d}UTU^{ŠI} ^{LÚ}*ṬE*$_4$-*MA I*]*Š-TU* ^{GIŠ}⸢MÁ⸣ *u-i-ya-nu-un*

§24' (A ii 79–86) [But when] I had bottled up Puranda for [N] days, [I attacked it ...] The Sun-Goddess of Arinna, My Lady, the Powerful Storm-God, My [Lord], Mezzulla, [and all the gods ran before me, so that] I defeated Puranda. [The captives whom I, My Majesty, brought to the royal establishment] numbered 16,000+. [The captives], cattle, and sheep that [the noblemen of Hattusa and the infantry] and [chariotry brought back were without number. I dispatched them to Hattusa, and they] were led [away].

§25' (A iii 1–12) [... was] in [the midst of the sea ... But Piyama-Kurunta], son of Uhha-ziti, [...] he [came out] from the sea, [and he entered (into exile)] with the King of **Ahhiyawa** [... And I, My Majesty], sent [a messenger to him] by ship, [...] and he was brought out. [The captives who] were brought out [with him, together with the captives of the cities of ...] and Lipa, [altogether] were [...] in number. I dispatched [them to Hattusa], and they were led away.

8. [...]*-ta na-an-kán* [*a*]*r-ḫa ú-wa-te-er*
9. [*kat-ti-iš-ši-ma-kán ku-in* NAM.RA.MEŠ *a*]*r-ḫa ú-wa-te-er*
10. [*na-aš IŠ-TU* NAM.RA ^{URU} ...] x *Ù IŠ-TU* NAM.RA.MEŠ ^{URU}*Li-pa*
11. [*an-da* 1*-e-et-ta* N SIG$_7$ N *LI-IM* N *ME*] NAM.RA *e-eš-ta*
12. [*na-an-kán* ^{URU}KÙ.BABBAR*-ši pa-ra-a n*]*e-eḫ-ḫu-un na-an ar-ḫa ú-wa-te-er*

§26'

13. [GIM*-an-ma-kán I-NA* KUR ^{ÍD}*Še-e-ḫ*]*a* EGIR*-pa ú-wa-nu-un nu-kán I-NA* ŠÀ ^{ÍD}*Še-e-ḫa*
14. [^{m}*Ma-na-pa-*^{d}U*-aš ku-iš* EN*-aš e*]*-eš-ta ma-a-na-an za-aḫ-ḫi-ya-nu-un nu-mu ma-aḫ-ḫa-an*
15. [^{m}*Ma-na-pa-*^{d}U*-aš iš-ta*]*-ma-aš-ta* LUGAL KUR *Ḫat-ti-wa ú-iz-zi*
16. [*na-aš na-aḫ-šar-ri-y*]*a-at-ta-at na-aš-mu nam-ma me-na-aḫ-ḫa-an-da*
17. [*Ú-UL ú-it nu-m*]*u-kán* AMA*-ŠU* $^{LÚ.MEŠ}$ŠU.GI $^{MUNUS.MEŠ}$ŠU.GI*-ya*
18. [*me-na-aḫ-ḫa-an-da*] *pa-ra-a na-iš-ta na-at-mu ú-e-er* GÌR.MEŠ*-aš kat-ta-an*
19. [*ḫa-a-li-i-e-er*] *nu-mu* MUNUS.MEŠ *ku-it* GÌR.MEŠ*-aš* GAM*-an ḫa-a-li-i-e-er*
20. [*nu A-NA* MUNUS.MEŠ] *ḫa-a-an-da ka-a-ri ti-ya-nu-un nu nam-ma I-NA* ^{ÍD}*Še-e-ḫa*
21. [*Ú-UL p*]*a-a-un nu-kán* NAM.RA ^{URU}KÙ.BABBAR*-ti ku-iš I-NA* ^{ÍD}*Še-e-ḫa*
22. [*an-d*]*a e-eš-ta na-an-mu* ^{erasure} *pa-ra-a pí-i-e-er nu-mu* NAM.RA *ku-in*
23. *pa-ra-a pí-i-e-er na-aš* 4 *LI-IM* NAM.RA *e-eš-ta na-an-kán* ^{URU}KÙ.BAB-BAR*-ši*
24. *pa-ra-a ne-eḫ-ḫu-un* ^{erasure} *na-an ar-ḫa ú-wa-te-er* ^{m}*Ma-na-pa-*^{d}U*-an-ma-za*
25. KUR ^{ÍD}*Še-e-ḫa-ya* ARAD*-an-ni da-aḫ-ḫu-un*

§27'

26. *nam-ma I-NA* KUR ^{URU}*Mi-ra-a pa-a-un nu* KUR ^{URU}*Mi-ra-a A-NA* ^{m}*Maš-ḫu-i-lu-wa AD-DIN*
27. KUR ^{ÍD}*Še-e-ḫa-ma A-NA* ^{m}*Ma-na-pa-*^{d}U *AD-DIN* KUR ^{URU}*Ḫa-pal-la-ma A-NA* ^{m}*Tar-ga-aš-na-al-li*
28. *AD-DIN nu-za-kán ke-e* KUR.KUR.MEŠ ⌈*pé*⌉*-e-di-iš-ši* ARAD*-na-aḫ-ḫu-un*
29. *nu-uš-ma-aš-kán* ÉRIN.MEŠ *iš-ḫi-iḫ-ḫu-un nu-mu* ÉRIN.MEŠ *pí-iš-ki-u-an da-a-ir*

§26' (A iii 13–25) [When] I came back [to the land of the Seha River], I would have given battle to [Manapa-Tarhunta, who] was lord in the land of the Seha River. But when [Manapa-Tarhunta heard] that the King of Hatti was coming, [he took fright, and did not come out] again against me, but dispatched to me his mother, old men, and old women. They proceeded [to cast themselves] down at my feet. And because the women cast themselves down at my feet, I had compassion [for the women and did not] go again into (the land of) the Seha River. The captives of Hatti who were [in] (the land of) the Seha River were turned over to me. Those captives turned over to me numbered 4,000. I dispatched them to Hattusa, and they were led away. I accepted Manapa-Tarhunta and the land of the Seha River into vassalage.

§27' (A iii 26–41) Then I went to the land of Mira. I gave the land of Mira to Mashuiluwa, the land of the Seha River to Manapa-Tarhunta, and the land of Hapalla to Targasnalli. I subjugated these lands in place, and imposed troop levies upon them, and they began to provide troops to me. And because I spent the winter in Arzawa, for two years the Sun-Goddess of Arinna, My Lady, the Powerful Storm-God, My Lord, Mezzulla, and all the gods ran before me, so that I conquered Arzawa. Some (of the population of) Arzawa I brought back to Hattusa and some I subjugated in place, imposing troop levies upon them—and they began to send me troops. Because I conquered all of Arzawa, the capti-

30. *nu-kán I-NA* ŠÀ KUR ^{URU}*Ar-za-u-wa* ⌈*ku-it*⌉ *erasure* ŠE$_{12}$*-ya-nu-un I-NA* MU.2.KAM*-ma-mu*

31. ⌈^{d}UTU⌉ ^{URU}TÚL*-na* GAŠAN*-YA* ^{d}U NIR.GÁL EN*-YA* ^{d}*Me-ez-zu-ul-la-aš* DINGIR.MEŠ*-ya*

32. *ḫu-u-ma-an-te-eš pí-ra-an ḫu-u-i-e-er nu-za* KUR ^{URU}*Ar-za-u-wa tar-aḫ-ḫu-un*

33. ⌈*nu-za*⌉ *ku-it* ^{URU}KÙ.BABBAR*-ši ar-ḫa ú-da-aḫ-ḫu-un ku-it-ma-za-kán pé-di-iš-ši*

34. ARAD*-na-aḫ-ḫu-un nu-uš-ma-aš-kán* ÉRIN.MEŠ *iš-ḫi-iḫ-ḫu-un nu-mu* ÉRIN.MEŠ *pé-eš*[*-ki*]*-u-an*

35. *da-a-ir nu-za* KUR ^{URU}*Ar-za-u-wa ku-it ḫu-u-ma-an tar-aḫ-ḫu-un nu-za* ^{d}UTU$^{\check{S}I}$ *ku-in*

36. NAM.⌈RA⌉ *I-NA* É.LUGAL *ú-wa-te-nu-un na-aš an-da* 1*-e-et-ta* 6 SIG$_7$ 6 *LI-IM* NAM.RA

37. *e-eš-ta* ^{URU}KÙ.BABBAR*-aš-ma-za* EN.MEŠ ÉRIN.MEŠ ANŠE.KUR.RA.MEŠ*-ya ku-in* NAM.RA GUD UDU*-ya*

38. *ú-wa-te-et nu-uš-*⌈*ša*⌉*-an kap-pu-u-wa-u*[40]*-wa-ar* NU.GÁL *e-eš-ta*

39. *nu-za* ⌈*ma*⌉*-aḫ-ḫa-an erasure* KUR ^{URU}*Ar-za-u-wa ḫu-u-ma-an tar-aḫ-ḫu-un*

40. *nam-ma* ^{URU}KÙ.BABBAR*-ši ar-ḫa ú-wa-nu-un nu-*⌈*kán*⌉ *I-NA* KUR ^{URU}*Ar-za-u-wa ku-it*

41. *an-da gi-im-ma-an-da-ri-ya-nu-un nu ki-i I-NA* MU.1.KAM DÙ*-nu-un*

---

40. C iii 4' omits.

ves whom I brought to the royal establishment numbered altogether 66,000. The captives, cattle, and sheep that the noblemen of Hattusa and the infantry and chariotry brought back were without number. And when I had conquered Arzawa, I came back once again to Hattusa. Because I had spent the winter in Arzawa, I accomplished this in one year.

AhT 1B

Extensive Annals (CTH 61.II)

A.[41] *KUB 14.15 + KBo 16.104*
B. KUB 14.16
C. KBo 16.5 + KUB 19.40
D. KBo 12.37

A i

---

§1'

23. *ma-aḫ-ḫa-an ḫa-me-eš-ḫa-an-za ki-ša-at nu* ^{m}*U-uḫ*[*-ḫa-*LÚ*-iš ku-it A-NA* LUGAL **KUR *A-aḫ-ḫi-ú-wa-a*** EGIR*-an ti-ya-at*]
24. *nu-kán* KUR ^{URU}*Mi-il-la-wa-an-da A-NA* LUGAL **KUR *Aḫ-ḫi-ú*[*-wa-a*** … *nu* ^{d}UTU$^{\check{S}I}$ …]
25. *nu-kán* ^{m}*Gul-la-an* ^{m}*Ma-la-*LÚ*-in* ÉRIN.MEŠ A[NŠE.KUR.MEŠ*-ya*] ⸢*pa-ra-a*⸣ *n*[*e-eḫ-ḫu-un na-aš* KUR ^{URU}*Mi-il-la-wa-an-da*]
26. GUL*-aḫ-ḫi-ir na-at IŠ-TU* NAM.RA.MEŠ GU[D.ME]Š UDU.ḪI.A *ša-ra-a da-a-ir* [*na-at* ^{URU}KÙ.BABBAR*-ši ar-ḫa ú-da-a-ir*]

---

§2'

27. ⸢^{m}*Maš*⸣*-ḫu-i-lu-wa-aš-ma* LU[GAL ^{URU}*Mi-i*]-⸢*ra*⸣*-a* ⸢*ku*⸣*-i*[*t*] ^{URU}*Im-pa-a-an ḫar-ta nu-uš-ši* ^{m}SUM[-^{d}LAMMA*-aš*]
28. [DUMU] ⸢^{m}⸣*U-uḫ-ḫa-*LÚ *za-a*[*ḫ-ḫi-ya ti-ya-at*] *nu A-NA* ^{m}*Maš-ḫu-i-lu-wa am-me-el* DINGIR.MEŠ *pí-ra-an* ⸢*ḫu-u-i-e-er*⸣
29. [*na-aš-za*] ⸢^{m}⸣SUM-^{d}[LAMMA*-an* DUMU ^{m}*U-uḫ-ḫa-*LÚ *ta*]*r-aḫ-ta na-an ḫu-ul-li-i-e-et nu-za ma-aḫ-ḫa-an*
30. [^{m}*Maš-ḫu-i-lu-wa-aš* ^{m}SUM-^{d}LAMMA*-an* D]UMU ^{m}*Uḫ-ḫa-*LÚ *tar-aḫ-ta* ⸢*nam-ma*⸣[*-aš*] ⸢*pa-it-pát nu*⸣ [KUR ^{URU}]⸢*Ḫa-pa-a-nu*⸣*-wa-an*
31. [GUL*-aḫ-ta* … *ŠA* K]UR ^{URU}*M*[*i-ra*]*-a ME-ŠE-IL-ŠU* ⸢*IŠ-TU*⸣ ^{m}*Maš-ḫ*[*u-i-lu-wa*]
32. [*ti-ya-at* …] *na-aš-za ŠA* KUR <URU>KÙ.BABBAR*-ši* DÙ*-at*

(uninscribed space for approximately 6 lines follows; then gap of uncertain length)

41. Transliteration of Texts A and B is based upon the copies in KUB 14 as well as upon Götze's corrections included in his edition of 1933.

§1' (A i 23–26) When spring arrived, [because Uhha-ziti had supported the King of **Ahhiyawa**] and […] the land of Millawanda to the King of **Ahhiyawa**, [I, My Majesty, …] and [dispatched] Gulla and Mala-ziti, infantry [and chariotry, and they] attacked [the land of Millawanda]. They captured it, together with civilian captives, cattle, and sheep, [and brought them to Hattusa].

§2' (A i 27–32) Because Mashuiluwa, [King of Mira], occupied the town of Impa, Piyama-Kurunta, [son] of Uhha-ziti, [met him in battle]. My gods ran before Mashuiluwa, [so that] he defeated [Piyama-Kurunta, son of Uhha-ziti], and crushed him. And when [Mashuiluwa] had defeated [Piyama-Kurunta], son of Uhha-ziti, he indeed went further and [attacked] the town of Hapanuwa. […] Half [of] the land of Mira [supported] Mashuiluwa, […] And it became part of the land of Hatti.

(gap)

B ii

§3'

1'. […] x x […]

2'. […]-⸢*a*?⸣ *an*-⸢*da a*?⸣[- …]

3'. […]-*ra-am e-ep-t*[*a* …]

4'. [… -*mu*] *za-aḫ-ḫi-ya an-da* [*Ú-UL ti-ya-at*]

5'. [… *pí-ra-a*]*n ar-ḫa tar-na-aš*

6'. [… ^{URU}*Pí*?- … -*š*]*a-an ar-ḫa*^{er} *wa-ar-n*[*u-nu-un*]

7'. [*na-an IŠ-TU* NAM.RA.MEŠ GUD.MEŠ UDU.ḪI.A *ša-ra-a da-aḫ-ḫu-u*]*n na-an* ^{URU}*Ḫa-at-tu-ši ar*-⸢*ḫa*⸣ [*ú-da*]-⸢*a*?-*aḫ*?-*ḫu*?-*un*⸣

---

§4'

8'. [(GIM-*an-ma* ^{URU}*Pí*?)- … -*az* ^{URU}*Ḫa-at-tu-ši*] EGIR-*pa ú-wa-nu-un nu-mu* ^{URU}*Pal-ḫu-iš-ša-aš*

9'. [*ku-it ku-u-ru-ri-ya-aḫ-ḫa-an ḫar-ta nu* (*I*)]-⸢*NA*⸣ ^{URU}*Pal-ḫu-iš-ša pa-a-un nu* ^{URU}*Pal-ḫu-iš-ša-an*

10'. [*a*(*r-ḫa wa-ar-nu*)-*nu-un nu-kán I-NA* ^{URU}*Pal-ḫu-iš-ša*] *še-er-pát tu-uz-zi-ya-nu-un nu-uš-ši ḫal-ki*$^{\mathrm{ḪI.A}}$[42]-*uš*

11'. [*a*(*r-ḫa ḫar-ni-i*)*n-ku-un ku-it-ma-an-m*]*a-za I-NA* ^{URU}*Pal-ḫu-iš-ša e-šu-un*

12'. [*ḫal-ki*$^{\mathrm{ḪI.A}}$-*uš-ma-aš-ši a*(*r-ḫa ḫa*)]*r-ni-in-ki-iš-ki-nu-un* ^{LÚ}KÚR ^{URU}*Ga-aš-ga-aš-ma-mu*

13'. [GUL-*aḫ-ta*? *n*(*a-aš ḫu-u-m*)]*a-an-za an-da wa-ar-re-eš-še-eš-ta nu-za-kán* ^{URU}*Ku-za-aš-ta-ri*-⸢*na*⸣-*an*

14'. [*e-ša-at ma-an ma-a-an*] *i-ya-aḫ-ḫa-at ma-an-mu-kán iš-ki-ša*-⸢*az*⸣

15'. [GUL-*aḫ-ta*? *ma-a*]*ḫ-ḫa-an*[43]-*ma-an-za-an-kán* EGIR-*pa u-uḫ-ḫu-un*

16'. [*nu-uš-ša-an pé-e-di* (*wa-aḫ*)]-*nu-nu-un nu-uš-ši za-aḫ-ḫi-ya-pát an-da ti-i-ya-nu-un*

17'. [(*nu-mu*[44] DINGIR.MEŠ *p*)*í-ra-an ḫu-u-i-e-er*] ^{d}U NIR.GÁL *BE-LÍ-YA* ^{d}UTU ^{URU}*A-ri*-⸢*in*⸣-*na*[45] GAŠAN-*YA*

18'. [^{d}U ^{URU}*Ḫa-at-ti* ^{d}LAMMA ^{URU}*Ḫa-at*]-*ti* ^{d}U[46] KARAŠ ^{d}U *MUL-TAR*[-*RI-Ḫ*]*U* ^{d}*IŠTAR* LÍL

19'. [*n*(*u-za* ^{LÚ})]KÚR *tar-aḫ-ḫu-un na-an-kán ku-e*-⸢*nu-un*⸣ *nu* ^{LÚ}KÚR

---

42. C:6' omits.

43. C:12': [G]IM-*an*.

44. D ii 5' omits.

45. D ii 6': ^{URU}TÚL[-.

46. C:16': ^{d}IŠKUR.

§3' (B ii 1'–7') [... did not meet me] in battle, [...] yielded [...] I burned down [the town of ... , and captured it, together with civilian captives, cattle, and sheep], and brought them to Hattusa.

§4' (B ii 8'–22') But when I came back [from ... to Hattusa, because] the town of Palhuissa [had become hostile] to me, I went to Palhuissa and burned Palhuissa down. I camped up [in Palhuissa] and destroyed its crops. [But while] I was in Palhuissa destroying [its crops], the Kaskaean enemy [attacked(?)] me, and every one of them came as allies. [They occupied] the town of Kuzastarina. [If I had] marched out, they would have [attacked(?)] me from the rear. But when I saw them from behind, I wheeled around [in place] and met them in battle. Then the gods—the Powerful Storm-God, My Lord, the Sun-Goddess of Arinna, My Lady, [the Storm-God of Hatti, the Tutelary Deity of Hatti], the Storm-God of the Army, the August Storm-God, Shaushga of the Field—ran before me, so that I defeated the enemy, and destroyed them. The enemy [died] in droves, [and] I crossed over to the town of Anziliya. I [subjugated once more ...] all the lands [that] had been hostile to me, and they began to provide me with troops.

20'. [(*pa-an-ga-ri*)-*it* BA.ÚŠ *nu-kán*] *I-NA* URU*An-zi-li-ya pa-a-ri-ya-an pa-a-un*

21'. [(*nu-mu* KUR.KUR.Ḫ)I.A *ku-i-e-eš ḫu*(-*u-m*)]*a-an-te-eš ku-u-ru-ur e-šir*

22'. [*na-aš-za* … *da-a-an* EGIR-*pa* ARAD-*n*]*a-aḫ-ḫu-un nu-mu* ÉRIN.MEŠ *pé-eš-ki-u-wa-an da-a-ir*

---

§5'

23'. [*ma-aḫ-ḫa-an-ma-za ke-e* KUR.KUR.ḪI.A *tar-aḫ-ḫu-un*] *na-aš-za* EGIR-[(*pa* ARAD-*aḫ-ḫu-un*)]

24'. [*nam-ma a-pé-e-da-ni-pát* MU*TI* *I-NA* KUR URU*Ar*-(*za-u-w*)]*a pa-a-un nu* [(*ma-aḫ-ḫa-an I-NA* ÍD*Še-ḫi-ri-ya*)]

A ii

2'. [*a-ar-ḫu-un nu-za* dU NIR.GÁ]L *pa-ra-a ḫa-an-ta-an-*⌈*da*⌉*-tar ti-ik-ku-uš-nu-ut*

3'. [*nu* GIŠ*kal-mi-iš-na-a*]*n ši-ya-it na-an-kán* EGIR-*an-da* KUR URU*Ḫa-at-ti uš-ki-it*

4'. [*me-na-aḫ-ḫa-an-d*]*a-ma-an-kán* KUR *Ar-za-u-wa uš-ki-it nu* GIŠ*kal-mi-iš-na-aš pa-it-pát*

5'. [*nu* URU*A*]-⌈*pa-aš*⌉*-ša-an ŠA* m*Uḫ-ḫa*-LÚ URU-*an* GUL-*aḫ-ta* m*U-uḫ-ḫa*-LÚ-*in-na* GUL-*aḫ-ta*

6'. *na-an i-da-lu-uš* GIG-*aš iš-tar-ak-ta na-aš gi-nu-uš-ši du-ud-*⌈*du-wa-re*⌉*-eš-ta*

7'. dUTU*ŠI*-*ma ma-aḫ-ḫa-an i-ya-aḫ-ḫa-at nu ma-aḫ-ḫa-an* ⌈*A*⌉*-NA* URU*Šal-la-*⌈*pa*⌉ [*a-ar-ḫu-un*]

8'. *nu A-NA* mLUGAL-dXXX-*uḫ ku-it* ŠEŠ-*YA* LUGAL URU*Kar*-[*g*]*a-miš ḫa-*⌈*at*⌉[*-ra-a-an ḫar-ku-u*]*n*

9'. *na-aš-mu* ÉRIN.MEŠ ANŠE.KUR.RA.MEŠ *I-NA* URU*Šal-la-pa pí-ra-*⌈*an*⌉ *ša-ra-a* ⌈*ú*⌉[*-da-aš nu-uš-ši-za ú-wa*]*-a-tar*

10'. *I-NA* URU*Šal-la-pa i-ya-nu-un nam-ma I-NA* KUR URU*Ar-za-u-wa* ⌈*i*⌉[*-ya-aḫ-ḫa-at nu ma*]*-aḫ-ḫa-an*

11'. *I-NA* URU*A-*⌈*ú-ra*⌉ *a-ar-ḫu-un nu* m*Maš-ḫu-i-lu-wa-aš ku-iš* URU[*Im-pa-a--an ḫa*]*r-ta*

12'. *nu-mu me-na-aḫ-ḫa-*[*a*]*n-da u-un-ni-iš-ta na-an pu-u-nu-uš-šu-un* [*na-aš-mu me-mi-iš-t*]*a*

13'. ⌈m*U-uḫ-ḫa*-LÚ-*in-na*⌉[*-wa*] ⌈BÚN⌉ DINGIR*LIM* GUL-*aḫ-ta nu-*⌈*wa*⌉*-ra-an* [*i-da-a-lu-uš* GIG-*aš i*]*š-tar-ak-ki-ya-at-ta-at*

14'. [*nu-wa-ra-aš gi-nu-uš-ši*] ⌈*du-ud-du-wa*⌉*-ri-iš-ta nu-*⌈*wa ma-a*⌉[*-an* …]

15'. […] x *ka-ru*[*-ú* …]

16'. […] x *uš* x […]

§5' (B ii 23'–24', A ii 2'–41') [When I had defeated those lands] and subjugated them once more, [in the very same year] I went [again to] Arzawa. And when [I arrived] at the Sehiriya River, [the Powerful Storm-God] made manifest [his] providence. He launched [a lightning bolt], and Hatti watched it go, while Arzawa watched it coming [at them]. The lightning bolt indeed traveled and struck Apasa, the city of Uhha-ziti. It struck Uhha-ziti, so that he became gravely ill; his knees collapsed. When I, My Majesty, marched and [arrived] at the town of Sallapa—because [I had written] to Sharri-Kushuh, my brother, King of Carchemish, he brought up infantry and chariotry to me before Sallapa. I held a review (of the troops) in Sallapa and [marched] further into Arzawa. [And] when I arrived at the town of Aura, Mashuiluwa, who [had occupied the town of Impa], drove out to meet me. I questioned him, [and he told me]: "The lightning bolt struck Uhha-ziti, so that he became [gravely] ill; [his knees] collapsed. And if already [... " ...] fortified camp [...] that one [... on the one side ...], but on the other side [...] one league [...]

(gap)

(gap of around 22 lines; only a few ends of lines preserved)

38’. BÀD K[ARAŠ …]

39’. *a-ši-ma*^{er} [… *ke-e-ez* …]

40’. *ke-e-ez-za-m*[*a* …]

41’. 1 DANNA *ki*[- …]

---

§6’

42’. *ma-aḫ-ḫ*[*a-an* …]

(gap of around 40 lines)

A iii

§7’

24’. *nu-wa ne*-x[- …]

25’. ŠEŠ-*YA-ya* x [o o]-*uš-ki-it* [… *na-an*]

26’. ZI-*an wa-ar-ši-ya-nu*-<*nu*>-⸢*un*⸣ […]

---

§8’

27’. *am-mu-uk-ma-kán* ⸢NAM⸣.RA.MEŠ *ku-it pí-ra-an* ⸢*ar*⸣-*ḫa* [*pár-še-er nu A-NA* ^{m}LUGAL-^{d}XXX-*uḫ* ŠEŠ-*YA kiš-ša-an ḫa-at-ra-a-nu-un*]

28’. NAM.RA.MEŠ-*wa-mu-kán ku-i-e-eš pí-ra-an ar-ḫa pár*-⸢*še-er* NAM.RA ^{URU}*Ḫur*⸣[-*ša-na-aš-ša-kán* NAM.RA ^{URU}*Šu*]-⸢*ru-ta*⸣

29’. *Ù* NAM.RA.MEŠ ^{URU}*At-ta-ri-ma an-da ú*-⸢*e-er nu*⸣-*wa*-⸢*ra-at*⸣ *ku-w*[*a-pí* … *-an-ta-a*]*t*

30’. *ar-ḫa-wa-ra-at-za* ⸢*šar*⸣-*ra-an-da-at nu-wa*-⸢*kán ták*⸣-*ša-an* ⸢*šar*⸣-*r*[*a-an I-NA* $^{ḪUR.SAG}$*A-ri*]-⸢*in*⸣[-*na-a*]*n-ta*

31’. *še-er* NAM.RA.MEŠ ^{URU}*Ḫu*[*r-š*]*a-na-aš-ša-aš-ma*^{er}-*aš-kán* NAM.RA ^{URU}⸢*At*⸣-[*ta-ri-im-ma Ù*] ⸢NAM⸣.RA ⸢^{URU}*Šu-ru-da*⸣

32’. *an-da I-NA* ^{URU}*Pu*-⸢*ra-an*⸣-*ta-ya-wa-kán ták-ša-an šar-ra*-⸢*an*⸣ [*še-er*]

33’. NAM.RA ^{URU}*Ḫur-ša-na-aš-ša-ya-wa-aš*^{er}-*ma-aš-kán* NAM.⸢RA⸣ [^{URU}*At-ta-ri-im-ma*] ⸢*Ù* NAM.RA ^{URU}*Šu*⸣-*ru-ta an*-⸢*da*⸣

---

§9’

34’. *nu-mu-kán* NAM.⸢RA.ḪI.A⸣ *ku-it pí-ra-an ar-ḫa pár-še-er nu-uš-ma-aš*[-*kán* ḪUR.SAG.MEŠ *na-ak*]-⸢*ke-e-eš*⸣ EGIR-*pa*

35’. *e-ep-pí-ir*[47] [(*nu-za*)] ^{m}LUGAL-^{d}XXX-⸢*an*⸣ LUGAL ^{URU}*Kar-ga-miš* ŠEŠ-*YA* x [… *ta-pa*]-*ri-ya-an ti-it-ta-nu-nu-un*

36’. NAM.RA.Ḫ[I.A-*wa-ká*]*n ku-it pí-ra-an* ⸢*ar-ḫa*⸣ *pár-še-er nu-wa*-⸢*aš*⸣-*m*[*a-aš-ká*(*n* ḪUR.SAG)].MEŠ *na-ak*-⸢*ki*⸣-*ya-aš*

47. B iii 2’: -*i*]*r*.

§7' (A iii 24'–26') […] my brother was […] I calmed him […]

§8' (A iii 27'–33') [I wrote as follows to Sharri-Kushuh, my brother, about] the civilian captives who [had fled] before me: "The civilian captives who fled before me, the captives [of the towns of Hu(wa)rsanassa and Suruda] and the captives of the town of Attarimma came here, and when [they …], they split up. A portion is up on Mt. Arinnanda; among them are captives of Hu(wa)rsanassa, [Attarimma, and] Suruda. A portion is [up] in the town of Puranda; among them are (also) captives of Hu(wa)rsanassa, [Atarimma], and Suruda."

§9' (A iii 34'–52') The captives who fled before me took refuge in inaccessible [mountains]. I installed my brother, Sharri-Kushuh, King of Carchemish, as commander […], (saying): "The captives who fled before me have taken refuge in inaccessible mountains, and our time is short—let us proceed to encircle either one (of the groups) and carry them off." [Then I, My Majesty], went to Mt. Arinnanda. This Mt. Arinnanda is very inaccessible. It stretches out into the sea and furthermore is very high and thickly wooded. Finally, it is rocky and not suitable for the ascent of chariotry. All of the civilian captives occupied it, and

37'. EG[IR-*pa e-e*]*p-pir* MU.KAM-*za-ma-wa-an-na-aš* ⸢*še-er*⸣ *te-e-pa-u-*⸢*e*⸣*-e*[(*š-ša-an-za nu-wa-kán*)] *ú-wa-at-ten*

38'. 1[*-e-da-*(*ni ku*)]*-e-da-ni-ik-ki wa-ar-pa ti*[48]*-ya-*⸢*u*⸣*-e-ni nu-w*[(*a-ra-an-kán kat-ta*)] ⸢*ú*⸣*-wa-te-u-e-ni*

39'. [*nu* ^{d}UTU^{ŠI} (*I-N*)]*A* $^{ḪUR.SAG}$*A-ri-in-na-an-da pa-a-un a-ši-*⸢*ma*⸣ [($^{ḪUR.SA}$)^{G}*A-ri-i*(*n-na-an-da-a*)]*š me-ek-ki*

40'. [(*na-ak-ki*)]*-*⸢*iš*⸣ *a-ru-ni-ya-aš-kán pa*[49]*-ra-an-da* ⸢*pa-a-an-za*⸣ *na*[(*m-ma-aš me-ek-ki pár-ku-u*)]*š wa-ar-ḫu-i*[50]*-ša-aš*

41'. *nam-ma-aš* ^{NA_4}*pé*[51]*-ru-*⸢*na-an*⸣*-za nu-kán IŠ-*⸢*TU* ANŠE.KUR.RA.MEŠ⸣ *š*[(*a-ra-a pé-en-nu-ma-a*)]*n-za Ú-UL* DÙ*-ri*[52]

42'. NAM.RA.MEŠ*-ma-an pa-an-*⸢*ku-uš*⸣ *ḫar-ta* ⸢ÉRIN.MEŠ*-ya-kán pa-an-ku*⸣[(*-uš še-er e-eš-ta*)] *nu-kán* ⸢*IŠ-TU*⸣ ANŠE.KUR.RA[53]

43'. *ku-it ša-ra-a pé-*⸢*en-nu-ma-an*⸣*-zi* ⸢*Ú*⸣[(*-UL ki-ša-at nu* ^{d})UTU^{ŠI} *A*]*-NA* KARAŠ.ḪI.A GÌR-[(*i*)]*t*

44'. *pí-ra-an ḫu-u-i-ya-nu-un nu-*⸢*kán*⸣ [(*I-NA* $^{ḪUR.SAG}$*A*)*-ri-in-n*(*a-an-da* GÌR*-it š*)]*a-ra-a pa-a-un*

45'. *nu-kán* NAM.RA.MEŠ ⸢*ka*[54]*-aš*⸣*-ti ka-ni-*[(*in-ti an-da ḫ*)*a-at-ke-eš-nu-nu-*(*un nu*)]*-uš-ši ma-aḫ-ḫa-an*

46'. *ka*[55]*-aš-ti* ⸢*ka*[56]*-ni-in*⸣*-ti na-*⸢*ak-ke*⸣[(*-e-eš-ta nu-kán* NAM.RA.MEŠ *kat-ta*)] ⸢*ú*⸣*-e-er na-at-mu* ⸢GÌR.MEŠ⸣*-aš*

47'. *kat-ta-an ḫa*[57]*-li-ya-an-*⸢*da*⸣*-at BE*[(*-LÍ-NI-wa-an-na-aš le-e ḫar-ni-ik-ti*)] *nu*[(*-wa*)]*-an-na-aš-za BE-LÍ-NI*

48'. ARAD*-an-ni da-a nu-wa-an-na-aš*[(*-kán* ^{URU}*Ḫa-at-tu-ši ša-ra-a pé-e-ḫu*)*-t*]*e* [*nu-*(*m*)]*u* GIM*-an*[58] NAM.RA.MEŠ

49'. GÌR.ḪI.A*-aš kat-ta-an ḫa-a-*⸢*li*⸣*-y*[(*a-an-da-at nu-kán* NAM.RA.MEŠ *IŠ-TU* $^{ḪUR.SAG}$*A-ri-in*)]*-na-an-da kat-ta*

50'. ⸢*ú*⸣*-wa-te-nu-un nu-za am-mu-uk* 1[*-aš*[59] *I*(*-NA* É*-YA* 1) SI(G$_7$ 5 *LI-IM* 5 *ME* NAM.RA.M)]EŠ *ú-wa-te-nu-un*

48. B iii 6' inserts *-i-*.
49. B iii 8': *pár-*.
50. B iii 9': *-iš-*.
51. B iii 9': inserts *-e-*.
52. B iii 10': *ki-ša-at*.
53. B iii 11' adds MEŠ.
54. B iii 14' inserts *-a-*.
55. B iii 15' inserts *-a-*.
56. B iii 15' inserts *-a-*.
57. B iii 16' inserts *-a-*.
58. B iii 18': *ma-aḫ-ḫa-an*.
59. B iii 22' omits 1*-aš*.

all of the (enemy) infantry were up there. And because it was not suitable for the ascent of chariotry, I, [My Majesty], ran on foot before the army. I went up Mt. Arinnanda on foot. I kept exerting pressure on the captives through hunger and thirst, and when hunger and thirst weighed heavily upon them, the captives came down and fell down at my feet, (saying): "May you, our lord, not destroy us, but take us into your service! Take us up to Hattusa!" When the captives fell down at my feet, I brought the captives down from Mt. Arinnanda. I alone brought 15,500 captives to my household. The captives whom the infantry, chariotry, and *sarikuwa*-soldiers of Hattusa brought back were without number.

51’. ^{URU}*Ḫa-at-tu-ša-aš-ma-za* ÉRIN.MEŠ ANŠE.KUR.RA.M[E(Š ^{ÉRIN})].^{MEŠ}[(*ša-a-ri-ku-wa-aš-ša* NAM.RA *ku-i*)]*n*

52’. [(*ú-wa-te-et nu-uš*)-*ša-a*]*n kap-pu-u-wa-u-wa-ar* NU.GÁL [(*e-eš-ta*)]

B iii

§10’

23’. *nu-kán ma-aḫ-ḫa-an IŠ-TU* $^{ḪUR.SAG}$⸢*A-ri*⸣[-*in*(-*na-an-da* NAM.RA.MEŠ *kat*)]-*ta ú-wa-te-nu-un*

24’. *na-an-kán* ^{URU}KÙ.BABBAR-*ši pa-ra-a ne-eḫ-ḫu-u*[*n nu* ^{d}UTU^{ŠI} (*I-NA* ^{URU}*P*)]*u-u*[60]-*ra-an-da A-NA* N[AM.RA].M[EŠ]

25’. EGIR-*an-da pa-a-un ma-aḫ-ḫa-an-ma I-NA* ^{URU}[… (*a-ar-ḫu-un nu A-NA* LÚ.MEŠ) ^{URU}*Pu-u-ra*(-*an-da*)]

26’. *ḫa-at-ra-a-nu-un šu-me-eš-wa-aš-ma-aš* ARAD.MEŠ ⸢*A*⸣-*B*[*I-YA* (*e-eš-te-en nu-wa-aš-m*)*a-aš A-BU-Y*(*A da-a-aš*)]

27’. *nu-wa-aš-ma-aš A-NA* ^{m}*U-uḫ-ḫa*-LÚ ARAD-*an-ni pa-i*[*š-ta a-pa-a-aš-ma-wa A-NA* LUGAL **KUR *Aḫ-ḫi-*(*ú-wa-a*)]**

28’. EGIR-*an ti-i-ya-at nu-wa*<-*mu*> *ku-u-ru-ri-ya-a*[(*ḫ-ta*) *šu-me-eš-ma-za* EGIR-*pa am-me-el*]

29’. *ki-iš-du-ma-at nu-wa A-NA* ^{m}*U-uḫ-ḫa*-LÚ [(EGIR-*an*) *le-e nam-ma ti-ya-at-te-ni nu-wa-aš-ma-aš-kán*]

30’. *am-me-el ku-i-e-eš* ARAD.MEŠ-*YA* NAM.RA [(^{URU}*Ḫur-ša-na-aš-ša*) NAM.RA ^{URU}*Šu-ru-da*]

31’. *Ù* NAM.RA ^{URU}*At-ta-a-ri-im-ma* [*an-da ú-e-er* (*nu-wa*)-*ra-aš-m*(*u pa-ra-a*) *pé-eš-ten*]

32’. *a-pu-u-uš-ma-mu* EGIR-*pa ki-iš-ša*[-*an ḫa-at-ra-a-ir … -wa- …*]

33’. *ḫar*-⸢*u*⸣-*e-ni nu-wa-kán an-za-a-aš ku*-⸢*i*⸣[-*e-eš* ARAD.MEŠ-*KA an-da ú-e-er Ú-UL-wa-ra-aš-ta*]

34’. *pa-ra-a pí-i-ya-u-e-ni*^{er} *I*[-*NA* …]

35’. *ma-a-an-wa-ra-aš-kán a-ru-ni an*[-*da* …]

36’. *nu-wa-aš-ši* EGIR-*an-da u-i*[-*ya-u-e-ni* …]

37’. *tar-nu-um-me-e-ni am-mu*[-*uk-ma* …]

38’. *ŠU-U-RI-PU ku-it ka-r*[*u-ú ki-ša-at nam-ma* EGIR-*pa I-NA* ^{ÍD}*Aš-tar-pa*]

39’. *ú-wa-nu-un nu-za* BÀD [KARAŠ *I-NA* ^{ÍD}*Aš-tar-pa wa-aḫ-nu-nu-un*]

40’. ^{m}*U-uḫ-ḫa*-LÚ-*iš-ma k*[*a-* …]

41’. *iš-tar-ak-ki-ya-a*[*t-ta-at na-aš* BA.ÚŠ…]

42’. DAM-*SÚ-ma-aš-ši-ká*[*n* …]

43’. ⸢^{m}SUM-*ma*-^{d}⸣L[AMMA …]

(gap of uncertain length)

---

60. A iii 54’ omits -*u*.

§10' (B iii 23'–43') When I brought the captives down from Mt. Arinnanda, I dispatched them to Hattusa. [And] I, My Majesty, after [the captives] (had gone), went to Puranda. When I arrived at […], I wrote to the people of Puranda: "You were subjects of [my] father, and [my father] took you and gave you in service to Uhha-ziti. [But] he supported [the King of **Ahhiyawa**] and became hostile to me. (Now) you must become mine [again], and [no longer support] Uhha-ziti. And turn over to me my subjects—the civilian captives of Hu(wa)rsanassa and [Suruda] and the captives of Attarimma—who [came to you]." They [wrote] back to me as follows: "We hold […, and] we will [not] turn over [your subjects who came to us. …] If he is in the midst of the sea, […] we will send back to him […] we will release." I […] Because winter [had already arrived]. I came [back to the Astarpa River] and [pitched] camp [at the Astarpa River]. But Uhha-ziti […] became ill [and died. …] his wife to him […] Piyama-Kurunta […]

(gap)

A iv

§11'

14'. ^{m}*Ma-na-pa-*^{d}[U-*an-ma-kán ku-in* ŠEŠ.MEŠ-*ŠU IŠ-TU* KUR-*ŠU ar-ḫa wa-at-ku-nu-ir*]

15'. *na-an-kán am-mu*[*-uk A-NA*] ⸢LÚ⸣.MEŠ [^{URU}*Kar-ki-ša an-da*] *wa-tar-na-a*[*ḫ-ḫu-un*]

16'. *nam-ma-aš-ši* LÚ.MEŠ ^{URU}*Kar-*⸢*ki*⸣*-ša še-e*[*r pí-i-ya-an-ni-iš-k*]*i-nu-un* ⸢^{m}*Ma*⸣[*-na-pa-*^{d}U*-aš-ma*]

17'. *am-me-e-da-az Ú-UL ti-i-ya-at nu-mu* ^{m}*Uḫ-ḫa*[-LÚ-*i*]*š ku-it* [*ku-u-ru-ri-ya-aḫ-ta*]

18'. *na-aš-za IŠ-TU ŠA* ^{m}*U-uḫ-ḫa*-LÚ *ki-ša-at n*[*u-uš-ši*] EGIR-*an ti-i*[*-ya-at nu* ^{d}UTU^{ŠI} *I-NA* ^{ÍD}*Še-e-ḫa*]

19'. *pa-a-un ma-aḫ-ḫa-an-ma-mu* ^{m}*Ma-na-pa-*^{d}U*-aš* DUMU ^{m}*Mu-u-wa-*⸢UR.MAḪ⸣ *iš-ta-m*[*a-aš-ta* ^{d}UTU^{ŠI}*-wa*]

20'. *ú-iz-zi nu-mu*^{er} ^{LÚ}*ṬE*$_{4}$*-MA me-na-aḫ-ḫa-an-da u-i-ya-at nu-*⸢*mu*⸣ *kiš-ša-an ḫa*[*-at-ra-a-iš BE-LÍ-wa-mu*]

21'. *le-e ku-e-ši nu-wa-mu-za BE-LÍ* ARAD-*an-ni da-a nu-wa-mu-kán ku-it* LÚ.MEŠ [*an-da ú-e-er*]

22'. *nu-wa-ra-at A-NA*^{er} *BE-LÍ-YA pé-eš-ki-mi am-mu-uk-ma-aš-ši* [*k*]*i-iš-ša-an* EG[IR-*pa AQ-B*]*I*

23'. *an-ni*^{er}*-ša-an-wa-ták-kán ku-wa-pí* ARAD.MEŠ-*KA* KUR-*e-az ar-ḫa wa-at-ku-nu-ir*

24'. *nu-wa-ták-kán A-NA* LÚ.MEŠ ^{URU}*Kar-ki-ša an-da wa-a-tar-na-aḫ*[*-ḫu-u*]*n*

25'. *nam-ma-wa-at-ta* LÚ.MEŠ ^{URU}*Kar-ki-ša še-er pí-i-y*[*a-n*]*i-iš-ki-nu-un nu-wa a-pí-ya*

26'. *am-mu-uk* EGIR-*an Ú-UL ti-i-ya-at nu-wa A*[*-NA* ^{m}*Uḫ*]*-ḫa*-LÚ ^{LÚ}KÚR-*YA*

27'. *ti-i-ya-at ki-nu-na-wa-du-za* ARAD-*an-ni da*[*-aḫ-ḫi m*]*a-an-ši pa-a-un-pát ma-a-na-an* ⸢*ar*⸣*-ḫa*

28'. *ḫar-ni-in-ku-un nu-mu-kán* AMA-*ŠU me-na-aḫ-ḫa*[*-an-da pa-ra*]-⸢*a*⸣ *na-iš-ta na-aš-mu ú-it*

29'. GÌR.MEŠ-*aš kat-ta-an ḫa-li-ya-at-ta-at nu-mu k*[*iš-ša-a*]*n* ⸢*IQ*⸣*-BI BE-LÍ-NI-wa-an-na-aš*

30'. *le-e ḫar-ni-ik-ti nu-wa-an-na-aš-za* ⸢*BE*⸣*-LÍ-NI* ARAD-*an-*⸢*ni*⸣ [*da*]-⸢*a*⸣ *nu-mu* MUNUS^{TU_4} *ku-it*

31'. *me-na-aḫ-ḫa-an-da ú-it na-aš-mu* ⸢GÌR⸣.MEŠ-*aš* GAM-*an ḫa-li-ya*[(*-at*)]*-ta-at*^{er} *nu A-NA* MUNUS^{TI}

32'. *ka-a-ri ti-ya-nu-un nu*^{er} *nam-ma I-NA* ^{ÍD}*Še-e-ḫa* ⸢*Ú*⸣*-UL pa-a-un*

§11' (A iv 14'–33') I gave orders [to] the people [of the town of Karkisa] concerning Manapa-Tarhunta, [whom his brothers had caused to flee from his land], and furthermore, [I rewarded] the people of Karkisa because of him. [But Manapa-Tarhunta] did not take my side. Because Uhha-ziti [became hostile] to me and he became a partisan of Uhha-ziti and [supported him, I, My Majesty], went [to the (land of) the Seha River]. But when Manapa-Tarhunta, son of Muwa-walwi, heard [that My Majesty] was coming, he sent a messenger to meet me, [writing] to me as follows: "Do not kill [me, my lord]; take me into your service! I will give to my lord those people who [came] to me." I [answered] him as follows: "When formerly your subjects caused you to flee (your) land, I gave orders to the people of Karkisa concerning you, and furthermore I rewarded the people of Karkisa because of you. But then you did not take my side, but took the side of my enemy, Uhha-ziti. [Should I] now take you into my service?" I would have gone and destroyed him, but he dispatched his mother to meet me. She came to me and cast herself down at my feet, speaking [as follows]: "May you, our lord, not destroy us; may you, our lord, take us into your service!" And because the woman came to meet me and cast herself down at my feet, I had compassion for the woman and did not go again into (the land of) the Seha River. I accepted Manapa-Tarhunta and the land of the Seha River into vassalage.

33'. *nu-za* ^{m}*Ma-na*<*-pa*>-^{d}U-*an* KUR ^{ÍD}*Še-e-ḫa-ya* ARAD-*an-ni da-aḫ-ḫu-un*

---

§12'

34'. *nam-ma I-NA* KUR ^{URU}*Mi-ra-a* ⸢EGIR⸣-*pa ú-wa-nu-un nu* KUR ^{URU}*Mi-ra-a ta-ni-nu-nu-un*

35'. *nam-ma* ^{URU}*Ar-ša-ni-in* ⸢^{URU}⸣*Ša-a-ra-u-wa-an* ^{URU}*Im-pa*[61]*-an-na ú-e-te--nu-un na-aš* BÀD-*eš-na-nu-un*

36'. *na-aš* ÉRIN.MEŠ *a-ša-an-du-*⸢*lu-az*⸣ *e-ep-pu-un* ^{URU}*Ḫa-a-pa-nu-wa-an-na* ÉRIN.MEŠ *a-ša-an-du-la-za*

37'. *e-ep-pu-un nam-ma* [*I-N*]*A*[62] ^{URU}*Mi*[63]*-ra-a* ^{m}*Maš-ḫu-i-lu-wa-an* EN-*iz-na-an-ni ti-it-ta-nu-nu-un*

38'. *nu A-NA* ^{m}*Maš*^{aš}*-ḫu-i-l*[(*u-w*)]*a kiš*[64]*-ša-an me-ma-aḫ-ḫu-un zi-ik-wa-kán* ^{m}PÍŠ.TUR-*aš*[65]

39'. *PA-NI A-BI-YA* ⸢*pít-ti*⸣*-ya-an-ti-li an-da ú-it nu-wa-at-ta A-BU-YA ša-ra-a da-a-aš*

40'. *nu-wa-du-za* ^{LÚ}⸢*ḪA*⸣*-TÁ*[66]*-NU i-ya-at nu-wa-at-ta* ^{f}*Mu-u-wa-at-tin a-pé*[67]*-el* DUMU.MUNUS-*SÚ*

41'. NIN-*YA A-NA* DAM-*UT-TI-ŠU pé-eš-ta* EGIR-*an-ma-wa-ra-aš-t*[(*a*)] *Ú-UL ti-i-ya-at*

42'. [(*nu-wa-at-ták-kán*)] $^{\text{LÚ.MEŠ}}$KÚR^{er}*-KA še-er Ú-UL ku-en-ta nu-wa-ra-at-t*[(*a*)] *am-mu-uk* ⸢EGIR⸣*-an*

43'. [(*ti-i-ya-nu-u*)]*n nu-wa-ták-kán* $^{\text{LÚ.MEŠ}}$KÚR-*KA še-er ku-e-nu-un nam-*[*m*(*a*)]*-wa* URU.DIDLI.ḪI.A

44'. [(*ú-e-te-nu-u*)]*n nu-wa-ra-aš* BÀD-*eš*$_{17}$[68]*-na-nu-un nu-wa-ra-aš* ÉRIN.MEŠ *a-š*[*a-a*]*n-du-la-*[*a*]*z*

45'. [(*e-ep-pu-un*)] *nu-wa-at-ta I-NA* ^{URU}*Mi*[69]*-ra-a* EN-*an-ni ti-it-t*[(*a-nu-nu-u*)]*n*

---

61. B iv 8' inserts *-a*.
62. B iv 10' inserts KUR.
63. B iv 10' inserts *-i-*.
64. B iv 11': *ki-iš-*.
65. B iv 11': ^{m}*Maš-ḫu-i-lu-wa-aš*.
66. B iv 13' inserts *-A-*.
67. B iv 13' inserts *-e*.
68. B iv 16': *-eš-*.
69. B iv 17' inserts *-i-*.

§12' (A iv 34'–45') I came back to the land of Mira and set Mira in order. I rebuilt the towns of Arsani, Sarauwa, and Impa and fortified them. I provided them with garrisons. I provided Hapanuwa with a garrison. Furthermore, I installed Mashuiluwa in rule in Mira, saying to Mashuiluwa as follows: "You, Mashuiluwa, came to my father as a fugitive, and my father took you up and made you his son-in-law, giving you his daughter and my sister Muwatti in marriage. But he could not come to your assistance and defeat your enemies for you. (Now) I have come to your assistance and defeated your enemies for you. Furthermore, I have rebuilt towns, fortified them, and provided them with garrisons. I have installed you in rule in Mira."

§13'

46'. [*nam-ma-aš-ši* 6] *ME* ÉRIN.MEŠ *A-NA* SAG.DU-*ŠU uš-ki-iš-ga-at*[70]-⸢*tal*⸣[(*-la-an-ni p*)]*í-iḫ-ḫu-un*

47'. [*nu-uš-ši kiš-ša*]*-an me-ma-aḫ-ḫu-un* LÚ.MEŠ ^{URU}*Mi*[71]*-ra-*⸢*a-wa*⸣ [(*ku-it mar-š*)]*a-an-te-eš*

48'. [*nu-wa-at-ta*] *ka-a-aš* 6 *ME* ÉRIN.MEŠ SAG.DU-*i uš*[(*-ki-iš-ga-tal-la-aš e-eš*)]*-du A-NA* LÚ.MEŠ ^{URU}*Mi-ra-a*[(*-ma-wa-za*)]

49'. [*an-da le*]*-e ú-e-ri-ya-an-za pí-ra-an-na-wa*[(*-aš-ma-aš le-e ú-e*)*-ri-an-ni-i*]*š-ki-ši*

---

§14'

50'. ⸢*nu ma-aḫ-ḫa*⸣*-an* KUR ⸢^{URU}*Mi-ra-a*⸣ *ta-ni-nu-nu-un nu-kán* KUR ^{U}[^{RU} …]

51'. *nu ma-aḫ-ḫa-an I-N*[*A* ^{URU}*A*]⸢*ú-ra*⸣ *a-ar-ḫu-un nu-m*[*u* …]

52'. *nu A-NA* ^{m}*Maš-ḫu-i*[*-lu-wa* LUGAL KUR ^{URU}*Mi*]⸢*-ra*⸣*-a* KUR ^{URU}*Ku-wa-*⸢*li*⸣[*-ya-ya* EN-*an-ni AD-DIN nu A-NA* ^{m}*Ma-na-pa-*^{d}U]

53' DUMU ^{m}*Mu-u-wa-*UR[.MAḪ LUGAL] ⸢KUR ^{ÍD}⸣*Še-e-ḫa* KUR ⸢^{URU}⸣[*Ap-pa-wi-ya-ya* EN-*an-ni AD-DIN nu A-NA*]

54'. ^{m}*Tar-ga-aš-ša*[*-na-al-li* KUR] ⸢$^{URU?}$*Ḫa*?*-pa*?*-al*?*-la*?⸣ [EN-*an-ni AD-DIN* …]

55'. *an-da* x x […]

56'. *traces*

(text breaks off)

---

70. B iv 18': *-ki-*.

71. B iv 19' inserts *-i*.

§13' (A iv 46'–49') [In addition], I gave [him] 600 soldiers as his personal bodyguard, saying [to him as follows]: "Because the people of Mira are untrustworthy, these 600 soldiers shall be [your] personal bodyguard. They shall not conspire with the people of Mira, and you shall not conspire against them."

§14' (A iv 50'–56') When I had set Mira in order, [I ...] the land of [...] And when I arrived in Aura, to me [... I gave] the land of Kuwaliya to Mašhuiluwa, [King of Mira, to rule; I gave] the land [of Appawiya to Manapa-Tarhunta], son of Muwa-walwi, [King] of the Land of the Seha River, [to rule; and I gave the land] of Hapalla [to] Targasnalli [to rule ...]

Commentary

Shortly after his accession to the Hittite throne ca. 1322, Mursili II embarked on a series of military campaigns designed to reestablish Hittite authority throughout the territories over which his father Suppiluliuma I and his brother Arnuwanda II had held sway. These men had been his predecessors on Hatti's throne, and their unexpected deaths, particularly Arnuwanda's after only a brief reign, had provoked a serious crisis in the kingdom. There were widespread uprisings by subject states and enemy territories alike against the new regime. If the kingdom were to survive this crisis, a prompt and comprehensive response by its new ruler, demonstrating his fitness for royal power and his ability to meet all challenges to his authority, was essential.

Mursili spent his first two regnal years campaigning against the Kaska people, who occupied the Pontic regions north of the Hittite homeland. Then in his third year, he turned his attention westwards. We can sketch out some of the details of the campaigns which he conducted in western Anatolia during his third and fourth years by combining the information contained in his Ten-Year and his Extensive Annals for these years. These documents record defections by a number of Hatti's western subject territories and peoples at the beginning of Mursili's reign. Notable among them was the Land of Millawanda (Milawata) on the Aegean coast, which encompassed the territory of the later Classical city Miletus. From what we can reconstruct of a fragmentary passage in the Extensive Annals (§1'), it appears that Millawanda had formerly been subject to

Hatti, but had now switched its allegiance to the king of Ahhiyawa. So too, a man called Uhha-ziti, identified as a king of Arzawa, had allied himself with the Ahhiyawan king. Millawanda was brought back under Hittite control by two military commanders Gulla and Mala-ziti, dispatched by Mursili to attack and capture it. But a few years later, it was to come firmly under Ahhiyawan sovereignty (see AhT 4).

Of particular significance here is the reference to a king of Ahhiyawa. (Neither here nor in any of the texts which refer to Ahhiyawa is the name of any Ahhiyawan king preserved.) That is to say, in this context, the name Ahhiyawa is used specifically of a kingdom whose ruler became politically and perhaps militarily involved in western Anatolian affairs. This highlights an important aspect of the Ahhiyawa texts: if the equation between Ahhiyawa and the Mycenaean world is valid, then Mycenaean interest in western Anatolia was not merely commercial in nature, but had political and military implications as well. Inevitably, Ahhiyawa's and Hatti's overlapping spheres of interest in the west led to tensions and perhaps on occasion conflicts between them. It seems likely, however, that Ahhiyawa sought to expand its influence and control in western Anatolia through alliances with local rulers, often at the expense of ties which these rulers had with Hatti, rather than by direct military action.

The Arzawan king Uhha-ziti figures in the Annals as the chief target of Mursili's western campaigns, primarily because he had defied the Hittite king by refusing to hand back to him refugees from Hittite authority, namely, from the lands Attarimma, Huwarsanassa, and Suruda (1A §12, 1B §8'). These lands lay in southwestern Anatolia, in or near the the territory called Lukka or Lukka Lands in Hittite texts. We shall have more to say about Lukka below. The rebellion of the peoples of these lands and the refusal of the refugees' protector to give them up is symptomatic of the sharp decline in Hatti's authority in the west, as elsewhere in the Hittite realm, at the beginning of Mursili's reign. Providing sanctuary for refugees from Hittite authority was in the Hittite view tantamount to an act of war and in this case as in others provoked military retaliation. It was perhaps the chief catalyst for Mursili's western campaigns.

We can conclude from both the Ten-Year and the Extensive Annals that Uhha-ziti was king of a land called Arzawa. His capital, Apasa, is generally recognized as the forereunner of Classical Ephesus on the Aegean coast. Remains of what is probably a Late Bronze Age fortification wall unearthed on a hill called Ayasuluk near Ephesus were very likely part of the defences of Uhha-ziti's city. The term "Arzawa" is applied in Hittite texts to a number of countries in western Anatolia, including Mira(-Kuwaliya), the Seha River Land, Hapalla, and (sometimes) Wilusa. Uhha-ziti's kingdom may have been the epicenter of this complex, and is sometimes referred to as "Arzawa Proper" or "Arzawa Minor" to distinguish it from other members of the complex. "Arzawa" appears in some texts as a generic name for the complex as a whole. From the Annals, it is clear that the Arzawa countries were divided in their loyalties, with Mira's king Mashuiluwa taking Mursili's side in the conflict with Uhha-ziti. Mashuiluwa inflicted a crushing defeat on Uhha-ziti's son Piyama-Kurunta when the latter invaded his kingdom, which now became firmly attached, or reattached, to Hatti (1B §2').

Uhha-ziti was undoubtedly emboldened to engage in war with Mursili because of his alliance with the king of Ahhiyawa. But there is no indication that his ally gave him any more than moral support in the conflict that followed. Almost certainly there were strong incentives for Uhha-ziti to risk his kingdom by provoking hostilities with the Hittites, though we have no hint of such incentives from the texts themselves. At all events, Mursili considered Uhha-ziti a formidable opponent, and suspended full-scale operations against him until a later campaign in Arzawa in his third year, following his return to Hattusa and a further expedition into Kaska territory. When he resumed his campaign in the west, his army was reinforced by infantry and chariotry brought from Carchemish by his brother Sharri-Kushuh, who was the viceroy at Carchemish. The two armies joined forces at Sallapa, located somewhere in the vicinity of the Salt Lake (1B §5').

As the combined Hittite armies marched westwards, they received, according to Mursili's account, a helping hand from the Storm-God, who launched a lightning bolt against Arzawa. The divine weapon was seen by Mursili's troops as it passed over their heads on its way to Arzawa, where it struck Uhha-ziti's city and Uhha-ziti himself (1A §17', 1B §5'). Various scholarly attempts have been made to rationalize this peculiar episode. Whatever the explanation, Uhha-ziti was incapacitated by whatever it was that struck him, and was obliged to send his son Piyama-Kurunta in his place to meet the rapidly approaching Hittite forces. In a battle fought at the Astarpa river, which lay outside Arzawa's frontiers, Mursili won a decisive victory over Piyama-Kurunta and then pursued the defeated enemy into their own territory, invading and capturing their royal capital. Uhha-ziti himself escaped capture, when "he went across the sea to the islands and remained there." The likelihood is that the islands in question lay not far off the Aegean coast and belonged to the territory controlled by the king of Ahhiyawa. No doubt Uhha-ziti had arranged with the Ahhiyawan a safe haven in his territory when he formed an alliance with him, in anticipation of a "worst case scenario" in his conflict with the Hittites.

The Hittite occupation of Arzawa resulted in a mass flight of its population, according to Mursili; some sought refuge in a mountain stronghold called Mt. Arinnanda, perhaps to be identified with Classical Mycale on the Aegean coast north of Miletus, some in the city of Puranda, perhaps the fortified hill site now named Bademgediği, a few kilometers west of Torbalı, while others were granted refuge, along with their king Uhha-ziti, in Ahhiyawan territory "across the sea." It seems that this third group included the king's sons Piyama-Kurunta and Tapalazunawali. Mursili only had time to lay siege to and starve the occupants of the Arinnanda stronghold into submission before the onset of winter brought his campaigns for his third year to an end (1A §§18'–19', 1B §§8'–10'). He spent the winter months with his army on the banks of the Astarpa river, where he celebrated an annual religious festival and made ready for an early start to his final military operations in Arzawa the following spring.

It was about this time that the enfeebled Uhha-ziti died in his place of refuge, prompting his son Tapalazunawali to return to his homeland and take on leadership of the remnants of his father's army (perhaps at his father's request) for a final showdown with Mursili. Puranda provided the setting for the last confrontation, and Mursili's defeat of Tapalazunawali's forces and the capture of the city (1A §§20'–24') appear to have marked the end of Arzawan hostilities against Hatti for the rest of his reign. Indeed, scholars generally agree that Mursili may now have totally eradicated Uhha-ziti's kingdom, deporting according to his own account 66,000 of its population to the Hittite homeland, and probably reallocating much if not all of its territory to the neighboring kingdom of Mira, whose ruler Mashuiluwa had been loyal to him throughout the crisis. Tapalazunawali appears to have eluded his conquerors. But his brother Piyama-Kurunta may eventually have been given up to them. This we conclude from a fragmentary passage in the Ten-Year Annals (1A §25') that seems to say that in response to a Hittite delegation which Mursili sent him by ship, the Ahhiyawan king delivered Piyama-Kurunta into Hittite custody, along with a number of other Arzawans who had fled with him to Ahhiyawan territory. If the passage which records this information has been correctly restored and read, it seems to mark a dramatic turn-around in the relations between Ahhiyawa and Hatti, no doubt reflecting Mursili's firm reassertion of Hittite authority in the west and the annihilation of his chief enemy there. Ahhiyawan interests in the region would now best be served by establishing friendly relations with the Hittite king who had for the forseeable future made himself the undisputed overlord of the region.

Mursili completed the consolidation of his authority in this region by diplomatic settlements with the rulers of the other Arzawan kingdoms, setting the appropriate atmosphere by sparing the capital of the Seha River Land, which he had set out to plunder and destroy in retaliation for the support its king Manapa-Tarhunta had given to Uhha-ziti. As he was on the point of attacking the city, he made a last-minute decision to accept Manapa-Tarhunta's appeal for mercy, delivered by his mother before the city-gates (1A §26', 1B §11'), and drew up with him a treaty which confirmed his status as a Hittite vassal. Similar treaties were concluded with Mashuiluwa, king of Mira, and Targasnalli, king of another

Arzawan state, Hapalla. The Targasnalli and Manapa-Tarhunta treaties are still extant (Beckman 1999: 69–73, 82–86).

AhT 2

Treaty between Tudhaliya IV of Hatti and Shaushga-muwa, king of Amurru (CTH 105)

This document is the last known of a series of treaties concluded between Hatti and Amurru. The junior partner, Shaushga-muwa, king of Amurru, was also a Hittite prince, brother-in-law (§6) as well as nephew, of his lord Tudhaliya IV. Perhaps for this reason it was apparently not necessary to translate the treaty into Akkadian, the usual language for agreements and correspondence between the Hittite Great King and his vassals in Syria. In any event, both copies which have come down to us are in Hittite: Text A, which is shown to be a rough draft by its numerous erasures, insertions, and careless placement of text on the tablet, and Text B, which is extremely fragmentary.

The preserved provisions of the text deal almost exclusively with the loyalty demanded by Tudhaliya from Shaushga-muwa toward himself against other potential claimants to the Hittite throne, and toward Hatti against other great powers of the day. It is striking that Tudhaliya admonishes his treaty partner not to conduct himself like an earlier vassal and royal brother-in-law, whose disloyalty toward Urhi-Teshshup (Mursili III) had helped Tudhaliya's own father Hattusili III seize power in Hatti (§§7-8). Also of interest are the restrictions that the Hittite Great King seeks to impose on the trade of his Assyrian enemy (§13).

A. 93/w (+) KUB 23.1 + KUB 31.43 (+) KUB 23.37 (+) 720/v (+) 670/v
B. 1198/u + 1436/u + 69/821 + KUB 8.82

A i
§1

1. [*UM-MA Ta-ba-ar-na* ^{m}*Tu-ud-ḫa-l*]*i-ya* LUGAL.GAL
2. [LUGAL KUR ^{URU}*Ḫ*(*a-at-ti* UR).SAG *NA*-(*RA-AM* ^{d}UT)]U ^{URU}*A-ri-in*[-(*na*)]
3. [DUMU ^{m}*Ḫa-at-tu-ši-li* LUGAL.GAL LUGAL KUR ^{URU}*Ḫ*]*a-at-ti* UR.S[AG]
4. [DUMU.DUMU ^{m}*M*(*u-ur-ši-l*)*i* LUGAL.G(AL LUGAL KUR ^{URU}*Ḫa-at-ti* UR.SAG)][72]

72. B obv. inserts paragraph stroke and skips to A i 8.

PREAMBLE

§1 (A i 1–7) [Thus says the Tabarna, Tudhaliya], Great King, [King of] Hatti, Hero, beloved of the Sun-Goddess of Arinna; [son of Hattusili, Great King, King] of Hatti, Hero; [grandson of] Mursili, Great [King], King of Hatti, Hero; [descendant] of Tudhaliya, [Great King, King] of Hatti, Hero:

5. […] ^{erasure} […]
6. [NUMUN *ŠA* ^{m}*T*]*u-ud-ḫa-li-ya* L[UGAL.GAL]
7. [LUGAL KUR ^{URU}*Ḫ*]*a-at-ti* UR.SAG

---

§2
8. [*tu-uk* ^{md}]⸢*IŠTAR*⸣*-mu-u-wa-an* ^{d}UTU^{Š}[^{I} ŠU-*ta AṢ-BAT*]
9. [*nu-ud-du-za* ^{L}]^{Ú}*ḪA-DA-A-NU i-ya-n*[(*u-un*)]
10. [(*nu-ut-ta iš*)]*-ḫi-ú-la-aš ku-it* [*tup-pí*]
11. [*i-ya-nu-un*] *nu-kán tup-pí-aš* [*me-mi-ya-nu-uš*]
12. [*le-e wa-aḫ*]*-nu-ši*

--- [73]

§3
13. [*an-ni-iš-ša-an*] KUR ^{URU}*A-mur-ra*[74] ⸢*Ú*⸣[*-UL*[75] (*IŠ-TU* ^{GIŠ}T)]UKUL
14. [(*ŠA* KUR ^{URU}*Ḫa*)]*-at-ti tar-aḫ-ḫ*[*a-an*] *e-eš-ta*
15. [^{m}*A-zi-ra-aš ku-w*]*a-pí IT-TI A-BI A-BI* ^{d}UTU^{ŠI}
16. [^{m}*Šu-up-pí-lu*]*-*⸢*li*⸣[*-(u-m)*]*a I-NA* KUR ^{URU}*Ḫa-at-ti*
17. [(*ú-it nu*)] KUR.KUR.ḪI.⸢A⸣ ^{URU}*A-mur-ru*[76] *nu-u-wa*
18. [*ku-u-ru-u*]*r e-eš-ta* ARAD.MEŠ *ŠA* LUGAL *Ḫur-ri-at*
19. [*e-eš-ta*] *nu-uš-ši* ^{m}[*A*]*-zi-ra-aš QA-TAM-MA*
20. [(*pa-aḫ-ḫa-aš-t*)]*a-at IŠ*[*-(T)*]*U* ^{GIŠ}TUKUL*-ma-an-za-an*
21. [*Ú-UL tar*]*-aḫ-ta nu* [^{m}*A*]*-zi-ra-aš A-BA-A-BI-KA*
22. [^{m}*Šu-up-pí*]*-lu-li-u-ma-an AŠ-ŠUM* EN*-UT-TA*[77] PAP*-aš-ta*
23. [KUR ^{URU}*Ḫa-a*]*t-ti-ya pa-aḫ-ḫa-aš-ta*
24. *kat-ta-ya* ^{m}*Mu-ur-ši-li-in AŠ-ŠUM* EN*-UT-TA*
25. *pa-aḫ-ḫa-aš-ta* KUR ^{URU}*Ḫa-at-ti-ya* PAP*-aš-ta*
26. *nu IT-TI* KUR ^{URU}*Ḫa-at-ti Ú-UL ku-it-ki*
27. *wa-aš-ta-aš*

---

§4
28. GIM*-an-ma* ^{m}NIR.GÁL*-iš* ⸢ŠEŠ⸣ *A-BI* ^{d}UTU^{ŠI}
29. LUGAL*-iz-zi-at nu-uš-ši* LÚ.MEŠ KUR ^{URU}*A-mur-ra*[78]
30. IGI*-an-da*[79] *wa-aš-te-er nu-uš-ši a-pa-a-at*
31. *wa-a-tar-na-aḫ-ḫi-ir a-aš-ši-ya-an-na-aš-wa-an-na-aš*

73. B obv. omits.
74. B obv. 5: *-ri*.
75. B obv. 5: [*na-at*]*-ta*.
76. B obv. 6: KUR *A-*⸢*mur*⸣*-ri*.
77. B obv. 8: *-TIM*.
78. B obv. 10: *-ri*.
79. B obv. 10: *me-na-a*[*ḫ-ḫa-an*]*-da*.

§2 (A i 8–12) I, My Majesty, [have taken you], Shaushga-muwa, [by the hand], and have made [you my] brother-in-law. And you [shall not alter the words] of the treaty tablet which [I have made] for you.

Historical Introduction

§3 (A i 13–27) [Earlier] the land of Amurru had not been defeated [by] the force of the arms of Hatti. When [Aziru] came to the (great-)grandfather of My Majesty, [Suppiluliuma], in Hatti, the lands of Amurru were still [hostile]. They [were] vassals of the King of Hurri, and Aziru correspondingly was loyal to him. But although he did [not] defeat him by force of arms, Aziru, your (great-great-) grandfather, became loyal to Suppiluliuma in regard to authority, and he was loyal to Hatti. Later on he was also loyal to Mursili in regard to authority, and he was loyal to Hatti. In no way did he commit an offense against Hatti.

§4 (A i 28–39) But when Muwattalli, uncle of My Majesty, became king, the people of Amurru committed an offense against him, informing him thus: "We were vassals out of affection. Now we are no longer your vassals." And they went over to the King of Egypt. Then My Majesty's uncle Muwattalli and the King of Egypt fought over the people of Amurru. Muwattalli defeated him, destroyed the land of Amurru by force of arms, subjugated it, and made Shapili king in the land of Amurru.

32. ARAD.MEŠ *e-šu-en ki-nu-un-ma-wa*[80]*-tu-za Ú-UL*[81] ARAD.MEŠ
33. *na-at-kán A-NA* LUGAL KUR[82] ^{URU}*Mi-iz-za-ri-i* EGIR-*pa-an-da*
34. *ti-i-e-er nu* ŠEŠ *A-BI* ^{d}UTU$^{\check{S}I}$ ^{m}NIR.GÁL-*iš*
35. LUGAL KUR ^{URU}*Mi-iz-za*[83]*-ri-ya A-NA* LÚ.MEŠ KUR *A-mur-ra*[84]
36. *še-er za-aḫ-ḫi-ir na-an-za-an* ^{m}NIR.GÁL-*iš*
37. *tar-aḫ-ta* KUR ^{URU}*A-mur-ri-ya IŠ-TU* ^{GIŠ}TUKUL
38. *ar-ḫa ḫar-ga-nu-ut na-at-za* ARAD-*na*[85]*-aḫ-ta*
39. *nu I-NA* KUR ^{URU}*A-mur-ri* ^{m}*Ša-pí-li-in* LUGAL-*un* DÙ-*at*[86]

---

§5

40. GIM-*an-ma-za* ^{m}NIR.GÁL-*iš* ŠEŠ *A-BI* ^{d}UTU$^{\check{S}I}$
41. DINGIR^{LIM}-*iš ki-ša-at nu A-BI* ^{d}UTU$^{\check{S}I}$
42. ^{m}*Ḫa-at-tu-ši-li-iš* LUGAL-*iz-zi-at*
43. *nu* ^{m}*Ša-pí-li-in ar-ḫa ti-it-ta-nu-ut*
44. ^{m}*Pé-en-te-ši-na-an A-BU-KA I-NA* KUR *A-mur-ri*
45. LUGAL-*un* DÙ-*at*[87] *nu A-BI* ^{d}UTU$^{\check{S}I}$ PAP-*aš-ta*
46. KUR ^{URU}KÙ.BABBAR-*ti Ú-UL ku-it-ki*
47. *ua-aš-ta-aš*

--- [88]

A ii

§6

1. [*nu-ut-t*]*a* ^{d}⌈UTU$^{\check{S}I}$⌉ LUGAL.GAL *tu-uk* ^{d}*IŠTAR*-A.A-*an* ŠU-*ta AṢ-BA*[*T*]
2. [*nu-u*]*d-du-za* ^{LÚ}*ḪA-DA-A*[89]*-NU* DÙ-*nu-un*[90] *nu-ut-ta* NIN-*YA* DAM-*an*[-*ni*]
3. *pí-iḫ-ḫu-un nu-ut-ta I-NA* KUR ^{URU}*A-mur-ri* LUGAL-*un* DÙ-*nu-un*
4. *nu AŠ-ŠUM* EN-*UT-TI* ^{d}UTU$^{\check{S}I}$ PAP-*ši kat-ta-ya* DUMU.MEŠ DUMU.DUMU.MEŠ
5. NUMUN *ŠA* ^{d}UTU$^{\check{S}I}$ *AŠ-ŠUM* EN-*UT-TI* PAP-*ši*
6. *ta-ma-i-in* EN-*UT-TA le-e i-la-li*[-*ya-š*]*i*
7. *ka-a-aš-ta me-mi-aš ŠA-PAL NI-EŠ* DINGIR^{LIM} *ki-it-ta-ru*

---

80. B obv. 11 inserts *-at-*.
81. B obv. 11: *n*[*a-at-t*]*a*.
82. B obv. 11 omits.
83. B obv. 12 omits.
84. B obv. 12: *-ri*.
85. B obv. 13 omits.
86. B obv. 14: [*i-y*]*a-at*.
87. B obv. 16: *i-ya-at*.
88. B obv. omits.
89. B obv. 18 omits.
90. B obv. 18: *i-y*[*a-nu-un*].

§5 (A i 40–48) But when Muwattalli, the uncle of My Majesty, became a god (that is, died), the father of My Majesty, Hattusili, became King. He deposed Shapili and made Benteshina, your father, king in the land of Amurru. He was loyal to the father of My Majesty, and he was loyal to Hatti. In no way did he commit an offense against Hatti.

LOYALTY TO HITTITE DYNASTY

§6 (A ii 1–6) [And] I, My Majesty, Great King, have taken you, Shaushga-muwa, by the hand [and] have made you my brother-in-law. I have given you my sister in marriage and have made you king in the land of Amurru. Be loyal to My Majesty in regard to authority. And later on be loyal to the sons, grandsons, and progeny of My Majesty in regard to authority. You shall not desire some other authority for yourself. Let this matter be placed under oath for you.

---

§7

8. *tu-uk-ma-za* [^{m}]^{d}*IŠTAR*-A.A-*an* ^{LÚ}*ḪA-DA-A-NU ku-it* DÙ-*nu-u*[*n*]
9. *nu* ^{d}UTU^{ŠI} *AŠ-Š*[*UM* E]N-*UT-TI pa-aḫ-ši kat-ta-ya* DUMU.MEŠ DUMU.DUMU.MEŠ
10. NUMUN *ŠA* ^{d}⸢UTU⸣^{ŠI} *AŠ-*⸢*ŠUM*⸣ EN-*UT-TI pa-aḫ-ši* ŠEŠ.MEŠ ^{d}UTU^{ŠI}-*ma*
11. *ku-i-e-eš* [*š*]*a-ku-wa-šar-ru-*⸢*uš*⸣ DUMU.MEŠ $^{MUNUS.MEŠ}$*I-ŠAR-TI-ya ku-i-*⸢*e*⸣*-eš*
12. *ŠA A-BI* ^{d}UTU^{ŠI} *nam-ma-*⸢*ya*⸣ *ku-*⸢*it*⸣ *ta-ma-i* NUMUN LUGAL-*UT*[*-TI*]
13. $^{LÚ.MEŠ}$*pa-*⸢*aḫ*⸣*-ḫur-ši-iš-ta ku-i-e-*⸢*eš*⸣ *nu-za a-pí-ya*
14. *AŠ-ŠUM* EN-[*U*]*T-TI le-e ku-in-ki i-*⸢*la*⸣*-li-ya-ši*
15. *Š*[*A* ^{m}*M*]*a-aš-*⸢*tu*⸣*-ri i-wa-ar le-e i-ya-ši*
16. [^{m}*M*]*a-aš-tu-ri-iš ku-iš* LUGAL KUR ^{ÍD}*Še-e-ḫa e-eš-ta*
17. *na-an* ^{m}NIR.GÁL-*iš da-a-aš na-an-za-an* ^{LÚ}*ḪA-DA-NU* DÙ-*at*
18. *nu-uš-ši* ^{f}DINGIR.MEŠ.IR NIN-*ŠU* DAM-*an-ni pé-eš-ta*
19. *na-an I-NA* KUR ^{ÍD}*Še-e-ḫa* LUGAL-*un i-ya-at*

---

§8

20. GIM-*an-ma-za* ^{m}NIR.GÁL-*iš* DINGIR^{LIM}-*iš* ⸢*ki-ša*⸣*-at*
21. ⸢*nu*⸣ ^{m}*Úr-ḫi-*^{d}<U>-*up-aš* DUMU ^{m}NIR.GÁL LUGAL-*iz*[*-z*]*i-at*
22. [*nu A-BI-Y*]*A* ⸢*A-NA*⸣ ^{m}*Úr-ḫi-*^{d}U-*up* LUGAL-*iz-na-*⸢*tar*⸣ *ar-ḫa* ME-*a*[*š*]
23. *erased*
24. [^{m}*Ma-aš-d*]*u-ri-iš-ma-kán ku-pí-ya-ti-in ku-up-ta*
25. ⸢*na-an da*⸣*-at-ta ku-iš* ^{m}NIR.GÁL-*iš*
26. ^{LÚ}*ḪA-DA-NU-y*[*a-a*]*n ku-iš* DÙ-*at nu nam-ma a-pé-el* DUMU-⸢*ŠU*⸣
27. ^{m}*Úr-ḫi-*^{d}U-*up-an Ú-UL pa-aḫ-ḫa-aš-ta*
28. $^{er\rightarrow}$*nu-kán* ⸓*ku-pí-ya-ti-in* ⸓*ku-up-ta*$^{\leftarrow er}$ *na-aš A-NA A-BI-YA* EGIR-*an ti-ya-at*
29. ^{LÚ}*pa-aḫ-ḫur-ši-in-pát pa-aḫ-ḫa-aš-ḫi* ^{LÚ}*pa-ḫur-ši-ya-aš-ma-wa* ⸢DUMU⸣.NI[TA] *ku-it* DÙ-*mi nu zi-iq-qa ku-at-qa*
30. *ŠA* ^{m}*Ma-aš-tu-ri i-wa-ar i-ya-ši*
31. *nu A-NA* ^{d}UTU^{ŠI} *ku-iš-ki na-aš-ma A-NA* DUMU.MEŠ DUMU.DUMU.MEŠ
32. ⸢NUMUN⸣ *ŠA* ^{d}UTU^{ŠI} *ú-wa-i ku-iš-ki*^{er} *ú-da-i*
33. *zi-ik-ma ma-a-an* ^{m}*IŠTAR*-A.A-*aš*
34. *QA-DU* DAM.<M>EŠ-*KA* DUMU.MEŠ-*KA* ÉRIN.MEŠ-*KA* ANŠE.KUR.RA.MEŠ-*KA*

§7 (A ii 8–19) Because I have made you, Shaushga-muwa, my brother-in-law, be loyal to My Majesty in regard to authority. And later on be loyal to the sons, grandsons, and progeny of My Majesty in regard to authority. You shall not desire anyone for authority from among those who are legitimate brothers of My Majesty, sons of concubines of the father of My Majesty, (or) even other royal progeny who are (to be regarded) by you as bastards. You shall not behave like Masturi: Muwattalli took Masturi, who was king of the Land of the Seha River, and made him his brother-in-law, giving him his sister Massanuzzi in marriage. And he made him king in the Land of the Seha River.

§8 (A ii 20–38) But when Muwattalli became a god, then Urhi-Teshshup, son of Muwattalli, became King. [Then my father] wrested the kingship away from Urhi-Teshshup. But Masturi committed treachery. (Although) it was Muwattalli who had taken him up and had made him (his) brother-in-law, afterwards he (Masturi) was not loyal to his son Urhi-Teshshup, but went over to my father (thinking): "Will I be loyal even to a bastard? Why should I act (on behalf of) the son of a bastard?" Will you perhaps behave like Masturi? And (if) someone brings difficulties upon My Majesty, or upon the sons, grandsons, or progeny of My Majesty, and you, Shaushga-muwa, together with your wives, your sons, your infantry, and your chariotry, do not help wholeheartedly, and are not ready to die for him, together with [your] wives and your children—let these things be placed under oath for you.

35. *ša-ku-wa-šar-ri-*⸢*it* ZI⸣*-it Ú-UL wa-ar-iš-ša-at-te*
36. *nu-uš-ši QA-DU* DAM[.MEŠ-*KA* D]UMU.ME[Š-*K*]*A še-er Ú-UL ak-ti*
37. *ne-et-ta ŠA-PAL NI-E*[*Š* DINGIR^{LI}]^{M} GAR-*ru*
38. *erased*

---

§9
39. ^{d}UTU^{ŠI} *AŠ-ŠUM* EN-*UT-*⸢*TI*⸣ *pa-aḫ-ši kat-ta*[*-ya* N]UMUN ⸢*ŠA*⸣ [^{d}UTU^{ŠI}]
40. *AŠ-ŠUM* EN-*UT-TI pa-aḫ-ši ta-ma-i*[*-in*]
41. *AŠ-ŠUM* ⸢EN⸣-*UT-TI le-e i-la-l*[*i-ya-ši*]
42. *ma-*⸢*a*⸣*-an-na-kán I-NA* KUR ^{UR}[^{U}*Ḫa-at-ti*]
43. *ša-ra-a iš-pár-za-zi* […]
44. *nu-kán pa-ra-a le-*⸢*e*⸣ […]
45. KUR-*KA wa-ar-i*[*š-ša-* …]
46. *nu A-NA* ^{d}UTU^{Š}[^{I} …]
47. *A-NA* ^{d}UTU^{ŠI} […]
48. *nu ma-*⸢*a*⸣[*-an* …]
49. ⸢*ma-a*⸣[*-an*? …]

A iii
1. […]
2. […]
3. *nu* x […]
4. *ki-iš-t*[*a*(-) … *nu ka-a-aš me-mi-aš*]
5. *ŠA-PAL NI-*⸢*IŠ* DINGIR⸣^{L}[^{IM} GAR-*ru*]

---

§10
6. *A-NA* LÚ.MEŠ ^{URU}*Ḫa-at-ti-ya* […]
7. *an-da ú-e-ri-at-ta-at* […]
8. *nu-ut-ták-kán ma-a-an* LÚ ^{URU}*Ḫa-*⸢*at*⸣*-t*[*i ku-iš-ki*]
9. *an-da ta-me-ek-zi na-aš-šu* ŠEŠ.LU[GAL]
10. *na-aš-ma* DUMU.LUGAL *na-*<*aš*>*-ma BE-LU na-aš-ma* ⸢EGIR-*iz*⸣*-z*[*i-iš*]
11. *ḫa-an-te-*⸢*ez*⸣*-zi-iš* UN-*aš*
12. *nu-ut-ták-kán ŠA* ^{d}UTU^{ŠI} *ku-it-ki*
13. ⸗*ku-ug-gur-ni-ya-u-wa-ar* EGIR-*pa an-da ú-da-*⸢*i*⸣
14. *na-aš-ma-ták-kán* ^{d}UTU^{ŠI} *ku-it-ki*
15. ḪUL$^{!}$-*an-ni* ⸢*kat*⸣*-ta ma-ni-ya-aḫ-zi*
16. *nu-kán* INIM-*an A-NA* ^{d}UTU^{ŠI} *le-e*
17. *ša*[*-an-n*]*a-at-ti A-NA* ^{d}UTU^{ŠI}*-an me-mi*
18. *n*[*u ka-a-aš*] *me-*⸢*mi*⸣*-aš ŠA-PAL NI-EŠ* DINGIR<^{LIM}> GAR-*ru*

---

§9 (A ii 39–iii 5) Be loyal to My Majesty in regard to authority. [And] later on be loyal to the progeny of [My Majesty] in regard to authority. You shall not desire [anyone] else in regard to authority. If [some conspiracy] breaks out [in Hatti ...], then you shall not [... Rather, together with your army] and your land, help [...] For My Majesty [...] to My Majesty [... (*The next six or seven lines have been almost completely lost.*) ... Let this matter be placed] under oath (for you).

§10 (A iii 6–18) [...] became involved with the Hittites. [...] If [some] Hittite attaches himself to you—either a brother of the King, a prince, a nobleman, or a man of lowest (or) highest rank—and he brings up again some slander concerning My Majesty, or he subjects My Majesty to malice in some way before you, you shall not cover up the matter before My Majesty. Tell it to My Majesty! Let [this] matter be placed under oath (for you).

(*approximately twenty lines have been largely or totally lost, rendering §11 [A iii 19–29] and the first portion of §12' unintelligible*)

§11

19. [… *AŠ-ŠUM* E]N-⌈*UT*⌉-*TI pa-aḫ-ši*
20. [… LUGAL-*i*]*z-za-na-tar*
21. [… *z*]*i*-[*i*]*k-za* LUGAL ^{URU}KÙ.BABBAR-*ti e-eš*
22. […]
23. [… .M]EŠ-*KA*
24. [… *wa-a*]*r-i*[*š-š*]*a*
25. […] *a-ak*
26. […] x x
27. […]-⌈*a*⌉ ^{LÚ}KÚR $^{\text{d!}}$UTU$^{\check{S}I}$
28. […]
29. [*nu ka-a-aš me-mi-aš ŠA-PAL NI-EŠ* DINGIR^{LIM} GA]R-⌈*ru*⌉

(approximately eight lines lost)

§12'

38'. […] -⌈*at*⌉ *le-e* ⌈*tar-na*⌉[- …]
39'. [… KUR ^{URU}*Mi-iz-za*]-*ri-i*
40'. [… *le*]-⌈*e*⌉ *ku-in-ki*
41'. *kat*-⌈*ta*⌉ […]x-*tar-na-aḫ-ti*
42'. *ma-a-an* L[UGAL KUR ^{URU}*Mi-iz*]-*za-ri-i*
43'. *A-NA* ^{d}UTU$^{\check{S}I}$ *ták*[-*šu-ul*] ⌈*tu*⌉-*uq-qa-aš ták-šu*-⌈*ul*⌉
44'. *e-eš-du ma-a-an*[-*ma-aš*] ⌈*A*⌉-*NA* ^{d}UTU$^{\check{S}I}$
45'. *ku-u-ru-ur tu*[-*uq-qa-aš ku-u-r*]*u-u*[*r*] *e-eš-du*

A iv

§13'

1. LUGAL.MEŠ-*ya-mu ku-i-e-eš* ^{LÚ}*MI-IḪ-R*[*U-T*]*I* […]
2. LUGAL ^{URU}*Mi-iz-ri-i* LUGAL KUR *Ku-ra-an-du-ni-aš*
3. LUGAL KUR *Aš-šur* $^{er\rightarrow}$LUGAL KUR ***Aḫ-ḫi-ya-u-wa-ya***$^{\leftarrow er}$[91]
4. *ma-a-an* LUGAL KUR *Mi-iz-ri-i A-NA* ^{d}UTU$^{\check{S}I}$ *ták-šu-ul*
5. *tu-uq-qa-aš ták-šu-ul e*-⌈*eš*⌉-*du*
6. *ma-a-an-ma-aš A-NA* ^{d}UTU$^{\check{S}I}$ *ku-ru-ur*
7. *tu-uq-qa-aš ku-ru-ur e-eš-du*
8. *ma-a-an-na* LUGAL KUR *Ka-ra-an-du-ni-aš*
9. *A-NA* ^{d}UTU$^{\check{S}I}$ *ták-šu-ul tu-uq-qa-aš*
10. *ták-šu-ul e-eš-du ma-a-an-ma-aš A-NA* ^{d}UTU$^{\check{S}I}$
11. *ku-ru-ur tu-uq-qa-aš ku-ru-ur e-eš-du*
12. LUGAL KUR *Aš-šur A-NA* ^{d}UTU$^{\check{S}I}$ GIM$^{!}$-*an ku-ru-ur*
13. *tu-uq-qa-aš QA-TAM-MA ku-ru-ur e-eš-du*

---

91. The scribe has erased the designation of this final ruler.

ALLIANCE

§12' (A iii 38'–45') ... If [the King] of Egypt is the [friend] of My Majesty, he shall be your friend. [But] if [he] is the enemy of My Majesty, he shall be [your enemy].

§13' (A iv 1–18) And the Kings who are my equals in rank are the King of Egypt, the King of Babylonia, the King of Assyria, *and the King of **Ahhiyawa**.*[91] If the King of Egypt is the friend of My Majesty, he shall be your friend. But if he is the enemy of My Majesty, he shall be your enemy. And if the King of Babylonia is the friend of My Majesty, he shall be your friend. But if he is the enemy of My Majesty, he shall be your enemy. Since the King of Assyria is the enemy of My Majesty, he shall likewise be your enemy. Your merchant shall not go to Assyria, and you shall not allow his merchant into your land. He shall not pass through your land. But if he should come into your land, seize him and send him off to My Majesty. [Let] this matter [be placed] under [oath] (for you).

14. *tu-el-kán* ^{LÚ}DAM.GÀR ŠÀ KUR *Aš-šur le-e*
15. *pa-iz-zi a-pé-el-ma-kán* ^{LÚ}DAM.GÀR
16. ŠÀ KUR-*KA le-e tar-na-at-ti*
17. KUR-*KA-aš-kán iš-tar-na ar-ḫa* ⸢*le*⸣*-e pa-iz-zi*
18. *ma-a-an-ma-aš-ták-kán* ŠÀ KUR-*KA-ma ú-iz-zi na-an* ⸢*an*⸣*-da e-ep na-an A-NA* ^{d}UTU^{ŠI} *ar-ḫa up-pí ka-a-aš-ta* INIM-*aš* GAM *N*[*I-EŠ* DINGIR^{LIM} GAR-*ru*]

---

§14’

19. ^{d}UTU^{ŠI}*-ya ku-it* LUGAL KUR *Aš-šur ku-ru-ra-an-ni da-aḫ-ḫu-un nu-za* ^{d}UTU^{ŠI} GIM-*an* KARAŠ ANŠE.KUR.RA
20. 𒑱*ti-eš-ša-eš-ki-*[*m*]*i A-NA* ^{d}UTU^{ŠI}*-ya-aš* GIM-*an* 𒑱*ḫu-u-ta-aš* 𒑱*ú-pa-ḫi-le-eš-ša tu-uq-qa-aš QA-TAM*[*-MA*]
21. 𒑱*ḫu-u-ta-aš* 𒑱⸢*ú*⸣*-pa-ḫi-le-eš-ša e-eš-du nu-za* KARAŠ ANŠE.KUR.RA *ša-ku-wa-aš-ša-ri-it* Z[I-*it*]
22. *ti-eš-ša-eš-ki ka-a-aš-ta* INIM-*aš* GAM *NI-EŠ* DINGIR^{LIM} GAR-*ru*

---

§15’

23. [*ŠA* KUR ***Aḫ-ḫ***]***i-***⸢***ya***⸣***-u-wa****-aš-ši* ^{GIŠ}MÁ *pa-a-u-an-zi l*[*e-e tar-na-ši*$^{?}$]
24. [o o o] x *pa-ra-a-ma-aš-kán ku-wa-pí na-*⸢*a*⸣[*-i*$^{?}$ …]
25. [o o o o] x x x ⸢DINGIR⸣^{LUM} *ŠA* KUR^{TI}*-K*[*A* …]
26. [o o o o o o o o o o o] x É.[GA]L⸢^{LIM}⸣ *p*[*í*$^{?}$*-* …]

(approximately 3–5 lines lost)

§16’

30’. *nu-kán* […]
31’. GÙB-*li* […]
32’. *le-e* […]
33’. KUR ^{URU}KÙ[.BABBAR-*ti* …]
34’. *da-aš-*x […]
35’. *ka-*⸢*a*⸣[*-aš-ta me-mi-aš* GAM *NI-EŠ* DINGIR^{LIM} GAR-*ru*]

---

§17’

36’. LUGAL.MEŠ […]
37’. *nu-za i*[*š*$^{?}$*-* …]
38’. *le-*⸢*e*⸣ [… *i-l*]*a-li-ya-ši* ARAD.MEŠ[*-YA*$^{?}$ …]
39’. *ku-*⸢*i*⸣[*-e-eš*$^{?}$ o o o o] *A-NA* KUR ^{URU}KÙ.BABBAR-*ti k*[*u-* …]
40’. x [o o o o o o o o *-š*]*a-i nu da-me-e-da A-N*[*A* …]
41’. [o o o o o o o o E]GIR-*pa an-da ú-iz-zi* […]
42’. [o o o o o o o o] ⸢*le*⸣*-e-wa-an-na-aš ŠA* KUR ^{U}[^{RU} …]

§14’ (A iv 19–22) Because I, My Majesty, have begun hostilities with the King of Assyria, and as I, My Majesty, am forming(?) an army and a unit of chariotry for myself—just as it is (a matter of) urgency and … for My Majesty, let it likewise be (a matter of) urgency and … for you. With alacrity form(?) an army and a unit of chariotry for yourself. Let this matter be placed under oath for you.

§15’ (A iv 23–26) [You shall not allow(?)] any ship [of] **Ahhiyawa** to go to him (that is, the King of Assyria) […] When he dispatches(?) […] the deity of your land […] the palace […]

Short gap followed by the badly damaged §16’ (A iv 30’–35’), which ends with the familiar formula: [Let] this [matter be placed under oath (for you)].

§17’ (A iv 36’–47’) The kings […] You shall not desire [… My(?)] servants, who […] to the land of Hatti […] And elsewhere, to […] He comes back into […] not to us, of the land [of …] You shall not conceal him, but rather seize him—[together with] his wife and his son—and dispatch [him] to My Majesty. This matter [shall be placed] under oath for you. [The …, which] you fortify and those who […] the grain harvest […] Fortify and protect it continuously. In the face of the enemy [come(?)] to Hattusa! You shall not protect [another man(?)]! This will be placed under oath for you.

43'. [o o o o *m*]*a*$^{?}$*-an le-e ša-an-na-at-ti*
44'. [*na-an QA-DU*] ⸢DAM⸣-*ŠU* DUMU-*ŠU an-da e-ep*
45'. [*na-an*]*-kán A-NA* ^{d}UTU^{ŠI} *pa-ra-a na-a-i*
46'. [*ka*]-⸢*a*⸣*-aš-ta me-mi-aš* GAM *NI-EŠ* DINGIR^{LIM} [GAR-*ru* …]
47'. [*ku-i-e-e*]*š*$^{?}$ *ša-ḫe-eš-na-eš-ki-ši ḫal-ki-ya-za* ⸢*ku*⸣*-i-e-eš* […]

A left edge

1. *na-an-za-an*$^{!}$ *ša-ḫe*$^{!}$*-eš-ni-eš-ki* PAP-*nu-uš-ki A-NA* ^{LÚ}KÚR IGI-*an-da* ^{URU}GIDRI-*ši* [*e-ḫu*$^{?}$ *ta-ma-i-in*$^{?}$ *le*]-⸢*e*⸣ PAP-*nu-uš-ki-ši*
2. *ka-a-aš-ta* INIM-*aš* GAM *NI-EŠ* DINGIR^{LIM} GAR-*ri*

(*gap of uncertain length*[92])

B rev.

§18'

1'. […] (-)*pa*-x […]
2'. […]x-*ra* […]
3'. [… IN]IM$^{?}$ ^{d}UTU^{ŠI} x […]

4.' […]

---

§19'

5'. [… KUR ^{URU}*Ḫa-at*]*-ti pa-aḫ-ši*
6'. [… *IT-T*]*I* ^{d}UTU^{ŠI} *nu*[- …]
7'. […]

---

§20'[93]

8'. […] ^{d}U KI.LAM
9'. [… ^{d}U ^{URU}*Ḫi*]*-iš-ša-aš-ša-pa*
10'. [… ^{URU}*Ḫa*]*-at-ti*
11'. [… ^{URU}*Ḫa-a*]*t-ti*
12'. […] ^{d}A.A ^{d}*AL-LA-TUM*
13'. […] x ^{d}*Aš-ka-še-pa-aš*
14'. [… ^{d}*IŠTAR* ^{URU}*Ḫa-a*]*t-ta-ri-na*
15'. [… ^{d}ZA.BA$_{4}$.BA$_{4}$ ^{URU}*El-la-ya*] ^{d}ZA.BA$_{4}$.BA$_{4}$ ^{URU}*Ar-zi-ya*
16'. […] ^{d}*Ḫa-tág-ga-aš* ^{URU}*An-ku-wa*

---

92. The continuation of Text A onto a second tablet has not been recovered and the single-tablet rescension of Text B is too fragmentary to allow calculation of how many lines have been lost.

93. Restorations here are drawn from the parallel god lists KBo 12.31 iv (CTH 132) and KBo 1.4 iv (CTH 53).

(gap of uncertain length followed by mutilated §§18'–19' [B rev. 1'–7'])

DIVINE WITNESSES

§20' (B rev. 8'–25') [...] the Storm-God of the Market [... , the Storm-God] of Hissassapa, [...] of Hatti, [...] of Hatti, [...] Ea, Allatum, [...], Askasepa, [... , Shaushga] of Hattarina, [... , the War-God of Ellaya], the War-God of Arziya, [...], Hatagga of Ankuwa, [...], Huwassanna of Hupisna, [... of Ishupitta, the Lady] of Landa, [Kuniyawani of Landa, Mount Lebanon, Mount Sarissiya, Mount Pisaisa], the mountain-dweller deities, [the mercenary deities, Ereshkigal, all the male and female deities of the land] of Hatti, all [the male] and female deities [of the land of Amurru, Nara, Napsara, Munki, Tuhusi], Ammunki, [Ammizzadu, Alalu, Antu, Anu, Apandu], Enlil, Ninlil, [the mountains, the rivers, the springs, the great sea—they shall be witnesses] to these stipulations [and this oath. And if] you alter the words of this tablet, [then these gods shall utterly destroy you].

17'. [... ^{d}GAZ.B]A.A.A-*aš* ^{URU}*Ḫu-piš-na*

18'. [... ^{URU}*Iš-ḫu-pí-it-ta* ^{d}*BE-EL-TI* $^{\text{U]RU}}$*La-a-an-da*

19'. [^{d}*Ku-ni-ya-wa-ni-iš* ^{URU}*La-a-an-da* $^{\text{ḪUR.SAG}}$*La-ab-la-na* $^{\text{ḪUR.SAG}}$*Ša-ri-iš-ši-ya* $^{\text{ḪUR.SAG}}$*Pí-ša-i-ša*] DINGIR.MEŠ *Lu-la-ḫi*[*-iš*]

20'. [DINGIR.MEŠ *Ḫa-pí-ra-aš* ^{d}EREŠ.KI.GAL DINGIR.MEŠ LÚ.MEŠ DINGIR.MEŠ MUNUS.MEŠ *ḫu-u-ma-an-te-eš* *ŠA* KUR ^{URU}*Ḫa-a*]*t-ti* [DINGIR LÚ.MEŠ] DINGIR MUNUS.MEŠ *ḫu-u-ma-an-te-eš*

21'. [*ŠA* KUR ^{URU}*A-mur-ri* ^{d}*Na-ra-aš* ^{d}*Na-ap-ša-ra-aš* ^{d}*Mu-un-ki-iš* ^{d}*Tu-ḫu-ši-i*]*š* ^{d}*Am*[*-mu-un-ki*]*-iš*

22'. [^{d}*Am-mi-iz-za-du-uš* ^{d}*A-la-lu-uš* ^{d}*A-an-tu* ^{d}*A-nu* ^{d}*A-pa-an-du-uš*] ^{d}EN.LÍL ^{d}NIN.LÍL

23'. [ḪUR.SAG.MEŠ ÍD.MEŠ TÚL.ḪI.A A.AB.BA GAL DINGIR.MEŠ *ḫu-u-ma-an-te*]*-eš* *ke-e-da-aš me-mi-ya-na-aš*

24'. [*ke-e-da-ni li-in-ga-i ku-ut-ru-we-ni-eš a-ša-an-du nu-kán ma-a-an ke-e*]*-el tup-pí-aš* INIM.MEŠ *wa-aḫ-nu-š*[*i*]

25'. [*nu-ut-ták-kán ku-u-uš* DINGIR.MEŠ *ar-ḫa ḫar-ni-in-kán-du*]

Commentary

The term Amurru was one of variable extension. In the third- and early-second millennia, it was applicable to much of the region covered by modern Syria, but in the Late Bronze Age its use was restricted to the territory lying between the Orontes River and the central Levantine coast. In the fifteenth century, this territory was incorporated into the Egyptian empire by the pharaoh Tuthmosis III. But its attachment to Egypt was a tenuous one, and by and large anarchy prevailed throughout the region until power was seized in it by a local warlord called Abdi-Ashirta. Nominally acknowledging the pharaoh as his overlord, Abdi-Ashirta united local semi-nomadic groups called the Habiru into an effective fighting force, which terrorized and plundered neighboring states until their leader was captured and probably executed by the Egyptian authorities. His son Aziru inherited his role, and like his father nominally accepted Egyptian sovereignty while plundering the territories of his neighbors. Eventually, he recognized that his interests would best be served by joining the Hittites, who were becoming an increasingly powerful presence in the region, and declared his allegiance to the Hittite king Suppiluliuma I. Thenceforth Amurru became a subject-ally of Hatti as reflected in a treaty that Suppiluliuma drew up with Aziru (Beckman 1999: 36–41).

Amurru remained Hittite subject territory until the pharaoh Seti I wrested it from his Hittite counterpart Muwattalli II in a (first) battle fought at Qadesh on the Orontes River ca. 1290. It subsequently reverted to Hittite control following a second engagement at Qadesh fought in 1274 between Muwattalli and Seti's successor Ramesses II, and remained subject to Hatti until the end of the Hittite empire in the early-twelfth century. Amurru's continuing attachment to Hatti is reflected in treaties drawn up between the Hittite king Hattusili III, brother and second successor of Muwattalli, and the current Amurrite king Benteshina (Beckman 1999: 100–103), and between Hattusili's son and successor Tudhaliya IV and Benteshina's son(?) and successor Shaushga-muwa—the treaty translated here.

The introduction to the treaty is one of our main sources of information about Amurru's history from the reign of Aziru onwards, with particular reference to the contest between Hatti and Egypt for control over the region (§4). The treaty also highlights the increasing instability of the Hittite monarchy in the last decades of the Hittite empire. In no small measure, this instability was a legacy inherited by Tudhaliya from his father along with the kingship. Hattusili had usurped the throne from its rightful occupant Urhi-Teshshup (Mursili III), and the latter and his family had constantly sought to get it back, calling on the assistance of foreign kings in their attempts. In the explicit terms he imposes upon Shaushga-muwa, Tudhaliya highlights the risks he constantly faced from pretenders to the throne from among the ranks of collateral branches of his own family, and is ever alert to the threats of conspiracies against him (§§7–10). The specific admonition to Shaushga-muwa not to follow the example of Masturi is ironic, since it was Masturi's treachery that had helped Tudhaliya's father seize the throne—in so doing inevitably creating a precedent for future bids for royal power through conspiracy and treachery. That was one of Tudhaliya's greatest fears. The marriage of his sister to Shaushga-muwa was an attempt to shore up support from his Syrian vassal against the threat of a coup like that the dispossessed Urhi-Teshshup had suffered.

In the final sections of the treaty, Tudhaliya moves from internal matters to external affairs. Of particular interest here is a reference to the king of Ahhiyawa in the list of foreign rulers whom Tudhaliya considers his equals (§13'). Unsurprisingly, the rulers of Egypt, Babylonia, and Assyria are included in the list. And originally the list also contained the king of Ahhiyawa—the name subsequently being erased. This erasure has generated much debate. Clearly the scribe had made a mistake in including the name in the first place, and the Ahhiyawan king is not included in subsequent references in the treaty to Tudhaliya's royal peers. But that leaves us with the question of why the mistake occurred in the first place. A possible conclusion is that the Ahhiyawan king had indeed enjoyed the status of one of the Great Kings of the Late Bronze Age world, at least in Hittite diplomatic terminology, but had recently lost this status. The scribe who drafted this version of the treaty may initially have copied the list of Great Kings from an earlier document, not picking up the mistake until the out-of-date name had already been inscribed on the clay. We know from the so-called Tawagalawa Letter (AhT 4), probably authored by Tudhaliya's father Hattusili III, that the current Ahhiyawan king, the letter's recipient, was accorded peer status by his correspondent. By the time of the Shaushga-muwa treaty, Ahhiyawa's ruler no longer had this status, and Bryce (2005: 308-9) has suggested that his loss of it may be connected with the loss of Ahhiyawan control over the land of Millawanda/Milawata, which had hitherto served as the major base for Ahhiyawan activities in western Anatolia. The reestablishment of Hittite sovereignty over Millawanda by or during the reign of Tudhaliya is implied in the so-called Milawata letter, commonly ascribed to Tudhaliya (AhT 5).

In §13' of the Shaushga-muwa treaty, the Amurrite vassal is told that he must regard the king of Assyria as his enemy, since Assyria is at war with Hatti, and that he must ban any trade contacts between his kingdom and Assyria. In effect, this means Amurru's ports or other trading centers are not to be used for the transhipment of goods and commodities either to or from Assyria, to or from other parts of the Near Eastern and Aegean worlds. In §15', Tudhaliya imposes a further prohibition, instructing his vassal thus: "[You shall not allow(?)] any ship [of Ahh]iyawa to go to him (that is, to the king of Assyria)." It was of course literally impossible for an Ahhiyawan ship to travel to Assyria, and the passage—if it has been correctly restored and read (for an alternative restoration and reading, see Steiner 1989[94])—is generally interpreted as a further reference to a ban on trade between Ahhiyawa and Assyria, presumably involving merchandise brought by ship to the Levantine coast before being conveyed overland into Mesopotamia. It would thus relate to the ban already stipulated in §13' on trading contacts between Amurru and Assyria. But we should note that Tudhaliya turns from trade matters in §13' of the treaty to military matters in §14', and it may be that the prohibition in §15' belongs to a military rather than a mercantile context. Bryce (2010: 50) comments that there could well have been shiploads of freebooting Mycenaeans trawling the Mediterranean at this time, in search of plunder or military service in the hire of a foreign king; it is against the prospect of Ahhiyawans/Mycenaeans such as these entering the forces of Assyria that Tudhaliya's ban is imposed. That is to say, it is Mycenaean mercenaries rather than Mycenaean merchandise that Tudhaliya is attempting to prevent from reaching Assyria via the ports of the Syro-Palestinian coastlands.

94. Steiner's proposal to restore [*la-aḫ-ḫ*]*i-ya-u-wa-aš-ši* ^{GIŠ}MÁ ("warship") in place of [*Aḫ-ḫ*]*i-ya-u-wa-aš-ši* ^{GIŠ}MÁ ("ship of Ahhiyawa") in A iv 23 (§15') has not met with scholarly acceptance.

AHT 3

INDICTMENT OF MADDUWATTA (CTH 147)

This document, composed during the reign of Arnuwanda I, constitutes the opening portion of an extensive recounting of the duplicitous activities of a Hittite vassal in western Anatolia during the first decades of the fourteenth century, a time of relative weakness for the Hittite state. The absence of a heading as well as the presence of a substantive erasure (§36') and alternative formulations of a single sentence (§22') indicate that this is a preliminary draft. The purpose of the text is uncertain: Is it a warning to be sent to Madduwatta to encourage him to change his behavior, or a summary of evidence to be employed in a legal proceeding at the Hittite court?

Many of the events narrated in this text had taken place under the preceding king, Tudhaliya I/II, and records from his reign are frequently adduced here. In several instances, direct quotations from these documents have been carelessly edited, so that Tudhaliya refers to himself as "the father of My/His Majesty" (e.g., §§4, 6–7).

This text describes how Tudhaliya had rescued Madduwatta from an attack by Attarissiya of Ahhiya (§§1–3), assigned him the land of Mount Zippasla to rule (§§4–5), and imposed upon him an oath of vassalage (§§6–7). Later, against the explicit command of Tudhaliya, Madduwatta attempted to expand his territory at the expense of Kupanta-Kurunta of Arzawa, but the latter ruler soon gained the upper hand (§§8–9), only to be repulsed by a Hittite army sent to the aid of Madduwatta (§§10–11). Finally, a second offensive by Attarissiya again threatened Madduwatta, necessitating yet another Hittite intervention on his behalf (§12).

But rather than show his gratitude for Tudhaliya's benevolence, Madduwatta proceeded to engage in intrigues against his Hittite overlord (§§13–15)—even plotting with their former common enemy Kupanta-Kurunta (§§16–20')—extending his realm (§§22'–23'), seizing Hittite towns (§24'), refusing to extradite fugitives from Hatti (§§25', 30'–32'), and inciting other Hittite vassals to rebellion (§26').

The present tablet concludes with an account of the mission of Arnuwanda's envoy Mulliyara (§§29'–36') to the prevaricating Madduwatta, followed by a curious paragraph (§37') presenting an animal fable, unfortunately too broken for certain interpretation, but probably somehow reflecting on the conduct of

Madduwatta. Undoubtedly the text did not end at this point, but we have not recovered any further tablets. We are also ignorant of the ultimate fate of Madduwatta, for this petty ruler does not appear in any other Hittite records.

KUB 14.1 + KBo 19.38[95]

obv.

§1

1. [*tu-uk-k*]*a* ^{m}*Ma-*⸢*ad-du*⸣*-wa-at-ta-an t*[*u-e*]*l* KUR-*ya-az* ^{m}*At-*⸢*ta-ri-iš-ši*⸣*-ya-aš* **LÚ** ^{URU}***A-a*[*ḫ-ḫi-y*]*a-a*** *ar-*⸢*ḫa pár-aḫ-ta*⸣

2. [*nam-ma*]*-aš-ták-kán* ⸢EGIR⸣*-an-pát ki-*⸢*it-ta-at*⸣ *nu-ut-ta* [*pá*]*r-ḫi-iš-ki-it nu t*[*u*]*-*⸢*e*⸣*-el ŠA* ^{m}*Ma*[*-ad-du-wa*]*-at-*⸢*ta*⸣ [*i-da-a*]*-*⸢*lu*⸣ *ḫi-in-*⸢*kán ša-an*⸣*-ḫi-iš-ki-it*

3. [*ma-an-t*]*ák-kán ku-en-ta* \ *nu-uš*[*-ša-a*]*n zi-ik* ^{m}⸢*Ma-ad-du*⸣*-wa-*⸢*at-ta*⸣*-aš an-da A-NA A-B*[*I* ^{d}UTU^{ŠI} *pí*]*d-*⸢*da-iš*⸣ *nu-ut-*[*ták-ká*]*n A-BI* ^{d}UTU^{ŠI}

4. ⸢*ḫi-in*⸣[*-ga*]*-na-az ḫu-iš-nu-ut nu-*⸢*ut-ták-kán*⸣ ^{m}*At-ta-*⸢*ri-iš-ši*⸣*-ya-*⸢*an*⸣ EGIR*-an* ⸢*ar*⸣*-ḫa ka*[*r-aš-ta ma*]*-a-an Ú-UL-ma* ⸢*ma-an*⸣*-ta* ^{m}*At-tar-ši-ya-aš*

5. [*Ú*]*-*⸢*UL*⸣ *da-li-eš-ta* [*m*]*a-an-t*[*ák-k*]*án ku*[*-en-ta*]

---

§2

6. ⸢*nu-ut*⸣*-ta A-BI* ^{d}UTU^{ŠI} *ma-aḫ-ḫa-an* ^{m}[*At-ta-ri-iš-ši-y*]*a-an* EGIR-⸢*an ar-ḫa*⸣ *k*[*ar-aš-ta nu-za-kán*] ⸢*A*⸣[*-BI*] ^{d}UTU^{ŠI} ⸢*tu-uk*⸣ ^{m}⸢*Ma-ad-du*⸣*-wa-at-ta-an*

7. *QA-DU* DAM.MEŠ*-KA* DUMU.MEŠ*-KA* ÉRIN.MEŠ*-KA* A[NŠE.KUR.RA.ḪI.A*-KA da-aš-ki*]*-*⸢*it nu-ut-ta* ^{GIŠ}GIGIR.ḪI.A⸣ [o o .ḪI.A] ŠE.ḪI.A ⸢NUMUN.ḪI.A⸣ *iš-*⸢*ḫu-eš-ni pí*⸣[*-iš-k*]*i-it*

8. KAŠ.GEŠTIN.ḪI.A*-ya-at-ta* DIM$_4$ BAPPIR.ḪI.A *EM-ṢA* [GA.KIN.AG.ḪI].⸢A⸣*iš-ḫu-eš-ni* ⸢*pí-iš*⸣[*-ki-it*] *nu tu*[*-uk* ^{m}*Ma-a*]*d-*⸢*du*⸣[*-wa*]*-*⸢*at-ta-an*⸣ *QA-DU* DAM.MEŠ*-KA*

9. [DUMU.MEŠ]*-KA* ÉRIN.MEŠ*-KA-ya A-BI* ^{d}UTU^{ŠI} *ki-*⸢*iš-du-wa-a-an*⸣[*-du*]*-*⸢*uš*⸣ *ḫu*[*-iš-nu-ut*]

---

95. This transliteration is based on Götze's hand copy in KUB 14, on his transliteration (1928), which includes corrections made after further collation of the tablet, and on Gary Beckman's own examination of the photos included with his edition. Since they are so numerous, and many of them had already been included in the *editio princeps*, divergences from the copy have not been specially marked here.

§1 (obv. 1–5) Attarissiya, the ruler of **Ahhiya**, chased [you], Madduwatta, out of your land. [Then] he harassed you and kept chasing you. And he continued to seek an [evil] death for you, Madduwatta. He [would] have killed you, but you, Madduwatta, fled to the father [of My Majesty], and the father of My Majesty saved you from death. He [got] rid of Attarissiya for you. Otherwise, Attarissiya would not have left you alone, but would [have killed] you.

§2 (obv. 6–9) When the father of My Majesty [got] rid of [Attarissiya] for you, [then] the father of My Majesty [took] you, Madduwatta, together with your wives, your children, your infantry, and [your chariotry]. He gave you chariots, […], barley, and seed in heaps, and he gave you young wine, malt, beer bread, rennet, and [cheese(?)] in heaps. And the father of My Majesty [saved] you, Madduwatta, together with your wives, your [children], and your troops, when you were hungry.

§3

10. ⸢*nu-ut-ták*⸣*-kán* ⸢*A-BI*⸣ ^{d}UTU^{ŠI} *IŠ-TU* GÍR ^{m}*At-tar-ši-ya* ⸢*ar*⸣[*-ḫa*] *ḫu-iš-nu-ut tu-ug-ga* ^{m}⸢*Ma-ad-du*⸣[*-wa-at-t*]*a-an QA-DU* DAM<.MEŠ>-*KA* [DUMU].MEŠ-*KA* SAG.GÉME.ARAD.⸢MEŠ-*KA*⸣

11. ⸢*Ù*⸣ *QA-DU* ÉRIN.MEŠ-⸢*KA*⸣ ANŠE.KUR.RA.ḪI.A-*KA A-BI* ^{d}UTU^{ŠI} *ḫu-iš-*⸢*nu-ut*⸣ *ma-a-an Ú-UL-ma* ⸢*ma-an-ša*⸣[*-ma*]*-*⸢*aš ka-a*⸣*-aš-ti pí-ra-an* UR.GI$_{7}$.⸢ḪI.A⸣ *ka-re-e-pí-ir*

12. ⸢*ma*⸣*-an-kán ma-*⸢*a*⸣*-an* ⸢*A-NA*⸣ ^{m}*At-tar-ši-ya ḫu-iš-ú-e-*⸢*te-en*⸣*-na* ⸢*ka*⸣*-a-aš-ti-ta-ma-an a-ak-te-en*

---

§4

13. *nam-ma-*⸢*az*⸣ *ú-it A-BI* ^{d}UTU^{ŠI} *tu-*⸢*uk*⸣ ^{m}*Ma-ad-du-wa-at-ta-an* ⸢*li-in*⸣*-ki-ya-aš-ša-aš i-e-et* ⸢*nu*⸣[*-ut-ta li-in*]*-ga-nu-*⸢*ut*⸣ *nu-*⸢*ut*⸣[*-ta*] *li-in-ki-ya*

14. [*ka*]*t-ta-an ke-e ud-da-*⸢*a-ar*⸣ *da-iš* ⸢*ka-a*⸣*-ša-wa-kán A-*⸢*BI*⸣ ^{d}⸢UTU⸣^{ŠI} [*tu-uk*] ^{m}*Ma-ad-du-wa-at-ta-an* [*IŠ-TU* GÍR] ⸢^{m}*At-tar*⸣*-ši-*⸢*ya*⸣ *ḫu-iš-nu-nu-un*

15. ⸢*nu-wa*⸣*-za ŠA A-BI* ^{d}UTU⸢^{ŠI}⸣ *Ù ŠA* KUR ⸢^{URU}*Ḫa*⸣*-at-ti e-eš nu-*⸢*wa-at*⸣[*-ta ka-a*]*-ša* KUR $^{ḪUR.SAG}$*Zi-ip-pa-aš-la*[*-a a-ša-a-an-na*] *pí-iḫ-ḫu-un*

16. [*nu-wa*] *zi-ik* ^{m}*Ma-ad-du-wa-at-ta-aš QA-DU* [ÉRIN].MEŠ-*KA I-NA* KUR $^{ḪUR.SAG}$⸢*Zi-ip*⸣*-pa-aš-la-a e-eš nu-wa-za-kán* ⸢*iš*⸣[*-ki*]*-*⸢*ša a-ap*⸣*-pa I-NA* KUR [$^{ḪUR.SA}$]^{G}*Zi-ip-pa-aš-la-a*

17. ⸢*ti-ya*⸣*-a-an ḫar-ak A-BI* ^{d}⸢UTU^{ŠI}⸣*-ma tu-uk A-NA* ^{m}*Ma-ad-du-wa-at-ta ki-iš-*⸢*ša-an*⸣*-na me-mi-iš-ki-it* ⸢*e-ḫu-wa*⸣*-za I-NA* KUR $^{ḪUR.SAG}$[*Ḫa-ri*]*-ya-ti e-eš-ḫu-ut*

18. *nu*[*-wa*]*-za A-*⸢*NA*⸣ KUR ^{URU}*Ḫa-at-ti-ya ma-an-ni-in-ku-wa-an* ^{m}*Ma-ad-du-wa-at-*⸢*ta-ša-az*⸣ KUR $^{ḪUR.SAG}$*Ḫa-ri-ya-ti a-ša-a-an-na mi-im-ma-aš nu ú-it*

19. ⸢*A-BI* ^{d}UTU^{ŠI}⸣ *A-NA* ^{m}*Ma-ad-du-wa-at-*⸢*ta*⸣ *ki-iš-ša-an nam-ma me-mi-*⸢*iš-ta*⸣ [*ka*]*-a-ša-wa-at-*⸢*ta*⸣ KUR $^{ḪUR.SAG}$*Zi-ip-pa-*⸢*aš-la-a AD*⸣[*-DIN*] *nu-*⸢*wa-za*⸣ *a-pu-u-un-pát e-ši*

20. ⸢*nam-ma-ma-wa*⸣[*-az*] ⸢*pa*⸣*-ra-a ta-ma-a-*⸢*in*⸣ *ḫa-pa-a-ti-in ta-ma-i* KUR-*e* ZI[*-it*] *le-e* [*e-eš*]*-ta-ri nu-wa-at-*⸢*ta*⸣ [KUR $^{ḪUR.SA}$]^{G}*Zi-*⸢*ip-pa*⸣*-aš-la-a* ZAG-*aš e-*⸢*eš-tu*⸣

21. *nu-*⸢*wa-za*⸣ *am*[*-me-el*] ⸢ARAD^{TUM}⸣ *e-eš* ÉRIN.MEŠ.ḪI.A-*KA-ya-wa am-me-el* ÉRIN.MEŠ.ḪI.A *a-*⸢*ša-an-du*⸣

---

§5

22. [^{m}*M*]*a-a*[*d-du-wa-at-ta-aš-ma*] *A-NA A-BI* ⸢^{d}UTU⸣^{ŠI} *ki-iš-ša-an me-mi-iš-*⸢*ta*⸣ [*zi-ik-wa-mu* EN]-⸢*YA* KUR $^{ḪUR.SAG}$⸣*Zi-i*[*p-pa-aš-la*] *a-ša-an-na pa-it-ta*

§3 (obv. 10–12) And the father of My Majesty saved you from the sword of Attarissiya. The father of My Majesty saved you, Madduwatta, together with your wives, your [children], your household servants, and together with your infantry and your chariotry. Otherwise, dogs would have devoured you from hunger. If you had escaped from Attarissiya, you would have died from hunger.

§4 (obv. 13–21) Furthermore, the father of My Majesty proceeded to make you, Madduwatta, his sworn ally. He caused [you] to swear an oath, and he placed these matters under oath for you, (saying): "I, the father of His Majesty, have now saved [you], Madduwatta, [from the sword] of Attarissiya. Be a partisan of the father of His Majesty and of Hatti. I have [now] given you the land of Mount Zippasla [to rule]. You, Madduwatta, occupy the land of Mount Zippasla, together with your [troops], and have your base of support established in the land of [Mount] Zippasla." The father of My Majesty repeatedly spoke thus to you, Madduwatta: "Come, occupy the land of Mount Hariyati, so that you will be near Hatti." Madduwatta refused to occupy the land of Mount Hariyati, so the father of My Majesty proceeded to say again as follows to Madduwatta: "I have now given you the land of Mount Zippasla, so occupy it alone! You shall not occupy in addition another river valley (or) another land on your own authority. [The land of Mount] Zippasla shall be your march. Be [my] servant, and your troops shall be my troops."

§5 (obv. 22–27) [But Madduwatta] said as follows to the father of My Majesty: "You, my [lord], have given [me] the land of Mount [Zippasla] to occupy, [so that I am] the border guard [and] the watchman [of this land. And whoever] speaks of a matter [of hostility] before [me, (or whenever) I myself] hear of a

23. [*nu-wa*]-*za* [*ke-e-e*]*l* [*ŠA* KUR^{TI}]^{M} ^{LÚ}*a-ú-ri-ya-la-aš* ^{LÚ}*uš-ki-iš-g*[*a-tal-la-aš-ša ú-uk nu-wa-mu ku-u-ru-ra-aš*] ⸢*me*⸣-*m*[*i-an ku-iš*] ⸢*pí*⸣-*ra-an me-ma-i*
24. [*ú-ka-k*]*a-wa-kán ku*[*-u-ru*]-*ra-aš me-mi-an ku-e-ez* KUR-*ya-az ar-ḫa* ⸢*iš-ta*⸣[*-ma-aš*]-*mi* [*nu-wa-ták-kán A-NA A-BI* ^{d}UTU^{ŠI} *a-pu-u-un an-tu*]-*uḫ-ša-an a-pa-a-at* KUR-*e*
25. [*Ú-UL ša-an-na-aḫ-ḫi n*]*u-wa-ra-aš-ta ḫa-at-*⸢*re*⸣*-eš-ki-mi-pát* <<LUGAL>> *ku-i-*⸢*ša*⸣-[*w*]*a* ⸢KUR⸣[*-e*]-⸢*an-za-ma-at*⸣[*-ta ku*]-*u-ru-u*[*r e-ep-zi nu-wa-aš-ša-an ku-it-ma-a*]*n ŠA* ^{d}UTU^{ŠI}
26. [ÉRIN.MEŠ *za-aḫ-ḫi-ya-at-ta*]-*ri ú-ga-wa-za ma-an-ni*[*-in-k*]*u-wa-an ku-it* [*nu-w*]*a-ra-*⸢*at*⸣ *ú-uk* ⸢*ḫu-u*⸣[*-da*]-⸢*a-ak*⸣ *wa-a*[*l-aḫ*]-⸢*mi*⸣ [*nu-wa-za QA-TE*^{MEŠ}*-Y*]*A ú-uk ḫu-u-da-a-ak*
27. ⸢*e*⸣[*-eš-ḫar-nu*]-⸢*mi*⸣ *nu li-ik-ta nu-za ke-e* ⸢*ud*⸣-*da-a-*⸢*ar*⸣ *ŠA-PAL NI-IŠ* DINGIR^{LIM} [*da-i*]*š*[*-ta*]

---

§6

28. ⸢*A*⸣-[*BI* ^{d}U]TU^{ŠI}*-ma-aš-ši ŠA-PAL NI-*⸢*IŠ*⸣ DINGIR^{LIM} *ki-iš-*⸢*ša-an*⸣*-na* ⸢*da*⸣*-iš ku-iš-wa A-*⸢*NA*⸣ [*A-BI* ^{d}UT]U^{ŠI} *Ù A*[*-NA* KUR ^{URU}]⸢*Ḫa*⸣*-at-ti me-*⸢*na*⸣*-aḫ-ḫa-an-ta ku-u-ru-ur*
29. [*tu-uk-ka*]-*wa-ra-aš A-NA* ^{m}*Ma*[*-ad-du-wa*]-*at-ta ku-u-ru-ur e-eš-tu nu-*⸢*wa-ra-an*⸣ *A-*⸢*BI*⸣ [^{d}UTU^{ŠI}] ⸢*ma-aḫ-ḫa-an*⸣ [*kar-ši*] ⸢*za*⸣*-aḫ-ḫi-ya-aḫ-ḫa-ri* ⸢*zi*⸣*-ig-ga-wa-ra-an*
30. ^{m}[*Ma-ad-du-w*]*a-at-*⸢*ta-aš*⸣ [ÉRIN.MEŠ-*KA*]-⸢*ya QA-TAM*⸣*-MA kar-ši za-aḫ-ḫi-ya-at*[*-tén*] ^{m}*Ku-pa-an-t*[*a-*^{d}LAMMA]-*ya*[*-aš-ma A-NA A-BI* ^{d}UT]U^{ŠI} *ma-aḫ-ḫa-an me-na-aḫ-ḫa-an-ta ku-u-ru-ur*
31. [*tu-uk-ka-wa-r*]*a-aš A-NA* ^{m}[*Ma-ad-du-wa-a*]*t-*⸢*ta*⸣ *QA-*⸢*TAM*⸣*-MA me-na-aḫ-ḫa-an-*⸢*ta ku-u-ru*⸣*-ur* ⸢*e-eš-tu*⸣ *nu-wa-r*[*a-an A-BI* ^{d}UTU^{ŠI}] *ma-aḫ-ḫa-an kar-ši za-aḫ-ḫi-ya-aḫ-ḫa-ri*
32. [*zi-ik-ka-wa*]-*ra-an* ^{m}*M*[*a-ad-du-wa*]-⸢*at-ta*⸣*-aš QA-TAM-MA kar-ši za-aḫ-ḫ*[*i-ya-aḫ-ḫu-ut*] ⸢*A*⸣*-NA* K[UR-*e-y*]*a-wa ḫa-lu-ki* [ZI-*i*]*t le-e ku-e-da-ni-ik-ki pí-i-e-ši*
33. [*ku-u-ru-ur*]-⸢*wa*⸣ *me-*⸢*na-aḫ*⸣[*-ḫa*]-*an*[*-ta* ZI]-⸢*it*⸣ *le-e ku-e-da-ni*[*-ki e-eš*$^{?}$]-⸢*ši*⸣ *ku*[*-ša*$^{?}$]-*zi-ya-tar-r*[*a-wa*] ⸢ZI⸣*-it me-na-aḫ-ḫa-an-ta le-e ku-e-da-ni-ki i-ya-ši*
34. [o o o o o]-*du* [o o o o] x [o o] *le-e tar-*⸢*ši-ik*⸣*-ki-*⸢*ši*⸣ [*ku-iš-wa-ták-kán*] ⸢*ŠA*⸣ KUR ^{URU}*Ḫa-at*[*-ti* ^{LÚ}]⸢*ḫu*⸣*-ya-an-za an-da ú-iz-*⸢*zi*⸣ *ma-a-na-aš* ^{LÚ}*BE-EL* ^{GIŠ}TUKUL
35. [*ma-a-na-aš*] x x [o o *nu-wa-ra-an*] *ša-an-na-at-ti-ya le-*⸢*e*⸣ *mu*[*-un-na*]-⸢*a-ši*⸣*-i*[*a*]-*wa-ra-an le-e* [*nam-ma*]-*ya-wa-ra-an-za ta-me-e-da-*⸢*ni*⸣ KUR-*ya le-e*

matter of hostility from some land, [then I will not conceal that] person or that land [from the father of His Majesty], but I will indeed always write about them. But whatever land [commences hostilities] against you, [while the troops] of Your Majesty [make war]—because I am nearby, I will attack it immediately, [and] I will immediately [bloody my hands]." You took an oath and [placed] these matters under oath.

§6 (obv. 28–36) But [the father] of My Majesty placed the following under oath for him: "The person who is an enemy to [the father of His Majesty] and [to] Hatti shall be an enemy [to you], Madduwatta. And as I, the father [of His Majesty] make war on him [without hesitation], you, [Madduwatta], and [your troops] shall likewise make war on him without hesitation. As Kupanta-Kurunta is an enemy [to the father of His Majesty], he shall likewise be an enemy [to you, Madduwatta], and as I, [the father of His Majesty], make war [on him] without hesitation, [you, Madduwatta], shall likewise make war on him without hesitation. [And] you shall not send (anyone) on a (diplomatic) mission to any [land on your own authority. You shall] not [be an enemy] to anyone [on your own authority], nor shall you display enmity against anyone on your own authority. You shall not speak [...] repeatedly. [Whatever] fugitive of Hatti comes [to you], whether he is a craftsman, [or ...], you shall not conceal [him], nor [hide] him, nor [release] him to another land. Always [seize] him and [send] him back to the father [of My Majesty]."

36. *a[n-da tar-na]-ši nu-⸢wa-ra-an⸣ [ap-pí-iš-k]i nu-wa-ra-an a-ap-pa A-NA A-⸢BI⸣* [^{d}UTU]$^{⸢ŠI⸣}$ *[up-pí-i]š-ki*

---

§7

37. *⸢i-da-a-lu-un-na-wa⸣-at-ta me-mi-an [ku]-iš pí-ra-an me-ma[-i] ⸢na-aš-šu-wa⸣-at-⸢ta ku⸣[-u-ru-r]a-⸢aš⸣ me-mi-an ku-iš-ki pí-ra-an ⸢me-ma-i⸣ na-aš-ma-wa-kán* LUGAL.MEŠ DUMU.MEŠ.LUGAL

38. *⸢ku-iš-ki za-am⸣-mu-ra-a-iz-zi z[i-ik-ka]-⸢wa⸣-ra-an le-e [ša-an]-⸢na-at⸣-ti nu-wa me-⸢mi-ya-an A⸣-NA* ^{d}UTU^{ŠI} *⸢ḫa-at-ra-a-i⸣ an-tu-⸢uḫ-ša⸣-an-na-wa e-ep*

39. *nu-⸢wa-ra⸣[-an A-NA] A-BI* $^{d⸢}$UTU$^{⸣ŠI}$ *up-⸢pí⸣ [A-N]A* ^{m}*At-tar-ši-ya-⸢ya⸣[-wa ḫa-lu-ki] le-e [u-i-ya-š]i ⸢ma-a-an⸣-wa-at-⸢ta⸣* ^{m}*⸢At⸣-tar-ši-ya-⸢ša?⸣ ḫa-lu-ki u-i[-ya-zi]*

40. *[zi-ga-wa]* ^{LÚ}*ṬE$_4$-MI ⸢e-ep⸣ nu[-wa-ra]-an A-NA A-BI* $^{⸢d⸣}$[UTU^{ŠI} *up-pí me-mi]-⸢ya⸣-an-na-wa-a[t-ták-kán ku-i]n ḫa-at-ra-⸢a-iz-zi⸣ nu-wa-ra-an le-e ša[-an-na-at-ti]*

41. *nu-wa-ra-an A-NA A-BI* ^{d}UTU^{ŠI} *ša-⸢ku⸣-wa-aš-šar ḫa-⸢at⸣[-ra-a-i* IGI.ḪI.A]-*⸢ma⸣-wa-kán a-ap[-pa A-NA] ⸢MA⸣-ḪAR* ^{m}[*At-tar-ši-ya*] ZI-*it le-e ⸢na⸣-i[t-ti]*

---

§8

42. *zi-ga-kán* ^{m}*Ma-ad-du[-wa-at-t]a-aš ⸢ŠA⸣ A-BI* ^{d}UTU[^{ŠI} *li-in-ga]-⸢a⸣-uš šar-ra-at-ta nu-⸢ut-ta⸣ A-BI* $^{⸢d}$UTU$^{⸣ŠI}$ *[a-ša]-⸢a⸣-an-na* ⸢KUR⸣ $^{ḪUR.SAG}$*Zi-ip[-pa-aš-la-a pa-iš]*

43. *nam-ma-⸢at⸣-ta li-⸢in-ga-nu⸣-ut nu-⸢ut-ta⸣ ŠA-⸢PAL⸣ [NI-IŠ* DINGIR]$^{⸢LIM⸣}$ *ki-iš-⸢ša⸣-an ⸢da-iš⸣ [ka]-⸢a⸣-ša-⸢wa-at⸣-ta* ⸢KUR⸣ [$^{ḪUR.SAG}$]*⸢Zi⸣[-ip-pa]-aš-la-a AD-DIN [nu-wa-kán a-pu-u-un-pát]*

44. *e-eš ⸢nam⸣[-ma]-⸢ma⸣-wa-az ⸢pa-ra-a⸣ ta-ma-a-⸢i⸣* KUR-*⸢e⸣ [ta-ma-a-i]n-na ḫa-pa[-a-ti-in* ZI-*i]t le-e e-eš-ta[-ri* ^{m}*Ma-ad-du]-wa-at-ta-ša* [KUR-*e*]

45. *ḫu-u-ma-an [IṢ]-BAT nam-m[a-a]t IŠ-TU* ÉRIN.MEŠ *⸢pa⸣[-an-ga]-⸢ri⸣-it ni-ni-ik[-ta nu-za A-NA* ^{m}*Ku]-⸢pa-an-ta⸣*-^{d}LAMMA *[za-aḫ-ḫi-ya pa]-it* ^{m}*K[u-pa-an-ta*-^{d}LAMMA-*aš-ma-at]*

46. *⸢ma⸣[-aḫ]-⸢ḫa⸣-an [IŠ]-ME ⸢na⸣-aš-ta [pa]-⸢it⸣* ÉRIN.MEŠ KUR $^{URU⸢}$*Ar⸣[-za-u-wa] ⸢kat⸣-ta-an ar-ḫa t[ar-na-aš] ⸢nu⸣* ÉRIN.MEŠ KUR $^{URU⸢}$*Ar-za-u⸣[-wa] A-NA* ^{m}*Ma-ad-[du-wa-at-ta]*

47. *⸢pa⸣[-a]-ir ⸢na⸣-aš-ta* ÉRIN.MEŠ ^{m}*Ma-ad-du-wa-at-ta [ḫu]-⸢u⸣-ma-an-ta-an-pát ar-ḫa ⸢ḫa-aš-pí-ir na-aš⸣[-ta* ^{m}*Ma-ad]-du-wa-at-ta-aš* ⸢1⸣[-*aš*]

48. *p[ár-aš-ta* KA]RAŠ-*za-kán ku-u-i-eš te-pa-u-eš i[š-pár]-⸢te-er⸣ a-pa-a-at-⸢ma⸣-kán ⸢ḫu-u-ma-an⸣ a[r-ḫa ḫa]-⸢aš-pí⸣-ir-pát*

§7 (obv. 37–41) "You shall not [conceal the person who] speaks an evil word before you—either whether someone speaks of a matter of hostility before you, or someone slanders the kings and princes. Write about the matter to My Majesty. Seize the person and send [him to] the father of My Majesty. You shall not [send] (someone) [on a mission to] Attarissiya. If Attarissiya sends (someone) on a mission to you, [you] seize the messenger and [send] him to the father [of My Majesty]. You shall not [conceal the matter about which] he writes [to you], but write about it scrupulously to the father of My Majesty. You shall not dispatch [the messenger] back to [Attarissiya] on your own authority."

§8 (obv. 42–48) You, Madduwatta, transgressed [the oaths] of the father of My Majesty. The father of My Majesty [gave] you the land of Mount Zippasla to occupy. Then he caused you to swear an oath, and placed the following under [oath] for you: "I have now given you the land [of Mount] Zippasla, [so] occupy [it alone]! You shall not occupy in addition another land (or) [another] river valley [on your own authority]." But [Madduwatta] seized the entire land, and then he mobilized [it en masse] with (its) troops. [He went in battle against] Kupanta-Kurunta, [but] when [Kupanta-Kurunta heard about it, he proceeded to turn loose(?)] the troops of the land [of Arzawa]. Then the troops of the land of Arzawa went against Madduwatta and disposed of absolutely all of the troops of Madduwatta. Madduwatta [fled alone. In regard to the army]—the few men who [escaped]—they also disposed of all of it.

---

§9

49. *nu*[*-za ŠA* ^{m}*Ma-ad-du*]*-wa-at-ta* DAM.⌈MEŠ-*ŠU*⌉ [DUM]U.M[EŠ-*ŠU*] ⌈NAM⌉.RA.ḪI.A-*SÚ-NU a-aš-*⌈*šu*⌉[*-u-y*]*a* EGIR-*an* ^{N}[$^{A4?}$ o o] x x [o] *e-eš-ta na-aš-ta* ^{m}*Ku-*⌈*pa-an-ta*⌉[-^{d}LAMMA-*aš*]

50. *up*$^{?}$[- o o o o]-⌈*ra*$^{?}$⌉ *nu-uš-ši* ⌈É-*ŠU*⌉ [o o -*r*]*a*$^{?}$*-an IṢ-BAT nu* DAM.MEŠ-⌈*ŠU*⌉ [DUMU.MEŠ-*ŠU* NAM.RA.ḪI.A]-⌈*SÚ-NU*⌉ [*a*]*-aš-šu-u-*⌈*ya*⌉ *ḫu-u-ma-an-ta-pát da-a-aš I-*[*NA*$^{?}$ … *ku-it*]

51. *ḫu*[*-u-ma-an-te-eš*$^{?}$] *A-NA NI-ŠI* DINGIR[^{LIM} *wa-aš-ta-an*]*-ni-iš-*⌈*ki*⌉*-ir nu*[*-uš* DINGIR.MEŠ *e-ep-pir*] ⌈*na*⌉*-aš-ta* ^{m}*Ma-ad-du-wa-at-ta-aš-pát ne-ku-ma-an-za* [*iš-pár-za-aš-ta*]

52. *kap-*⌈*pu-u*⌉[*-wa-an-te-eš-p*]*át an-tu-uḫ-še-eš iš-*⌈*pár-te*⌉*-er* [*a-pa*]*-*⌈*a-at-ma-kán*⌉ [*ḫu-u-ma*]*-an ar-ḫa ḫa-aš-pí-ir*

---

§10

53. ⌈*nu*⌉ [*A-BI*] ^{d}⌈UTU⌉[^{ŠI}]*-ma ma*[*-aḫ-ḫa-an IŠ-ME na-aš*] ^{m}*Pí-še-ni-in* [^{LÚ}*BE-LU*$^{?}$ *IŠ-TU*] ÉRIN[.MEŠ] ANŠE.KUR.RA.ḪI.A ⌈*A-NA*⌉ ^{m}*Ma-ad-du-wa-at-ta šar-di-ya IŠ-PUR na-aš-*⌈*ta*⌉ [*pa-a-ir*$^{?}$]

54. ⌈*ma-aḫ*⌉[*-ḫa-an-ma-a*]*š-ši* [*kat-ta ú-e-er na-aš*]*-*⌈*ta*⌉ *ŠA* ^{m}⌈*Ma*⌉[*-ad*]*-*⌈*du*⌉*-wa-at-*⌈*ta*⌉ [DAM].⌈MEŠ-*ŠU*⌉ <DUMU.MEŠ-*ŠU*> NAM.RA.⌈ḪI.A⌉-*SÚ-NU a-aš-šu-u-wa še-e-er* ^{URU}*Šal-la-u-wa-aš-ši ú-*⌈*e*⌉[*-mi-e-er*]

55. ⌈*na-at-ši a*⌉*-ap*[*-pa pí-i-e-er ŠA*] ^{m}*Ku-pa-an-ta-*^{d}[LAMMA]*-ya*<<*-ya-*>>*kán* [DAM.MEŠ-*ŠU* DUMU.MEŠ]-⌈*ŠU*⌉ NAM.RA.ḪI.A-*SÚ a-aš-šu-u-ya še-*<*e*>*-er* ^{URU}*Šal-la-u-wa-aš-ši* ⌈*ú*⌉[*-e-mi-e-er-pát*]

56. *nu* ⌈*a-pa-a-at-ta*⌉ [*A-NA* ^{m}*Ma-ad*]*-*⌈*du*⌉*-wa-at-*⌈*ta pí*⌉[*-i-e*]*-er nu* ⌈^{m}*Ku*⌉[*-pa-an-ta-*^{d}LAMMA*-ya-aš-pá*]*t A-ḪI-TI-ŠU a-ra-aḫ-za ḫa-an-da-a-it-ta-at na-aš-t*[*a* ^{m}*Ku-pa-an-ta-*^{d}LAMMA*-aš*]

57. 1-*iš* x x x x x ⌈*iš-pár-za-aš*⌉*-ta ke-e-kán* [*ḫu*]*-u-ma-an* ⌈*ar-ḫa ḫa-aš*⌉[*-pí*]-⌈*ir nu*⌉ ^{m}*Ma-ad-du-wa-at-ta-an ta-a-an pí-e-da-aš*[*-ša-aḫ-ḫi-ir*]

---

§11

58. ⌈*na*$^{?}$⌉-x x [o o]-⌈*kán* ^{URU}⌉*Šal-la-u-wa-aš-ši* ⌈*kat*⌉*-ta-an-*⌈*ta*⌉ $^{LÚ.MEŠ}$*BE-LU* GAL$^{⌈TIM⌉}$ *ku-*⌈*e*⌉[*-uš*] ⌈^{m}*Pí-še-ni*⌉*-in* ^{m}*Pu-uš-ku-ru-nu-wa-an-na* DUMU ^{m}*Aḫ*[- …]

59. x [o] x x [o]-⌈*ta-ra nu-uš*⌉*-ša-an A-NA* ^{m}⌈*Ma-ad*⌉*-du-*⌈*wa*⌉*-at-ta ku-it še-*<*e*>*-er za-*⌈*aḫ*⌉[*-ḫi*]-⌈*ir*⌉ [*ma-a*]*n-kán še-e-er A-NA* ^{m}*Ma-ad-du-wa-at-ta ku-e-nir*

---

§9 (obv. 49–52) And [Madduwatta's] wives, [his children], their civilian captives and goods were back [in ...] Then Kupanta-Kurunta [...], and he seized his [...] household, and took his wives, [his children], their [civilian captives], and absolutely all the goods. [... Because] they [all] sinned against the oath, [the gods seized them]. And Madduwatta [escaped] naked by himself. Only a few men escaped, but they (the Arzawans) disposed of all of it (that is, the army).

§10 (obv. 53–57) And [when the father] of My Majesty [heard, then] he sent Piseni, [the nobleman(?), ... together with] infantry and chariotry to the aid of Madduwatta. And [they went, but] when [they came] to him, [they found] Madduwatta's [wives], <his children>, their civilian captives and goods up in the city of Sallauwassi, and [they gave] them back to him. And [they even found the wives, the children], the civilian captives, and goods [of] Kupanta-Kurunta up in Sallauwassi, and these too they gave [to] Madduwatta. And [Kupanta-Kurunta] was kept apart by himself, and [Kupanta-Kurunta] fled [...] alone. All of this they disposed of, and [they installed] Madduwatta in his place once more.

§11 (obv. 58–59) The prominent noblemen Piseni and Puskurunuwa, son of Ah[...], whom [he sent(?)] down to Sallauwassi, made war on behalf of Madduwatta, and they [could have] been killed for Madduwatta.

§12

60. *a*[*-ap-pa*]-⸢*ma*⸣*-kán* ^{m}*At-tar-ri-iš-ši-ya-aš* ⸢**LÚ**⸣ ^{URU}***A-aḫ-ḫi-ya-a*** *ar-ḫa ú-it nu* ⸢EGIR-*an*⸣ *tu-uk-pát* ^{m}*Ma-ad-du-wa-at-ta-an ku-na-an-na ša-an-ḫ*[*i-iš-ki-i*]*t*

61. *A*[*-BI* ^{d}UT]U⸢^{ŠI}*-ma ma*⸣*-aḫ-ḫa-an IŠ-ME* ⸢*na-aš-ta*⸣ ^{m}*Ki-iš-na-pí-li-in* ÉRIN.MEŠ ANŠE.KUR.ḪI.A *A-NA* ^{m}*At-ta-ri-iš-ši-ya me-na-aḫ-ḫa-an-ta za-aḫ-ḫi-ya pa-ra-a* ⸢*na*⸣*-iš*

62. *nu* [*zi*]*-ik* ^{m}*Ma-*⸢*ad-du*⸣*-wa-at-ta-aš* ⸢*nam-ma* ^{m}*At*⸣*-ta-*⸢*ri*⸣*-iš-ši-ya-an Ú-UL ma-az-za-aš-ta nu-uš-ši pí-ra-an ar-ḫa tar-na-aš nu-ud-du-za ú-it* ^{m}*Ki-iš-na-pí-li-iš*

63. x x x *IŠ-TU* ⸢KUR⸣ ^{URU}*Ḫa-at-ti ḫu-i-*⸢*nu-ut*⸣ ^{m}*Ki-iš-*⸢*na*⸣*-pí-li-ša* ⸢*A-NA*⸣ ^{m}*At-ta-ri-iš-ši-ya me-na-aḫ-ḫa-an-ta za-aḫ-ḫi-ya pa-it* ⸢*nu ŠA*⸣ ^{m}*At-ta-ri-iš-ši-ya* 1 *ME* ^{GIŠ}G[IGIR N *LI-IM* ÉRIN.MEŠ *za-aḫ-ḫi-ya ti-i-e*]*-er nu za-aḫ-ḫi-ir*

64. *na-*⸢*aš-ta*⸣ *ŠA* ^{m}⸢*At-ta*⸣[*-ri-iš*]-⸢*ši*⸣*-ya-ya* 1 LÚ.SIG$_5$*-in ku-e-*⸢*nir*⸣ *an-ze-el-la-kán* 1 LÚ.SIG$_5$ ^{m}*Zi-da-a-an-za-an ku-e-nir* ⸢*nu* ^{m}*At-ta*⸣*-ri-iš-ši-ya-aš*

65. *A-NA* [^{m}*Ma*]-⸢*ad*⸣*-du-wa-at-ta* [o o o o] *ne-e-a-at* ⸢*na*⸣*-aš-za* ⸢*ar-ḫa I*⸣*-NA* KUR-*ŠU pa-it nu* ^{m}*Ma-ad-du-wa-at-ta-an nam-ma ta-a-an* ⸢*pé-e*⸣*-da-aš-ša-aḫ-ḫi-ir*

---

§13

66. *a-*⸢*ap-pa-ma*⸣ ^{URU}*Da-la-u-wa-aš* [*ku*]-⸢*u*⸣[*-ru*]*-ur* ⸢*IṢ-BAT*⸣ *nu* ^{m}*Ma-ad-du-wa-at-ta-aš A-NA* ^{m}*Ki-iš-na-pí-li ki-iš-ša-an ḫa-at-ra-a-it ú-uk-wa wa-al-ḫu-u-an-zi*

67. ^{URU}*Da-la-u-wa pa-i-mi* [*šu-me-eš-ma*]*-wa* ^{URU}⸢*Ḫi-in*⸣*-du-wa i-it-tén nu-wa ú-*⸢*uk*⸣ ^{URU}*Da-*⸢*la-u-wa-an*⸣ *wa-al-aḫ-mi nu-wa nam-ma* ÉRIN.MEŠ ^{URU}*Da-la-u-wa A-NA* ^{URU}*Ḫi-in-du-wa*

68. ⸢*šar*⸣*-di-ya Ú-UL ú-iz-z*[*i nu-wa-za* ^{UR}]^{U}*Ḫi-in-*⸢*du*⸣*-wa-an ḫar-ni-ik-te-ni nu* ^{m}*Ki-iš-na*[*-pí-li-i*]*š* ÉRIN.MEŠ-*an* ^{URU}*Ḫi-in-du-wa za-aḫ-ḫi-ya pé-ḫu-te-et*

---

§14

69. ⸢^{m}*Ma*⸣*-ad-du*[*-wa-at*]-⸢*ta*⸣*-ša* ⸢*nam-ma* ^{URU}⸣*Da-la-*⸢*u-wa*⸣ *za-aḫ-ḫi-ya Ú-UL ku-it pa-it na-aš-ta* ⸢*A-NA*⸣ LÚ.MEŠ ^{URU}*Da-la-u-wa im-ma kat-ta-an ar-ḫa ḫa-at-ra-a-it*

70. ⸢*ka-a*⸣*-aš-ma-*⸢*wa*⸣ [ÉRIN].MEŠ [^{UR}]^{U}*Ḫa-at-ti* ^{URU}*Ḫi-in-du-*⸢*wa*⸣ *za-*⸢*aḫ*⸣*-ḫi-ya pa-it* ⸢*nu-wa*⸣*-aš-ma-aš* ⸢KASKAL-*an*⸣ *pí-ra-an e-ep-tén nu-wa-ra-aš wa-al-aḫ-tén*

§12 (obv. 60–65) But [later] Attarissiya, the ruler of **Ahhiya**, came and was plotting to kill *you*, Madduwatta. But when the father of My Majesty heard, he dispatched Kisnapili, infantry, and chariotry in battle against Attarissiya. And you, Madduwatta, again did not resist Attarissiya, but yielded before him. Then Kisnapili proceeded to rush [...] to you from Hatti. Kisnapili went in battle against Attarissiya. 100 [chariots and ... thousand infantry] of Attarissiya [drew up for battle]. And they fought. One officer of Attarissiya was killed, and one officer of ours, Zidanza, was killed. Then Attarissiya turned [away(?)] from Madduwatta, and he went off to his own land. And they installed Madduwatta in his place once more.

§13 (obv. 66–68) Later the city of Dalauwa commenced [hostilities], and Madduwatta wrote thus to Kisnapili: "I will go to attack Dalauwa. You go to the city of Hinduwa. I will attack Dalauwa, and then the troops of Dalauwa will not (be able to) come to the aid of Hinduwa, [so that] you will destroy Hinduwa." And Kisnapili led troops to Hinduwa for battle.

§14 (obv. 69–72) Then because Madduwatta did not go to Dalauwa for battle, but in fact wrote away to the people of Dalauwa (saying): "[The troops] of Hatti have just gone to Hinduwa for battle. Block the road before them and attack them!" Then they deployed [the troops] of Dalauwa on the road. They proceeded to block the way [of our] troops and routed them. They killed Kisnapili and Partahulla. But [Madduwatta] laughed out loud about them.

71. ⸢*nu-uš*⸣*-ša-an* É[RIN.MEŠ ^{URU}]*Da-la-u-wa* ⸢KASKAL-*ši*⸣ *pa-*⸢*ra-a*⸣ *ú-wa-te-*⸢*e-er*⸣ *nu ú-e-er* ⸢*an*⸣*-z*[*e-el*] ÉRIN.MEŠ^{TI} KASKAL-*an e-ep-pir nu-uš ni-ni-in-ki-ir*

72. *na-aš-ta* ^{m}⸢*Ki*⸣[*-iš-na*]*-*⸢*pí-li-in*⸣ ^{m}*Pár-ta-ḫu-ul*⸣*-la-an-*⸢*na*⸣ *ku-en-nir* ^{m}*Ma*[*-ad-du-wa-at-t*]*a-aš-ma-aš-ma-aš-kán pa-ra-a ḫa-aḫ-ḫar-aš-ki-it*

---

§15

73. *nam-ma-kán* ^{m}*Ma-*⸢*ad-du-wa-at*⸣[*-ta-aš* L]Ú.M[EŠ ^{UR}]^{U}*Da-la-u-wa A-NA* KUR ^{URU}*Ḫa-at-*⸢*ti* EGIR⸣*-an* ⸢*ar*⸣*-ḫa-pát na-iš na-at IŠ-TU* $^{LÚ.MEŠ}$ŠU.GI^{TIM} *kat-ta-an a-pé-e-da-ni*

74. *i-ya-an-ni-wa-an* [*da-a-i*]*r* [*na-at-ši me-na-aḫ-ḫa*]*-an-ta li-*⸢*in-ga*⸣*-nu-ut* ⸢*nam*⸣[*-ma-aš*]*-ši* ⸢*ar*⸣[*-kam-ma*]*-an píd-da-a-an-ni-wa-an da-a-ir*

---

§16

75. ⸢*a*⸣[*-ap-pa-m*]*a* ^{m}[*Ku-pa-an-ta-*^{d}LAMMA*-aš A-NA*] *A-BI* ^{d}UTU^{ŠI} *me-na-aḫ-ḫa-an-ta ku*[*-u*]*-*⸢*ru*⸣*-ur e-eš-*⸢*ta zi-ga-aš-ši*⸣ ^{m}*Ma-ad-du-wa-at-ta-aš me-na-aḫ-ḫa-an-ta* ⸢*ták*⸣*-šu-la-a-eš*

76. [o o o o o o o o o o o o *n*]*u-uš-ši* DUMU.MUNUS-*KA A-NA* ⸢DAM⸣-*SÚ* [*pa*]*-*⸢*it*⸣*-ta A-NA* ^{d}[UTU]⸢^{ŠI}⸣*-ma ki-iš-ša-an ḫa-at-ra-a-eš ka-*⸢*a*⸣*-ša-wa-az* ^{m}*Ku-pa-an-ta-*^{d}LAMMA*-an*

77. [o o o o o o o o o o o o o o] *nu-wa-aš-ši* ⸢*ki-iš*⸣*-ša*[*-an*] *ḫa-*⸢*at-ra*⸣*-a-mi kat-ti-mi-wa e-ḫu nu-wa-at-ta* DUMU.MUNUS-*YA A-NA* DAM-*KA pí-iḫ-ḫi*

78. [*ma-a-an-wa-ra-aš-ma-kán kat-ti-mi ú-iz*]*-*⸢*zi*⸣ *nu-wa-*⸢*ra-an*⸣ [*e-ep*]*-mi* [*nu*]*-wa-ra-*⸢*an*⸣*-kán ku-e-mi nu-mu ma-aḫ-ḫa-an* ^{m}*Ma-ad-du-wa-at-ta-aš QA-TAM-MA ḫa-at-ra-a-it*

---

§17

79. [*nu-za* ^{d}UTU^{ŠI} *ki-iš-ša-an* EGIR-*pa me-mi-iš-ki*]*-nu-un nu-wa A-NA* ^{m}*Ma*[*-ad-d*]*u-wa-at-ta* ^{m}*Ku-*⸢*pa-an*⸣*-ta-*^{d}LAMMA*-aš ke-e-ma me-na-aḫ-ḫa-an-ta li-in-ga-an ḫar-zi*

80. [o o o o o o o o o o o o o o o o o o o o *nu-wa-aš*]*-ši ŠA* ŠÀ-*ŠU* [DUMU.MUNU]S-*SÚ A-NA* DAM-*ŠU ḫar-zi nu-wa a-pa-*⸢*a*⸣[*-aš*] *A-NA* ^{LÚ}*ḪA-AT-NI-ŠU ŠA* ŠÀ-*ŠU-ya*

81. [DUMU.MUNUS *me-na-aḫ-ḫa-an-ta i-da-a-lu ša-an-ḫi-iš-ki-zi nu-wa-aš*]*-ši* EGIR[*-an ḫi*]*-in-kán ḫa-an-te-eš-ki-zi nu-wa ú-iz-zi nam-ma ta-me-e-da-ni ge-en-*⸢*zu*⸣

82. [*ḫar-zi … nu-w*]*a* ^{m}*Ma-ad-du-wa-at-ta tu-e-ek-ku-uš an-da me-ek-ki a-ar-ḫu-un*

§15 (obv. 73–74) Furthermore, Madduwatta turned the people of Dalauwa away from Hatti, and at the (decision of their) elders [they began] to march with him. [And] he caused [them] to swear an oath [to him], and on top of that they began to pay him [tribute].

§16 (obv. 75–78) [But later Kupanta-Kurunta] was an enemy [to] the father of My Majesty, while you, Madduwatta, were at peace with him. […] And you gave him your daughter in marriage. But you wrote thus to [My Majesty]: "Now [I will …] Kupanta-Kurunta, and I will write to him as follows: 'Come to me, and I will give you my daughter in marriage.' [If he comes to me], then [I will seize] him [and] kill him." And when Madduwatta wrote to me thus,

§17 (obv. 79–83) [then, I, My Majesty, was thinking as follows]: "Kupanta-Kurunta has sworn these things to Madduwatta, [and] he has the former's own begotten [daughter] in marriage. [Would] he (Madduwatta) [be plotting evil against] his son-in-law and his own [daughter]? Would he be arranging his death? And furthermore, would he proceed [to have] an emotional tie to an outsider? [… And] I have very much gotten to the heart of the matter(?), O Madduwatta." [… I wrote back to him as follows]: "Do as seems right to you."

83. [… *ki-iš-ša-an-na-aš-ši* EGIR-*pa ḫa-at-r*]*a-a-nu-un ma-aḫ-ḫa-an-wa-at-ta a-aš-šu nu-wa QA-TAM-MA i-ya*

---

§18

84. […]-⸢*ni*$^{?}$ *kar*$^{?}$⸣[- o o *p*]*í-iḫ-ḫu-un* ^{m}*Pár-ta-ḫu-*⸢*ul*⸣*-la-aš ku-it* TI-*an-za e-eš-ta*

85. […]*-tu-u-ma-an* DUMU.MUNUS-*SÚ-ya ḫar-ta ú-uk* ^{m}*Pár-ta-ḫu-ul-la-aš*

86. […].ḪI.A *le-e iš-ša-at-ti* ^{m}*Ma-ad-du-wa-at-ta-ša-mu ki-iš-ša-an me-mi-iš-ta ŠA* KUR^{TI}*-wa-an-na-ša-at iš-ḫi-*⸢*ú*⸣[*-ul*]

87. […] ^{m}*Ma-ad-du-wa-at-ta-ša-*⸢*wa-mu ki-iš*⸣*-ša-an*

88. [*me-mi-iš-ta*$^{?}$ …]*-na-ya-ša* x [o o o o o o] x x

89. […]

90. […]

---

§19

91. […]

92. […]x-*ki*

93. […]

(lower edge and first three lines of rev. lost)

§20'

4. [… ^{m}*Ma-ad-du-wa*]*-at-ta-aš ki-iš-ša-an*

5. [*ḫa-at-ra-a-it*$^{?}$ …] x *ka-a-ša zi-ik*

6. [… *A-NA* ^{m}*Ma-ad-du-wa-a*]*t-ta* ^{m}*Ku-pa-an-ta-*^{d}LAMMA*-aš*

7. [*ki-iš-ša-an ḫa-at-ra-a-it*$^{?}$ … *-aš*$^{?}$]-⸢*ša*⸣*-wa-mu ku-it me-na-aḫ-ḫa-an-ta*

8. [… DUMU.MUNUS-*KA ar*]*-ḫa da-a nu-wa-ra-an-za A-NA* DAM-*YA ú-uk*

9. [*Ú-UL da-aḫ-ḫi*$^{?}$ … *ma-a-an-wa-r*]*a-aš kat-ti-mi ú-iz-zi nu-wa-ra-an e-ep-mi*

10. [*nu-wa-ra-an-kán ku-e-mi* …] x *ḫa-li-iḫ-la-i*

---

§21'

11. [… *nu-ut-ta ma-a*]-⸢*an*⸣ [*A-BI*] ^{d}UTU^{ŠI} *a-ša-a-an-na* KUR ^{ÍD}*Ši-ya-an-ta-ya pa-ra*]-⸢*a*⸣ [*pé-e*]*š*$^{?}$*-ta*

12. [o o o o o o o o o o o o o o o o o o *zi-ik-ma* ^{m}*Ma-ad-du-wa-at-t*]*a-aš A-NA* KUR.KUR.ḪI.A ^{LÚ}KÚR ^{LÚ}*a-ú-ri-ya-la-aš* ^{LÚ}*ša-pa-a-ša-al-*⸢*li-iš*⸣

13. [*Ú-UL e-eš-ta* o o o o o o *A-NA* ^{d}UTU^{ŠI} *ki-iš-š*]*a*$^{?}$-⸢*an*$^{?}$⸣ [*me-mi-iš-ta*$^{?}$] *nu-wa-mu ku-wa-pí* ^{d}UTU^{ŠI} *BE-LÍ-YA la-a-aḫ-ḫa ḫal-zi-iš-ša-at-ti*

§18 (obv. 84–90) [...] I gave. Because Partahulla was alive, [...] he had his ... daughter. I, Partahulla, [...] you shall not perform [...] But Madduwatta said to me as follows: "It is the custom of our land." [...] "Madduwatta [said(?)] this to me: [' ... ']"

(The final five lines of the obverse, those of the lower edge, and the initial three lines of the reverse are too fragmentary for translation, or have been altogether lost.)

§20' (rev. 4–10) [... Madduwatta wrote(?)] thus: [" ...] you now [... " Then] Kupanta-Kurunta [wrote(?) thus to Madduwatta: " ...] Because [...] against me, take [your daughter(?)] away! I [will not take(?)] her in marriage. [... If] she comes to me, I will arrest her, [and kill her(?)." ...] (S)he genuflects.

§21' (rev. 11–18) [... And when the father] of My Majesty [gave you] the Land of the Siyanta River to occupy, [... But you, Madduwatta, were not] a border guard and a scout against the foreign lands. [And although you said to the father of My Majesty as follows]: "As soon as you, Your Majesty, my lord, summon me to a campaign, [I will come immediately to your aid." When] the father of My Majesty gave [you] the Land of the Siyanta River to occupy, and then [caused] you [to swear an oath, and placed under oath for you as follows]: "The father of His Majesty has now given the Land of the Siyanta River to you. You be [a border guard] and [a scout of the father of His Majesty] against

14. [*nu-wa-ra-at-ta ḫu-u-da-a-ak šar-di-ya ú-wa-mi? ma-aḫ-ḫa-an-ma-at-t*]*a* *A-BI* ^{d}UTU^{ŠI} KUR ^{ÍD}*Ši-ya-an-ta a-ša-a-an-na pa-iš nam-ma-at-ta* [*li-in-ga-nu-ut*]

15. [*nu-ut-ta ŠA-PAL NI-IŠ* DINGIR^{LIM} *ki-iš-ša-an da-iš ka-a*]-*ša-wa-at*-⌈*ta*⌉ *A-BI* ^{d}UTU^{ŠI} KUR ^{ÍD}*Ši-ya-an-ta pa-iš zi-ga-wa-za A-NA* [KUR.KUR.ḪI.A ^{LÚ}KÚR]

16. [*ŠA A-BI* ^{d}UTU^{ŠI} ^{LÚ}*a-ú-ri-ya-la-aš* ^{LÚ}*ša-pa-a-ša*]-*al-le-eš-ša e-eš nu-wa-kán* KUR.KUR.ḪI.A ^{LÚ}KÚR *me-na-aḫ-ḫa-an-ta ḫar-ak nu-wa-a*[*t-ta ma-a-an me*]-⌈*mi*⌉-*an*

17. [*ku-ru-ra-aš ku-iš me-ma-i nu-wa A-NA A-BI* ^{d}UTU^{ŠI}] *le-e ku-it-ki ša-an-na-aš-ki-ši nu-wa-mu ḫu-u-ma-an ḫa-at-re-eš-ki* [*ma-a-an-wa* KUR-*e*]

18. [*ku-u-ru-ur e-ep-zi nu-wa-ra-an ḫu-u-da-a-a*]*k wa-al-aḫ nu-wa-za QA-TE*^{MEŠ}-*KA zi-ik ḫu-u-da-a-ak e-eš-ḫar-nu-ut*

---

§22’

19. [*nam*]-*ma-ma-wa-az IŠ*-⌈*TU*⌉ K[UR ^{ÍD}*Ši-ya-an-ta pa*]-⌈*ra*⌉-*a ta-ma-a-i* KUR-*e ta-ma-a-in-na ḫa-pa-a-ti-in* ZI-*it le-e* ⌈*e*⌉[-*eš-ta-ri*]

20. ^{m}*Ma-ad-du-wa-at-ta-ša-k*[*án A-N*]*A* ⌈*A*⌉-*BI* ^{d}UTU[^{ŠI}] ⌈*li*⌉-*in-ga-in šar-ra-at-ta-at nu-za* KUR ^{URU}*Ar-za-u-wa ḫu-u-ma-an da-a-aš na-a*[*t* o o o o o]

21. KUR ^{URU}*Ḫa-pa-al-la-ma-az* ⌈*li*⌉[-*in*]-*ki-ya kat-ta-an ki-iš-ša-an zi-ik-ke-eš* KUR ^{URU}*Ḫa-pa-a-al-la-ma-az* ^{m}*Ma-ad-du-wa-at-ta-aš li-i*[*n-ki-ya kat-ta-an*]

22. *ki-iš-ša-an zi-ik-ki-it*[96] [KUR] ^{URU}*Ḫa-pa-a-al-la-wa-kán na-aš-šu ku-e-mi na-aš-ma-wa-ra-at QA-DU* NAM.RA.ḪI.A GUD.ḪI.A UDU.ḪI.A *ar-nu-mi* [*na-at A-NA*] ⌈^{d}UTU⌉^{ŠI}

23. *pa-ra-a pí-iḫ-ḫi nam-ma-ma-kán* KUR ^{URU}*Ḫa-pa-a-al-la ku-en-ta-ya Ú-UL e-ep-ta-ya-at Ú-UL na-at A-NA* ^{d}UTU^{ŠI} *pa-ra-a* ⌈*Ú*⌉[-*UL pa-it-ta*]

24. *na-at-za* ^{m}*Ma-ad-du-wa-at-ta-aš da-a-aš*

---

§23’

25. ⌈*A-NA*⌉ GAL.GEŠTIN-*ma ki-iš-ša-an ḫa-at*-⌈*re*⌉-*eš-ki-zi A-NA* KUR ^{URU}*Ḫa-pa-a-al-la-wa-at-ta* 1-*e*-<*da*>-*az ti-ya-mi zi-ga-wa-mu-kán a-wa-an ar-ḫa* [*tar-na*]

26. *nu-wa-kán i-it* KUR ^{URU}*Ḫa-pa-a-la-wa-kán ku-e-ni na-aš-ma-wa-ra-at ar-nu-ut ma-aḫ-ḫa-an-ma-an-za-kán* GAL.GEŠTIN *a-wa-an ar-ḫa tar-na-aš*

---

96. Here the scribe has included two variant formulations of the same sentence.

[the foreign lands]. And hold off the foreign lands. [If someone speaks a] word [of hostility before you], you shall not conceal anything [from the father of His Majesty], but write me everything. [If a land commences hostilities], attack [it immediately], and you bloody your hands immediately."

§22' (rev. 19–24) "Furthermore, [you shall] not [occupy] another land or another river valley beyond [the Land of the Siyanta River]." But Madduwatta transgressed the oath [to] the father of My Majesty, and he took all the land of Arzawa, and [he ruled(?)] it. But you placed (the matter of) the land of Hapalla under oath as follows—Madduwatta placed (the matter of) the land of Hapalla [under oath] as follows:[96] "Either I will smite [the land] of Hapalla, or I will carry it off, together with civilian captives, cattle, and sheep, [and] I will turn [it] over [to] Your Majesty." But subsequently you did not smite the land of Hapalla, you did not capture it, and [you did not turn] it over to My Majesty. Madduwatta took it for himself.

§23' (rev. 25–28) He kept writing to the general: "I will approach the land of Hapalla through you (that is, through your territory) alone. You [let] me through, (saying): 'Go, smite the land of Hapalla, or carry it off!'" But when the general did let him through, he subsequently would have [blocked] his roads and would have attacked him in the rear. And in this matter even Antahitta, chief [of the …], and Mazlauwa, the ruler of Kuwaliya, were informers against him.

27. *nam-ma-ma-an-ši* EGIR-⸢*an* KASKAL⸣.MEŠ^{TIM} *I*[*Ṣ-BAT*] *ma-a-na-an-kán* EGIR-*an-ta wa-al-aḫ-ta nu-uš-ši ke-e-da-ni ud-da-ni-i* ^{m}*An-ta-ḫi-it-ta-a-aš-pát* G[AL o o o o]
28. ^{m}⸢*Ma*⸣-*az-la-u-wa-aš-ša* LÚ ^{URU}*Ku-wa-li-ya ḫa-an-ti-ti-ya-tal-le-eš*

---

§24'

29. x-*az ŠA* ^{d}UTU^{ŠI} *nam-ma a*-⸢*ša*⸣[*-a-a*]*n-ta* KUR.KUR^{TIM} *da-a-aš* KUR ^{URU}*Zu-u-ma-an-ti* KUR ^{URU}*Wa-al-la-ri-im-ma* KUR ^{URU}*Ya-la-an-ti* KUR ^{URU}[*Zu-u-mar-ri*]
30. ⸢KUR ^{URU}⸣*Mu-ú-ta-mu-ú-ta-aš-ša* KUR ^{URU}*At*-⸢*ta*⸣-*ri-im-ma* KUR ^{URU}*Šu-ru-ú-ta* KUR ^{URU}*Ḫu-u-ur-ša-na-aš-ša nu nam-ma ke-e-el ŠA* KUR.KUR^{TIM} ^{LÚ}[$^{.MEŠ}$*ṬE*$_4$*-MI*]
31. *M*[*A*]*-ḪAR* ^{d}UTU^{ŠI} *ú-wa-u-an-zi Ú-UL tar-n*[*a*]*-i* ÉRIN.MEŠ-*ya ke-e-el ŠA* KUR.KUR^{TIM} *MA-ḪAR* ^{d}UTU^{ŠI} *ú-wa-u-an-zi Ú-UL tar-na-i ku-e-da-ni-ya ku*[*-it e-eš-ta*]
32. *nu nam-ma MA-ḪAR* ^{d}UTU^{ŠI} *ar*-⸢*ga-mu*⸣-*uš-ša* [*ú*]-⸢*tum*⸣-*ma-an-zi Ú-UL tar-na-i nu-uš-za a-pa-a-aš da-aš-ki-it ŠA* ^{d}UTU^{ŠI}-*ya-kán* ANŠE.KUR.RA.ḪI.A *k*[*u-it a-pí-ya*] *e-eš-ta*
33. [*nu*]*-za a-pé-el* ANŠE.KUR.RA.ḪI.A-*ŠU A-NA* ^{GIŠ}A[PIN *ti*]*-it-nu-uš-ki-it*

---

§25'

34. [^{URU}]*Up-ni-ḫu-wa-la-an-ma-az* URU-*an* ZI-*it* [*e-eš*]*-ta-at nam-ma-ták-kán ŠA* KUR ^{URU}*Ḫa-at-ti ku-i-e-eš* $^{LÚ.MEŠ}$*pít-te-ya-an-te-eš an-da i-ya*[*-an-ta-at*]
35. ⸢^{m}*Ma*⸣-*ad-du-wa-at-ta-aš-ma-aš-za da-aš-ke-eš* [*A-BI* ^{d}]UTU^{ŠI}-*ma-at-ta* ^{d}UTU^{ŠI}-*ya* EGIR-*an-ta ḫa-at-re-eš-ki-ir zi-ga-aš a-ap-pa Ú-U*[*L pa-it-ta*]
36. [*nu-ut*]*-ta ma-a-an ši-e-ta-ni ud-da-ni-i* ⸢*a*?⸣[*-ap-pa ḫa*]*-at-ra-a-u-ni zi-ga-an-na-aš nam-ma ud-da-ni-i a-ap-pa ar-ku-wa-ar* ⸢*Ú*⸣[*-UL i-ya-ši*]
37. [*nu*]*-kán ta-ma-a-i ku-e-ek-ki ud-da-a-ar* [*me-mi-iš-ki-ši nu-u*]*n-na-aš* EGIR-*pa ta-ma-a-i ud-da-a-ar ḫa-at-re-eš-ki*[*-ši*]

---

§26'

38. ⸢*a-ap*⸣-*pa-ma-kán* ^{d}UTU^{ŠI} *IŠ*-⸢*TU*⸣ KUR ^{URU}*Šal-pa Ù I*[*Š-TU* KUR ^{URU} o o o]-*ša* ÉRIN.MEŠ ANŠE.KUR.RA.ḪI.A *ar-ḫa ú-wa-te-nu-un* ^{m}*Ma-ad-du-wa-at-t*[*a-aš-ma A-NA* ^{d}UTU^{ŠI}]
39. [*ŠA*] KUR ^{URU}*Pí-i-ta-aš-ša* ⸢^{LÚ}⸣*ta-pa-ri-ya-al*-⸢*li*⸣[*-uš Ù* $^{LÚ.MEŠ}$]⸢ŠU⸣.GI ^{URU}*Pí-i-ta-aš-ša-ya me-na-aḫ-ḫa-an-ta li-in-ga-nu-uš*-⸢*ki*⸣[*-it nu-uš pár-ra-an-ta*]

§24’ (rev. 29–33) [In addition(?)] he took for himself further lands belonging to My Majesty: the land of Zumanti, the land of Wallarimma, the land of Iyalanti, the land [of Zumarri], the land of Mutamutassa, the land of Attarimma, the land of Suruta, and the land of Hursanassa. And furthermore, he did not allow [the messengers] of these lands to come before My Majesty. Finally, he did not allow the tribute which [was incumbent] on anyone to be brought before My Majesty, but always took it himself. And he set to the plow the horses of My Majesty [that] were [there].

§25’ (rev. 34–37) But you [occupied] the city of Upnihuwala on your own authority. And furthermore, you, Madduwatta, kept taking for yourself the fugitives of Hatti who [traveled] to you. [The father] of My Majesty and My Majesty repeatedly wrote after (them) to you, but you did not [give] them back. [And] when we write back to you in one matter, you do [not] subsequently [present] a defense to us in the matter. [Then] you [speak] about some other matters. You always write us back about other matters.

§26’ (rev. 38–42) But later, I, My Majesty, brought infantry and chariotry out of the land of Salpa and [out of the land of ... But] Madduwatta caused the chieftains [of] the land of Pitassa [and] the elders of Pitassa to swear an oath against [My Majesty], and led [them astray, (saying)]: “Be my partisans! Occupy [the lands of His Majesty]! Attack Hatti!” Then they proceeded [to attack the lands of My Majesty], and they burned down fortified cities. I, My Majesty, [came back], and my own troops [displayed(?)] their triumphant heart. In those days Madduwatta hid his eyes and [...] forth to the people of Pitassa.

40. *ti-it-nu-ut am-me-el-wa-az e-eš-tén nu-wa-za-kán Š*[*A*? ^{d}UTU^{ŠI} KUR.KUR^{TI}]^{M} *e-eš-du-ma-at* KUR ^{URU}*Ḫa-at-ti-ma-wa wa-al-aḫ-te-en nu ú-e*[*-er ŠA* ^{d}UTU^{ŠI} KUR.KUR^{TIM} *wa-al-ḫi-ir*]

41. ⸢*nu*⸣ URU.DIDLI.ḪI.A BÀD *ar-ḫa wa-ar-nu-ir* ^{d}UTU^{ŠI}-⸢*kán*⸣ *a-a*[*p-pa u-wa-nu-un*] *nu-za-kán am-me-el-pát* ÉRIN.MEŠ.ḪI.A *tar-ḫu-i-la-uš ka-ra-a-ta*[*-uš* o o o o]

42. [^{m}*Ma*]*-ad-du-wa-at-ta-aš-ma-az a-pé-e-da-aš* UD.ḪI.A*-aš ša-*⸢*a*⸣*-k*[*u-wa mu-un*]*-na-a-it na-aš-kán A-NA* LÚ.MEŠ ^{URU}*Pí-i-ta-aš-ša pa-ra-a* […]

---

§27'

43. x x*-ma* ⸢*A*?*-NA*?⸣ ^{m}*Ku-pa-an-ta-*^{d}LAMMA*-ya ḫa-at-re-eš-ki-it* [o o]*-wa* [o o o o] x *a-pu-u-un-na pár-ra-an-ta ti-it-nu-ut* x [o o o o o o]

44. ⸢*a-pa-a-ša-at*⸣ *a-pa-a-ši-la-pát ŠA-PAL NI-IŠ* DINGIR^{LIM} *ki-iš-ša-an zi-ik*[*-ki-it ka-a*]*-ša-wa-az ke-e-da-aš A-NA* KUR.KUR^{TIM} [^{LÚ}*a-ú-ri-ya-la-aš*]

45. *uš-ki-iš-*[*g*]*a-tal-la-aš-ša ú-uk nu-wa-mu ma-a-an i-da-a-lu-un me-mi-an ku-iš* [*me-ma-i ú*]*-ga-wa-kán A-NA* ^{d}UTU^{ŠI} *Ú-U*[*L ku-it-ki ša-an-na-aš-ki-mi nam-ma-wa-ra-at*]

46. ⸢*a-ap-pa*⸣ *i-ši-ya-aḫ-ḫi-iš-ki-mi ma-a-an-wa* ⸢*ku-it*⸣ <KUR*-e*> *ku-u-ru-ur e-ep-zi nu-wa-aš-ša-an ku-it-*⸢*ma-an*⸣ *ŠA* ^{d}UTU^{ŠI} ÉRIN.M[EŠ *za-aḫ-ḫi-ya-at-ta-ri ú-ga-wa-za ma-an-ni-in-ku-wa-an ku-it*?]

47. ⸢*nu-wa-ra-at*⸣ *am-mu-uk ḫu-u-da-a-ak wa-al-aḫ-m*[*i nu-w*]*a-za* ⸢*QA-TE*⸣$^{ḪI.A}$*-YA am-mu-uk ḫu-u-da-a-ak e-eš-ḫar-nu*[*-mi*]

---

§28'

48. [*nu-za*] *ḫa-an-te-ez-zi* BAL^{LIM} ^{m}*Ma-ad-du*[*-wa*]*-at-ta-aš* [*a*]*-pa-a-ši-la-pát ŠA-PAL NI-IŠ* DINGIR^{LIM} *ki*[*-iš-ša-an da-a-iš* EGIR*-az-ma-aš li-in-ga-uš šar-ra-at-ta-at*]

49. ⸢*a-pa*⸣*-a-ša-aš nam-ma Ú-UL wa-al-aḫ-ta ša-a-ku-wa-pát mu-un-na-a-it* ^{d}UTU^{ŠI}*-ma-aš-ši A-N*[*A* …]

50. ^{m}*Ma-ad-du-wa-at-ta-aš-ma-at* EGIR*-an* [*ku-k*]*u-pa-la-an-ni i-e-et nu ŠA* KUR ^{URU}*Pí-i-ta-aš-ša ku*[- …]

51. *ka-ru-ú li-in-ki-iš-ki-it nu* 10 *ṢÍ*[*-I*]*M-D*[*I* ANŠ]E.KUR.RA.ḪI.A 2 *ME* ÉRIN.MEŠ*-ya A-NA* ^{m}*Zu-wa-a* LÚ ^{GIŠ}GIDRU *tar*[*-na-aḫ-ḫu-un* …]

52. [^{LÚ}]KÚR*-ya ŠA-PAL* ^{URU}*Ma-ra-a-ša a-ar*[*-aš na-aš*]*-ta* ^{m}*Zu-wa-a-an* LÚ ^{GIŠ}GIDRU *ku-en-nir A-NA* […]

53. ⸢*li*⸣*-in-ga-an ḫar-kán-zi nu A-NA* ÉRIN.MEŠ*-ŠU* [ANŠE.KUR.RA.ḪI.A]*-ŠU a-da-a-an-na a-ku-an-na pí-i-e-er* [o o o o o o o o o o o o o o o o] x *pa-ra-a* […]

§27' (rev. 43–47) But [...] he wrote again and again to Kupanta-Kurunta: [" ... "] and led him astray. [...] And he (Madduwatta) himself repeatedly placed it under oath as follows: "I am [now a border guard] and a watchman for these lands. And if a person [speaks] an evil word to me, I [will] not [conceal anything] from Your Majesty, [but] I will disclose [it] fully. If some <land> commences hostilities, while the troops of Your Majesty [make war—because I am nearby], I will attack it immediately, and I will immediately bloody my hands."

§28' (rev. 48–54) [And] initially Madduwatta himself [placed the preceding] under oath, [but later he transgressed the oath]. Subsequently he did not attack them, but rather even hid his eyes. I, My Majesty, [...] to [...] for him. But in response Madduwatta treated it underhandedly. And [concerning(?) the ...] of the land of Pitassa, he had already sworn an oath. I [turned over] ten [teams] of horses and 200 infantrymen to Zuwa, the staff-bearer [...] The enemy drew up below the city of Marasa, [and] they killed Zuwa, the staff-bearer. To [...] they have sworn. And they provided food and drink for his infantry and his [chariotry ...] Then they went away and put [the city of] Marasa to the torch. [They burned] it [down].

54. *na-at-za ar-ḫa pa-a-ir* ^{URU}*Ma-ra-a-*⸢*ša*⸣*-an* [URU-*an*] *kat-ta-an lu-uk-ke-e-er na-an a*[*r-ḫa wa-ar-nu-e*]*-er*

---

§29’

55. ⸢EGIR⸣-*an-ta-ma ú-wa-nu-un* ^{d}UTU$^{\check{S}I}$ *A-NA* ^{m}*Ma*[*-ad-du-wa-a*]*t-ta* ^{m}*Mu-ul-li-ya-ra-an* LÚ ^{GIŠ}GIDRU *ḫa-lu-ki AŠ-PUR na-an A-N*[*A* ^{m}*Ma-ad-du-wa-at-t*]*a ki-iš-ša-an ḫa-a*[*t-ra-a-nu-un*]

56. ⸢KUR ^{URU}⸣*Ḫa-pa-a-al-la-wa ŠA* ^{d}UTU$^{\check{S}I}$ *ku-it* KU[R-*e zi-ig*]-⸢*ga*⸣*-wa-ra-at ku-wa-at da-a-at-ta ki-nu-na-wa-ra-at-mu a-ap-pa* [*pa-a-i nu* ^{m}*Ma-ad-du*]*-wa-at-ta-ša A-NA* ^{m}*Mu-u*[*l-li-ya-ra*]

57. [*ki-i*]*š-ša-an me-ma-i* KUR ^{URU}*Ḫa-pa-al-la-wa* [o o o o] KUR-*e nu-wa-ra-at IŠ-TU ŠA* ^{d}UTU$^{\check{S}I}$ *e-eš-zi* KUR ^{URU}*I-ya-la*[*-an-ti-ma-wa-ra-az* KUR ^{UR}]^{U}*Zu-u-mar-ri* KUR ^{URU}*Wa-al-*⸢*la*⸣[*-ri-im-ma*]

58. [*IŠ-T*]*U* ^{GIŠ}TUKUL *tar-ḫu-un nu-wa-ra-at am-me-el* [*a-ša-an-zi*]

---

§30’

59. ⸢^{m}*Ni*⸣*-wa-al-la-a-aš-ma ŠA* ^{d}UTU$^{\check{S}I}$ ^{LÚ}*ṢA-A-I-*⸢*DU*⸣ [*ḫu-wa-iš*] ⸢*na*⸣*-aš IT-TI* ^{m}*Ma-ad-du-wa-at-ta pa-it* ^{m}*Ma-ad-du-wa*[*-at-ta-ša-an ša-ra-a da-a-aš nu*]*-uš-ši* ^{d}UTU$^{\check{S}I}$ *ḫa-an-te-ez-zi* BA[L^{LIM}]

60. EGIR-*an-ta ḫa-at-re-eš-ki-nu-un* ^{m}*Ni-wa-al-la-a*[*š-wa ŠA* ^{d}UTU]$^{\check{S}I}$ ^{LÚ}*ṢA-A-I-D*[*U*] ⸢*ḫu*⸣*-wa-iš nu-wa-ra-aš kat-ti-ti ú-it n*[*u-wa-ra-an e-ep nu-wa-ra-a*]*n-mu a-ap-pa pa-i*

61. ^{m}*Ma-ad-du-wa-at-ta-*⸢*ša*⸣ *ḫa-an-te-ez-zi* BAL^{L}[^{IM} o o o o] x-*a-an t*[*a*$^{?}$*-ar*$^{?}$]*-aš-ki-it-pát Ú-UL-wa-mu ku-iš-ki* [*ú-it*]

---

§31’

62. [*nu-u*]*š-ši-kán pa-it ki-nu-un* ^{m}*Mu-ul-li-*⸢*ya*⸣[*-ra-aš I-NA* É-*ŠU* ^{LÚ}*pít-te-ya-a*]*n-da-an ú-e-mi-it nu A-NA* [^{m}*Ma-ad-du-wa-at-ta ki-iš-ša-a*]*n me-ma-i*

63. [^{LÚ}*pít*]*-te-ya-an-ta-*⸢*aš-wa*⸣*-at-ta ut-tar ŠA-PAL* [*NI-IŠ* DINGIR^{LIM} *ki-iš-ša-an ki-it-ta-at*] *ku-iš-wa-ták-kán ŠA* KUR ^{URU}[*Ḫa-at-ti* ^{LÚ}*ḫu-ya-an-za ú*]*-i-iš-ki-it-ta-ri*

64. [*zi*]-⸢*ga*⸣*-wa-ra-an* ⸢*a-ap*⸣*-pa A-NA* ^{d}UTU$^{\check{S}I}$ ⸢*up*⸣[*-pé-eš-ki ki-nu-un-wa-at-ta* ^{m}*Ni-wa-al-la-a-aš-m*]*a ŠA* ^{d}UTU$^{\check{S}I}$ ^{LÚ}*ṢA-A-I*[*-DU píd-da-a-iš nu-wa-ra-aš kat-ti-ti ú-it*] ⸢^{d}⸣UTU$^{\check{S}I}$*-ma-wa-at-ta*

65. [*ḫa-a*]*t-re-eš-ki-it zi-ga-wa-ra-an ša-an*[*-na-at-ti nu-wa-ra-an mu-un-na-a-ši nu-wa-ra-a*]*n an-da* [*e-ep*]

---

§32’

66. [*nu* ^{m}*M*]*a-ad-du-wa-at-ta-ša A-NA* ^{m}*Mu-ul-l*[*i-ya-ra ki-iš-ša-an a-ap-pa*

§29' (rev. 55–58) But thereafter I, My Majesty, proceeded to send Mulliyara, the staff-bearer, on a mission to [Madduwatta], and [I gave] him [written instructions(?)] as follows for [Madduwatta]: "Why have you taken the land of Hapalla, which is a land of My Majesty? [Give] it back to me now!" [And Madduwatta] said as follows to [Mulliyara]: "The land of Hapalla is a […] land, and it is on the side of His Majesty, [but] I have conquered the land of Iyalanti, [the land] of Zumarri, and the land of Wallarimma [by] force of arms. They [belong] to me."

§30' (rev. 59–61) Niwalla, the huntsman of My Majesty, [ran off] and went to Madduwatta, and Madduwatta [took him in. Then] at first, I, My Majesty, wrote after him repeatedly: "Niwalla, the huntsman [of My Majesty], ran off and came to you. [Seize him and] give him back to me!" Initially Madduwatta […] kept saying: "No one [came] to me."

§31' (rev. 62–65) Now Mulliyara has gone to him and found [the fugitive in his household]. He said [as follows] to [Madduwatta]: "The matter of a fugitive [stands] under [oath] for you [thus]: 'You [shall always send] back to His Majesty whatever [fugitive] of [Hatti] comes to you.' [But Niwalla], the huntsman of His Majesty, [fled and came to you]. His Majesty has written to you repeatedly, but you conceal him [and hide him. Now seize him]!"

§32' (rev. 66–67) [Then] Madduwatta [replied as follows] to Mulliyara: "The huntsman [… and] he belongs to the household of Piseni. […] the house-

me-mi-iš-ta] *nu-wa* ^{LÚ}*ṢA-A-I*[*-DU* o o o o o o o o o *nu*]*-wa-ra-aš ŠA* É ^{m}*Pí-še-ni*

67. [o o o]*-wa* É ^{m}*Pí-še-ni am-me-el* DUMU-*Y*[*A* …]

68–70. *uninscribed*

---

§33’

71. [*ŠA*] É.ḪI.A ^{URU}*Ma-a-ḫar-ma-ḫa-ya-az da-*⸢*a*⸣[*-aš* o o o o o o o o o o o o o o o o]*-at* x [o o o o o o o o o *ki-iš-ša-an ḫa-at-ra*]*-*⸢*a*⸣*-nu-un*

72. ⸢*a-pu-u*⸣[*-un*]*-*⸢*wa*⸣*-za ku-wa-at da-a-at-ta* ^{m}*Uš-*x[- o o o o o o o o o o o o o o o]*-ru*? [o o o o o o o o o o o o o o o o o o o o]*-*⸢*du*?⸣

73. ⸢*ḫa-at-ra-a-it pa-a*⸣*-it-wa a-pé-e-ez kat-t*[*a* …] x*-tar*

74. [*A-NA*?] ⸢^{d}⸣UTU^{ŠI} ⸢*ú*⸣*-id-du nu-wa* x x […] x *up-pa-aḫ-ḫi*

75. [o o]*-pu*?*-wa* ^{m}*Mu-uk-šu-uš ku-it* […]*-lu*?

76. *erased traces*

---

§34’

77. [o o] x ^{m}*Ma-ad-du-wa-at-ta* […] x-x*-at*

78. [o]*-iš ši-pa-an-ta-an-za* […]

79. […]

---

§35’

80. [o o]*-ru-up-ša-az* x […]

81. [*I-NA*?] KUR ^{URU}*Ka-ra-ki-ša* x […] ⸢*IṢ-BAT*⸣ *ku-u-uš-kán*

82. [*A-NA*?] ^{d}UTU^{ŠI} *ku-wa-at ku-en-t*[*a* …] x*-wa* ^{m}*Ma-ad-du-wa-at-ta-aš*

83. [o o] x 6 É.ḪI.A EGIR*-pa* ⸢*pa*⸣[*-iš* …]

---

§36’

84. [o] x ^{m}*Mu-ul-li-ya-*⸢*ra-ma*?⸣ [*A-NA* ^{m}*Ma-ad-du-wa-at-ta tup-pí*] ⸢*AD*⸣*-DIN* ^{d}UT[U^{ŠI}*-wa* o o o o o o o o o o o o o] ⸢*ki*⸣*-iš-ša-an me-mi*[*-iš-t*]*a*

85. [KUR] ^{URU}*A-*⸢*la*⸣*-ši-ya-wa ŠA* ^{d}UTU^{ŠI} *ku-it* L[Ú?.MEŠ KUR ^{URU}*A-la-ši-ya-ya-wa-mu ar-kam-ma*]*-an píd-*⸢*da-a-an-zi*⸣ [*ku-wa-at-wa-ra-at wa-al-ḫa-an-ni-iš-ki-i*]*t* ^{m}⸢*Ma-ad-du-wa-at-ta*⸣[*-aš*]*-*⸢*wa*⸣

86. [*ki-iš*]*-*⸢*ša*⸣*-an me-mi-iš-ta* KUR ^{URU}*A-la-ši-ya-wa m*[*a-aḫ-ḫa-an* ^{m}*At-tar-aš-ši-y*]*a-aš* LÚ [^{URU}*Pí-ig-ga-ya-ya wa-a*]*l-*⸢*ḫa*⸣*-an-ni-iš-kir* *erasure*

87. *erasure*[97] *A-BI* ^{d}UTU^{ŠI}*-ma-wa-mu Ú*[*-UL ku-wa-pí-ki wa-a-tar-na-aḫ-ta*] ⸢^{d}⸣UTU^{ŠI}*-ma*[*-wa-mu Ú-UL*] *ku-wa-pí-ki wa-a-tar-na-aḫ-ta*

---

97. Text in erasure: *ú-ug-ga-wa-ra-*[*a*]*t* [*wa*]*-al-ḫa-an-ni-iš-ki-nu-un* “I often raided it too.”

hold of Piseni, my son [...]"

§33' (rev. 71–76) And he(?) took [some of] the households of the city of Mararmaha [... I wrote as follows]: "Why did you take that one?" [...] he wrote: "He went down from that (place) [...] He shall [come] to Your Majesty, and [...] I will send ... Because Muksu [...]"

§34' (rev. 77–79) Madduwatta [...] the sacrificed [...]

§35' (rev. 80–83) [... in(?)] the land of Karakisa [...] he seized. Why did you kill these persons [for(?)] My Majesty? [...] "Madduwatta [gave] back the six [...] households [...]"

§36' (rev. 84–90) [The report(?)] of Mulliyara: "I gave [the tablet to Madduwatta (saying)]: 'His Majesty said thus [...]: "Because [the land] of Alasiya belongs to My Majesty, [and the people of Alasiya] pay [me tribute—why have you continually raided it?"' But] Madduwatta said thus: '[When Attarissiya and] the ruler [of Piggaya] were raiding the land of Alasiya, *I often raided it too*.[97] But the father of His Majesty [had never informed] me, [nor] had His Majesty ever informed [me] (thus): "The land of Alasiya is mine—recognize it as such!" If His Majesty is indeed now demanding back the civilian captives of Alasiya, I will give them back to him.'" And given that Attarissiya and the ruler of Piggaya are rulers independent of My Majesty, while (you), Madduwatta, are a servant of My Majesty—why have you joined up with [them]?

88. KUR URU*A-la-ši-ya-wa am-*⌈*me-el*⌉ *nu-wa-ra-at* ⌈*QA-TAM*⌉*-MA* ⌈*ša-a-ak*⌉ *ki-*⌈*nu-na-wa ma*⌉*-a-an* ⌈dUTU*ŠI*⌉ NAM.RA.ḪI.A URU*A-la-ši-ya im-ma a-ap-pa ú-e-wa-ak-*⌈*ki*⌉[*-zi*]

89. *nu-wa-ra-an-ši* ⌈*a-ap-pa*⌉ *pí*[*-iḫ-ḫ*]*i nu* m*At-tar-ši-ya-aš* LÚ URU*Pí-ig-ga-ya-ya A-NA* dUTU*ŠI* LÚ.MEŠ*ku-re-e-wa-ni-eš ku-it* m*Ma-ad-du-wa-at-ta-aš-ma* ARAD dUTU*ŠI*

90. *a-*⌈*pé*⌉[*-e-d*]*a-aš-za an-da ku-wa-at ḫa-an-da-a-it-ta-at*

---

§37'

91. *nam-ma* ⌈URU*A*?⌉[- o o] x [o o]*-aš* [o o] x [o o]-⌈*ḫa-ri*⌉ [o o o] ⌈*ki*⌉[*-iš*]*-*⌈*ša*⌉*-an ú-da-aš a-li-ya-aš-wa Ú-UL wa-a-i Ú-UL-ma-wa wa-ak-ki Ú-UL-ma-wa iš-pár-ri-iz-zi*

92. x [o o o o o o o o o o o o o o o o o o o o o] ⌈*a*⌉*-li-ya-an pár-ḫa-at-ta-ri* ⌈ŠAḪ⌉*-ma-wa ú-i-wa-i ku-it nu-wa ku-iš A-NA* ŠAḪ!

93. *še*?[- o o o] x x x x x [o o o o o o o o o o o o]-⌈*ya*?⌉ *ku-en-zi nu-wa ú*[*-ug*]-⌈*ga* ŠAḪ⌉*-aš i-*⌈*wa-ar*⌉ *ú-i-ya-mi*

94. [*nam-ma-w*]*a ak-kal-lu* x [o o o o]

---

left edge, colophon

DUB.1.KAM *MA-AḪ-*⌈*RU-Ú ŠA*⌉ m[*Ma-ad-du*]*-wa-at-ta wa-aš-*⌈*du-la*⌉[*-aš*]

§37' (rev. 91–94) Furthermore, [...] brought [a message] as follows: "The stag does not cry out. He does not bite. He does not escape. [...] pursues the stag. But because the pig does cry out, the one who [...] to the pig [...] he kills. I will cry out like the pig, [and then] I shall die [...]"

Colophon: First tablet of the offense of [Madduwatta]

(the text must have continued on a further tablet, now lost)

Commentary

The so-called Indictment of Madduwatta, composed during the reign of Arnuwanda I, provides our earliest attestation in Hittite records of the name Ahhiyawa, in its reference to Attarissiya, a ruler of Ahhiya. "Ahhiya" is the older, shorter form of "Ahhiyawa," and is found only here and in the oracle text KBo 16.97 (AhT 22). Attarissiya, whom Forrer sought to identify with the legendary Mycenaean king Atreus, is one of only two (or possibly three) Ahhiyawan persons whose names are actually specified in the extant Hittite texts (Tawagalawa, AhT 3, and possibly Kagamuna, AhT 6, are the others). We cannot be sure what his status was, but his designation as a 'ruler' (LÚ) of Ahhiya(wa) suggests that he might not have been viewed as a king, for which the term LUGAL was customarily used. However, he was very likely a Mycenaean of high status, who had installed himself on the Anatolian mainland with a significant fighting force at his command. Niemeier (1999: 149) believes he may have been an aristocrat displaced by the emergence of a centralized palace system in mainland Greece, or the agent of one of the new expanding Mycenaean palace centers. In any case, it is clear that Mycenaeans had involved themselves in military operations in western Anatolia already by the late-fifteenth or early-fourteenth century B.C.E., during or before the reign of Tudhaliya I/II. Very likely Attarissiya's forces were largely of Anatolian origin. We do not know what provoked the conflict between him and Madduwatta (perhaps it arose from a dispute over territorial boundaries), which resulted in the latter being forced to flee the region with his family and a retinue of troops and chariots. He too was clearly a man of importance in his own land, which is not named in the text but must have lain somewhere in western Anatolia.

Madduwatta sought and was granted protection by Tudhaliya I/II, Arnuwanda's predecessor, who set him up as one of his vassal rulers in the mountain land Zippasla, after the refugee had declined the offer of an appointment to another region, and subsequently handed over to him an additional territory called the Siyanta River Land. Neither Zippasla nor the Siyanta River Land can be located with any degree of certainty, though very likely they lay on the western periphery of Hittite subject territory close to the Arzawa lands. The contingent of infantry and chariotry which Madduwatta brought with him was no doubt reinforced by Tudhaliya, to ensure adequate defense of the region over which his new vassal had been assigned control. Many of the treaty obligations imposed by Hittite kings upon their vassals were stipulated for Madduwatta, particularly military obligations (§6). He was also forbidden to invade or occupy any other land, at least without his overlord's approval, or to have diplomatic dealings with any other lands or their rulers, notably Attarissiya of Ahhiya. But in the reigns of both Tudhaliya and his successor Arnuwanda I, Madduwatta regularly violated his oath of allegiance, according to the "Indictment," as illustrated by his abortive invasion of the Arzawan kingdom of Kupanta-Kurunta (§§8-9), his failure to resist a second attack launched against him by Attarissiya, from whose consequences he was saved by timely Hittite military intervention (§12), and his treachery against Hittite forces in the region, particularly on the occasion when he ambushed a Hittite expeditionary force and killed its commander (§14).

Amazingly, it seems, he managed to avoid a military showdown with either Tudhaliya or Arnuwanda, maintaining that a number of his initiatives in apparent breach of his oath were undertaken in his overlords' interests; his alleged plot to assassinate the Arzawan king Kupanta-Kurunta while supposedly arranging a marriage alliance with him (§§16–17) was a case in point. He was nonetheless clearly intent on carving out a small empire of his own in southwestern Anatolia, and in the process continued to make inroads into Hittite subject territory. Sometimes he handed back lands he had occupied in response to a direct demand from Hattusa, as in the case of Hapalla (§29'); sometimes he refused to cede territories he had won by force of arms, including the lands Iyalanti, Zumarri, and Wallarimma, which lay in or near the region of Lukka.

When he had gained control over a large part of southwestern Anatolia, Madduwatta turned his attention to the land called Alasiya. Almost all scholars agree that this land is to be identified with Cyprus (or a part of it). If so, then to carry out the repeated raids on Alasiyan territory of which he was accused by Arnuwanda (§36'), Madduwatta must have had a fleet of ships at his disposal. Most likely these ships were of Lukka origin. Lukka-men were notorious for their piratical activities—their raids on Alasiyan coastal cities are attested several decades later in the reign of the pharaoh Akhenaten—and Madduwatta may well have won some form of control over the region from which they came, or entered into some form of mutually beneficial arrangement with its inhabitants. Arnuwanda claimed sovereignty over Alasiya; hence his complaint of Madduwatta's raids upon it. His claim is a surprising one. The landlocked kingdom of Hatti had no fleet of its own, and could not in fact have exercised any form of practical control over any lands separated from it by sea, unless it had at its disposal a navy supplied by one or more of its coastal vassal states. But apart from this single reference in the "Indictment," we know of no instance of Hittite political or military involvement with Alasiya before the reigns of Tudhaliya IV and Suppiluliuma II, in the last decades of the Hittite empire, when these kings conducted military operations upon and around the island. Madduwatta's statement that he did not know Alasiya was claimed by the Hittites may well have been a disingenuous one. But if Arnuwanda did in fact exercise some form of sovereignty over the island, it must have been nominal in the extreme.

Of particular significance for the study of Ahhiyawa is Attarissiya's reported involvement in the raids on Alasiya (§36'). Such raids would be entirely consistent with the image presented in the Homeric epics of Mycenaean plundering enterprises conducted through the Aegean and eastern Mediterranean regions, and may well account for much of the wealth that was accumulated in the Mycenaean palace centers. On this occasion, a Mycenaean warlord called Attarissiya, a ruler of Ahhiya, extended his military operations in western Anatolia to piratical raids off the southern Anatolian coast. Opportunistically, he appears to have coordinated his operations against the cities of Alasiya with his former enemy Madduwatta. Both benefited from the partnership.

To conclude, it is clear that during at least the early decades of the fourteenth century, the authority exercised by the Hittites in western Anatolia remained tenuous, little more than token in some of the territories to which they laid claim. This provided the opportunity for the expansion of Ahhiyawan/Mycenaean activity in the region, perhaps initially by freebooting military leaders like Attarissiya, who paved the way for a more substantial and more formal Ahhiyawan presence in the region by the end of the century. What authority the Hittites did possess in the region, they sought to maintain through local vassals who were pledged to allegiance to the Hittite crown and were obliged by the terms of this allegiance to defend the Great King's territories in the lands where they were installed. Madduwatta very effectively turned to his own advantage the forbearance which his successive overlords Tudhaliya and Arnuwanda displayed towards his continual violation of his obligations and his acts of outright treachery. Ultimately, they may have felt that their hold over the west was too insecure for them to do anything other than keep open the diplomatic channels with him, and while protesting about his flagrant misconduct, continue to allow him considerable latitude in the fulfilment of his own ambitions in the west.

AhT 4

Letter from a King of Hatti (Probably Hattusili III) to a King of Ahhiyawa—The "Tawagalawa Letter" (CTH 181)

Traditionally called the "Tawagalawa Letter," this third and probably final tablet of a long diplomatic dispatch from a Hittite Great King—probably Hattusili III—to his unnamed counterpart in Ahhiyawa is actually very little concerned with this eponymous individual. A far more important role in the relations between the two countries is played by Piyamaradu, a freebooter who enters greater Hatti to cause trouble, rebuffs the friendly overtures of the Hittite monarch, and then withdraws to land controlled by Ahhiyawa. Here the Hittite king asks that his correspondent use his influence either to assure Piyamaradu of his own good intentions or to deny the latter the use of Ahhiyawan territory as a base of operations. Incidentally, we learn that an earlier dispute between Hatti and Ahhiyawa over the land of Wilusa has now been settled amicably.

KUB 14.3

obv. i

§1

1. [o ^{m} o *-l*]*a-aš pa-it nu* ^{URU}*At-t*[*a*]*-⸢ri-im⸣-ma-a*[*n*] ⸢*ar-ḫa*⸣
2. [*ḫar-g*]*a-nu-ut na-an ar-ḫa wa-ar-nu-ut IŠ-TU* ⸢BÀD⸣ É.MEŠ LUGAL
3. [*nu*] *A-NA* ^{m}*Ta-wa-ga-la-wa* LÚ.MEŠ ^{URU}⸢*Lu*⸣*-uq-qa-a* G[IM]*-an* ZI*-ni*
4. [*a*]*r-nu-e-er na-aš* ⸢*ke*⸣*-e-da-aš* KUR*-e-aš ú-it ú-uq-qa QA-TAM-MA*
5. ZI*-ni ar-nu-e-er nu*^{er} *ke-e-da-aš* KUR*-e-aš* GAM *ú-wa-nu-un*
6. *nu* GIM*-an I-NA* ^{URU}*Šal-la-pa ar-ḫu-un nu-m*[*u* U]N*-an* IGI*-an-da*
7. *u-i-ya-at* ARAD*-an-ni-wa-mu da-a nu-wa-mu* ⸢^{LÚ}*tu*⸣*-uḫ-kán-ti-in*
8. *u-i-ya nu-wa-mu IT-TI* ^{d}UTU^{ŠI} *ú-wa-te-ez-*⸢*zi*⸣ *nu-uš-ši*
9. ^{LÚ}*TAR-TE-NU u-i-ya-nu-un i-it-wa-ra-an-za-an-*⸢*kán*⸣ *A-*⸢*NA*⸣ ^{GIŠ}GIGIR
10. GAM*-an ti-it-ta-nu-*[*u*]*t nu-wa-ra-an ú-wa-ti a*[*-pa-a-aš-š*]*a-kán*
11. ^{LÚ}*TAR-TE-NU* ⸢*ka*⸣*-ri-ya-nu-ut nu-za Ú-UL me-m*[*a-aš*] ^{LÚ}⸢*TAR*⸣*-TE-NU-ma*
12. *Ú-UL A-NA* ⸢LUGAL⸣ *a-ya-wa-la-aš* ⸢ŠU⸣*-an-ma-an ḫa*[*r-ta*] *nu-uš-ši-za* EGIR*-an*
13. *Ú-UL me-ma-aš na-an A-NA PA-NI* KUR.KUR.MEŠ *te-pa-wa*[*-a*]*ḫ-ta*$^{!}$
14. *nu a-pa-a-at nam-ma-pát IQ-BI* LUGAL^{UT-TA}*-wa-mu* ⸢*ka*⸣*-a pí-di-ši*
15. *pa-a-i ma-a-an-wa Ú-UL-ma nu-wa Ú-UL ú-wa-m*[*i*]

§2

16. GIM*-an-ma* AŠ ^{URU}*Wa-li-wa-an-da ar-ḫu-un nu-uš-ši AŠ-PUR*
17. *ma-a-an-wa am-me-el* EN^{UT-TA} *ša-an-ḫe-eš-ki-ši nu-wa* ⸢*ka*⸣*-a-ša*
18. *I-NA* ^{URU}*I-ya-la-an-da ku-it ú-wa-mi nu-wa-kán* ŠÀ $^{U[RU}$*I-y*]*a-la-an-da*
19. [*t*]*u-el* UN*-an le-e ku-in-ki ú-e-mi-ya-mi* [*zi-i*]*q-qa-wa-za-kán*
20. EGIR*-pa an-da le-e ku-in-ki tar-na-at-ti ta-pa-r*[*i-ya-wa*]*-*⸢*mu*⸣*-za-kán*
21. *le-e an-da ki-iš-ta-ti am-me-el-wa* ARAD.MEŠ [*ú-ki-la* EGIR*-a*]*n*$^{?}$
22. *ša-an-aḫ-mi* GIM*-an-ma I-NA* ^{URU}*I-ya-la-an-d*[*a ar-ḫu-un*]
23. *nu-mu* ^{LÚ}KÚR 3 *AŠ-RA za-aḫ-ḫi-ya ti-ya-at nu* [*a-pé-e*$^{?}$ *AŠ-RA*$^{?}$]
24. *ar-pu-u-wa-an nu-kán* GÌR*-it ša-ra-a pa-a-u-u*[*n nu a-pí-ya*]
25. ^{LÚ}KÚR *ḫu-ul-li-ya-nu-un nu-kán* UN.MEŠ*-tar a-pí-y*[*a*$^{?}$ …]
26. ^{m}*La-ḫur-zi-<iš>-ma-mu a-pé-el* ŠEŠ*-ŠU še-na-aḫ-*⸢*ḫa*⸣ [*pí-ra-an da-iš*]
27. *nu* ŠEŠ*-YA pu-nu-uš-pát ma-a-an Ú-UL kiš-an* ⸢^{m}⸣*L*[*a-ḫur-zi-iš-ša*]
28. *za-aḫ-ḫi-ya an-da Ú-UL e-eš-ta am-mu-uq-qa-an* [*I-NA* ŠÀ^{BI}]
29. KUR ^{URU}*I-ya-la-an-da Ú-UL AK-ŠU-UD a-pé-e*[*z-ma-za-aš pa-it*]
30. ⸢*ša*⸣*-ku-wa-aš-ša-ri* INIM ^{URU}*I-ya-la-an-da Ú-U*[*L-wa nam-ma*]
31. *I-NA* ^{URU}*I-ya-la-an-da pa-a-i-mi*

§1 (i 1–15) [...] went and destroyed the town of Attarimma. He burned it down together with the fortified royal compound. [Then] when the people of Lukka appealed to Tawagalawa, he went to those lands. They likewise appealed to me, so that I came down to those lands. When I arrived in the town of Sallapa, he (Piyamaradu) sent a man to meet me, (with the message): "Take me into (your) service! Send the Crown Prince to bring me to Your Majesty!" I sent the Crown Prince to him: "Go set him on the chariot with you in order to bring him here." But [that one] squelched the Crown Prince and refused. But isn't the Crown Prince the social equal of the King? He held his hand, but in response he refused. He belittled him before the lands. And on top of this he said: "Bestow kingship on me here on the spot! If not, I will not come."

§2 (i 16–31) But when I arrived in the town of Waliwanda, I sent to him: "If you desire my dominion—because I am now coming to the town of Iyalanda, let me not find any of your men in Iyalanda. You shall not allow anyone back in, nor become involved in my domain. I will look after my subjects [myself]!" But when [I arrived] in Iyalanda, the enemy engaged me in battle in three places. [These places] were rough terrain. I ascended on foot [and] fought the enemy [there]. The population there [...] But his brother Lahurzi [set] an ambush for me. Just inquire, my brother, if this isn't so. Wasn't [Lahurzi] in the battle? Didn't I encounter him [in] the territory of Iyalanda? [But he left there] in accordance with his candid statement about Iyalanda: "I will not go to Iyalanda [again]."

---

§3

32. *nu-ut-ta ke-e ku-e* INIM.MEŠ *AŠ-PUR nu* GIM-*an* [*ki-ša-at*]
33. *nu* LUGAL.GAL *li-in-ku-un* ^{d}U *iš-ta-ma-a*[*š-ki-id-du* DINGIR.MEŠ-*ya*]
34. *iš-ta-ma-aš-kán-du* GIM-*an ke-e A-WA-TE*^{ME}[^{Š} *ki-ša-at*]

---

§4

35. ⸢GIM⸣-*an* KUR ^{URU}*I-ya-la-an-da ar-ḫa* [*ḫar-ga-nu-un*]
36. *nu* KUR^{TUM} *ku-it ḫu-u-ma-*[*a*]*n ar-ḫa ḫar-g*[*a-nu-un a-pí-ya-ma*]
37. ^{URU}*At-ri-ya-an* 1^{EN} *ḪAL-ṢU A-NA* ^{URU}[…]
38. *ḫa-an-da-aš da-li-ya-nu-un nu-kán* EG[IR-*pa I-NA* ^{URU}*I-ya-la-an-da*]
39. ⸢*ša*⸣-*ra-a ú-wa-nu-un* KUR^{er} ^{URU}*I-ya*[*-la-an-da an-da ku-it-ma-an*]
40. *e-šu-un nu-kán* KUR^{TUM} *ḫu-u-ma-a*[*n* … *-za-kán*]
41. ⸓*ḫa-aš-pa-ḫa A-NA* NAM.RA[.MEŠ-*ma* …]
42. GIM-*an wa-a-tar* NU.GÁL ⸢*e*?⸣-[*eš-ta*? …]
43. *nu-mu-kán* KARAŠ.ḪI.A *t*[*e*?*-pa-u-wa-za e-eš-ta*? …]
44. EGIR-*an-da Ú-UL pa-a-u-u*[*n* …]
45. *ša-ra-a ú-wa-nu-un ma-a-n*[*a-* …]
46. EGIR-*pa-ma-a-na-an Ú-UL* […]
47. *nu-za-kán I-NA* ^{URU}*A-ba*-x[- …]
48. *nu I-NA* ^{URU}*Mé-el-la-wa-a*[*n-da A-NA* ^{m}*Pí-ya-ma-ra-du AŠ-PUR*]
49. *an-da-wa-mu-kán e-ḫ*[*u* o] x x [… *MA-Ḫ*]*AR* ZAG
50. *AŠ-PUR ke-e-da-ni-y*[*a-wa-ra-a*]*n me-mi-*⸢*ni*⸣ *AṢ-BAT ki-i-wa-mu*
51. ^{m}*Pí-ya-ma-ra-d*[*u-uš* KUR^{TUM} *k*]*u-it wa-al-aḫ-ḫe-eš-ki-iz-zi*
52. *nu-wa-ra-at* ŠE[Š-*YA I-DI nu-w*]*a-ra-at Ú-UL-ma I-DI*

---

§5

53. GIM-*an-ma-mu* [^{LÚ}*ṬE*$_{4}$*-MU ŠA* ŠEŠ-*Y*]*A an-da ú-e-mi-ya-at*
54. *nu-mu Ú-U*[*L aš-šu-la-an ku-in-ki*] *ú-da-aš Ú-UL-*⸢*ya-mu*⸣ *up-pé-eš-šar*
55. *ku-it-ki* [*ú-da-aš ki-iš-ša-an-m*]*a IQ-BI A-NA* ^{m}*At-pa-wa IŠ-PUR*
56. ^{m}*Pí-y*[*a-ma-ra-du-un-wa-ká*]*n A-NA* LUGAL ^{URU}*Ḫa-at-ti* ŠU-*i da-a-i*
57. x [o o o o o o *erasure*]-*un*
58. *n*[*u I-NA* ^{URU}*Mé-el-l*]*a-wa-an-da pa-a-u-un pa-a-u-un-ma*
59. [*ke*]-⸢*e-da*⸣-*n*[*i-y*]*a me-mi-ni ḫa-an-da-aš A-NA* ^{m}*Pí-ya-ma-ra-du-wa*
60. [*ku-e*] *A-WA-TE*^{MEŠ} *me-ma-aḫ-ḫi nu-wa-ra-at* ARAD.MEŠ ŠEŠ-*YA-ya*
61. [*iš-t*]*a-ma-aš-ša-an-du nu-kán* ^{m}*Pí-ya-ma-ra-du-uš* ^{GIŠ}MÁ-*za*
62. [*ar-ḫ*]*a ú-it na-an A-NA A-WA-TE*^{MEŠ} *ku-e-da-aš ḫar-ku-un*
63. [*na-a*]*t* ^{m}*At-pa-aš-š*[*a*] <<*iš-ta-ma-aš-ki-it*>> ^{m}*A-wa-ya-na-aš-ša*
64. [*iš*]*-ta-ma-aš-kir nu-uš-ma-ša-aš* ^{LÚ}*E-MI-ŠU-NU ku-it*

§3 (i 32–34) I, Great King, have sworn that these things about which I have written to you (indeed) took place. May the Storm-God listen, [and] may [the (other) gods] listen to how these things [happened].

§4 (i 35–52) When [I had destroyed] the land of Iyalanda, seeing as I had destroyed the entire land, I left [there] the single fortress of Atriya out of concern for the town of […] Then I came [back] up [to Iyalanda. While] I was [in] the land of Iyalanda, I destroyed […] the entire land. [But] to the civilian captives […] When there was no more water […] My forces [were small …] I did not pursue […] I came up […] If […] not back […] In the town of Aba[…] And [I wrote to Piyamaradu] in Millawanda: "Come here to me!" [And to …] on(?) the border I wrote: "I have lodged a complaint against him in this matter, that Piyamaradu keeps attacking this [territory] of mine." Does [my] brother [know] it or not?

§5 (i 53–ii 8) But when [the messenger of] my brother met me, he did not bring me [any greetings] or any gift. He just spoke [as follows]: "He has written to Atpa: 'Turn [Piyamaradu] over to the King of Hatti!'" […] Then I went to Millawanda; I went because of this matter: "May the subjects of my brother hear the words [that] I will speak to Piyamaradu." Then Piyamaradu departed by ship, while Atpa and Awayana listened to the charges that I made against him. Why are they covering up the matter—because he is their father-in-law? I made them take an oath that they would report the whole business to you. Didn't I send over the Crown Prince (saying): "Go drive over there, take him by the hand, set him on the chariot [with] you in order to bring him here before me"? He refused. When Tawagalawa himself, (as the representative of?) the Great King, crossed over to Millawanda, Kurunta was [already(?)] here. The Great King drove to meet you—wasn't he a mighty king? Didn't he [travel(?) …] under a pledge of

65. [*n*]*u-wa me-mi-an ku-wa-at ša-an-na-an-zi*
66. *na-aš li-in-ga-nu-nu-un nu-ut-ta me-mi-an ša-ku-wa-šar*
67. *me-ma-an-du Ú-UL-kán* ^{LÚ}*TAR-TE-E-NU pa-ri-ya-an*
68. *u-i-ya-nu-un i-it-wa-kán pa-ri-ya-an pé-en-ni*
69. ⸢*nu*⸣*-wa-ra-an* ŠU*-an e-ep nu-wa-ra-an-za-an-kán A-NA* ^{GIŠ}GIGIR
70. [GAM-*a*]*n ti-it-ta-nu-ut nu-wa-ra-an-mu* IGI*-an-da ú-wa-ti*
71. [*Ú-U*]*L me-ma*^{er}*-aš* ^{m}⸢*Ta*⸣*-wa-ga-la-wa-aš-pát-kán*^{er} *ku-wa-pí* LUGAL.GAL
72. [*A-N*]*A* ^{URU}*Mé-el-la-wa-an-da ta-pu-ša ú-it*
73. [*ka-ru*]-⸢*ú*⸣*-ma* ^{md}LAMMA*-aš ka-a e-eš-ta nu-ut-ta* LUGAL.GAL
74. [IGI*-an-d*]*a u-un-né-eš-*⸢*ta*⸣ *Ú-UL-aš šar-ku-uš* LUGAL*-uš e-eš-ta*

ii

1. *na-aš Ú-*⸢*UL*⸣*-ma* ⸗⸢*za-ar-ši-ya*⸣ […]
2. *a-pa-a-aš-mu ku-wa-at Ú-UL* [o o] x […]
3. *ma-a-an-ma ki-i me-ma-i* [INI]M [*ku-na-an-na-aš-wa*] ⸢*na-aḫ*⸣-[*ḫu*]*-un*
4. *nu-uš-ši Ú-UL* DUMU*-YA* $^{\text{LÚ}\,er}$*TAR-TE-*⸢*NU*⸣ IGI*-an*⸣*-da* ⸢*u-i*⸣*-ya-nu-un*
5. *na-an ki-i wa-tar-na-aḫ-ḫu-un* ⸢*i-it-wa-aš-ši*⸣
6. *li-in-ki nu-wa-ra-an* ŠU*-an* ⸢*e-ep*⸣ *nu-wa-*⸢*ra*⸣*-an-mu*
7. IGI*-an-da ú-wa-ti ku-na-an-na-aš-*⸢*ma*⸣*-aš me-mi-ni* [*k*]*u-e-*[*d*]*a-ni*
8. *na-aḫ-ta* ^{erasure} *e-*⸢*eš*⸣*-ḫar A-NA* KUR ^{URU}⸢KÙ.BABBAR*-ti*⸣ *a-a-ra* ⸢*na-at Ú*⸣*-UL*

---

§6

9. GIM*-an-ma-mu* ^{LÚ}*ṬE*$_4$*-MU ŠA* ŠEŠ*-*⸢*YA me-mi-an IQ-BI*⸣
10. *a-pu-u-un-wa* UN*-an da-a le-e-wa-*⸢*ra-an*⸣ […]
11. *nu ki-i AQ-BI ma-a-an-wa-mu*^{er} *am-me-el* x x x ⸢*ku-iš-ki*⸣
12. *IQ-BI na-aš-šu* ŠEŠ*-YA ma-a-an-wa a-*⸢*pé-el-la*⸣ x x
13. *me-mi-an AŠ-MI ki*$^{!}$*-nu-na-wa-mu* ŠEŠ*-YA* ⸢LUGAL.GAL *am-me-el*⸣
14. *an-na-*⸢*ú*⸣*-li-iš IŠ-PUR nu-wa am-me-e*[*l an-na-ú-li-ya-aš*]
15. *me-mi-an Ú-UL iš-ta-ma-aš-mi nu* ⸢*ú*⸣[*-ki*]*-la* […]
16. *pé-en-na-aḫ-ḫu-un ma-a-an ma-a-an* x […] x
17. *ma-an* ŠEŠ*-YA nam-ma IQ-BI* ⸢*am*⸣*-m*[*e-el-wa me-mi-a*]*n Ú-*⸢*UL*⸣ *IŠ-MÉ*
18. *Ú-UL-wa-ra-aš-mu ka-a-ri t*[*i*]*-*⸢*ya-at*⸣ x x x ⸢EGIR⸣*-an UL*
19. *pu-nu-šú-un-ma-an UL* ŠEŠ*-YA ki*$^{!}$*-i* […] *ka-a-ri* ^{erasure}
20. *ti-ya-at ú-ug-ma pa-a-u-un-pát nu-kán* ⸢*a-pí-ya ku-wa-pí pa*⸣*-ra-a*
21. *ti-ya-nu-un nu A-NA* ^{m}*At-pa-a A*[*Q*]*-B*[*I* … *-y*]*a-wa-*⸢*at-ta*⸣ *ku-it*
22. *IŠ-PUR i-it-wa-ra-an A-NA* LUGAL KUR^{er} [^{URU}KÙ.BABBAR*-ti pé*]*-e-ḫu-te*
23. *nu-wa-ra-an ú-wa-ti nu-wa-za-kán* x x [o o o o] x x

safe-conduct? Why did he not [meet(?)] me? If he says this: "I feared an assassination plot"—didn't I send my son, the Crown Prince, to meet him? I instructed him: "Go swear an oath for him, take him by the hand, and bring him before me." As for the assassination plot about which he was afraid—is bloodshed permissible in Hatti? It is not!

§6 (ii 9–50) But when the messenger of my brother said to me: "Take that person; don't [...] him," I said this: "If some [...] or my brother had spoken to me, I would have heard his [...] word. But now my brother, a Great King, my peer, has written to me—should I not listen to the word of my [peer]?" And I myself drove out [to ...] If [...], my brother would once more have said: "He hasn't listened to my [message]; he hasn't accommodated me." Would I have not in reply asked my brother this: "Did [...] comply?" I actually went, and when I set foot there, I said to Atpa: "Because [...] sent to you: 'Go take him to the King [of Hatti],' bring him here. Then without hesitation he wiped out the [...] command. He will without hesitation [again(?)] wipe out the command. [And if he says]: 'I am afraid,' I am ready to send a nobleman, or I'll send a brother. Let [this person] remain in his place (as a hostage). But he still kept saying: 'I continue to be afraid.'" Then Atpa said to me: "O, Your Majesty, give a hand to the heir!" [...] gave to that one. Then with that [...] If [...] had done much [...], I would have left [him] alone under a guarantee. Then I made [Atpa] swear an oath [to me] and gave him a hand, [saying to him]: "I will place you [...] I will [...] the matter to you. [...] I will place. [I will write(?)] about it to [my]

24. *me*^{er}*-mi-an* DUḪ-*ši* ⸗*pa-ši-ḫa-*⌈*a*⌉*-it* x [o o o o]-x[-*wa*]-*za-kán*
25. *me-mi-an* DUḪ-*ši* ⸗*pa-ši-*⌈*ḫa*⌉*-a-*⌈*ti*⌉ x […]
26. *na-aḫ-mi-wa nu-wa ka-a-ša* 1^{EN} *BE-L*[*U ú-i-ya-mi*]
27. *na-aš-ma-wa* ŠEŠ *u-i-ya-mi nu-wa*[*-ra-aš-ši a-pa-a-aš*] ⌈*pé-di-eš-ši*⌉
28. ⌈*e*⌉*-ša-ru a-*⌈*pa*⌉*-a-aš-ma nu-u-wa-pát me-m*[*i-iš-ki-it*]
29. [*w*]*a-aḫ-ḫe-eš-ki-mi-wa nu-mu* ^{m}*At-pa-a*[*-aš ki-iš-ša-a*]*n I*[*Q-BI*]
30. [^{d}]UTU^{ŠI}*-wa* ŠU*-an A-NA* IBILA *pa-a-i* […]
31. [*a-p*]*é-e-da-ni pé-eš-*⌈*ta*⌉ *nu a-pád-da* x […]
32. [o] x *ma-a-an me-ek-ki-pát i-ya-at* […]
33. [⸗*za-a*]*r-ši-ya* GAM$^{!}$*-an da-li-ya-nu-un* [*nu-za* ^{m}*At-pa-a-a*]*n*
34. [*li-in-g*]*a-nu-nu-un nu-uš-ši* ŠU*-an AD-*⌈*DIN*⌉ x […]
35. [o o o *-wa-ra-at-t*]*a* ⌈*te*⌉*-ḫi nu-wa-ra-at-ta* INIM [o o o*-m*]*a-wa*<*-ra*>*-at-* *-ta* x x
36. [o o o o o o o] *te-eḫ-ḫi nu-wa-ra-at A-NA* ŠE[Š*-Y*]*A* ⌈LUGAL⌉ [^{KUR}***Aḫ-ḫ*]*i-ya-wa-a***
37. [*ḫa-at-ra-a-mi na-a*]*t-za UL me-em-ma-aš* x [o] x x x
38. [o o o o o o o] x x ⌈*am-me*⌉*-el ak-kán-*⌈*ta-an kat*?⌉*-ta*
39. [o o o o KUR ^{URU}]⌈*Ḫi-mu*⌉*-uš-ša* KUR ^{URU}*Da-aḫ*[*-d*]*a-aḫ-ḫu*
40. [o o o o o o o] ⌈(-)*tu-wa*?⌉*-li* LUGAL^{UT-TA} *am-mu-uk*
41. […] x-⌈*du*⌉-x[-o]-*ki-ya-nu-un*
42. [… *a*]*r-ḫa ti-ya-zi*
43. [… *-a*]*z* LUGAL^{UT-TA}
44. [… LUGAL^{U}]$^{T-TA}$ *p*[*a*]⌈*-i*⌉
45. […] *me-mi*
46. [… *k*]*u-it* ⌈*Ú*⌉*-UL ú-*⌈*it*⌉
47. […] x x
48. […] x […]
49. x […]
50. x x […]

---

§7

51. *a-pé-e-el-*⌈*ma*⌉ UN*-aš* INIM […]
52. É*-ir-ši-kán ku-it ti-*[…]
53. *am-me-el le-en-ga-uš* x […]
54. *ku-iš-ki* ⌈INIM*-az*⌉ *pé-ra-an* x […]
55. DINGIR^{LUM}*-an ku-iš-ki* SIG$_5$*-u-i pa-ra-*[*-a* …]

---

brother, the King of **Ahhiyawa**." [But] he refused […] my dead, down […] the towns of Himusa and Dahdahhu […] Kingship to me […]

(lines ii 41–50 too fragmentary for translation)

§7 (ii 51–54) But that person's man […] the matter […] Because his household […] and my oaths […] someone because of the matter, before […] some deity will […] him in favor.

§8

56. *nu nam-ma-pát A-NA* ŠEŠ[-*Y*]*A ḫa-an-da-aš Ú-UL ma-a*[*n-qa i-ya-nu-un nu ma-a-an*]

57. ŠEŠ-*YA ku-wa-at-qa da-ri-*[*y*]*a-nu-zi A-NA* LUGAL ^{KUR}*Ḫa*[*t-ti-wa pa-a-i-mi*]

58. *nu-wa-mu-kán* KASKAL-*ši da-a-ú nu ka-a-aš-ma* ^{m}*Da-ba-l*[*a*-^{d}U-*an*]

59. ^{LÚ}*KAR-TAP-PU u*<*-i*>*-ya-nu-un* ^{m}*Ta-ba-la*-^{d}U-*aš-ma Ú-UL k*[*u-iš-ki*]

60. ⸢EGIR⸣-*iz-zi-iš* UN-*aš* TUR-*an-na-aš-ma* ^{LÚ}*KAR-TAP-PU A-NA* ^{GIŠ}GIGIR

61. GAM-*an ti-iš-ki-iz-zi A-NA* ŠEŠ-*KA-ya-aš-kán A-NA* ^{m}*Ta-wa-ka-la-*⸢*wa*⸣ [*A-NA* ^{GIŠ}GIGIR]

62. GAM-*an ti-iš-ki-it nu A-NA* ^{m}*Pí-ya-ma-ra-du* *za-ar-ši-ya-an* x [… *AD-DIN*]

63. *za-ar-ši-ya-aš-ma I-NA* ^{KUR}*Ḫat-ti kiš-an ma-a-an* NINDA *ši-ya-an-ta-y*[*a*?]

64. ⸢*ku*⸣*-e-da-ni up-pa-an-zi nu-*⸢*uš*⸣*-ši-kán* ḪUL *UL ták-*⸢*ki*⸣*-iš-ša-an-*⸢*zi*⸣

65. *za-ar-ši-ya-ma*^{er} *še*$^{!}$*-er ki-i ar-nu-nu-un e-ḫu-ma* ⸢*nu*⸣*-wa-mu-*⸢*za*⸣ *ar-*⸢*ku*⸣*-w*[*a-ar*]

66. *i-ya nu-wa-ták-kán* KASKAL-*ši te-eḫ-ḫi* KASKAL-*ši-ma-wa-ták-kán* GIM-*an te-eḫ-*[*ḫi*]

67. *nu-wa-ra-at A-NA* ŠEŠ-*YA ḫa-at-ra-a-mi nu-ut-ta ma-a-an* ZI-*an-za*

68. *wa-ar-ši-ya-zi e-eš-du-wa ma-a-an-ma-wa-at-ta* ZI-*an-za*

69. *Ú-UL wa-ar-ši-ya-zi nu-wa ú-it* GIM-*an* EGIR-*pa-ya-wa-at-ta*

70. *I-NA* **KUR** ^{URU}***Aḫ-ḫi-ya-wa-a*** *am-me-el* UN-*aš QA-TAM-MA pé-*<*e*>*-ḫu-*⸢*te*⸣*-ez-zi*

71. *ma-a-an-ma-wa Ú-UL-ma nu-wa-aš-ši ka-a-aš* ^{LÚ}*KAR-TAP-PU*

72. *pé-di-ši e-ša-ru ku-*⸢*it*⸣*-ma-*⸢*na*⸣*-*<*wa*>*-aš ú-iz-zi ku-it-ma-na-*<*wa*>*-aš*

73. *a-pí-ya* EGIR-*pa ú-iz-zi* ⸢*ka-a*⸣*-aš-ma* ^{LÚ}*KAR-TAP-PU ku-iš*

74. *ŠA* MUNUS.LUGAL-*za ku-it ŠA* MÁŠ^{TI} *ḫar-zi I-NA* KUR ^{URU}*Ḫat-ti ŠA* MUNUS.LUGAL

75. MÁŠ^{TU_4} *me-ek-ki šal-li na-aš-mu Ú-UL im-ma* ^{LÚ}*ḪA*$^{!}$*-*<*DA*>*-NU*

76. *nu-uš-ši a-pa-a-aš pé-e-di-eš-ši e-ša-ru ku-it-ma-na-aš ú-*⸢*iz-zi*⸣

76a. \\ *ku-it-ma-na-aš* EGIR-*pa ú-*[*zi*]*-*⸢*zi*⸣

iii

1. ŠEŠ-*YA-ya-*⸢*an-za*⸣*-an ḫa-an-za* ⸢*e-ep*⸣ *na-an tu-*⸢*e-el*⸣ [UN-*aš*]

2. *ú-wa-te-ed-du nam-ma-aš-ši* ⸢ŠEŠ-*YA* *za-ar-ši-ya-an*⸣

3. *ki-iš-ša-an a-ša-an-ta-an* ⸢*up-pí le-e-wa IT-TI* ^{d}UTU^{ŠI}⸣

4. *nam-ma ku-it-ki wa-aš-ta-*⸢*ti*⸣ […] *nam-ma*

5. *an-da tar-na-aḫ-ḫi na-an* x […] -x-*zi*

§8 (ii 55–iii 6) And yet again, out of consideration for my brother, [I have done] nothing at all. [And if] my brother should perhaps complain: "[I will go] to the King [of Hatti] so that he might send me on my way," I have herewith sent Tapala-Tarhunta, the charioteer. Tapala-Tarhunta is not a person of low rank: (even) in (my) youth he mounted the chariot with me, and as a charioteer he often mounted [the chariot] with your brother Tawagalawa. And [have I not offered ...] Piyamaradu a pledge of safe-conduct? In Hatti (the practice of) safe-conduct is as follows: If they send bread [and] beer(?) to someone, they may inflict no harm upon him. In (the spirit of) safe-conduct, I brought these things, (saying): "Come! Give me an explanation and I will send you on your way. And when I send you on your way, I will write about it to my brother. If you are satisfied, let it be! If you are not satisfied, then my man will take you to **Ahhiyawa** just as you(!) came. If that's not acceptable, then let this charioteer remain (as a hostage) in your(!) place, while you(!) come and return there." Who is this charioteer? Because he has married into the Queen's family—and in Hatti the family of the Queen is very important—isn't he more than an in-law to me? Let him remain in his place while he comes and returns. Take care of him, my brother, and let your [man] bring him. Convey my trustworthy pledge of safe-conduct to him as follows: "Do not cause any further offense to His Majesty! [...]" I will turn [him] loose again, and [...] will [...] him. [My brother should know that] I will send him on his way.

6. *na-an* KASKAL-*ši* GIM-*an te-ḫi* [… -*d*]*u*$^{?}$

---

§9

7. *ma-a-an-ma ke-e Ú*-⸢*UL*⸣ […]
8. *nu* ŠEŠ-*YA ke-e-el* […]-x-*an i-ya*
9. NAM.RA.MEŠ-*kán me-ek-ki* [*A*]-*N*[*A* KUR]-*YA ta-pu-ša*
10. ⸢*ú*⸣-*it* 7 *LI-IM* NAM.RA.MEŠ[-*ya*]-*mu* ŠEŠ-*YA d*[*a*$^{?}$-*at-t*]*a*$^{?}$
11. *nu am-me-el* UN-*aš ú-iz-zi* ⸢*nu-za*⸣ ŠEŠ-*YA*
12. *BE-LU*^{MEŠ} *pé-ra-an* GAM *da-a*-⸢*i*⸣ GEŠPÚ-*za-kán ku-it* […]
13. *ta-pu-ša ú-wa-te-et nu* ŠEŠ-*YA* […]
14. *am-me-el-la* UN-*aš ar-ta*-⸢*ru*⸣ [*nu ma-a-an* …]
15. *me-ma-i AŠ-ŠUM MU-NAB-TI-wa-ká*[*n* …]
16. *na-aš a-pí-ya e-eš-du ma*[-*a-an-ma me-ma-i*]
17. GEŠPÚ-*aḫ-ta*-⸢*wa-mu*⸣ *n*[*a-aš*(-) … EGIR-*pa*$^{?}$ *an-da*$^{?}$ *ú-id-du*$^{?}$]
18. *ma-a-an* x […]
19. *ar-ḫa ta*[*r*$^{?}$- …]
20. x […]
21. […]

---

§10

22. *a-pa-a*-⸢*aš-ma*⸣ […]
23. *me-ek-k*[*i* …]
24. ⸢*MU-NAB*⸣-*TU*$_4$ x […]
25. *ar-ḫa p*[*é*- …]
26. *le-e* […]
27. ⸢*am-me*⸣-*e*[*l* …]
28. […]
29. […]
30. […]

---

§10a[98]

31. […]
32. […]
33. […]
34. […] x
35. […]
36. [… *n*]*a-an* x x
37. […] x *ki* [o] x -*ta*(-)[…]

98. Copy and photo show a double rule approximately after iii 30.

§9 (iii 7–21) But if he doesn't [accept(?) these (words of assurance)], then, my brother, make […] of its […] Many civilian captives have slipped across to your(!) [territory], and you, my brother, have [taken(?)] 7000 civilian captives from me. My man will come and you, my brother, must line up your noblemen! Because he, with force, brought […] Then, my brother, […] And my man shall be present. [If …] he says: "I came as a fugitive," he shall remain there. [But if he says]: "He compelled me," then [he shall return(?)] If […]

(lines iii 22–37 too fragmentary for translation)

§10a (iii 38–51) […] they march back in […] with whom he is angry […] keeps allowing in […] it belongs [to …]-ili. The son of Sahurunuwa […] Let a fugitive come [back] to my brother. Whether he is a nobleman or [a slave]—it is allowed. Did the Great King, my peer, […] that … to that one? When my fugitives crossed over to him, then Sahurunuwa […] to his son. He stepped up and went to that one, but he released him once more. Will you, my brother, [charge] him in that matter? If some servant of mine flees [from me], will you […] run after that one?

38. [… EGI]R-*pa an-da i*-⸢*ya-an-ta-ri*⸣
39. […] x *ku-e-da-ni* TUKU.TUKU-*eš*-⸢*zi*⸣
40. […] x-*an-da tar-ni*-[*iš-k*]*i-iz-zi*
41. [… *A-NA* ^{m} …]-DINGIR^{LÌ}-*ya-at* ⸢DUMU⸣ ^{m}*Ša*-⸢*ḫu*⸣-*r*[*u-nu*]-*wa-kán*
42. [o o o o o o o ^{L}]^{Ú}*MU-NAB-TU*$_4$-*kán* ⸢*A-NA*⸣ ŠEŠ-[*Y*]*A*
43. E[GIR-*pa an-d*]*a ú-id-du ma-a-na-aš BE-LU ma-a-na-aš* [ARAD-*ma*}
44. *tar*-⸢*na-na-at*⸣ LUGAL.GAL-*za am-me-el an-na*-[*ú-li-iš*]
45. ⸢*kar-ga-ra*⸣-*an-ti a-pé-e-da-ni a-pa*[-*a-at*] x x [o o]-⸢*a-it*⸣
46. *am*-[*me*]-*el-ši*-⸢*kán*⸣ *ku-wa-pí* ^{LÚ}*MU-NAB-T*[*I pár-r*]*a*-⸢*an-da*⸣
47. *pa-it*^{er} ⸢*nu-kán*⸣ ^{m}*Ša-ḫu-ru-nu-wa-aš A-N*[*A* DUMU]-*ŠU* x […]
48. ⸢*a*⸣-*pa-a-aš-ma* ⸢*ša-ra-a*⸣ *ti-ya-at na-aš*-⸢*kán*⸣ *a-pé*-⸢*e*⸣[-*da-ni*]
50. *tar*-⸢*na-aš* ŠEŠ-*YA-ya-mu*⸣ *a-pé-e-da-ni* INIM-*ni* [*e-e*]*p-ši*
51. ⸢*ma-a-an*⸣-*m*[*a-mu-kán*] ⸢ARAD-*YA ku-iš-ki*⸣ *ḫu-u-ya-zi nu*-⸢*kán*⸣ […] x

---

§11

52. *nam-ma ka-a-ša-aš-ši-ya ki*$^{!}$-*i*<<*wa*>> *me-mi-iš*[-*ki-iz-zi*]
53. ŠÀ ^{KUR}*Ma-a-ša-wa-kán* ^{KUR}*Kar-ki-ya pár-ra-an*-⸢*da*⸣
54. *pa-a-i-mi* NAM.RA.MEŠ-*ma-wa-za* DAM-*SÚ* DUMU.MEŠ ⸢É⸣[^{TU_4}-*ya*]
55. *ka-a ar-ḫa da-li-ya-mi na-aš* GIM-*an ka*-⸢*a-aš*⸣
56. *me-mi-aš* DAM$^{!}$-*SÚ-ši ku-wa-pí* DUMU.MEŠ É^{TU_4}-*ya*
57. *ŠA* ŠEŠ^{er}-*YA* ŠÀ KUR^{TI} *ar-ḫa da-li-ya*-⸢*zi*⸣
58. *na-an-kán tu-el* KUR-*e-an-za* ⸢*ḫa-an*⸣-*ti-ya*-⸢*iz-zi*⸣
59. ⸢*a*⸣-*pa-a-aš-ma* KUR^{TI}-*YA wa*-⸢*al-aḫ-ḫe*⸣-*eš-ki-iz-zi*
60. ⸢*na*⸣-*aš* EGIR-*pa* AŠ KUR-*KA ú-i*[*z*]-*zi*
62. ŠEŠ-*YA-za ma-la-a-ši* ⸢*ki-nu-un ki-i*⸣ x x x-*eš*

---

§12

63. *nu-uš-ši* ŠEŠ-*YA a-pa-a-at* 1-*an ḫa-at-ra-a-i*
64. *ma-a-an Ú-UL nu-wa ša*-⸢*ra*⸣-*a* ⸢*ti-i-ya*⸣
65. *nu-wa I-NA* ^{KUR}*Ḫat-ti* ⸢*ar-ḫa i-it*⸣
66. EN-*KA-wa-at-ta* EGIR-*an* ⸢*kap*⸣-*pu-u*-[*wa-i*]*t*
67. ⸢*ma-a-an-ma-wa*⸣ *UL nu-wa* AŠ ^{KUR}⸢***Aḫ-ḫi-ya-wa***⸣***-a***
68. [*a*]*r-ḫa* ⸢*e*⸣-*ḫu nu-wa-at-ta* ⸢*ku-e-da-ni*⸣ *pé-d*[*i*]
69. [GAM-*a*]*n a-ši-ša-nu-mi* […]

iv

1. […] x-*wa*(-)[…]
2. […] .MEŠ? x [… *ša-ra-a*] ⸢*ti-i-ya*⸣
3. [*nu-wa-kán dam-me*]-*e-da-ni pé-di* GAM *e-eš* [*nu-wa-za*] *A-NA* LUGAL ^{KUR}*Ḫa-at-ti*

§11 (iii 52–62) Further, he keeps saying this […]: "I will cross over to the land of Masa or the land of Karkiya, but I will leave behind here the civilian captives, my(!) wife, children, [and] household." Will it (indeed) be like this plan? While he leaves behind his wife, children, and household in my brother's land, will your land support him? This person keeps attacking my territory. But if I … it to him, he returns to your land. Do you approve, my brother? Did you now […] this?

§12 (iii 63–iv 15) O, my brother, write to him this one thing, if nothing (else): "Get up and go off to Hatti. Your lord has reconciled with you. If not, then come over to **Ahhiyawa**, and in whatever location I settle you, […] Get up [and] resettle in [another] location. So long as you are hostile to the King of Hatti, be hostile from another land! Do not be hostile from my land. If you(!) would rather be in Karkiya or Masa, go there. The King of Hatti has persuaded me about the matter of the land of Wilusa concerning which he and I were hostile to one another, and we have made peace. Now(?) hostility is not appropriate between us." [Send that] to him. If you/he were [to …] Millawanda, then my servants would flee en masse to that […] one. And, my brother, I have […] over against the land of Millawanda.

4. *⸢ku-wa-pí ku-ru⸣-ur nu-wa-za da-me-⸢da-za⸣* KUR-*e-za ku-ru-ur e-eš*
5. *am-me-ta-za-ma-wa-za-kán* KUR-*e-za ar-ḫa le-e ku-ru-ur*
6. *ma-a-an-wa-ši I-NA* ^{KUR}*Kar-ki-ya* ^{KUR}*Ma-a-⸢ša⸣* ZI-*za*
7. *nu-wa a-pí-ya ⸢i-it⸣* LUGAL ^{KUR}*Ḫa-at-ti-wa-an-na-aš-kán ú-uk*
8. *ku-e-da-ni A-NA* [INI]M ^{URU}*⸢Wi$_5$-lu-ša⸣ še-er ku-ru-⸢ur⸣*
9. *e-šu-u-en nu*[*-wa-m*]*u a-p*[*é-e-d*]*a-ni* INIM-*ni la-a*[*k-nu-ut*]
10. *nu-wa ták-šu-l*[*a-u-en k*]*i-nu*$^{!?}$*-na*$^{!?}$*-*[*ma-wa-an-n*]*a-aš ku-ru-ur UL ⸢a-a⸣-*
-ra
11. *nu-uš-ši a-p*[*a-a-at ŠU-PUR m*]*a-a-an-ma-an* ^{URU}*Mé-el-la-wa-an-da-ma*
12. *ar-ḫa d*[*a-li-ya-zi n*]*u-kán* ARAD.MEŠ-*YA a-pé-e-⸢da⸣-ni*
13. *⸗kar-ga-r*[*a-an-t*]*i* [EGIR-*pa-a*]*n-⸢da píd-da-iš-kán-zi⸣*
14. *nu* ŠEŠ-*⸢YA⸣* [… *A-N*]*A* ^{KUR}*Mé-el-la-⸢wa-an⸣-da*
15. IGI-[*an-da* … *-y*]*a-an* [*ḫ*]*ar-zi*

---

§13

16. [o o o o o o o o o] ^{m}*Pí-ya-ma-ra-du*
17. x [o o o o o o o o o] *nu-mu* ŠEŠ-*YA me-mi-ya-ni*
18. x [o o o o o o o o o] x *na-at-mu ŠU-PUR*
19. *nu* [*ŠA* ^{URU}*Wi$_5$-lu-ša ku-e-da-ni me*]*-mi-ni še-er ku-ru-ri-iḫ-ḫu-e-en*
20. *nu-za-k*[*án ku-it ták-šu-la-u-en nu na*]*m-ma ku-it*
21. *ma-a-*[*an-za-kán* ^{LÚ}*TAP-PU A-NA* ^{LÚ}]*TAP-PÍ-ŠU pé-ra-an wa-aš-túl*
22. *tar-na-i* [*na-aš-za-kán ku-it A-NA* ^{LÚ}*TAP-P*]*Í-⸢ŠU⸣ pé-ra-an*
23. *wa-aš-túl ta*[*r-na-i na-an-kán ar-ḫa*] *⸢Ú⸣-UL pé-eš-ši-ya-iz-zi*
24. *am-mu-uq-⸢qa⸣*[*-za-kán am-me-el ku-it wa-aš-tú*]*l A-NA* ŠEŠ-*YA pé-ra-an*
25. *tar-na-aḫ-ḫu-u*[*n* o o o o o o *na-a*]*t A-NA* ⸢ŠEŠ⸣-*YA*
26. *le-e nam-m*[*a* …]

---

§14

27. *nu ma-a-an* ŠEŠ[-*YA* o o o o o o](-)*an*(-)⸢*da*⸣(-)[…]
28. *nu-mu* EGIR-*pa ŠU-P*[*UR*$^{?}$ o o o o o o …] x x […]
29. *ŠA* ARAD-*YA ku-wa*[*-pí*$^{?}$ …]
30. *ar-ḫa pé-eš-ši-y*[*a*(-) …]
31. *na-at* UN.MEŠ-*an-ni-ma* […]

---

§15

32. ŠEŠ-*YA-ma-mu ka-ru*[*-ú ki-iš*]*-š*[*a-an IŠ-PUR* …]
33. GEŠPÚ-*wa-mu up-pé-eš-ta a*[*m-mu-uk-ma-za nu-u-wa*]
34. TUR-*aš e-šu-un ma-a-an* x […]
35. *ú-uk AŠ-PUR Ú-UL-⸢ma⸣*[*-at* …]

§13 (iv 16–26) […] Piyamaradu […] And to me, my brother, in the matter […] Send it to me. And concerning the matter [of Wilusa] about which we were hostile—[because we have made peace], what then? If [a certain ally] confesses an offense before his ally, [because he confesses] the offense before his [ally], he does not reject [him. Because] I have confessed [my offense] before my brother, [… And] let it […] no further to my brother.

§14 (iv 27–31) And if [my] brother […], then send(?) back to me […] while the […] of my servant […] rejects […] and them(?) to the population […]

§15 (iv 32–57) But my brother already [wrote to me as follows: " …] You have used force against me." [But I was still] young. If […] I wrote, was [it] not […]? If likewise to me […] such [an utterance] comes from his(?) mouth […], the troops will be angry […] is crazy. And from that […] he speaks. Why [will] I […] them? Such an utterance [… before] the Sun-God. If this

36. *ma-a-an-mu QA-TAM-MA a-*⸢*ša*?⸣[-
37. *a-pé-e-ni-šu-u-an-za-kán* ⸢*me*⸣[*-mi-aš* …]
38. KAxU-*za i-ya-at-ta-ri* x […]
39. ^{LÚ}ÉRIN.MEŠ *šu-ul-li-ya-zi* […]
40. *mar-le-eš-ša-an-za nu a-pé-*⸢*ez*⸣ [INIM-*za* …]
41. *me-ma-i am-mu-uq-<qa>-aš-kán ku-wa*[*-at*? …]
42. *a-pé-e-ni-iš-šu-u-an-za me-mi-aš* ^{d}UT[U-*i pé-ra-an* …]
43. *ma-a-an-kán a-pa-a-aš me-mi-aš am-mu-uk* […]
44. GEŠPÚ $^{\textit{erasure}}$ *up-pa-aḫ-ḫu-un* ⸢*ki*⸣*-nu-na-ma* [*ŠA* ŠEŠ-*YA ku-iš*]
45. *me-mi-aš* KAxU-*za ú-it* ⸢*A-NA* LUGAL.GAL⸣[*-ma-aš* …]
46. *ú-it nu-za a-pa-a-at DI-NU pé-<ra>-an* GAM [*ti-ya-u-e-ni nu* ŠEŠ-*YA*]
47. *tu-el ku-in-ki* ARAD^{DUM} *u-i-ya nu-u*[*t-ta a-pu-u-un me-mi-an ku-iš*]
48. *ú-da-aš a-pa-a-aš* INIM-*aš ḫar-kán-*⸢*na*⸣ x x[99] *na-an-kán ka-a ḫa-an-ti* [*ti-ya-mi nu-kán a-pu-u-un* UN-*an*]
49. SAG.DU-*an ku-ra-an-du ma-a-an-ma-a*[*t-ta tu-el* UN-*aš* INIM-*an wa-aḫ-nu*]-⸢*ut*⸣
50. *nu-kán a-pu-u-un* UN-*an* SAG.DU-*an k*[*u-ra-an-du-pát* SAG.DU-*an-m*]*a*
51. *ku-in ku-ra-an-zi na-an-kán mar-*⸢*ri*⸣[*-ya-an-du* …]
52. *nu a-pa-a-at e-eš-ḫar ku-wa-pí pa-iz-z*[*i nu a-pu-u-un ku-it* INIM-*an*]
53. [A]RAD-*KA me-mi-iš-ta nu-kán a-pa-a-aš* 1-*aš* [*a-ki ma-a-na-at-ta me-mi-aš*]
54. KAxU-*za Ú-UL ú-it na-an-kán* ARAD^{DUM} x […]
55. *UL-an-kán tu-uk* SIxSÁ-*at ma-a-na-an* LU[GAL.GAL *am-me-el*]
56. *an-na-*⸢*wa*⸣*-li-iš me-mi-iš-ta* ARAD^{DUM}*-ma-na-an*[- …]
57. *a-pa-a-aš-kán* INIM-*aš* 1-*an-ki ma-*⸢*an-qa*⸣ *ne-pí-š*[*a-* …] x

---

colophon

58. 3 DUB *Q*[*A-TI*?]

99. This sentence inserted above line.

utterance [is ...] for me, [...] I have used force. But now the message [of my brother that] came orally, came to the Great King [... We will set] this legal dispute down before ourselves. You, [my brother], send me one of your servants. The one [who] brought you [that message]—that message is corrupted—I [will set] it (down) here separately. [And] let [that man] be beheaded. If your man has altered your message, let that man be beheaded [too]. Let them stew(?) [and ... the head] that they cut off. And where will that bloodshed lead? Because your servant spoke [this (false) message], he alone [must die. If the message] did not come from your mouth, then the servant [...] it. Did he not determine it on your behalf? If [the Great King, my] peer, had spoken it, the servant would have [...] it. That message somehow once [...]

Colophon (iv 58): Third tablet, [finished(?)].

COMMENTARY

The document commonly referred to by scholars as the "Tawagalawa Letter" was written by a Hittite king to his Ahhiyawan counterpart. In it, the writer complains of the activities of a renegade Hittite subject Piyamaradu, who had been raiding Hittite vassal territory in western Anatolia and stirring up resistance against his overlord; the addressee of the document had apparently given tacit support to these activities, and granted Piyamaradu refuge in Ahhiyawan territory, to prevent his falling into Hittite hands. Neither the author's nor the addressee's name is preserved in what remains of the document—only the third of the three tablets which once made it up. Most scholars assign authorship to Hattusili III, thus giving the document a mid-thirteenth century date, though O. R. Gurney in an article published posthumously (2002) has revived an earlier view that Muwattalli II, brother and predecessor-but-one of Hattusili, was the king in question. (We shall, however, assume for the sake of the discussion below that it was Hattusili.) Similarly, we do not know the identity of the Ahhiyawan king. The text does, however, refer to his brother Tawagalawa, who had apparently come to western Anatolia to receive and transport to Ahhiyawan territory local rebels who had sought protection from Hittite authority. ("Tawagalawa" is commonly assumed to represent the Greek name Eteokles, Mycenaean *E-te-wo-ke-le-we*). But as Itamar Singer first pointed out (1983), the document makes only brief reference to Tawagalawa and is much more concerned with its author's list of complaints against Piyamaradu.

The letter mildly rebukes the Ahhiyawan king for the support he has given Piyamaradu in the past, but its main purpose is to win Ahhiyawan cooperation in curbing the renegade's anti-Hittite activities in the future. This accounts for its author's largely conciliatory tone. Hattusili refers to an ultimately unsuccessful campaign he had conducted in the west. At the point where the broken text begins, he claims that he had marched to the west to quell an uprising in the Lukka lands, where loyalties appear to have been divided; some of the Lukka people had appealed to Tawagalawa and had been brought to him by Piyamaradu, presumably to arrange relocation in Ahhiyawan territory; others who had apparently been forcibly removed from their homeland by Piyamaradu had appealed to their Hittite overlord to rescue them. Gurney (1997) proposed that the events referred to here are those also attested in the fragmentary remains of Hattusili's Annals, which refer to a major rebellion in Lukka. In any case, it is clear from the letter that Piyamaradu was seen as the fomenter and leader of the anti-Hittite movements in the west and was the chief target of the Hittites' western campaign on this and probably other occasions. An attempted diplomatic settlement with him, initiated by Hattusili through his envoys while he was already on the march westwards, came to nothing when Piyamaradu allegedly quibbled over peace terms and remained defiant. His forces were eventually flushed out of a stronghold called Iyalanda after putting up vigorous resistance to their attackers, but Piyamaradu himself escaped capture and fled to Millawanda.

The Hittite king pursued him to Millawanda, but entered its territory only after Piyamaradu had refused his demand to give himself up. This prompted Hattusili to send an appeal to the Ahhiyawan king, who allegedly responded by ordering Millawanda's local ruler Atpa (Piyamaradu's son-in-law) to hand over the renegade (§5). But when Hattusili entered Millawanda, Piyamaradu had already gone, taking flight from Millawanda by ship. He reestablished himself in Ahhiyawan territory, presumably on one of the islands controlled by the Ahhiyawan king off the western coast of Anatolia—beyond the reach of the Hittites, but close enough to continue his attacks on Hittite territory once Hattusili's forces had left the area. Hence Hattusili's approach now to the Ahhiyawan king. He suggested three courses of action the Ahhiyawan might take: a) persuade Piyamaradu to surrender to the Hittite authorities; b) allow him to stay in Ahhiyawan territory, on the clear understanding that he would remain there and engage in no further anti-Hittite activities; c) compel him to move to another country, taking his family and retinue with him (§12).

The outcome of Hattusili's appeal is unknown. But it is unlikely, in view of subsequent events, that Ahhiyawan support of anti-Hittite activities in western Anatolia was in any way curtailed by the appeal. If anything, the Ahhiyawan king and his successor(s) continued to strengthen their influence in the region. Of particular significance is the fact that by this time Millawanda had become Ahhiyawan territory. That is evident from Hattusili's negotiations with his Ahhiyawan counterpart over Piyamaradu after the latter had fled to Millawanda, and from the fact that the local ruler of Millawanda at the time, Atpa, was clearly subject to the Ahhiyawan king's authority. We have seen that Mursili II had firmly reasserted Hittite sovereignty over Millawanda in his third regnal year (ca. 1319) after it had unsuccessfully sought to align itself with Ahhiyawa. But subsequently, it had come under Ahhiyawan control, perhaps during the reign of Mursili's successor Muwattalli II (ca. 1295–1272), and perhaps with Muwattalli's agreement as he sought to stabilize affairs in the west before his showdown with the Egyptians in Syria. Archaeological evidence indicates a significant Mycenaean presence in Millawanda in this period. That ties in well with the textual evidence that indicates the consolidation of Ahhiyawan political control over this important western Anatolian territory. Millawanda was henceforth to serve as the base for the further spread of Ahhiyawan/Mycenaean influence on the mainland. It was in fact to remain the only major center of Ahhiyawan power on the Anatolian mainland.

The letter provides us with some interesting information about earlier relations between its author and its recipient. Hostilities had apparently broken out between them over the country called Wilusa (§§12–13), which lay in northwestern Anatolia. (We shall have more to say about Wilusa below.) This is the only occasion in the Ahhiyawa corpus where there is a reference to what appears to have been direct conflict between Hatti and Ahhiyawa. In all other cases, hostile action by Ahhiyawa against Hatti appears to have been limited to support for the activities of local insurrectionists like Piyamaradu. However, we do not know what the nature or the scale of the hostilities was on this occasion, whether it amounted to outright war, a skirmish or two, or merely a verbal dispute conducted through diplomatic channels. (The verb *ku-ru-ri-iḫ-ḫu-e-en* used in this context could mean any of these things.) In any case, if Hattusili's claim that he was young at the time can be taken at face value, it may indicate that the episode in question occurred early in his regnal career, or perhaps even during the reign of his brother Muwattalli. Already at that time Hattusili exercised considerable political and military authority within the Hittite kingdom.

We should also note the significance of Hattusili's regular references to his Ahhiyawan counterpart as a "Great King," and as "my brother," "my peer" (e.g., §6). These terms were not used lightly in international royal terminology. In the Near Eastern context, "Great Kingship" was confined to the rulers of Hatti, Egypt, Babylon, Mitanni and (after Mitanni's fall) Assyria. And only "Great Kings" addressed their peers as "my brother." Thus the Ahhiyawan king is accorded by Hattusili a status that must have far exceeded his actual importance in the Near Eastern world in general, particularly when compared to the pharaoh of Egypt and the rulers of Mesopotamia, from whom there is not a single reference to a king or kingdom of Ahhiyawa. The Ahhiyawan king of the Tawagalawa letter was but one of a number of rulers of the small kingdoms of the Late Bronze Age Greek world, albeit one whose territory included islands off the Anatolian mainland and a major base on the mainland. From Hattusili's point of view, he had become an important participant in the Near Eastern scene, to the extent that he warranted acknowledgement as a Great King and royal brother—terminology that implied full diplomatic equality between the two kings, and might serve a useful purpose in the Hittite's attempts to win over a man whose cooperation he was so anxious to secure. Indeed the "Great King" tag for the Ahhiyawan ruler appears to have survived in Hittite records for some time, perhaps until it was struck out of diplomatic parlance during the drafting of Tudhaliya IV's treaty with Shaushga-muwa of Amurru.

AhT 5

Letter from a king of Hatti (probably Tudhaliya IV) to a western Anatolian ruler (Tarkasnawa, king of Mira?)— The "Milawata Letter" (CTH 182)

Although the preserved portion of this letter does not mention Ahhiyawa, it does treat several individuals and political entities deeply involved in the rivalry between Hatti and that country, namely, the rogue Piyamaradu, the land of Wilusa, and the city of Milawata. The name of the recipient, surely a ruler in the west of Anatolia, has been lost in the damaged salutation (§1), and the identity of the Hittite ruler remains hidden behind his title, "My Majesty" (^{d}UTU^{ŠI}). However, the reinstallation of Walmu as king of Wilusa (§7') leads us to conclude that the Great King here was probably one of the successors of Muwattalli II, in whose reign Wilusa was governed by Alaksandu. The most likely author of the dispatch is Tudhaliya IV.

KUB 19.55 + KUB 48.90

obv.

§1

1. ⸢*UM-MA*⸣ ^{d}UTU^{ŠI}-*MA A-N*[*A* … DUMU-*YA QÍ-BÍ-MA*]

---

§2

2. ^{d}UTU^{ŠI}-*ya* DUMU-*YA* UN-*an* [*ša-ra-a da-aḫ-ḫu-un nu-mu-za AŠ-ŠUM BE-LU-TÌ*]
3. *ša-ak-ta nu-ut-ták-kán* [*ŠA A-BI-KA* KUR-*e pé-eḫ-ḫu-un* … *-za A-BU-KA-ma*]
4. ZAG.MEŠ-*YA i-la-liš-ki*[*-it* …]
5. GIM-*an-ma-kán ar-*[…]
6. *nu-za A-BU-KA* GIM-*an* […]
7. GAM ME-*iš* ^{d}UTU^{ŠI}-*ya* […]
8. *nu* ^{d}UTU^{ŠI}-*ya ku-u-r*[*u-ur-ri-ya-aḫ-ḫu-un nu-za A-BU-KA tar-aḫ-ḫu-un*]
9. *nu-ut-ta*^{er} ^{d}UTU^{ŠI} [… DUMU-*YA ša-ra-a da-aḫ-ḫu-un*]
10. *nu-ud-du-za* ŠEŠ-*aḫ-ḫ*[*u-un* …]
11. *nam-ma* GAM ^{d}UTU AN⸢*E*⸣ [… *li-in-ku-e-en*]
12. *nu-za zi-ik* ^{d}UTU^{ŠI} [*AŠ-ŠUM BE-LU-TÌ ša-ak-ta* …]
13. EG[IR]-*pa a-ru-nu-un* ⸢*A*⸣[*-NA* ZAG-*YA* DÙ-*nu-un* …]
14. ⸢*ku*⸣-*i-e-eš* ḪUL-*u-i-eš* [UN.MEŠ-*eš* …]
15. *nu nam-ma A-BU-KA* […]
16. *iš-dam-ma-aš-ta n*[*u*? …]
17. *A-NA* LUGAL KUR ^{URU}*Ḫat-ti* x [… *na-at*?]
18. *ša-an-né-eš-ta-ya k*[*u*?- …]
19. *A-BU-KA pa-ra-a i*[*m-ma*? …]

---

§3

20. *ki-nu-un-ma-mu A-BU-KA* […]
21. ⸢*ku*⸣-*it* DUMU-*YA* SIG$_5$-*tar* PAP[*-aš-ti* …]
22. [KUR]-⸢*e*?-*ma*⸣-*mu-za* ⸢*le-e*⸣ *i*[*-la-li-ya-ši* …]
23. [o o o o]-x-*ma*?-x ⸢*da*?⸣-*a*[*ḫ*?- …]
24. [o o o o] ⸢*A*⸣-*BU-KA ku*-⸢*wa*⸣-[*pí* …]
25. [o o o o *-m*]*u*? *A-BU-KA A-NA* LU[GAL-*UT-TÌ*? …]
26. [o o o o *-z*]*a*?-*kán* ŠÀ-*ta* x […]
27. [*Š*]*A*? ZAG-⸢*YA*⸣ RA-*an-zi nu-k*[*án*? … *NI-IŠ* DINGIR^{LÌ}]
28. [*š*]*ar-ra-at-ti nu am-mu-uk A-BU-K*[*A* GIM-*an* DÙ-*at nu-mu QA-TAM-MA le-e*]

§1 (obv. 1) Thus says My Majesty: [Say] to [..., my son]:

§2 (obv. 2–19) [I], My Majesty, [have taken up] (you), my son, an ordinary man, [and] you have recognized [me as overlord. I gave the land of your father] to you. [But your father ...] had always desired my border territories. [...] When [...], and when your father [marched against the town of ...], he subdued [the town of ...], and [he ...] My Majesty, [...] Then I, My Majesty, opened hostilities [and defeated your father]. But I, My Majesty, [took you up, ... , my son], and treated you in a brotherly fashion. [...] Furthermore, under the Sun-God of Heaven [we swore an oath ...] You [recognized] My Majesty [as overlord. I, My Majesty, thereby established] once more the sea [as my frontier ...] Whatever evil [persons ...] And furthermore, your father [...] he heard. [They became hostile] to the King of Ḫatti [and ..., but] he kept quiet [about it. ...] Your father [indeed ...]

§3 (obv. 20–30) But now, your father [...], because [you], my son, protect [my] well-being. [... You] shall not [desire] my [land ...] while your father [...] your father for [kingship(?) ...] he [took(?)] to heart [... of(?)] my border territory they will attack, then [...] you will transgress [the oath]. You [shall not] treat [me as] your father treated me. And if [you] go away, [and ...], I, My Majesty, [will not lend] you [assistance(?)].

29. DÙ-*ši nu-kán ma-a-an ar-ḫa ú-w[a-ši …]*
30. ⸢^{d}⸣UTU^{ŠI}-*ma-ta pé-ra-an* UGU-*ya U[L*$^{?}$ …]

---

§4
31. *am-mu-uk-ma A-BU-KA ku-it ku-i[t* ḪUL-*lu* DÙ-*at* …]
32. *ka-a-aš* INIM-*aš* SAG.DU-*aš* INIM ^{URU}*[U-ti-ma Ù* ^{URU}*At-ri-ya* …]
33. *Ú-UL e-eš-ta* ^{erasure} *nu ku*$^{!}$*-u-un* INIM ^{URU}*[U-ti-ma Ù* ^{URU}*At-ri-ya* ^{d}UTU^{ŠI}]
34. *A-NA A-BU-KA AŠ-PUR na-at-kán Ú*$^{?}$*[-UL … ma-a-an-ma* …]
35. DUMU-*YA wa-aš-ti na-at-*⸢*kán*⸣ *A-NA [ŠA-PAL NI-IŠ* DINGIR^{LÌ} *ki-it-ta-ru]*

---

§5
36. *A-BU-KA-ma am-mé-el* ḪUL-*u-i* x […]
37. *A-NA* ^{d}UD.SIG$_{5}$ ḪUL.⸢ḪI.A⸣ x x EN$^{?}$ […]
38. *še-ek-ká[n-zi*$^{?}$ …]

(a total of 15–20 lines has been lost at the bottom of the obverse and the top of the reverse)

rev.
§6'
1'. [*ma*]-*a-an* DUMU-*YA me-ma-*⸢*ti*⸣ ^{d}UTU^{ŠI}-*wa UL* […]
2'. [*nu-w*]*a*$^{?}$ *ku-it* BAL-*nu-un ma-a-an* DUMU-*YA* INIM ^{m}⸢*A*⸣[*-ga-pu-ru-ši-ya ša-ra-a*]
3'. ⸢*ú*$^{?}$⸣*-it* INIM ^{LÚ}*MU-NAB-TI-ma* ^{d}UTU^{ŠI} *ku-it-ki m[u*$^{?}$*-* …]
4'. ^{LÚ}*MU-NAB-TU*$_{4}$*-ma* EGIR SUM-*u-an-zi UL a-a-ra* […]
5'. *nu* GAM ^{d}⸢IŠKUR⸣*-ma ku-it-ki ti-ya-u-en* ^{LÚ}*MU-NAB-TU*$_{4}$*-wa* [EGIR-*pa* SUM-*u-e-ni* …]
6'. *A-BU-KA ku-it* ^{LÚ}SANGA ^{URU}*Ta-a-*⸢*al*$^{?}$*-wi*$^{?}$⸣*-[šu*$^{?}$*]-*⸢*an*⸣*-ta*$^{?}$ [*UL e-ep-ta nu-mu* …]
7'. EGIR-*an-ta ap-pé-eš-ta ar-[ḫ]a* x x x […]
8'. *na-an-ši-kán an-*⸢*da*⸣ *UL tar-[na-aḫ-ḫu-un* …]
9'. *ma-an ma-a-an* ^{m}*A-ga-pu-ru-ši[-ya* …]
10'. ^{m}*Pí-ya-ma-ra-du-uš ku-wa-p[í* …]
11'. *ar-ḫa-wa-za* ⸢*pa*⸣*-a-i-mi* […]
12'. ^{m}*A-ga-pu-ru-ši-ya-an-n[a*$^{?}$ …]
13'. *ma-an* DUMU-*YA ša-a[k-ta* …]
14'. *n[u-u]š-ši wa-tar-na-a[ḫ-ḫu-un* …]
15'. [*na-a*]*n-za* EGIR[- …]
16'. ⸢*ša-ku-wa*⸣*-ša-*⸢*ri*⸣*[-it* ZI-*it* …]

§4 (obv. 31–35) But whatever [evil] your father [committed] against me [...], this matter is a capital crime. In respect to the question of the towns of [Utima and Atriya] he was not [...]. I, [My Majesty], wrote to your father [...] concerning this matter of [Utima and Atriya], but [he did] not [resolve] it. [If you do not resolve it], you, my son, will commit an offense. It shall [be placed under oath].

§5 (obv. 36–38) But your father [...] in evil against me [...] the evil matters until (his) dying day [...] they know [...]

(a total of 15–20 lines has been lost at the bottom of the obverse and the top of the reverse)

§6' (rev. 1'–17') But if you, my son, should say: "Your Majesty [did] not [...] How have I risen in revolt?" If, my son, the matter [of Agapurusiya ...] has come up—I, My Majesty, have somehow [...] the matter of the fugitive. [...] Is it not right to return a fugitive? [...] We have placed something under (the oath of?) the Storm-God: "[We will return] a fugitive." Because your father [did not capture] the priest of the town of Talwisuwanta(?), he sent [to me] later: "[He ran] away [... " And when he asked me for the fugitive so-and-so], did I not [release] him to him? If Agapurusiya were [...] At the time when Piyamaradu [...] "I will go away!" [...] Agapurusiya [...] If [you], my son, [knew ... I] have informed him: ["... "] And him in return [...] wholeheartedly [...] the matter [of Agapurusiya ...]

(gap of approximately fifteen lines)

17'. ⸢INIM⸣ ^{m}*A-ga-p[u-ru-ši-ya* …]

(gap of approximately fifteen lines)

§7'

32'. [*nu-u*]*š-ši ḫ/z*[*a*$^{?}$- …]

33'. ⸢*a*⸣-*pa-a-aš-ma ki*[*š-an* …] x x x […]

34'. [*nu*] ⸢*nam*⸣-*ma* ÉRIN.M[EŠ … *ar-ḫ*]*a*$^{?}$ *pa-it*

35'. ⸢*na*⸣-*aš-kán* GE$_{6}$-*za* ⸢GAM$^{?}$⸣ x […] KUR-*e UL* x […]

36'. [*n*]*u-kán* GIM-*an* EN-*ŠÚ* ⸢*me*⸣-*m*[*i-* …] x-⸢*an*$^{?}$-*ti*$^{?}$⸣ *ḫu-u-wa-a-i*[*š*]

37'. [*nu*]-*uš-ma-aš dam-ma-*⸢*in* EN⸣-*a*[*n da-a-ir* …-*ma-za* …] x ḪUL$^{!?}$-*an UL ša-qa-ḫu-u*[*n*]

38'. *A-NA* ^{m}*Wa-al*$^{!}$-*mu-ma ku-e* ^{GIŠ}ḪUR[.ḪI.A DÙ-*un na-at*] ^{m}KARAŠ.ZA *pé-e ḫar-ta*

39'. *na-at ka-a-aš-ma IT-TI* DUMU-⸢*YA*⸣ [*kat-t*]*a-an* x [o] *ú-da-i na-at a-ú ki-nu-un-ma* DUMU-*Y*[*A*]

40'. *ku-wa-pí ŠA* ^{d}UTU^{ŠI} SIG$_{5}$-*tar* PAP-*aš-ti tu-e-el-za* SILIM-*an* ^{d}UTU^{ŠI} *ḫa-a-mi*

41'. *nu-mu-kán* DUMU-*YA* ^{m}*Wa-al*$^{!}$-*mu-un pa-ra-a na-a-i na-an* EGIR-*pa I-NA* ^{KUR}⸢*Wi*$_{5}$-*lu*⸣-*ša*

42'. LUGAL-*iz-na-ni te*$_{9}$-*eḫ-ḫi na-aš ka-ru-ú* GIM-*an* LUGAL ^{KUR}*Wi*$_{5}$-*lu-ša e-eš-ta ki-nu-na-aš*<-*ša-aš*> *QA-TAM-M*[*A e-eš-du*]

43'. *nu-wa-na-ša-aš ka-ru-ú* GIM-*an* ARAD^{DUM} ⸢*ku-la*⸣-*wa-né-eš* ⸢*e*⸣-[*eš-ta k*]*i-nu-na-aš*-<*ša-aš*> *QA-TAM-MA*

44'. ARAD *ku-la-wa-né-eš e-eš-du*

---

§8'

45'. ZAG ^{KUR}*Mi-la-wa-*⸢*ta*⸣-*ma-na-aš* ^{d}UTU^{ŠI} DUMU-*YA-ya* GIM-*an* GIN-*u-en* [o o o o *t*]*u-e-e*[*l* SILIM-*an le-e*]

46'. *kar*$^{!}$-*ša-nu-ši* ^{d}UTU^{ŠI}-*za tu-e-*⸢*el*⸣ SILIM-*an ša-ku-wa-aš-ša-r*[*i-it* ZI-*it ḫa-a-mi nu*]-*ut-ták-k*[*án* …]

47'. *A-NA* ZAG ^{KUR}*Mi-la-wa-ta an-da ku-it UL pé-eḫ*[-*ḫu-un* …] x […]

---

lower edge

§9'

1. ⸢*A*⸣-*BU-KA-*⸢*za*⸣ [o o o] *ku-iš am-mé-el* ḪUL-*u*^{er}-*wa*^{er} *i-la-liš-ki-z*[*i A-NA* ^{d}UTU^{ŠI}-*ma*]

2. ḪUL-*u-wa-aš* INIM.MEŠ-*aš ku-iš* INIM-*aš* SAG.DU-*aš nu-mu a-pa-a-at iš*[- … *A-BU-KA-ma-za-kán*]

§7' (rev. 32'–44') […] to him […] But he [thus … And] furthermore the troops […] he went [away]. Then by night he [went(?)] down. […] He did not […] the land. And when his lord … […] he fled to [… Then they took] for themselves another lord. [But] I did not recognize […] the evil one. Kulana-ziti retained possession of the wooden tablets that [I made] for Walmu, and he has now brought them [down] to (you), my son. Examine them! Now, my son, as long as you look after the well-being of My Majesty, I, My Majesty, will put my trust in your good will. Turn Walmu over to me, my son, so that I may reinstall him in kingship in the land of Wilusa. [He shall] now be king of the land of Wilusa, as he was formerly. He shall now be our military vassal, as he [was] formerly.

§8' (rev. 45'–47') As I, My Majesty, and (you), my son, have established the borders of the land of Milawata, you shall [not] withhold your [good-will]. I, My Majesty, [will put my trust] wholeheartedly in your good-will. [And the …] that I did not give to you within the border territory of the land of Milawata […]

§9' (lower edge 1–left edge 6) Your father […], who always wished for my misfortune, and who was the primary factor in unfortunate affairs [for My Majesty, …] that to me. [Your father] boasted about my servants. And earlier, while he was boasting about the city of Arinna, [he said to me: "…] I will retain [them]." But when your father did not give me the hostages of the cities of Utima and Atriya, then I [did not go(?)] there, but I sent Kulana-ziti. You too […] the

3. *am-mé-el* ARAD$^{!}$-*iš wa-li-at nu-za-kán ka-ru-ú ku-wa-pí* ^{URU}PÚ-*na-an wa-*⸢*li*⸣-*a*[*t nu me-mi-iš-ta … -uš-wa*(-) …]
4. *ši-*⸢*wa*⸣-*ri-ya-wi*$_5$ GIM-*an-ma-mu A-BU-KA* ^{LÚ}*LI* ^{URU}*U* ^{URU}*At*[100] NU SUM *nu an-d*[*a UL pa-ḫu-ḫu-un*$^?$]
5. *nu* ^{m}KARAŠ.ZA *u-i-ya-nu-un*

left edge

1. [… *zi-i*]*q-qa* INIM ^{URU}*A-wa-ar-na Ù* ^{URU}*P*[*í-na* …]-x-*kán* ^{d}UTU^{ŠI} ⸢*am*$^?$⸣-[*me*]-*el*$^?$ DU[MU$^?$-*YA*] x x […]
2. […] x ^{GIŠ}TUKUL <<*u*>> *tar*$^{!?}$-*aḫ*$^{!?}$-*ḫa*$^{!?}$-<*an*$^?$>-*te-eš*[101] *UL an-da u-uḫ-ḫu-u*[*n* …] x x *IŠ-TU* ^{GIŠ}TUKUL ^{GI}GAG.⸢Ú⸣[.TAG.GA-*a*]*z*$^?$ […]
3. [… *tu-e-e*]*l* SIG$_5$-*an-*⸢*ni*⸣ *še-er an-da UL u-uḫ-ḫu-u*[*n* o o o o *pa-r*]*a-a u-uḫ-ḫu-un* INIM ^{URU}*A* ^{URU}*Pí zi-ig-*⸢*ga*⸣ [*me-mi-iš-ta*]
4. […] x ^{LÚ}*LI- ṬÙ-TU*$_4$ ^{URU}*A-wa* ^{URU}*Pí-na pa-a*[*-i ú-uq-qa*]-*wa-ta* ^{LÚ}*LI-ṬÙ-TU*$_4$ ^{URU}*U-ti-ma* ^{URU}*At-ri-ya pa-ra-a* [*pé-eḫ-ḫi*]
5. *nu-ut-ta* ^{d}UTU^{ŠI} ^{LÚ}*LI* [^{URU}*U* ^{URU}*At p*]*a-ra-a-pát AD-DIN zi-ik-*⸢*ma*⸣-*mu* NU x […]
6. ⸢*na-at*⸣ *UL i*[*m-ma a-a-ra nu tu*]-⸢*e-el*⸣ ḪUL *ŠA* ZI x x ḪUL ⸢ḪUL$^?$⸣ x x x

---

100. Abbreviation for ^{LÚ}*LI-ṬÙ-TU*$_4$ ^{URU}*U-ti-ma* ^{URU}*At-ri-ya*; cf. left edge 3–5.
101. The first portion of this line is written over an erasure.

matter of the cities of Awarna and [Pina]. I, My Majesty, [...] (you), my [son ...] Therein I did not see the [...] subdued by force of arms(?). [...] by means of mace and arrow [...] Out of consideration for [your] well-being I did not look [...]; I looked away. Concerning the matter of Awarna and Pina, you also [said]: "Give [me] the hostages of Awarna and Pina. [I will give] the hostages of the cities of Utima and Atriya over to you." I have given the hostages [of Utima and Atriya] over to you, but you [have] not [given the hostages] to me. It is not [at all right. And] your evil ...

COMMENTARY

The document commonly known as the "Milawata Letter" is so called because the boundaries of the land of Milawata/Millawanda figure among the topics dealt with in it. But its coverage extends to other western Anatolian regions as well, providing us with several important, though fragmentary, pieces of information about the history of these regions during the last centuries of the Late Bronze Age. Its value as a historical source has been significantly enhanced by H. A. Hoffner's discovery of a fragment in the Hittite tablet collection in Berlin that fitted precisely along one of the broken edges of what was till then the only recognized piece of the document (KUB 19.55, transl. in Garstang and Gurney 1959: 114–15). Hoffner's text join (Hoffner 1982) made possible the correlation of a number of scraps of information contained in the originally separate fragments, and provided a basis for a partial reconstruction of some of the document's most broken passages. The name of neither the author of the document nor its recipient appears in the surviving parts of the text. But there is general agreement that the former was Tudhaliya IV, and among the various candidates suggested for the latter, the most likely is Tarkasnawa, ruler of the Arzawan kingdom called Mira (thus Hawkins 1998: 19), which lay directly north of Milawata. We shall henceforth identify the author and recipient of the document by these names, on the understanding that there is as yet no hard proof for either identification.

From the letter's more substantial remains, we learn that Tudhaliya had engaged in military conflict with Tarkasnawa's father, the former king of Mira (whose name was perhaps Alantalli; see Hawkins 1998: 18), who had seized Hittite frontier territories bordering his land and taken hostages from towns subject to Hittite sovereignty. Tudhaliya had defeated and deposed him, appointing his son Tarkasnawa in his place as the new ruler of Mira, one of the Arzawa lands that had been Hittite vassal territory from at least the early years of Mursili II's reign. Tudhaliya seems to have formed a kind of partnership with Tarkasnawa, in which the latter assumed the role of a regional overlord, with immediate authority over a number of Hittite vassal territories in the west, while still remaining a subject of and directly answerable to the Hittite king. Such an arrangement would have been unprecedented in the imperial organization of the Hittite world, and may well have been prompted by the Hittites' increasing difficulties in maintaining their authority unlitaterally throughout their western territories.

Consistent with the new arrangement, Tudhaliya established in consultation with Tarkasnawa new boundaries for the land of Milawata, which bordered upon Mira to its north. From what we can make out from the broken text, Milawata was to remain independent of Tarkasnawa's authority. We have noted that at the time of the Tawagalawa letter, it was subject to the sovereignty of a king of Ahhiyawa. The absence of any reference to Ahhiyawa in the new arrangements made for Milawata's boundaries indicates that this was no longer the case. Milawata had by now been lost to the Ahhiyawan king and reverted to Hittite sovereignty, in circumstances unknown to us but perhaps as a result of one of Tudhaliya's western campaigns. With its loss, Ahhiyawa must have ceased to exercise any effective influence anywhere on the Anatolian mainland. This may provide the context for the erasure of the Ahhiyawan king from the list of Great Kings in the Shaushga-muwa treaty (**AhT 2**).

An important feature of Hoffner's text join is the contribution it makes to the small body of information we have about the kingdom of Wilusa (§7'). This too was a Hittite vassal state, which most scholars now locate in northwestern Anatolia, in the region of the Classical Troad— thus supporting Kretschmer's equation of the Hittite name Wilusa with Homeric (W)Ilios. From the join, we learn that a man called Walmu, already known from KUB 19.55, was in fact a king of Wilusa who had been driven by rebels from his land and had sought refuge with Tarkasnawa. Walmu was in Mira when Tarkasnawa received the letter from his Hittite overlord. It was accompanied by a royal Hittite envoy called Kulana-ziti (previously read Kuwatna-ziti), who presented the local king with wooden tablets authenticating the refugee's claim to Wilusa's throne. This was to pave the way for the reinstatement of Walmu in Wilusa, after Tarkasnawa had handed him back to Tudhaliya; Walmu would henceforth resume his role as a "military vassal" (so Beckman translates the term *kulawaniš*) of both kings. Thus Tarkasnawa's role as regional overlord would have extended north along the Aegean coast and hinterland to the far northwest of Anatolia. He may also have exercised authority over the Seha River Land, which lay between his kingdom and Wilusa, but there is no reference to this land in what survives of the document.

Despite the powers he assigned to Tarkasnawa, Tudhaliya did not fully trust him. An issue still to be resolved was his continuing detention of the hostages that his father had taken from the Hittite subject towns Utima and Atriya. That issue is raised by Tudhaliya in the final section of the letter before the text breaks off.

The reference to Piyamaradu in a very broken passage in the letter would seem to indicate that this man, one of the Hittites' most dangerous enemies in the west, was still alive and active, and no doubt continuing his anti-Hittite activities in the region. But the fragment that mentions him (§6' rev. 10') reveals nothing about him beyond his name.

AhT 6

Letter from a King of Ahhiyawa to a King of Hatti (probably Muwattalli II) (CTH 183)

This text represents a translation into Hittite of a message sent to the Great King of Hatti by his peer, the king of Ahhiyawa. Once again, damage to the salutation (§1) and the use of a title obscure the identities of the correspondents, but the historical context makes it likely that he was Muwattalli II. Discussion in the remaining portion of this badly damaged letter is primarily concerned with the rightful ownership of a group of islands that had seemingly formed part of a dowry in a previous generation.

KUB 26.91

obv.

§1

1. [*UM-MA* ^{m} o o o o o o o LUGAL.GAL LUGA]L ⌈^{KUR}⌉***Aḫ-ḫi-ya-w***[***a***-*ma* *A-NA* ^{d}UTU^{ŠI} LUGAL KUR ^{URU}*Ḫat-ti QÍ-BI-MA*]

---

§2

2. [o o o o o o o o o] x ⌈*ku-e*⌉*-ša-an n*[*a*?- …]
3. [o o] x x [o o] x x x x *-a ku-ru-ur iš-tar-na* [*ki-ša-at* …]
4. [*nu ki*]⌈*-i*⌉ *ki-ša-at nu ak-kán-ta-aš* *ar*-x[- …]

---

§3

5. [*pa*?]*-ra-a-an-ni* MU.KAM-*ti-mu* ŠEŠ-*YA ḫa-at-r*[*a-e-eš* …]
6. [*t*]*u-e-el* *gur-ša-wa-ra ku-e z*[*i*?*-ik* … *nu-wa-ra-at*]
7. ^{d}U ARAD-*an-ni am-mu-uk pa-iš* LUGAL ^{KUR}*A-aš*[*-šu-wa* …]
8. *erasure* <m>*Ka-ga-mu-na-aš-za*^{er}*-kán*^{er}*A-BA A-BA A-B*[*I-ŠU*? …]
9. *pí-ra-an ḫa-ma-ak-ta nu-za* ^{m}*Tu-ud-ḫ*[*a-li-ya-aš A-BA A-BA A-BI-KA* LUGAL ^{KUR}*A-aš-šu-wa tar-aḫ-ta*]
10. ⌈*na*⌉*-an-za-kán* ARAD-*na-aḫ-ta nu* *k*[*ur-ša-wa-ra ka-ru-ú ŠA* LUGAL ^{KUR}***Aḫ-ḫi-ya-wa*** *e-eš-ta-pát nu A-NA* ŠEŠ-*YA a-pád-da-an*]
11. *še-er ḫa-at-ra-a-nu-un A-N*[*A* ^{m} … *-ma* …]
12. *Ù*$^{!er}$ *ŠA*$^{!er}$ LUGAL ^{KUR}⌈***Aḫ***⌉***-ḫi-***⌈***ya***⌉[***-wa*** …]

§1 (obv. 1) [Thus says ... , Great King, King] of **Ahhiyawa**: [Say to His Majesty, King of Hatti]:

§2 (obv. 2–4) [...] which [...] hostility [occurred] therein. [... And this] occurred. Then the [...] of the dead [...]

§3 (obv. 5–20) In the previous year my brother wrote to me: ["...] As for your islands that [you ...]—the Storm-God gave them to me in subjugation." The King of Assuwa [...] Kagamuna, [his(?)] great-grandfather, [...] married previously. Then Tudhaliya, [your great-grandfather, defeated the King of Assuwa] and subjugated him. [The islands formerly indeed belonged to the King of **Ahhiyawa**, and] I have now written [to my brother] on account [of this. But] to [...] and of the King of **Ahhiyawa** [...] But in the past [...] then [...] in the land [of Hatti(?) ...] against [...] these [...] to [...]

(gap of uncertain length)

13. *an-ni-ša-an-ma* […]
14. LUGAL ^{KUR}*A-aš-šu-w*[*a* …]
15. *nu-kán d*[*u-* …]
16. *I-NA* KUR ^{URU}[*Ḫa-at-ti*$^{?}$ …]
17. *me-na-aḫ-ḫa*[*-an-da* …]
18. *ke-e* x […]
19. *A-NA* […]
20. *a-*[…]

rev.

§4’

1’. *traces*
2’. [*n*]*am-ma* […]
3’. [*n*]*u* ARAD-*Y*[*A* …]
4’. *an-da* x […]
5’. [E]GIR-*pa* x […]
6’. [Z]AG-*aš-ši* x […]
7’. [Ḫ]UL-*lu ku*[- …]
8’. [*a*]*m-me-el an-n*[*a-* …]
9’. [*I*]*Š-TU* ^{KUR}*Mé-e*[*l-la-wa-an-da* …]
10’. [U]N-*ša-an* UN.MEŠ[*-aš*$^{?}$ …]
11’. [*I*]*-NA QA-QA-RI-Y*[*A* …]

---

§5’

12’. [*am*]*-mu-uk-ma-an-kán* […]
13’. ŠEŠ-*YA uš-ki nam*[*-ma* …]
14’. ⸢É$^{?}$⸣ ŠEŠ-*YA* ARAD.MEŠ$^{!}$[*-KA-ya*$^{?}$ …]
15’. [o o o]⸢*-zi*$^{?}$⸣ […]

§4' (rev. 1'–11') Further [...] Then my servant [...] in [...] back [...] his(?) border [...] evil [...] my [...] from the land of [Millawanda ...] a person among(?) persons [...] in my territory [...]

§5' (rev. 12'–15') But I [...] him [...] examine, my brother! Further, [...] the household(?) of my brother and(?) my brother's servants [...]

(text breaks off)

COMMENTARY

This is one of the very few letters in the Ahhiyawa corpus that can be assigned to the authorship of an Ahhiyawan king. Unfortunately once again the broken text contains neither the name of the king nor that of his Hittite addressee. From the context, however, it is clear that the latter was a king of Hatti. He is linked in the text with a man called Tudhaliya, designated as his "great-grandfather," who had defeated and subjugated a king of Assuwa. Without doubt, the Tudhaliya in question was Tudhaliya I/II, an early New Kingdom ruler of Hatti (late-fifteenth–early-fourteenth century B.C.E.) well known for his destruction of a coalition of twenty-two countries, commonly referred to by scholars as the "Assuwan Confederacy" and extending along Anatolia's western coast and through part of its hinterland. A further reference to Tudhaliya's defeat and subjugation of it is inscribed on a sword that was discovered in Hattusa in 1991, but was probably produced in a western Anatolian workshop and subsequently taken to Hattusa as part of the spoils of Tudhaliya's victory. The inscription reads: "As Tudhaliya the Great King shattered the Assuwan country, he dedicated these swords to the Storm-God, his lord" (see Cline 1996).

The surviving portion of the letter is concerned primarily with disputed ownership over a group of islands, which presumably lay off Anatolia's Aegean coast. It seems that in the past, Assuwa's, Ahhiyawa's, and Hatti's rulers had all laid claim to them. A diplomatic marriage between the Ahhiyawan king's "great-grandfather," perhaps the man called Kagamuna in the text,[102] and an Assuwan princess may have resulted in the islands being transferred by the Assuwan king to the bridegroom as part of the dowry. The Hittites apparently claimed that Tudhaliya's victory over Assuwa had given *them* possession of Assuwa's offshore territories. But according to the letter's author, this was after these territories had already been presented to Ahhiyawa. Now the Ahhiyawan king was seeking to reaffirm his claims to the islands and to win Hittite acceptance of these claims through diplomatic means. (The diplomatic tone of the letter is clear from its author's use of the term "my brother" in addressing his Hittite counterpart.)

That brings us to the identity of the Hittite king addressed in the letter. Historical and palaeographical considerations have led most scholars to believe that the man in question was Muwattalli II. The letter may belong within the context of a number of negotiations that, perhaps, Muwattalli conducted with his Ahhiyawan counterpart over a distribution of territories between them in the west. Among the results of these were perhaps the formal establishment of Ahhiyawan sovereignty over Milawata/Millawanda and the reaffirmation of Ahhiyawan control over islands off the western coast. This view would be reinforced if the events referred to here can be linked to those of the Manapa-Tarhunta letter (**AhT 7**), as several scholars have suggested (see Hoffner 2009: 291), in which Muwattalli was also the addressee. But Muwattalli was not literally the great-grandson of Tudhaliya I/II, the conqueror of Assuwa. He was five generations removed from this Tudhaliya, and thus his great-great-great grandson. There must have been a similar relationship between the Ahhiyawan king who was allegedly given the islands by Assuwa and his descendant who reported the matter in his letter. In both cases, the term "great-grandfather" should presumably be assigned the more general meaning "ancestor."

Like all the documents in the Ahhiyawa corpus from Boğazköy, the letter is written in Hittite. This is possibly an indication that the author's palace estab-

102. A small gap in the text at this point makes it uncertain whether Kagamuna is the ancestor of the Ahhiyawan king (the letter writer) or the Assuwan king. The former is implied by Hoffner's reading and translation *A-BA A-BA A-B*[*I-YA*?...], "[my] great-grandfather," the latter, more tentatively, by Beckman's *A-BA A-BA A-B*[*I-ŚU*?...], "[his?] great-grandfather."

lishment included scribes of Hittite or Luwian origin, fluent in both Greek and Hittite. And it may be that the original document was in fact written in Hittite by a Hittite-speaking scribe in the Ahhiyawan king's service. Contra this, Hoffner (2009: 290–91) believes that the text "is probably a translation into Hittite of a communication between trusted bilingual emissaries at the common border between Ahhiyawan and Hittite territory. It is not a translation into Hittite made at the court of the Ahhiyawan king, but one made by the Hittite emissary and conveyed by him to the court of Hattusa and delivered together with his oral recollections of the communication from the Ahhiyawan emissary."

AhT 7

Letter from Manapa-Tarhunta of the Seha River Land to a king of Hatti (probably Muwattalli II) (CTH 191)

The main topic of what remains of this letter is the defection of a group of skilled Hittite craftsmen, dyers, to a ruler by the name of Atpa. Although Ahhiyawa is not mentioned in the preserved lines, the missive definitely belongs to our corpus, as demonstrated by the appearance of Piyamaradu, Wilusa, and Lazpa (Lesbos).

KUB 19.5 + KBo 19.79

obv.

§1

1. [*A-NA* ^{d}UTU^{ŠI} EN-*Y*]*A QÍ-BI-MA U*[*M-M*]*A* ^{m}*Ma-na-pa-*^{d}U ARAD-*KA-MA*

---

§2

2. [*ka-a-ša-kán* ŠÀ KUR]^{TI} *ḫu-u-ma-an* SIG$_5$-*in*

---

§3

3. [^{m}*Kaš-šú-ú-uš*] *ú-it* ÉRIN.MEŠ ^{KUR}*Ḫat-ti-ya ú-wa-te-et*
4. [*na-at* GIM]-*an* EGIR-*pa* ^{KUR}*Wi*$_5$-*lu-ša* GUL-*u-wa-an-zi pa-a-ir*
5. [*am-mu-uk-m*]*a iš-tar-ak-zi* GIG^{er}-*zi-ma-mu* ḪUL-*lu*^{er} GIG-*aš-mu*
6. [*me-ek-ki*] *ta-ma-aš-ša-an ḫar-zi*

---

§4

7. [^{m}*Pí-ya-m*]*a-ra-du-uš-ma-mu* GIM-*an lu-ri-ya-aḫ-ta nu-mu-kán* ^{m}*At-pa-a-an*
8. [*pí-ra-an* U]GU *ti-it-ta-nu-ut nu* ^{KUR}*La-az-pa-an* GUL-*aḫ-ta*
9. [*nu* o o ^{LÚ}]$^{.MEŠ}$*ṢA-RI-PU-TI ku-e-eš ku-e-eš am-mé-el e-še-er*
10. [*nu-uš-ši-kán ḫu*]-*u-ma-an-*⸢*du*⸣-*uš-pát an-da ḫa-an-da-ir ŠA* ^{d}UTU^{ŠI}-*ya ku-e-eš* [*e-š*]*e*[-*er na-at* o o o o o o]
11. [$^{LÚ.MEŠ}$*ṢA-R*]*I-PU-TI na-at-kán ḫu-u-ma-an-du-uš-pát an-da ḫa-an-da-ir*

§1 (obv. 1) [Thus says] Manapa-Tarhunta, your servant: Say [to His Majesty, my lord]:

§2 (obv. 2) [At the moment] everything is fine [in the land].

§3 (obv. 3–6) [Kassu] came (here) and brought the troops of Hatti. [And when] they went back to attack Wilusa, [I was] ill. My illness is terrible; the sickness has beaten me down [severely].

§4 (obv. 7–36) When Piyamaradu humbled me, he installed Atpa over me. Then he attacked Lazpa. [And] absolutely all of the dyers who belonged to me went over [to him]. Those who [belonged] to Your Majesty [were ...] dyers, and all without exception went over. [And] the household member, a waiter, [of the household of] Huha who had been appointed over the dyers arranged their defection. The dyers [of the household] of Huha made a [representation] to Atpa as follows: "We are persons subject to tribute, [and] we have come across the sea. We want [to deliver] our tribute. Siggauna may have committed a crime, but

12. [*nu ŠA* É ^{m}]*Ḫu-ḫa-aš ku-iš* ^{LÚ}AMA.A.TU LÚ $^{<\text{GIŠ}>}$BANŠUR *A-NA* $^{\text{LÚ.MEŠ}}$*ṢÉ-RI-PU-TE-kán*
13. [*an-da ú*]*-*⸢*e-ri*⸣*-ya-an-za e-eš-ta nu-kán* ⸢*a*⸣*-pu-u-uš-ša an-*⸢*da* SIxSÁ⸣*-at*
14. [*ŠA* É ^{m}]*Ḫu-ḫa-aš* $^{\text{LÚ.MEŠ}}$*ṢÉ-RI-PU-TI-*⸢*ma*⸣ *A-NA* ^{m}*At-pa-a kiš-ša-an*
15. [*ar-ku-w*]*a-ar* ⸢*i*⸣[*-e*]*-er an-za-aš-wa-an-na-aš ar-kam-ma-na-al-*⸢*li-iš*⸣
16. [*nu-wa-kán*] A.AB.BA *p*[*ár-ra*]*-an-ta ú-wa-u-en nu-wa-an-na-aš ar-kam-ma-an*
17. [*píd-da-u*]*-*⸢*e*⸣*-ni nu-wa* ⸢^{m}⸣*Ši-ig-ga-ú-na-aš wa-aš-ta-aš*
18. [*an-za-aš-ma-w*]a ⸢*Ú*⸣*-U*[*L*] *ku-*⸢*it*⸣*-ki* ⸢*i*⸣*-*[*y*]*a-u-en nu-uš-ma-aš* GIM*-an*
19. [*ar-kam-m*]*a-an* ⸢*ar*⸣*-ku-wa-a*[*r*] ⸢*i-e*⸣*-er* $^{m!}$*At-pa-a-aš-ma*<<*-wa*>>*-aš*
20. [*Ú-UL a*]*r-nu-ut ma-a-an-wa-ra*[*-aš a*]*r-ḫa tar-ni-iš-ta*
21. [^{m}*Pí-ya-ma*]*-ra-du-uš-ma*[*-aš-š*]*i*$^{!}$ ^{m}*Ši*[*-ig-ga-ú-na-a*]*n IŠ-PUR nu-uš-ši kiš-ša-an*
22. [*me-mi-iš*]*-ta tu-uk-wa* ^{d}U*-aš*$^{!}$ [*pí-y*]*a-na-it* EGIR*-pa-wa-ra-aš* ⸢*ku-wa*⸣*-at*
23. [*pí-eš-ti*] ^{m}*At-pa-a-aš-ma* GIM*-an* INIM ^{m}*P*[*í-y*]*a-ma-ra-du IŠ-ME*
24. [*na-aš*] EGIR*-pa Ú-UL pé-eš-ta k*[*i-n*]*u-na-kán* GIM*-an* ^{m}*Kaš-šú-ú-uš*
25. [*ka-a an-da*] ⸢*a*⸣*-ar-aš* ^{m}*Ku-pa-an-ta-*^{d}LA[MMA*-aš-m*]*a A-NA* ^{m}*At-pa-a IŠ-PUR*
26. [$^{\text{LÚ.MEŠ}}$*ṢA-RI-PU-T*]*I*$^{\text{ḪI.A}}$*-wa ku-e-eš ŠA* ^{d}U[TU^{ŠI}] ⸢*a*⸣*-pí-ya* *erasure*
27. [*nu-wa-ra-aš ar-ḫa*] *tar-ni*$^{!}$ *nu* $^{\text{LÚ.MEŠ}}$⸢*ṢA-RI*⸣[*-PU-TI ŠA*] DINGIR.MEŠ ⸢*ku-e*⸣*-eš ŠA* ^{d}UTU^{ŠI}
28. [*ku-e-eš e-še-er n*]*a-aš ḫu-u-ma-a*[*n-du-uš-pát ar-ḫ*]*a* [*tar-n*]*a-aš*
29. [*nu-mu* ^{m}*Ku-pa-a*]*n-ta-*^{d}[LAMMA*-aš kiš-ša-an IŠ*]*-PUR*
30. [*nu-wa i-ya-u-en*] ⸢*tu-uk*⸣[*-wa-mu ku-it TÁQ*]*-BI*
31. [*A-NA* ^{m}*At-pa-a-wa … ŠU*]*-PUR A-NA* ^{m}*At-pa-a-wa*
32. [… *AŠ*$^{?}$*-P*]*UR*
33. […] ^{LÚ}AD.KID*-ta-ra-aš-wa*<*-ra*>*-aš-*⸢*kán*⸣
34. [… *A-N*]*A* ^{m}*Ku-pa-an-ta-*^{d}LAMMA
35. [*kiš-ša-an* EGIR*-pa AŠ-PUR* …] EN*-YA*
36. [… EG]IR*-pa* GUL*-ḫu-un*
37. *traces*

we haven't done anything!" When they made their representation [concerning tribute], Atpa [did not] deport them. He would have released [them], but Piyamaradu sent [Siggauna to him, saying] as follows: "The Storm-God [has given] (them) to you—why [will you return] them?" When Atpa heard the message of Piyamaradu, he did not give [them] back. And now that Kassu has arrived [here], Kupanta-Kurunta sent to Atpa: "Release [the dyers] there who belong to [His Majesty]!" He released every [last one] of the dyers who belonged [to] the gods or to Your Majesty. [Then Kupanta-Kurunta sent to me: "We have done what] you [told me:] 'Write [to Atpa ... ' I did write] to Atpa [...] The reed-worker [...] them [... ." I wrote back as follows to] Kupanta-Kurunta: [" ...] my lord [...] I struck back [... "]

(text breaks off)

Commentary

The Seha River Land was part of the western Anatolian complex known as the Arzawa Lands. From information provided by our texts, it has been located in the northwestern segment of Anatolia, between Mira to the south and Wilusa to the north. The Seha River is probably to be identified with the Classical Caicus (modern Bakir) or the Hermus (modern Gediz). Manapa-Tarhunta, ruler of the land, first appears in Hittite records as a rebel against Hittite sovereignty at the beginning of Mursili II's reign (**AhT 1**). After Mursili accepted his submission and reinstated him on his throne, he remained a faithful Hittite subject through Mursili's reign, and the reign of his successor Muwattalli II until the latter deposed him and installed his son(?) Masturi in his place. His removal from power was due not to any apparent act of treachery or disloyalty by him, but to his failure to provide the Hittites with effective support in his region against insurrectionists like Piyamaradu. His excuse for not supporting a Hittite military expedition to Wilusa may have been genuine enough—he was no longer a young man and may well have been enfeebled by advancing years—but he was clearly becoming a serious liability to his overlord, at a time when Muwattalli needed to ensure strong and stable leadership among his western vassals as he prepared for his forthcoming campaigns in Syria. His illness may have served as the final catalyst for his removal from his throne.

We do not know precisely why Muwattalli sent a Hittite expeditionary force to Wilusa. Kassu's task as the leader of the force was perhaps to liberate it from a foreign invader, or perhaps to put down an uprising by the local population. The passage reporting the episode is too broken to be sure of this. Piyamaradu was certainly active in the region at this time, but he does not appear in the text until after Manapa-Tarhunta has apparently completed his report of the Wilusa episode. Marking this in his letter with a paragraph divider, the Hittite vassal then moves on to an account of Piyamaradu's activities against his own country, the Seha River Land. Piyamaradu inflicted a humiliating defeat upon Manapa-Tarhunta, and then appointed his son-in-law Atpa as his superior, thus the *de facto* ruler of his kingdom. He next proceeded to attack the island of Lazpa (Classical Lesbos), a dependency of the Seha River Land. A group of craftsmen from the island defected to Atpa as a consequence. We know from the Tawagalawa Letter that Atpa (there attested as the son-in-law of Piyamaradu) was the ruler of Milawata, under the overlordship of the king of Ahhiyawa, at the time the letter was composed. He may have occupied this position already at the time of Manapa-Tarhunta's letter, and if so, his installation as ruler of the Seha River Land marked a significant extension of the territory over which he held authority. It may be that in addition to the Seha River Land and its dependency Lazpa, Mira was also absorbed within this newly created kingdom of western Anatolian states, since it lay between the Seha River Land and Milawata. Kupanta-Kurunta, the current ruler of Mira, is mentioned in a fragmentary passage at the end of the surviving portion of the letter. (He also appears in the same context as Piyamaradu in KBo 19.78.) Piyamaradu may have set his sights on Wilusa as well, if the broken passage about Wilusa in Manapa-Tarhunta's letter does in fact belong to the same context as the Seha River Land episode that follows it.

We have no record of the outcome of the Hittite expedition to the region. But it evidently succeeded in reasserting Hittite authority over both Wilusa and the Seha River Land, in view of the treaty that Muwattalli drew up with Alaksandu, vassal ruler of Wilusa (Beckman 1999: 87–93), and the appointment of Masturi as Hittite vassal ruler in the Seha River Land in place of Manapa-Tarhunta. But Piyamaradu himself eluded the Hittites' grasp. On this as on other occasions, Ahhiyawa was probably the driving force behind his activities as he sought to eliminate Hittite authority throughout the western Anatolian lands, no doubt with the intention of paving the way for the establishment of Ahhiyawan dominance in the region.

AḫT 8

Letter from a Hittite official to a king of Hatti (Hattusili III?) (CTH 209.12)

KBo 2.11

obv.

§1'

1'. […]-⸢*an*⸣
2'. […]-*ša-an*[(-)]
3'. [… AN]ŠE$^{?}$.KUR$^{?}$.R[A]
4'. [… KUR$^{?}$ ^{U}]^{RU}*Ḫa-at-*⸢ *ti*⸣
5'. […]
6'. […] x-*ma* SUM$^{?}$-*aš*
7'. [… *ki*$^{?}$]-*ša-ru*
8'. [… *Š*]*A* ^{d}U *pí-ša*[*-i-ša-ap-ḫi*$^{?}$ …]
9'. [… -*i*]*š-ki*$^{!}$*-it* EN$^{!}$-*UT*$^{!}$*-TI*
10'. […] x-*YA-y*[*a*]
11'. […] GIM$^{!}$-*an pé-di Ú-UL*
12'. […]-*a ni-ni-ik-zi*
13'. […] x *IŠ-TU* EME
14'. […] x-*ya* DINGIR.MEŠ EGIR-*an*
15'. [… *ḫal*$^{?}$*-z*]*i-ya-an-du*

---

§2'

16'. [… *k*]*i*-[*i*]*t-ki* GAM-*an e-eš-du*
17'. […] x
18'. […] *ŠA* LUGAL-*UT-TÌ-YA*-[*m*]*a-na-at*
19'. […] x *im-ma ku-wa-pí-*⸢*ik-ki*⸣
20'. […] ⸢*e*⸣*-eš-ta*
21'. […] x *ku-*⸢*en*⸣*-m*[*i*]

(obv. too fragmentary for translation)

rev.

§3'

1'. [... *k*]*a*$^{?}$ x x x [...]

2'. [o] x-*ta-na-ya-ri na*-x x [...]

3'. [o ^{ḪI}]$^{\text{.A}}$-*ma-⸢kán⸣* ŠÀ KUR.KUR.MEŠ *mi-⸢i⸣-eš-ša-an* x [...]

4'. [*z*]*i-ik-ma-za ⸢ka⸣-ru-ú ka-ru-ú a-pí-ya nam-⸢ma-at*$^{?}$*-za⸣* [*ku-e* KUR.KUR. MEŠ]

5'. [*zi-ik e-e*]*p-ta nu-za a-pé-e* KUR.KUR.MEŠ EGIR *ar-ḫa da-a*[*-aš*$^{?}$]

---

§4'

6'. [^{d}UT]U^{ŠI}-*ma-mu ku-it kiš-an TÀŠ-PUR ku-it-wa e-eš-ša-at-ti ku-e-uš-⸢wa⸣* x [o] x x

7'. [*nu-wa k*]*u*$^{?}$*-e-da-ni-pí Ú-UL-za-kán* ^{URU}KÙ.BABBAR-*ši š*[*a*]*-ra-a nu-za* KASKAL ^{KUR}*Mi-iz-ri-i*

8'. [*e-ep-m*]*i nu-za* 𒑱*an-ta-ri-iš* 𒑱*ga-ši-in i-la-liš*$^{!}$*-k*[*i-i*]*z-zi*

9'. [*ki*]*-nu-un-ma*$^{!}$*-an ka-ru-ú* ZAG-*an ḫar-mi I-NA* [ITI$^{?}$.N].KAM-*kán ku-wa-pí-ik-ki*

10'. ⸢*a*⸣*-aš-šu Ú-NU-TU*$_{4}$ ^{URU}KÙ.BABBAR *kat-ta* KASKAL-*aḫ*$^{!}$-[*mi*]

---

§5'

11'. [*ŠUL-M*]*AN* LUGAL ***Aḫ***$^{!}$***-ḫi-ya-wa****-ma-mu ku-⸢it⸣ TÀŠ-PUR nu a-pa-a-at ku-it*$^{!}$ *UL I-DI*$^{!}$

12'. [^{LÚ}*ṬE*$_{4}$*-MI-Š*]*U*$^{?}$ *ma-a-an ú-da-aš ku-it-ki ma-a-an UL nu-kán ka-a-aš-ma BI-IB-RU* KÙ.BABBAR

13'. [*BI-IB-RU* KÙ.S]IG$_{17}$ *MAŠ-LU IŠ-TU ŠUL-MAN* ^{KUR}*Mi-iz-ri-i ar-ḫa ⸢da⸣-aḫ-ḫu-un*

14'. [*nu-uš-ši ke-e up*]*-⸢pa**⸣*-aḫ-ḫu-un nu-ut-ták-kán ku-it* ZAG-*na*$^{!}$ *nu a-pa-a-at up-pí*

15'. [*nu-mu* o o o o KÙ].⸢SIG$_{17}$⸣ *e-eš-zi-pát UL ku-it-ki* ⸢KÙ⸣.BABBAR-*ya-mu na*$^{!}$*-w*[*i*$_{5}$]

16'. [*ú-da-aš ma-a-an-ma-a*]*n-mu*$^{!}$ KÙ.BABBAR-*ma ú-da-an ⸢e⸣-eš-ta*

17'. [*BI-IB-RU* KÙ.BABBAR-*ma*]*-an UL a-an-ni-iš-ki-nu-⸢un⸣ ki-nu-un-ma-m*[*u* KÙ.BABBAR NU.GÁL]

---

§6'

18'. [... ^{m} ...]x-*ni-iz-zi-iš ú-it na-an ša*[- ...]

19'. [...] x *IŠ-TU* KASKAL ^{KUR}*Mi-iz-ri-i* ^{m}*Ša*[- ...]

20'. [...] x ^{URU}*Ta-at-ta-aš-ša-za ma-ni*<*-ya*>*-aḫ-ḫ*[*u-un*]

21'. [... *IŠ-TU*$^{?}$] KASKAL ^{KUR}*Mi-iz-ri-i* EGIR-*pa a-aš-z*[*i* ...]

§3' (rev. 1'–5') [...] have become favorable(?) in the lands [...] But you are already there, and furthermore he has taken back whatever lands you seized.

§4' (rev. 6'–10') In regard to the fact that you, My Majesty, wrote to me as follows: "What will you do? Which (pl.) [...]? In what place?" Aren't you up in Hattusa? [I will set out] for Egypt. The *antari* desires the *gaši*.[103] Now I have already got it successfully in hand. At some point, in the [...th month], I will dispatch fine goods from Hattusa.

§5' (rev. 11'–17') [Concerning the diplomatic gift] intended for the King of **Ahhiyawa** about which you wrote to me, because I don't know about it—whether [his messenger] brought anything or not—I have now taken a silver rhyton and [a rhyton] of refined [gold] from the diplomatic gift intended for Egypt, and I have sent [these to him]. Send me whatever seems right to you. [I] have no [gold here(?)], and [he has] not yet [brought] me silver. [If] silver [had] been brought to me, would I not have fabricated [silver rhyta]? But I now [have no silver].

§6' (rev. 18'–23') [...]nizzi came, and him [...] from the journey to Egypt [...] I governed Dattassa on my own behalf [...] remains behind [from] the journey to Egypt [...] ... When to(?) me [...]

103. Perhaps a proverbial expression.

22’. […] x-⸢*aḫ*⸣-[*t*]*a* GIM$^{!}$-*an-mu* […]
23’. […] x x *ni* x […]

---

lower edge
§7’
24’. […] x *k*[*a*$^{?}$- …]
25’. […] x-*mi* KÙ[.BABBAR$^{?}$ …]
26’. […] *I-N*[*A* …]

(remainder too fragmentary for translation)

COMMENTARY

This fragmentary passage comes from a letter dated to the thirteenth century and written by an unknown author to a king of Hatti. The passage refers to the dispatch of gifts to Egypt and to the king of Ahhiyawa, within the context of the conduct of diplomatic relations between the Hittite king and his counterparts in Egypt and Ahhiyawa. The author of the document may have been one of Hatti's royal envoys, shortly to set out for Egypt on a diplomatic mission. Gifts regularly accompanied such missions, their richness, range, and quality carefully calculated, for presentation to the ruler to whom the mission was directed. International diplomatic protocol required that gifts presented by a ruler to a foreign peer equate precisely in value to those which he had received from him. The Hittite king had informed the author of the current letter, who evidently had responsibility for such matters, that he was to send an appropriate gift to the king of Ahhiyawa. The official was apparently in some doubt as to what he should send, since he did not know whether the Ahhiyawan king's envoy who had arrived at the Hittite court had brought with him gifts for the Hittite king—the nature and value of which would have helped the official to determine what should be sent back to the Ahhiyawan king. He decided, however, to extract a silver rhyton and a gold rhyton from the gifts assembled for the pharaoh, and dispatch them to Ahhiyawa. The problem was that he had no current supply of silver or gold with which duplicates of the original items could be made. So he had requested that his king send him whatever materials he considered appropriate to make up the shortfall in the consignment for the pharaoh.

It is clear that at the time of the letter's composition, the Hittite king who was its recipient enjoyed peaceful relations with both Egypt and Ahhiyawa. This makes it likely that the man in question was Hattusili III, and that the letter is probably to be dated to the period shortly before or in the aftermath of the treaty which he concluded with the pharaoh Ramesses II in 1259. Relations between Hatti and Ahhiyawa seem also to have been peaceful, if strained, around this time, if we can so judge from the largely conciliatory tone of the so-called Tawagalawa Letter.

AhT 9

Letter from a king of Hatti(?) (perhaps Mursili II or Hattusili III) to a king of Ahhiyawa(?) (CTH 209.16)

KUB 23.95

iii

§1'

1'. […]
2'. […] ⸢URU⸣KÙ.BA[BBAR …]

---

§2'

3'. […] KAxU-*za me-mi-*⸢*aš*⸣
4'. [*nu-mu … ki-iš-ša-a*]*n TÀŠ-PUR*
5'. [… *IŠ-TU*? KUR***Aḫ-ḫ*]*i-ya-u-wa*** *ú-te-er*
6'. […] ⸢*Ú*?⸣-*UL i-ya-nu-un*
7'. […] x-*ya-at-za-kán* GAM *da-a-i*
8'. […] x x x-*ša nu* KA$_5$.A KUN-*ZU* x […]
9'. […] x-⸢*ki*⸣-*ši ku-en-zu-um-na-aš-za*
10'. […] x-*a*?-*ša-ma-aš* DINGIR.MEŠ *A-BI-ŠU*
11'. [… *-za* …] x-*na ma-la-it*
12'. […] x x ⸢UN⸣-*ši* EGIR-*an ti-ya-*⸢*at*⸣
13'. […] x ⸢*DI*⸣-*NU im-*⸢*ma*⸣-*ak-ku* EGIR-*pa*
14'. […] x *e-ep-ta PA-NI* DINGIR.MEŠ-*ma-at* GIM[-*an*]
15'. [… *am-mu-u*]*k me-ma-aḫ-ḫi-ya Ú-UL*
16'. […] *ḫar-ga-nu-ši ku-wa-at-ta še-er*
17'. [… Ḫ]UL-*aḫ-ḫu-un nam-ma-at-ta AŠ-PUR*
18'. […] x *ka-a-aš-ma ṬUP-PÍ-za* GIM-*an AŠ-PUR*

---

§3'

19'. [… *pa/ša-r*]*a-a pa-a-i na-an ar-ḫa ú-wa-*⸢*da-an-du*⸣
20'. […] x *a-uš-du ma**-*a-an-ma Ú-UL na-an ú-da-an-d*[*u*]
21'. […] UN.MEŠ-*uš le-e kat-ta* *erasure?*
22'. […] x-*zi an-za-a-aš-ma-an-na-aš* ⸢ŠEŠ*.MEŠ*⸣ SIG$_5$-*in*
23'. [… -*t*]*a*? *nam-ma da-*⸢*ma*?⸣-x x

§1' (iii 1'–2') […] Hattusa […]

§2' (iii 3'–18') The word from [your(?)] mouth […] You wrote [to me …] as follows: "[…] they brought [from] **Ahhiyawa** […] I did not do [… "] He set down […] Then the fox […] his tail.[104] […] you […] Someone from whatever place […] the gods of his father […] them […] he approved […] he stepped back to the man […] and indeed a legal dispute again […] he seized. But when before the gods they […] I will not speak […] You will ruin […] up in whatever place […] I mistreated. Furthermore I wrote to you […] I have now sent by means of a tablet.

§3' (iii 19'–23') [If(?)] he goes [up/forth], let them carry him away. […] let him see. But if not, let them bring him […] the people not down […] But we the brothers for ourselves well […] Furthermore, another(?) […]

104. Perhaps again a proverbial expression.

COMMENTARY

From §2' it is clear that this document contains the remnants of a letter that was one of a series of written communications between its author and its recipient. The surviving portion of the letter appears to deal with someone, or something, brought from Ahhiyawa to another place. There is reference to a legal dispute, and to a tablet perhaps connected with it that the writer has separately dispatched to his addressee. In the final lines of the fragment, the words "we the brothers" may indicate a peer diplomatic relationship between writer and addressee.

It is possible that like other surviving letters of the fourteenth and thirteenth centuries, this one has to do with the repatriation or extradition of Hittite subjects who have been relocated in a country outside Hittite authority. Within such a context, the letter writer is most likely a Hittite king. We may further speculate, from §2', that his addressee is a king of Ahhiyawa from whose country the Hittite subjects are to be, or have mostly been, returned. In diplomatic parlance, he is the 'brother' of the Hittite king. Hattusili III thus addresses his Ahhiyawan counterpart in the "Tawagalawa Letter" (**AhT 4**).

The circumstances of this letter may have been similar to some of those outlined in the Tawagalawa letter. Indeed, it is just conceivable that both letters refer to the same set of circumstances: Hattusili was seeking the repatriation of Hittite subjects who had been removed voluntarily or forcibly from his territory into Ahhiyawa, and above all the extradition of the Hittites' archenemy in the west Piyamaradu (if his anti-Hittite activities could not be curbed by other means). It is possible that the reference to a legal dispute and the dispatch of a tablet to the recipient, perhaps in support of the writer's claims, belong to this context. Piyamaradu may be the specific unnamed third person referred to in the letter, which may form part of the small corpus of texts that relate to his activities—activities that spanned much of the thirteenth century.

AhT 9 is perhaps a fragment of one of the first two missing tablets of the Tawagalawa Letter. But Sommer (1930: 264) considered this unlikely. As he rightly pointed out, negotiations over the exchange and repatriation of fugitives and prisoners of war were relatively common occurrences within the context of diplomatic relationships between the Bronze Age powers. A further illustration of this is a passage from Mursili II's Ten-Year Annals (**AhT 1A**), which could indeed provide another possible context for the letter. §25' of the document appears to refer to the Ahhiyawan king's surrender to Hittite custody of the Arzawan prince Piyama-Kurunta and other Arzawans who had sought refuge in Ahhiyawa. This was the response to a Hittite envoy sent by Mursili and arriving by ship, perhaps with documents on tablets of the kind referred to in **AhT 9**.

AHT 10

LETTER (CTH 209.17)

KUB 23.98

i$^{?}$

1’. […] x *a* x […]
2’. […] *ma-az-za-aš-t*[*a* …]
3’. […]-⸢*ki*⸣ *pár-ra-an-ta* […]
4’. [… *n*]*u*$^{?}$*-kán tu-uq-qa* x […]
5’. [… *-y*]*a ku-it na-*⸢*ak*⸣[- …]
6’. […] *nu-mu me-mi-an k*[*a*$^{?}$- …]
7’. […] *na-at-*⸢*kán*⸣ *A-N*[*A* …]
8’. […] ⸢*A*⸣*-NA* ŠEŠ-*YA* LUGAL ^{KUR}***A*[*ḫ*$^{?}$*-ḫi-ya-wa-*(*a*)** …]
9’. […] x-*ma*(-)*ni* ⸢*ták-šu-la-aš*⸣ […]
10’. […]-*aḫ-ḫu-un na-*⸢*at*⸣*-za-kán* […]
11’. [… -*š*/*t*]*a*$^{?}$-⸢*ma*⸣*-aš-kán* ŠEŠ-*KA* […]
12’. […] x-*kán iš-*⸢*tar*⸣[*-na*$^{?}$ …]
13’. […] x x […]

(too fragmentary for translation or commentary)

AhT 11

Offenses of the Seha River Land (Royal Edict of Tudhaliya IV?) (CTH 211.4)

This proclamation of the Great King announces and justifies the replacement of the vassal king of the Seha River Land in western Anatolia.

KUB 23.13

obv.

§1

1. [*UM-MA Ta-ba-ar-na* ^{m}*Tu-ud-ḫa-li-ya* o o o o o LUGAL.GA]L$^{?}$ KUR ^{ÍD}*Še-e-ḫa-aš* EGIR-*pa* 2-*ŠU wa-aš-*⸢*ta*⸣*-aš*
2. [o o o o o o o *ka-ru-ú-wa-an-na-aš-za A-BI A*]-*BI A-BI* ^{d}UTU$^{\check{S}I}$ *IŠ-TU* ^{GIŠ}TUKUL *UL tar-*⸢*aḫ*⸣*-ta*
3. [*nu-za A-BI A-BI* ^{d}UTU$^{\check{S}I}$ *ku-wa-p*]*í* KUR.KUR *Ar-*⸢*za*⸣-[*u-wa tar*]-*aḫ-ta an-za-a-aš-ma-wa-za IŠ-TU* ^{GIŠ}TUKUL
4. [*UL tar-aḫ-ta tar-aḫ-ta-ma-an-wa-a*]*n-na-aš-za nu-wa-aš-ši* ⸗*wa-aš-da-az-za iš-ḫu-na-aḫ-ḫu-u-en*
5. [EGIR-*an-da-ma* ^{md}U-*na-ra-du-u*]*š ku-u-ru-ri-ya-aḫ-ta nu-za-kán* LUGAL KUR ***Aḫ-ḫi-ya-u-wa*** EGIR-*pa e-ep-ta*
6. [*nu-za-kán* $^{\mathrm{NA4}}$*ḫé-gur Ḫa-a-ra-na-an* E]GIR-*pa e-ep-ta* LUGAL.GAL-*ma i-ya-an-ni-ya-nu-un*
7. [o o o o o o o o o o o ^{N}]$^{\mathrm{A4}}$*ḫé-gur Ḫa-a-ra-na-an-kán kat-ta da-aḫ-ḫu-un nu-kán* 5 *ME* ANŠE.KUR.R[A.ḪI.A]
8. [N ERÍN.MEŠ-*ya kat-ta*$^{?}$ *ú-w*]*a-te-nu-un* ^{md}U-*na-ra-du-na QA-DU* DAM.MEŠ-*ŠU*
9. [DUMU.MEŠ-*ŠU-ya I-NA* KUR ^{URU}*Ḫa-at-ti*] x *ar-nu-nu-un na-an* ^{URU}TÚL-*na* ^{d}UTU-*aš* URU-*ri* ⸢*ú-wa*⸣*-te-nu-un*

---

§2

10. [o o o o o o o *IŠ-TU* U_4-*UM* ^{m}*Ta-b*]*a-ar-na* LUGAL.[GA]L KUR-*TUM UL* ⸢*pa-it*⸣ *nu* NUMUN ^{m}⸢*Mu*⸣-[*u-wa*-UR.MAḪ]
11. [(PN) o o o o o o o o o o o LUGAL-*u*]*n i-ya-a-nu-un* [*n*]*u-uš-ši-kán* R[U$^{?}$-o-]x ANŠE.KUR.RA.[ḪI.A ÉRIN.MEŠ-*ya*]

§1 (obv. 1–9) [Thus says Tabarna Tudhaliya, Great King]: The Land of the Seha River offended once more, for the second time, (saying): "[... the great-] grandfather of His Majesty did not conquer [us earlier] by force of arms, [and when the grandfather of His Majesty] conquered the Arzawa lands, [he did not conquer] us by force of arms. [He would have conquered] us, but we eliminated the offense against him." [But afterwards, Tarhuna-radu] became hostile and relied upon the King of **Ahhiyawa**. He took refuge [on Eagle Peak]. Then I, the Great King, set out, [...], and captured Eagle Peak. I brought [down] 500 teams of chariotry [and (so many) infantrymen]. I brought Tarhuna-radu, together with his wives [and his children, to Ḫatti], and led him to Arinna, city of the Sun-Goddess.

§2 (obv. 10–12) [From the time of] Tabarna, no Great King had gone (into this) land. I made [...], descendant of [Muwa-walwi], king [there] and [imposed] upon him (the obligation to provide) chariotry [and infantry].

12. [*iš-ḫi-ya-nu-un*]

---

13. [...] x [...]

Commentary

This passage begins by providing some historical background to recent developments that had taken place in the Seha River Land. Its author, Tudhaliya IV, recalls an earlier occasion when the vassal kingdom had joined other Arzawa countries in taking up arms against Mursili II, Tudhaliya's grandfather, as recorded by Mursili in his Annals for his third and fourth years (**AhT 1A** and **1B**). Mursili had launched a punitive expedition against Manapa-Tarhunta, the Seha River Land's ruler, but had called off his attack at the last minute when Manapa-Tarhunta begged for mercy, via his mother, and repledged his allegiance to the Hittite crown. This was the first occasion on which the kingdom had "offended" against its Hittite overlord. The contrite vassal had "eliminated the offense" by his submission, and henceforth remained loyal to Hatti until he was deposed by Mursili's successor Muwattalli II, who installed Masturi (Manapa-Tarhunta's son?) in his place. The Seha River Land appears to have continued its allegiance to Hatti through the reigns of Muwattalli II, Urhi-Teshshup (Mursili III), and Hattusili III, and up to some point in the reign of Tudhaliya IV, Hattusili's son, when there was a fresh outbreak of rebellion. On this occasion, the uprising was led by a man called Tarhuna-radu, who may have unseated Masturi or seized the kingdom after his death. (We know that Masturi was still alive at the beginning of Tudhaliya's reign since he was one of the witnesses to the treaty which Tudhaliya drew up around that time with his cousin Kurunta, ruler of the land of Tarhuntassa [Beckman 1999: 114–24].)

The likelihood that Masturi died without issue may well have prompted Tarhuna-radu, apparently an upstart, to make his bid for the throne. He was encouraged in this venture by support he received from the king of Ahhiyawa. The nature of this support is not clear—was it military, political, logistical, or purely moral? Whatever its nature, it was clearly an important catalyst for the action taken by Tarhuna-radu, and demonstrates Ahhiyawa's continuing interference in western Anatolian affairs, despite any peace initiatives that Hattusili may have attempted, down into Tudhaliya's reign. Tudhaliya succeeded in crushing the rebellion, capturing its ringleader Tarhuna-radu, and deporting him and his family to the city of the Sun-Goddess of Arinna in the Hittite homeland. He then restored the vassal throne to its previous line of rulers by installing upon it a "descendant of Muwa-walwi"; the latter was the father of Manapa-Tarhunta.

It may well be that Ahhiyawan support for the rebellion finally induced Tudhaliya to force a military showdown with the Ahhiyawan regime—an action that may have resulted in the elimination of Ahhiyawa's sovereignty over Milawata, and the end of an effective Ahhiyawan political and military presence anywhere in western Anatolia.

Note that the term Tabarna/Labarna used here in reference to Tudhaliya is a traditional royal title for Hittite kings, adopted from Labarna, the name of the man most scholars believe to have been the founder of the Hittite royal dynasty.

AhT 12

Prayer of Mursili II/Muwattalli II/ Urhi-Teshshup(?) (CTH 214.12.A)

This fragmentary text seems to constitute a self-justification of the speaker, certainly a Hittite king, before the gods and thus may be classified as a prayer.

KUB 14.2

obv.

§1'

1'. _traces_

2'. DINGIR*.MEŠ*-_ma ku_⸢-_i-e_-⸣_eš_ UG*-_da_-*$^{??}$x-x […]

3'. _na-aš_ EGIR-_pa e-eš-še-er at_[- … DINGIR.MEŠ$^{?}$]

4'. _ku-u-i-e-eš_ UN.MEŠ-_an-za da-a_[-_aš_$^{?}$ …]

5'. _nu ki-iš-ša-an i-ya-nu_[-_un_ …]

6'. [_k_]_u-iš_ UN-_aš ŠA_ DINGIR^{LIM} ^{URU}[…]

7'. [_n_]_u-uš-ši-kán ŠA_ DINGIR^{LIM} _ar-kam-m_[_a-an_ … _pí-iḫ-ḫu-un_$^{?}$]

8'. _nu A-NA_ DINGIR^{LIM} _ar-kam-ma-an_ ⸢_zi_$^{?}$⸣[- …]

9'. _ku-iš-ma-za_ UN-_aš Š_[_A_] DINGIR^{LIM} _a_[_r-kam-ma-an_ …]

10'. ⸢_Ú_⸣-_UL me-em-ma-aš na-an-kán_ […]

11'. [_Ú-U_]_L u-i-iš-kán-zi_ ^{URU}[…]

12'. [o o o]-_ši a-aš-ši-iš-ki_[-_iz-zi_ …]

13'. [o$^{?}$ _ku-i-_]⸢_e_⸣-_eš_ DINGIR.MEŠ _ka-ru_-⸢_ú_⸣ […]

14'. [o o o-_m_]_a-kán ku-e-da_⸢-_aš_$^{?}$⸣ […]

15'. [o o o] _na-at nu_-⸢_u_⸣-_wa_ x […]

16'. [o o-_t_]_a-ri na-at-mu_ […]

17'. [_Ú-UL_] _ku-it-ki i-ya_[-_nu-un_ …]

rev.

1. [_n_]_u-mu ḫar-ga-an-na pa-ra-a le_[-_e tar-na-at-ti_ … _le-e_]

2. [_tar-n_]_a-at-ti_ ⸢_A-BU_⸣-_YA-ma-za at-t_[_u-uš-_ …]

---

§2'

3. _ku-it-ma-an-na A-BI-YA_ TI-_an-z_[_a e-eš-ta_ … PN$^{?}$ …]

4. [_n_]_a-aš IT-TI_ AMA-_YA ku_-⸢_it_⸣ [_ku-ru-ri-ya-aḫ-ta_$^{?}$ …]

5. [_n_]_a-an I-NA_ KUR ^{URU}**_Aḫ-ḫi-ya-w_**[**_a_**$^{?}$ … _a-ru-na-aš_]

§1' (obv. 1'–rev. 2) […] The gods who(m) … […] They again worshipped them regularly. […] the gods whom the populace took(?) […] I did as follows: [… I gave …] the contribution due to the deity to whichever person of the deity of the city [of …]. And […] the contribution to the deity […] Whatever person [… the contribution] of the deity […] did not refuse. And him/her […] they do [not] send. The city [of …] … Whichever gods formerly […] to whom […] And it(?) still […] And it(?) to me [… I] did [not] do anything […] Do not [abandon] me to destruction; [do not] abandon me [to …] But my father […] the (fore)fathers.

§2' (rev. 3–6) And while my father [was] (still) alive, [so-and-so …], and because (s)he [became hostile] to my mother, […] he dispatched him/her to the Land of **Aḫḫiyawa**, beside [the sea].

(remainder too fragmentary for translation)

6. [*t*]*a-pu-ša* ⌈KASKAL-*ši*⌉-*aḫ-ta* […]
7. *traces*
8–15. *(a single sign, mostly illegible, at the beginning of each line)*

Commentary

Since much of the right-hand side of the tablet on which this text appears is missing, its reading and the identity of the persons referred to (but not named) in it are much in doubt. Paragraph 2' appears to have contained some significant historical information, but all that survives of it is a reference to the father of the text's author in one line, a reference to his mother in the next, and following upon that the dispatch of a person to the Land of Ahhiyawa. There is general consensus among scholars that what the text is recording is the banishment of a Hittite queen to Ahhiyawa. But which queen and by whom was she banished? Connected with this, who is the author of the text? In the past, authorship has been assigned to Mursili II. If so, then the father referred to was Suppiluliuma I. We know that Suppiluliuma's first wife, Henti, was the mother of Suppiluliuma's five sons, including Mursili, but that she was subsequently supplanted by a new chief wife, the Babylonian princess who assumed the name Tawananna as a personal name. (It was otherwise used as a title for the chief consort.) The abrupt disappearance of Henti from Hittite records has led to the suggestion that Suppiluliuma removed her from the scene to make way for his new wife by banishing her to Ahhiyawa (see Bryce 2005: 159–56).

Alternatively, the person banished may have been Tawananna herself. We know from other texts that after Suppiluliuma's death, his sons and successors-in-turn Arnuwanda II and Mursili II became openly hostile to their stepmother, regarding her as a dangerously disruptive influence in the land, and Mursili charged her with the murder of his own wife. This he tells us in one of his prayers (CTH 71). He goes on to inform us that in accordance with oracular advice, he stripped Tawananna of office, but did not execute her, though the oracle had advised this too. Instead, he dismissed her from the palace and "gave her a place of residence" somewhere. We are not told its location.

There is an ominous similarity between the behavior and the fate of Mursili's stepmother and those of his second wife Danuhepa. The latter too survived her husband's death and had a tension-fraught relationship with her stepson, in this case Muwattalli II, Mursili's son and successor. The disputes between them came to a head when the king put his stepmother on trial, ostensibly for acts of profanation. She was found guilty, stripped of office, and apparently banished from the court and city. These events are reported by Muwattalli's son Urhi-Teshshup (Mursili III), who emphatically denied any involvement in them (as did his uncle and successor Hattusili III), and repeatedly prayed that he would not suffer any fallout from them: "May no evil, whatsoever, jeopardise me!" (Houwink ten Cate 1974: 132).

So if the text does refer to a banishment (and this is not entirely clear), there are at least three possible candidates: a) Suppiluliuma's first wife Henti, in which case the author of our text was Suppiluliuma's son Mursili; b) Suppiluliuma's second wife Tawananna, stripped of office by Mursili; in this case Mursili's son Muwattalli was the text's author; c) Mursili's last wife Danuhepa, stripped of office by Muwattalli; in this case the text was authored by Muwattalli's son Urhi-Teshshup.

In any of these scenarios, we should not miss the significance of Ahhiyawa being the designated place of exile. The banished person could only have been sent there by arrangement with the Ahhiyawan king, and such an arrangement implies some form of accord between Hatti and Ahhiyawa at this time. It has been suggested above (Commentary on **AhT 6**; see also Bryce 2005: 224) that a diplomatic understanding between Hatti and Ahhiyawa over territorial issues may have been reached during Muwattalli's reign, continuing perhaps through the reign of Urhi-Teshshup into that of Hattusili III. That might favor the third of the above scenarios. But we cannot rule out the first two. Henti in particular might well be reconsidered as the victim of banishment, particularly if §2' of our text refers to hostility between two women (a possibility allowed for in Beckman's reading) resulting in the banishment of one of them while the author's father was still alive. That would fit well with the scenario of the emergence of Suppiluliuma's new wife Tawananna, apparently around the same time as Henti's disappearance.

AhT 13

Memorandum(?) (CTH 214.12.B)

KUB 21.34

obv.

§1

1. [o o LUGAL$^{?}$ KUR ^{URU}***A*]*ḫ-ḫi-ya-wa***-*ma kiš*[-*an*]
2. [*me-ma-i*$^{?}$ o o *k*]*u-wa-pí ú-wa*[-*an-zi*$^{?}$]
3. [o o o o o -*l*]*i*$^{?}$-*in* [(X)$^{?}$]
4. [o o o o o o -*ma*]*r*$^{?}$-*na-aš pa-i*[*t*$^{?}$]
5. [o o o o o o o o] *u-i-*⸢*ya*⸣-[*at*$^{?}$]
6. [o o o o o o o o] x [o o o]

rev.

§2'

1'. [o o o o o] x 1 ⸢SISKUR$^{?}$⸣ *UL* ⸢*ti*$^{?}$⸣-[…]
2'. [o o o o o] x x $^{LÚ.MEŠ}$*LI-Ṭ*[*Ù-TI*]
3'. [o o o o o o o o o]-*za*$^{?}$
4'. [o o o o o o o o o] DUMU.MEŠ *EL-*⸢*LU*⸣-[*TI*]
5'. [o o o o]-*an-da nu ku-it A-NA* [o o o]
6'. [o o o] x GEŠTIN *pé-ḫu-te-er*$^{!}$
7'. [o o o] ⸢*I*⸣-*NA* KUR ^{URU}*Ḫat-ti*
8'. [o o o] URU^{LIM}.ḪI.A *ŠA* LUGAL ^{KUR}*Mi-ra-*⸢*a*⸣
9'. [o o]-x-*na-ir nu* INIM KUR^{TI}

upper edge

1. [*I-N*]*A*$^{?}$ É.GAL^{LIM} *še-ek-kán-du*
2. [*na-a*]*t-kán ta-me-en-kán-*⸢*du*⸣

§1 (obv. 1–6) [The king(?) of the Land] of **Aḫḫiyawa** [says(?)] as follows: "When they come(?) […] went(?) […] sent(?) […]"

§2' (rev. 1'–upper edge 2) […] one ritual(?), not […] hostages […] free persons […] And because to […] they brought wine […] in Hatti […] They […] the cities of the king of the Land of Mira. May the matter of the land be known [in] the palace, and may they care about(?) it (viz., the land).

COMMENTARY

Beyond noting the references to Ahhiyawa and the Land of Mira in the same context and the reference to hostages, little can be said about this document.

AhT 14

Extract from a letter(?) from a king of Hatti(?) (Tudhaliya IV?) concerning Urhi-Teshshup (CTH 214.12.C)

This piece reports on the doings of Urhi-Teshshup (Mursili III), probably after he had been driven from the throne by Hattusili III. Since it begins so abruptly, it was probably preceded by at least one earlier tablet.

KBo 16.22

obv.

1. [… *me-ma*$^{?}$]-⸢*i*$^{?}$⸣ *A-NA* ^{m}*Tal-me-*^{d}U*-up-wa*
2. [*ku-wa-pí* ^{m}*Úr-ḫi-*^{d}U*-up-aš* ^{m}*Ši-ip-pa-*LÚ*-iš-ša an-d*]*a ú-e-er nu-wa-aš-ši* ARAD.MEŠ-*ŠÚ* [GIM-*an*]
3. [*a-pí-ya Ú-UL wa-ar-re-eš-šir ki-nu-na-wa A-NA* ^{m}*Úr*]-⸢*ḫi*⸣-^{d}U*-up* LUGAL KUR ^{URU}***Aḫ-ḫi-ya-wa***
4. [*Ù* LUGAL KUR ^{URU} … *Ú-UL wa-ar*]*-re-eš-šir* ^{m}*Ši-ip-pa-*LÚ*-iš-ša*
5. [*A-NA* ^{m}*Úr-ḫi-*^{d}U*-up IŠ-PUR IŠ-TU* ^{URU} … *-w*]*a pa-ra-a e-*[*ḫ*]*u*
6. [GIM*-an-ma* ^{m}*Úr-ḫi-*^{d}U*-up-aš ke-e A-WA-TE*]^{MEŠ} *IŠ-ME nu* ^{m}*A-na-ni-pí-* *-ya-an*
7. [*A-NA* LÚ.MEŠ ^{URU}*Ḫal-la-wa ú-i-ya-at i-it-wa-ká*]*n* ^{URU}*Ḫal-la-wa pé-* *-en-ni*
8. […] *nu-wa-ra-aš* <*ni-*>*ni-in-ga-nu-ut*
9. […] x *ar-ḫa* ⁝*ḫa-aš-pa-ti*$^{!}$ *nu IŠ-*⸢*ME*⸣
10. [… ^{URU}*Ku-u*]*š-šu-úr-ri-ya pár-ra-an-*⸢*da*⸣
11. [… *A-N*]*A* LÚ.MEŠ ^{URU}*Ku-uš-šu-ri-*⸢*ya*⸣
12. [… *IŠ-PUR*$^{?}$ *A-N*]*A* $^{LÚ.MEŠ}$GAL *ŠA* ^{I7}SIG$_7$
13. […] x KUR^{TU_4} *wa-al-aḫ-*⸢*te*⸣*-en*
14. [… ERÍ]N.MEŠ ^{GIŠ}GIGIR.<MEŠ> *an-da e-ep-ta*
15. […] x *nu-wa-za-kán I-NA* ^{URU}*Ḫal*[*-la-wa*]
16. […] x*-ni pa-ra-an-da*
17. [… *-u*]*n-*⸢*na pár*⸣*-ra-an-da*
18. […]*-a-*⸢*i*⸣
19. […] x

(rev. uninscribed)

[... says(?): "When Urhi-Teshshup and Sipa-ziti] came to Talmi-Teshshup, then [just as] his subjects [at that time did not come] to his [aid, so now] the king of **Aḫḫiyawa** [and the king of ... have not] come to the aid of Urhi-Teshshup." Sipa-ziti [wrote to Urhi-Teshshup]: "Depart from [(the city of) ... !" When Urhi-Teshshup heard these words, he sent] Anani-piya [to the people of (the city of) Hallawa: "Go], drive to Hallawa, [...], and mobilize them!" [...] destroyed utterly. And he listened [...] across to (the city of) Kussurriya [...] to the people of Kussurriya [... wrote(?)] to the nobles of (the Land of) the Green River: "[...] Attack the land!" [...] assembled infantry and chariotry. [...] "To Hallawa [...] across [to ...] across [to ...] ... "

Commentary

Following Urhi-Teshshup's removal from the Hittite throne by his uncle Hattusili III, the deposed king was assigned a place of banishment in the Nuhashshi Lands in Syria. He was determined, however, to get his throne back, and in his bid to do so sought the support of both foreign kings and his former vassal rulers. We learn from other sources of approaches he made to the Babylonians and to the Assyrian king Shalmaneser I, as well as to the pharaoh Ramesses II. The Babylonians and Assyrians appear to have been sympathetic to his cause, since their kings apparently snubbed the usurper, at least early in his reign, and for a time Urhi-Teshshup was granted asylum in Egypt, where he had fled when Hattusili attempted to move him to a new place of exile. But none of the foreign rulers provided material assistance for his bid, and Ramesses eventually came down on the side of Hattusili by declaring that he was Hatti's rightful king.

From the passage above, it seems that Urhi-Teshshup had also made approaches to the king of Ahhiyawa (and to the king of another land whose name is now lost). Once again, his bid was unsuccessful. This is indicated after the reference to a visit he made to a man called Talmi-Teshshup, in company with a certain Sipa-ziti. The latter had been a loyal supporter of Urhi-Teshshup—and an implacable enemy of Hattusili as had been his father Arma-Tarhunta—throughout the conflicts between uncle and nephew which preceded Hattusili's seizure of the throne. He subsequently joined Urhi-Teshshup in exile, where he continued to work closely with him in his efforts to regain the kingship. The name Talmi-Teshshup is elsewhere attested as that of the last Hittite viceroy of Carchemish, the great-great grandson of Suppiluliuma I. His predecessor in the viceregal office had been his father Ini-Teshshup, an appointee of Hattusili, who still occupied his post during at least the early years of Tudhaliya's reign. On the assumption that the Talmi-Teshshup of our passage is the viceroy of Carchemish, our text can probably be dated to Tudhaliya's reign. This would mean that Urhi-Teshshup continued his bid to regain his throne for more than three decades—if we date his overthrow to ca. 1267 and the accession of Tudhaliya to ca. 1237. After his sojourn in Egypt (the length of which is unknown), it seems that Urhi-Teshshup returned to Syria or settled somewhere in southeastern Anatolia, where he continued to elude the man who had seized his throne.

The reference to Talmi-Teshshup in the same context as the king of Ahhiyawa is curious, if the former was in fact the viceroy of Carchemish. No doubt the reason for mentioning the two together would have been clear if we had more context. In any case, Urhi-Teshshup's approach to the Ahhiyawan king suggests that Ahhiyawa still had a significant presence in the Near Eastern world, albeit in the westernmost part of it—though its king was not willing to support a deposed ruler of Hatti who had lost his throne many years before and had failed to win support from any other foreign ruler. It may have been some time after the events recorded in this passage that Ahhiyawa lost what status and influence it had enjoyed in the Near East, perhaps as a result of one final decisive campaign by Tudhaliya against its western Anatolian territories.

AHT 15

LETTER FROM A KING OF HATTI (HATTUSILI III?) TO ANOTHER GREAT KING (CTH 214.12.D)

KUB 26.76

ii

§1'

1'. […] x(-)*e* […]

2'. […] x-*mu* $^{\text{LÚ.M[EŠ]}}$ x […]

3'. […] x $^{\text{[URU]U}}$*Kar*-⸢*ga*⸣-*miš* $^{\text{LÚ.MEŠ}}$*ṬE*$_4$-*ME* x […]

4'. [… -*š*/*t*]*a*$^?$ *ú-e-mi-ya-at ma-an-m*[*u*(-) …]

5'. […] x-⸢*da*$^?$⸣ *u-i-ya-at A-NA* ^{m}*Pí-y*[*a-ma-ra-du-ma*$^?$(-) …]

6'. [… LUGAL KUR ^{URU}*Ḫa-at*]-*ti-ma A-NA* LUGAL KUR ^{URU}*Mi-iz-ri* [*IŠ-PUR*$^?$…]

7'. […] x *A-BU*^{er}*-NI A-BI A-BI-NI nu-uš* […]

8'. […]-*za me-mi-aš an-zi*^{er}*-la-aš* […]

9'. […] x TI*-*wa-an-na-aš an-za-aš k*[*u*$^?$- …]

10'. […] x DINGIR.MEŠ KI^{TI*}*a-aš-šu wa-aš*-x […]

11'. […] x-*ma A*-[*N*]*A* LUGAL KUR ^{URU}***Aḫ-ḫi-y*[*a-wa-*(*a*)** …]

12'. […] *pa-a*-⸢*i*⸣-*mi nu-wa-mu-k*[*án** …]

13'. […] x-*mu i-ya-zi* […]

14'. *traces*

iii

§2'

1'. […] x […]

2'. […] x x x x […] x *mar š*[*a*$^?$(-) …]

3'. [… -*ḫ*]*a*$^?$*-ša-wa am-me-e*$^!$*-e*[*l* ŠE]Š$^?$-*YA* EN […]

4'. […]-*e an-da ka**-*l*[*i*$^?$-o-*t*]*a*$^?$ *nu-za* KUR.KUR.ḪI.A […]

5'. […]-*ik am-me-e-el* x x x x x-*ya-aš* KUR$^?$ […]

6'. […] x-*aš ma-a-an me-ma-an-zi* ⸢*li**⸣[-*i*]*n-ga-en*[- …]

7'. [*ma-a-an-ma*$^?$ …] ⸢*Ú*⸣-*UL me-ma-an-zi ki-nu-na* ⸢*ku*⸣-*u-un* […]

8'. […] x-*wa-mu-kán ka*-x-*iš-zi* ⸢ŠEŠ-*YA*⸣[(-) …]

9'. […] x-*ki* UN-*aš* ⸢*e*⸣-*eš-ta* ⸢*nam*$^?$-*ma*$^?$-*kán*$^?$⸣ […]

10'. [… *m*]*a-a-an* Ù^{TU_4} *a*-⸢*uš-ta*⸣ x x […]

§1' (ii) […] messengers [of(?)] Carchemish […] he met. If to(?) me […] he sent […] to Piyamaradu(?) [… the King of Hatti wrote(?)] to the King of Egypt: "[…] our fathers and our grandfathers. And them […] the matter, our […] the healthy one to(?) us [… may] the Gods of the Earth favorably […] to the King of **Ahhiyawa** […] I will go. Then to(?) me […] he will do for(?) me […]"

§2' (iii 1'–14') ["…] my brother, lord of […"] he …, and the lands for himself […] my … […] If they speak, the oath [… If …] they do not speak. Now this […] "He … to me. My brother […"] he was a human. Furthermore […] If he had a dream […] hostility, his father … […] he continues to seek […] the King of **Ahhiyawa** to me […] I will write(?) [to the King] of Egypt.

11'. [… *k*]*u-ru-ur A-*^{er}*BI-ŠU pí*^{er}-x x x […]
12'. […]-*an nu-u-wa ša-an-*⸢*ḫi-iš-ki*⸣*-i*[*z***-zi* …]
13'. […] *nu-mu* LUGAL KUR ^{URU}⸢***Aḫ-ḫi***⸣***-ya-w*[*a-*(*a*)** …]
14'. [… *A-NA* LUGAL KUR ^{UR}]^{U} ^{er}*Mi-iz*^{er}*-ri* x$^{?}$ ⸢*ḫa*⸣*-at-*⸢*ra-a*$^{?}$⸣[*-mi* …]

--- [a]

§3'
15'. [… -*ḫ*]*a*$^{?}$*-ap-ra-*x ⸢*e-eš*⸣*-ta a*[- …]
16'. […] x *i-ya-mi nu*$^{?}$*-mu*$^{?}$ ŠEŠ-*Y*[*A*$^{?}$ …]
17'. […]-*a*$^{?}$ *ša*-x […]
18'. *traces*

[a] So photo.

§3' (iii 15'–18') He was ... [...] I will do, and to me, my brother, [...]

Commentary

This letter is too fragmentary for any attempt at reconstruction of its contents. It was possibly written by Hattusili III within the context of his attempts to win recognition from foreign rulers as the rightful king of Hatti and to secure their cooperation in ending the activities of particular individuals opposed to his regime. The author refers to a letter which he wrote to the king of Egypt, perhaps one of the series of communications exchanged between Hattusili and Ramesses II, a number of which had to do with Hattusili's efforts to have Urhi-Teshshup extradited from Egypt. The author also refers to his communications with the king of Ahhiyawa, and to Piyamaradu, who long acted as an agent of Ahhiyawan interests in the west. Presumably the reference to Piyamaradu was a hostile one and the Hittite king was seeking support from his peers against him. But without more text, it is impossible to determine the reason for the references to these kings in the same passage, the specific reason for mentioning Piyamaradu here, or the reason for the appearance of Carchemish in this passage.

AHT 16

FRAGMENT (CTH 214.12.E)

KBo 19.83

obv.?

1'. […] x
2'. [… URU*Ḫa-a*]*t-ti*
3'. […]

4'. […]-*en*
5'. [… KUR URU***A*]***ḫ-ḫi-ya-u-wa***
6'. […] x-*kán*
7'. [… *a*]*r*?-*nu-wa-an-te-eš*
8'. […] *ar-ḫa*
9'. [… -*y*]*a-aš*

rev.?

1'. […]-*aš*?
2'. […]
3'. […] x x

(too fragmentary for translation or commentary)

AhT 17

Fragment (CTH 214.12.F)

KUB 31.30

§1' 1'. *nu* LUGAL KUR URU*Me-r*[*a-a* ...]

---

§2' 2'. *nu* LUGAL ⌈KUR ***Aḫ***⌉***-ḫi-ya-wa***[***-(a)*** ...]

---

§3' 3'. [*nu* LUGAL KUR] x x-*ma* [...]

(§1') Then the king of Mira [...]; (§2') then the King of **Ahhiyawa** [...]; (§3') [then the king of] ... [...].

Commentary

There is nothing to note here beyond the reference to the king of Mira and the king of Ahhiyawa in the same passage. As we mentioned earlier (commentary on **AhT 5**), the land of Mira lay immediately to the north of Millawanda, which from the late-fourteenth or early-thirteenth century had come under the control of the king of Ahhiyawa. The known kings of Mira in the thirteenth century are a) Kupanta-Kurunta, appointed by Mursili II and still alive and active in the 1260s, as indicated by a letter Ramesses wrote to him in response to one from him regarding the kingship of Hatti; b) Tarkasnawa, the last king of Mira, who served under Tudhaliya IV as a kind of regional overlord in the west; and c) Tarkasnawa's father Alantalli(?) (see Hawkins, 1998: 18), who was hostile to the Hittites and had seized Hittite frontier territories.

AHT 18

"BOUNDARY" LIST(?). REIGN OF HATTUSILI III OR TUDHALIYA IV(?) (CTH 214.16)

KUB 31.29

obv.

§1' 1'.[… Z]AG-*m*[*a* …]

§2' 2'.[…] ZAG-*ma* ⸢*ku*⸣-*i*[*š* …]

§3' 3'.[… LU]GAL? ZAG *ku-iš* […]

§4'. 4'.[… KUR] URUdU-*aš-ša-ma* […]

§5' 5'.[… KUR] URU*Me-ra-a-ma* x […]

§6' 6'.[…] KUR URU***Aḫ-ḫi-ya-*⸢*wa*⸣*-a*** […]

§7' 7'.[…] KUR ⸢URU⸣ x x […]

§8' 8'.[…] ⸢KUR?⸣ x […]

(§1') […] border […] (§2') […] border which […] (§3') […] the king(?). The border which […] (§4') [… the land] of Tarhuntassa […] (§5') [… the land] of Mira […] (§6') […] the land of **Ahhiyawa** […] (§7') […] the land of … […] (§8') […] the land [of …].

COMMENTARY

The references to borders in this text followed by references to the lands of Tarhuntassa, Mira, and Ahhiyawa, plus other lands whose names are now lost, may indicate that we have here a fragment of a document that defines the boundaries between a number of kingdoms of western and southern Anatolia. That Ahhiyawan-controlled territory in western Anatolia bordered on the kingdom of Mira can be inferred from the fact that a king or kings of Ahhiyawa exercised for a time sovereignty over the land of Millawanda, which lay directly south of Mira. The kingdom of Tarhuntassa lay further to the southeast, extending through the regions called Pamphylia and Cilicia in Classical sources (and perhaps extending as far north as Classical Lycaonia). Clearly, Tarhuntassa shared frontiers with neither Mira nor Ahhiyawa, so that if the document in its complete form provided a comprehensive list of lands and their boundaries in western and southern Anatolia, then the names missing from it must have been those of countries that lay in between. But the nature of the document and the significance of the list that it contains remain matters for conjecture (see most recently Heinhold-Krahmer 2007).

Ahhiyawa's inclusion in the text along with the Anatolian kingdoms of Tarhuntassa and Mira may indicate that Ahhiyawa still controlled territory in western Anatolia at the time the document was drawn up, and if so the document should be dated some time before the loss of this sovereignty during Tudhaliya IV's reign. This of course involves the assumption that all the countries listed in the document—and only three names survive—were Anatolian, or had territories in Anatolia. It is conceivable that foreign countries were included as well. If so, the nature of the document may have been quite different to what we have suggested.

AhT 19

Inventory (CTH 243.6)

An inventory of the contents of a storeroom in the palace, this listing includes some exotic goods, including a special type of copper vessel of Ahhiyawan type or manufacture.

KBo 18.181

obv.

§1

1. [2 T]ÚG GAL ŠÀ.BA 1 *Ḫ̮A-ŠÁR-TI* 1 BABBAR ⸢3 ^{TÚG}⸣*maš-ši-aš* ŠÀ.BA 1 ZA.GÌN 2 LÍL-*aš*
2. ⸢9⸣ TÚG.GÚ *Ḫ̮UR-RI ti-ya-la-an* ŠÀ.BA 2 SIG 1 GAD *ŠU-UḪ̮-RU* 2 GAD SIG 1 *a-*⸢*du-up-li*⸣ x-*bu*?
3. 1 *ka-pí-it-ta-šàm-na* 3 TÚG.GÚ *Ḫ̮UR-RI i-la*-na-aš* ⸢ŠÀ.BA 2⸣ *Ḫ̮AŠ-MAN-NI* 1 LÍL-*aš*
4. 7 TÚG.GÚ *Ḫ̮UR-RI* ŠÀ.BA 2 *MAŠ-LU* DIB-*an* 1 *MAŠ-*⸢*LU*⸣ x [o o o o o o] ⸢5⸣ TÚG.GAB ŠÀ.B[A 2 o o] ⸢LÍL⸣ 3 GAD SIG
5. 4 ^{TÚG}ÍB.LAL ŠÀ.BA 2 *MAŠ-LU* 2 GAD 7 TÚG [o o o o o o o o N TÚ]G? TUR
6. 3 ^{TÚG}E.ÍB.⸢GÍR⸣ ŠÀ.BA 2 SA$_5$ 1 GAD 5 T[ÚG o o ŠÀ.BA 4 o o o o] ⸢1? ZA.GÌN⸣
7. 2 ^{TÚG}SAG.DUL 2 ^{TÚG}*MAR-ŠUM* SAG[.DUL …]
8. 1 ^{TÚG}*še-pa-ḫ̮i-iš* 1 TÚG.GÚ *Ḫ̮UR-R*[*I* …]
9. 2 ^{TÚG}SAG.DUL SÍG GE$_6$ ŠÀ.B[A …]
10. 2 ^{TÚG}*MAR-ŠUM* ZA.GÌN 3 TÚG […]

---

§2

11. *traces*
12. [N TÚG].⸢GÚ⸣ [*Ḫ̮UR-RI* …]
13. 1 GAD *ŠU-UḪ̮-RU* 1 GAD x […]
14. 2 [TÚ]G? [o]-*pát* 2 ^{TÚG}*tar-r*[*i-ya-na-liš* …]
15. *A-NA LI-U*$_5$ *i-pu-ra-u*[*-aš* …]
16. 2 URUDU *wa-ar-pu-aš* 2 UR[UDU? …]

§1 (obv. 1–10) [2] large garments, among them 1 green and 1 white; 3 waist-bands, among them 1 blue and 2 of natural color; 9 *tiyala* Hurrian shirts, among them 2 fine, 1 of plain linen, and 2 of fine linen; 1 … sash; 1 *kapittašamna*; 3 flounced(?) Hurrian shirts, among them 2 blue-green and 1 of natural color; 7 Hurrian shirts, among them 2 trimmed and gathered, 1 trimmed […]; 5 "breast cloths," among them 2 of natural color and 3 of fine linen; 4 tunics, among them 2 trimmed and 2 of linen; 7 […] garments; [… N] small garments; 3 dagger belts, among them 2 red and 1 of linen; 5 [… garments, among them 4 …] and 1 blue; 2 scarves and 2 cords for scarves; […]; 1 herdsman's garment; 1 Hurrian shirt; […]; 2 scarves of black wool, among them […]; 2 blue straps; 3 […] garments.

§2 (obv. 11–17) [… N Hurrian] shirts […]; 1 of plain linen and 1 of […] linen; […]; 2 […] garments, 2 garments of third quality; […]—(these are listed) on the record of booty […]; 2 copper bath tubs; 2 copper(?) […]; <N> Watarma kilims. In [the possession of …].

17. <N> ^{TÚG}*pár-na-aš wa-tar-ma-aš*<*-ši*$^{?}$> *Š*[*A* ŠU ^{m} …]

---

§3

18. 3 TÚG GAL ŠÀ.BA 2 *ḪAŠ-MAN-NI* 1 ⸢ZA⸣.G[ÌN …]
19. 12$^{!}$ TÚG SIG ŠÀ.BA 7 GAD *nu* 1 ZA.GÌN 4 BABBAR […]
20. ŠÀ.BA 1 *ka-pí-ta-šàm-na* 3 *ŠU-UḪ-RU* GAD ⸢1$^{?}$⸣ […]
21. 5 TÚG.GÚ *ḪUR-RI i-la*$^{!}$*-na-aš* ŠÀ.BA 3 *ḪAŠ-MAN-NI* ⸢2 ZA⸣[.GÌN …]
22. 4 TÚG.GÚ *ḪUR-RI* BABBAR ŠÀ.BA 1 *MAŠ-LU* DIB-*an* 1 *MAŠ-LU* BABBAR [2 …]
23. 3 ^{TÚG}SAG.DUL ŠÀ.BA 1 BABBAR$^{!?}$ 1 ^{TÚG}*MAR-ŠUM* SAG.DU[L …]
24. ⸢5⸣ ^{TÚG}ÍB.LAL ŠÀ.BA 3 *MAŠ-LU* 2 GAD 5 ^{TÚG}E.Í[B …]
25. 2 ^{TÚG}E.ÍB GÍR ŠÀ.BA 1 SA$_5$ 1 GAD 6 TÚG x […]
26. ⸢3⸣ ^{TÚG}BAR.DUL$_5$ ŠÀ.BA 2 ZA.GÌN 1 *ḪAŠ-MAN-NI* 6 TÚG GAD […]
27. [3 ^{T}]^{ÚG}*MAR-ŠUM* ŠÀ.BA 2 *ḪAŠ-MAN-NI* 1 ZA.GÌN 7 ⸢TÚG⸣ […]
28. [N T]ÚG.GÚ *ḪUR-RI še-pa-ḫi-ya-aš* […]
29. [N] TÚG.GÚ *ḪUR-RI tab-ri-aš ti-ya-*⸢*la*⸣[*-an* …]
30. [N] ^{TÚG}SAG.DUL GEŠTU LÍL-*aš* 2 ^{TÚG}*MAR*[*-ŠUM* …]
31. ⸢N⸣ ^{TÚG}BAR.DUL$_5$ LÍL-*aš* 2 ^{TÚG}GAD.DAM LÍL[*-aš* …]
32. ⸢m⸣[o o] x-*nu-uš* ^{SISKUR}*pu*[- …]

rev.

§4'

1'. [o o o o o N *l*]*a-*⸢*ku-ša*⸣[*-a*]*n-za-*⸢*ni*⸣[- …]
2'. [o o o o o] x ^{GIŠ}TÚG GÌR ZU$_9$ *ma-*x[- …]

---

§5'

3'. [o o o o o]*-za* ŠÀ.BA 1 GAD 4 ^{TÚG}*ta-ri-y*[*a-na-liš* …]
4'. [o o N ^{TÚG}*še-p*]*a-ḫi-iš* ŠÀ.BA 2 GAD 4 TÚG x […]
5'. [o o o 1$^{?}$ ^{GIŠ}*k*]*ar-na-ša-aš* GAM-*an* SUD-*u-aš* […]
6'. [o o 1$^{?}$ ^{GIŠ}*kar-n*]*a-aš-ša* 1 ^{GIŠ}GÌR.GUB […]
7'. [o o o o o *-l*]*u kar-na-ša* BABBAR-*aš*

---

§6'

8'. [o o o o o] 3 ^{TÚG}*tar-ri-ya-na-liš* x x […]
9'. [N *la-ak-ku*]*-ša-an-za-ni-iš MA-YA*[*-LI* …][105]
10'. [*ŠA* ŠU] ^{m}*At-ta-a*

---

105. This line of text is followed by a pair of wavy lines.

§3 (obv. 18–32) 3 large garments, among them 2 blue-green and 1 [blue; ...]; 12(!) fine garments, among them 7 of linen—and 1 blue and 4 white [are ...; N ...], among them 1 *kapittašamna*, 3 of plain linen, 1(?) [...]; 5 flounced(?) Hurrian shirts, among them 3 blue-green and 2 blue; [...]; 4 white Hurrian shirts, among them 1 trimmed and gathered, 1 trimmed in white, [and 2 ...]; 3 scarves, among them 1 white; 1 cord for a scarf; [...]; 5 tunics, among them 3 trimmed and 2 of linen; 5 belts [...]; 2 dagger belts, among them 1 red and 1 of linen; 6 [...] garments; 3 ...-garments, among them 2 blue and 1 blue-green; 6 linen garments [... ; 3] straps, among them 2 blue-green and 1 blue; 7 [...] garments; [N] Hurrian shirts in herdsman style; [... ; N] *tiyala* Hurrian shirts (for wearing on) the throne(?) [... ; N] scarves covering the ear, of natural color; 2 straps [...]; N ...-garments of natural color; 2 pairs of leggings of natural color; [...] Responsibility of(?) [...]nu, (for the) *pu*[...]-offering.

(gap)

§4' (rev. 1'–2') [... N] (bed) sheet(s); [...] of boxwood, with ivory feet [...]

§5' (rev. 3'–7') [...], among them 1 of linen and 4 of third quality; [... N] herdsman's garments, among them 2 of linen; 4 [...] garments; [... ; 1(?) wooden] chair, tapered below; [... 1(?) wooden] chair; 1 wooden footstool; [...] a white chair.

§6' (rev. 8'–10') [...] 3 garments of third quality; [... ; N] bed sheet(s) [... In the possession] of Atta.

---

§7'

11'. [N TÚG GAL] ⌈N⌉ ^{TÚG}*maš-ši-aš* 8 TÚG.GÚ *Ḫur-⌈ri⌉* GAD *ti-y*[*a-la-an* …]

12'. [ŠÀ.BA N] *ka-⌈pí⌉-ta-šàm*$^{!}$*-na* 2 *tap-pa-aš-pa* 1 x […]

13'. [o o o] 3 ^{TÚG}⌈ÍB⌉.LAL GAD 7 TÚG.GAB ŠÀ.BA 3 SI[G 4 …]

14'. [o o] x ŠÀ.BA 2 *a-du-up-li* GAD *ti-ya-la-an* […]

15'. [N ^{TÚG}*k*]*u-re-eš-šar* ŠÀ.BA 2 GAL 7 ⌈TÚG⌉ […]

16'. [N ^{TÚG}B]AR.DUL$_5$ 8 ^{TÚG}GAD.DAM 1 TÚG x […]

17'. [N GAD] ⌈*ar*⌉*-ru-um-ma-aš* 2 GAD *a*-x[- …]

18'. [N GA]D $^{\langle\text{GIŠ}\rangle}$*ḫa-ap-ša-al-li*[*-ya-aš* …]

19'. [N GAD] ⌈EGIR$^{!}$⌉ *ar-ḫa* S[UD*-u-aš* …]

20'. [o o] x 1 ⌈GAD$^{?}$⌉ […]

21'. […] x [o] x x […]

22'. […] x ⌈2 ^{TÚG}*tar*⌉*-ri-ya-na-liš* 1 […]

23'. 1 ^{TÚG}*la-ku-ša-an-za-ni-iš* 1 ^{GIŠ}N[Á …]

24'. <1$^{?}$> $^{\text{TÚG!}}$*pár-na-aš tab-ri-aš*

---

§8'

25'. 1 GAD EGIR *ar-ḫa* SUD*-u-aš* 1 GAD <*ar*>-⌈*ru*⌉*-um-ma-aš* 2 [GAD …]

26'. 4 GAD *an-da dam-ma-aš-šu-aš* 2 GAD *kar-ta-u-aš* 2 ⌈GAD⌉ […]

27'. ⌈3⌉ GAD IGI ŠÀ.BA 2 LÚ.SAG 3 GAD *gi-nu-wa-aš* […]

28'. [N G]AD *ta-ni-pu-ú-⌈liš⌉* 1 GAD ^{GIŠ}ŠÚ.A 1 GAD ^{GIŠ}BAN[ŠUR …]

29'. [N o]*-na-a-aš* KÙ.BABBAR 1 [^{GIŠ}]GA.ZUM ZU$_9$ AM.SI

30'. [*A-NA LI*]*-U*$_5$ *i-pu-r*[*a-u*]*-aš* 6 URUDU *wa-ar-pu-aš*

31'. [N o o] AN.BAR 1 ^{URUDU}⌈NÍG.ŠU⌉.LUḪ.ḪA AN.BAR

upper edge

32'. [N … Š]À.BA 1 AN.BAR 1 $^{\text{URUDU DUG}}$SILÀ.ŠU.DUḪ.A AN.BAR

33'. […1$^{?}$] ^{URUDU}ŠU.TÚG.LÁ ^{KUR}***Aḫ-ḫi-ya-u-wa-a*** 1 URUDU UGU *la-ḫu-aš*

34'. *ŠA* ŠU ^{m}*A-pal-lu-ú* 1 ^{URUDU}ÚTUL ^{KUR}*Mi-iz-⌈ri⌉*

§7' (rev. 11'–24') [N large garments]; N waistbands; 8 *tiyala* Hurrian shirts; [... , among them N] *kapittašamna* and 2 *tappašpa*; 1 [...]; 3 linen tunics; 7 "breast cloths," among them 3 fine [and 4 ... ; ...], among them 2 *tiyala* linen sashes; [... ; N] cowls, among them 2 large; 1 [...] garment; [N linen] wash-cloths; 2 linen [... ; N] linens for the footstool; [N ...] linen(s) "for pulling away"; [...] 1 linen [...]; 2 garments of third quality; 1 [...]; 1 (bed) sheet; 1 [...] bed; 1 kilim for the throne.

§8' (rev. 25'–34') 1 linen "for pulling away"; 1 washcloth; 2 [linens for ...]; 4 linens "for pressing in"; 2 linens for cutting; 2 linens [for ...]; 3 linens for the face(?), among them 2 for the eunuchs; 3 linen napkins; [... ; N] *tani-puli* linens; one linen chair covering; one linen tablecloth; [... N] ... of silver; 1 comb of ivory—(these are listed) [on] the record of booty; 6 copper bath tubs; [N ...] of iron; 1 iron basin for hand-washing; [N...], among them 1 of iron; 1 iron goblet for the cupbearer; [... 1(?)] copper ...-vessel from **Ahhiyawa**[106]; 1 copper vessel for pouring out; 1 copper pot from Egypt. In the possession of Apallu.

COMMENTARY

As Cline (1994) has demonstrated, the evidence we have for cultural or commercial contacts between the Late Bronze Age Greek-Aegean and the Hittite worlds is extremely limited. Cline notes that archaeological investigations have produced only a handful of artifacts imported from Late Bronze Age Anatolia into the Aegean world, and Aegean imports into Anatolia, while more plentiful, are confined almost entirely to Anatolia's western and southern coasts. Written

106. Or: in the style of Ahhiyawa.

evidence for such contacts is even sparser, indeed almost nonexistent. For this reason, the reference in this inventory text to a copper vessel from Ahhiyawa, or a vessel of Ahhiyawan type, among a list of exotic items recorded in the palace archives is worth mentioning. But it is otherwise of little significance. We have no idea how the item was acquired—whether through trade, as a gift perhaps presented to the palace by a traveller returning from the west, or by other means. It may not in fact have been of Ahhiyawan/Greek origin, but rather an item produced locally, or in western Anatolia, inspired by an original Greek design.

For the possibility that contacts other than political or military were in fact more frequent than is indicated in either the written or the archaeological evidence, see Bryce 2003b.

AhT 20

Oracle Report (CTH 570.1)

The Hittites believed that most unfortunate occurrences in their world were manifestations of the displeasure of one or more deities angered by human misbehavior, negligence, or active practice of the arts of black magic. In order to determine the precise cause of divine chastisement, Hittite diviners employed a number of techniques: most frequently extispicy (examination of the entrails of a sacrificed sheep or bird, e.g., AhT 20, §§3′, 52′), augury (observation of the flight of birds over a demarcated area, e.g., AhT 20, §18′), and the little-understood "lot" oracle in which various persons, concrete and abstract nouns are said to act upon one another (e.g., **AhT 23**, §6′).

The practitioners left meticulous records of their research, which was structured as a series of binary alternatives. In these reports a sequence of yes-or-no questions is posed and each time the expert arbitrarily stipulates whether he or she will understand a positive or negative result as a confirmation. That is, a "positive" result (in terms of the internal logic of the system of divination) to an inquiry requesting a "negative" outcome would be taken as a "no." The investigation proceeds by a process of elimination until finally the deity in question provides a "yes" to the query, "Is there anything else bothering you?"

KUB 5.6 + KUB 18.54 + KBo 53.103 (+) KUB 50.123

§1'
i
1'. […] x x x

---

§2'
2'. [… *I*]*T-TI* ^{d}UTU^{ŠI}-*ma-aš*
3'. […] x-*ši* BAR-*ri še-er*
4'. [… *zi a-r*]*i*? ⌈10?⌉ ^{ŠÀ}*TIR* SIG_5
5'. [… *ka-ru*]-*ú pa-ra-a* ⌈SUM⌉-*ir*

---

§§1'–2' (i 1'–5') *(too fragmentary for translation)*

§3'

6'. [^{d}*Iš-ḫa-ra*?]-*aš*? *ku-iš* SIxSÁ-*at na-aš-*⸢*kán*⸣ ŠÀ É.DINGIR^{LIM} SIxSÁ-*at*

7'. [ŠÀ É.ŠÀ?] ⸢DINGIR⸣^{LIM}-*ya-aš* SIxSÁ-*at nu-kán* ŠÀ É.DINGIR^{LIM} *wa-aš-ku-i-e-eš ú-e-mi-ir*

8'. [*na-aš*] ⸢*ka-ru*⸣-*ú* EGIR-*pa* SIG$_5$-*ya-aḫ-ḫi-ir iš-ḫi-ú-ul-la-za ŠA* ^{f}*Mi-iz-zu-ul-la*

9'. ⸢*i-wa-ar mar*⸣-*ki-ya-at nu iš-ḫi-ú-ul ŠA* ^{URU}*Aš-ta-ta ša-an-aḫ-ta*

10'. *nu a-píd-da še-er TE*^{MEŠ} *pu-u-ra-mi-im-ma ER-kir* IGI-*zi TE*^{MEŠ}

11'. ^{GIŠ}ŠÚ.A-*ḫi* ZAG-*an nu-uš-ši pu-u-ma-ri-iš pí-ra-an* EGIR-*pa* NU.SIG$_5$

erasure

12'. EGIR-*zi TE*^{MEŠ} *ni-eš-kán* ZAG-*na* GÙB-*la pí-iš-ši-ya-at še-er-ma-aš-ši*

13'. *a-dam-ta-ḫi-iš* GÙB-*la-za* RA^{IṢ} 10 ^{ŠÀ}*TIR* SIG$_5$ *IŠ*-[-*T*]*U* ^{MUNUS}ŠU.GI-*ya* NU.SIG$_5$

---

§4'

14'. *zi-la-aš-ma TE*^{MEŠ} *pu-ra-mi-ma* IGI-*zi TE*$^{ME<Š>}$ SIG$_5$-*ru* EGIR-*ma* ⸢NU.SIG$_5$⸣-*du* IGI-*zi TE*^{MEŠ} *ni ši ta ke-ti* ZAG[-*na*] GÙB-*la-za* RA^{IṢ}

15'. 10 ^{ŠÀ}*TIR* SIG$_5$ EGIR-*zi TE*^{MEŠ} 8 ^{ŠÀ}*TIR* NU.SIG$_5$ *I*[*Š-T*]*U* ^{MUNUS}ŠU.GI-*ma*

16'. KIN 3-*ŠÚ* SIG$_5$

---

§5'

17'. *pa-a-an-zi* DINGIR^{LUM} *ŠA* ^{URU}*Aš-ta-ta i-wa-ar e-eš-šu-wa*!-*an*! ⸢*ti*⸣-*an-zi*

18'. *ma-a-an-ma zi-la-du-wa* DINGIR^{LUM} *ŠA* ^{f}*Mi-iz-zu-ul-la i-wa-ar*

19'. *Ú-UL ku-it-ki ša-an-aḫ-ti nu IŠ-TU TE*^{MEŠ} NU.SIG$_5$<-*du*> KIN-*ya* NU.SIG$_5$

---

§6'

20'. *A-NA* DINGIR^{LIM} *ku-it iš-ḫi-ú-ul ŠA* LÚ ^{URU}*Aš-ta-ta i-wa-ar* SIG$_5$-*at*

21'. *nu* LÚ ^{URU}*Aš-ta-ta ku-iš* 1 EZEN *ḫar-pí-ya-aš* 1 EZEN *ŠA* ITI.10.⸢KAM⸣ *IQ-BI*

22'. *na-at IŠ-TU ṬUP-PÍ ma-aḫ-ḫa-an a-ni-ya-an-te-eš na-aš QA-TAM-MA*

23'. *e-eš-šu-wa-an ti-i-ya-an-zi ŠA* ^{f}*Mi-iz-zu-ul-la-ya i-wa-ar ku-it*

24'. *iš-ḫi-ú-ul ke-e-da-aš A-NA* SISKUR.ḪI.A *an-da* SIxSÁ-*at nu-kán ma-a-an* DINGIR^{LUM}

25'. EZEN *a-ya-a-ri ke-e-da-aš A-NA* EZEN.ḪI.A *ŠA* ^{f}*Mi-iz-zu-ul-la*

26'. *i-wa-ar an-da ša-an-aḫ-ta nu* SIxSÁ-*at*

---

§3' (i 6'–13') (In respect to the fact that) [the deity Ishhara(?)] was identified by oracle (as the source of the illness of His Majesty), in particular in her temple, and most particularly [in her cella(?)]—transgressions have been uncovered in the temple, [and] they have already rectified [them]. Have you, (O deity), rejected the regimen in the style of (the priestess) Mezzulla and sought the regimen in the style of the city of Ashtata? They performed *puramimma*-extispicies about this. First extispicy: 'throne' on the right and *pumari* in front and behind it. Result: unfavorable. Second extispicy: *nipašuri* (flap of the liver?) displaced to the right and the left, and *adamtaḫiš* striped to the left on top of it; ten intestinal coils. Result: favorable. (Checked) by the Old Woman: unfavorable.

§4' (i 14'–16') Prognostication by means of *puramimma*-extispicies: Let the first extispicy be favorable and the second unfavorable. First extispicy: *nipašuri*, *šintaḫi* ('emplacement'), *tanani* ('strength'; lower ridge of the liver?), *keldi* ('well-being'; pancreas?) striped to the left; ten intestinal coils. Result: favorable. Second extispicy: eight intestinal coils. Result: unfavorable. (Checked) by the Old Woman three times by lot oracle: favorable.

§5' (i 17'–19') They proceed: They will begin to worship the deity in the style of Ashtata. But if in future, O deity, you do not desire anything in the style of Mezzulla, then (let) the extispicy (be) unfavorable and the lot oracle unfavorable.

§6' (i 20'–26') Because the regimen in the style of the man of Ashtata was established by oracle, and the man of Ashtata mentioned one harvest festival (lit. 'of the grain pile') and one festival in the tenth month, they will begin to celebrate them as they are set down on the tablet. Because the regimen in the style of Mezzulla was (also) established for these festivals, whether you, O deity, among these festivals desired an *ayari*-festival in the style of Mezzulla was established by oracle.

§7'

27'. *nu me-na-aḫ-ḫa-an-ta A-NA* 2 EZEN.MEŠ *ŠA* ^{URU}*Aš-ta-ta Ù A-NA* EZEN

28'. *ŠA* ^{f}*Mi-iz-zu-ul-la i-wa-ar ḫa-an-za ap-pa-an-na-aš TE*^{MEŠ} *ER-kir*

29'. IGI-*zi TE*^{MEŠ} *ni ši ta ke* GÙB-*la-za* RA^{IṢ} SIG$_5$ EGIR-*zi TE*^{MEŠ}

30'. *ni ši* ^{ŠÀ}*TIR*$^{ḪI.A}$ *ḫi-ri-iḫ-ḫi-iš ta-a-li-in tu-nu-ta-me-et-ta* NU.SIG$_5$

---

§8'

31'. *A-NA* DINGIR^{LIM} *ma-al-du-wa-ar ŠA* ^{d}UTU^{ŠI} SIxSÁ-*at nu* 1 GU$_4$ 46 UDU-*ya* SIxSÁ-*at*

32'. *nu-za-kán ka-ru-ú ma-al-ta-aš ma-aḫ-ḫa-an-ma* ^{d}UTU^{ŠI} SIG$_5$-*ri*

33'. *na-at pí-i-ya-an-zi* ^{erasure}

---

§9'

34'. *A-NA* DINGIR^{LIM} *ŠA* ^{f}*Mi-iz-zu-ul-la i-wa-ar kar-tim-mi-ya-ad-du-uš*

35'. *še-er ar-ḫa da-an-zi nam-ma-kán* ⸢^{d}UTU^{ŠI}⸣ *A-NA* DINGIR^{LIM} 1 GU$_4$ <4>6 UDU-*ya*

36'. ^{URU}KÙ.BABBAR-*aš i-wa-ar ši-ip-pa-an-ti* DINGIR^{LIM}-*za QA-TAM-MA ma-la-a-an ḫar-ti*

37'. *nu TE*^{MEŠ} SIG$_5$-*ru ni ši ta ke zi a-ri* 10 ^{ŠÀ}*TIR* SIG$_5$ *ka-ru-ú* SUM-*an*

---

§10'

38'. *A-NA* DINGIR^{LIM} *ku-i-e-eš wa-aš-ku-i-e-eš* SIxSÁ-*an-ta-at na-aš* EGIR-*pa* SIG$_5$-*ya-aḫ-ḫi-ir*

39'. *nu ku-it-ma-an A-NA* ^{LÚ}AZU *pa-a-an-zi ku-it-ma-an* ^{LÚ}SANGA

40'. ^{URU}*Aš-ta-ta-za ú-wa-da-an-zi ku-it-ma-an ú-wa-an-zi ŠA* DINGIR^{LIM}

41'. *ša-ak-la-uš ta-ni-nu-wa-an-zi ma-a-an-ma-kán* DINGIR^{LUM} *ke-e-da-ni* ^{erasure}

42'. *A-NA* GIG ^{d}UTU^{ŠI} ḪUL-*an-ni pár-ra-an-ta Ú-UL nam-ma ku-it-ki ša-li-ik-ti*

43'. *nu* KIN SIG$_5$-*ru* KIN 3-*ŠÚ* SIG$_5$

---

§11'

44'. LÚ.MEŠ ^{URU}*Aš-ta-ta ku-it ú-wa-te-er na-aš ŠA* DINGIR^{LIM} *ša-ak-la-i*

45'. *pu-nu-uš-šir nu me-mi-ir ma-a-an-wa* DINGIR^{LUM} UN-*ši me-na-aḫ-ḫa-an-da* TUKU.TUKU-*an-za*

46'. *iš-tar-ak-zi-wa-ra-an nu-wa ku-it-ma-an* DINGIR^{LUM} *a-ri-ya-an-zi*

47'. *ku-it-ma-an-wa-ra-an-kán* KASKAL-*ši ti-an-zi ku-it-ma-an-wa ir-ma-la-an-za*

§7' (i 27'–30') As a countercheck concerning the two festivals of Ashtata and the *ayari*-festival in the style of Mezzulla, they performed extispicies of confirmation. First extispicy: *nipašuri*, *šintaḫi*, *tanani*, *keldi* striped to the left. Result: favorable. Second extispicy: *nipašuri*, *šintaḫi*; the intestinal coils were *ḫiriḫḫiš talin tanu tametta*. Result: unfavorable.

§8' (i 31'–33') It was established by oracle that His Majesty should make a vow to the deity; one ox and 46 sheep were indicated. He has already performed the vow, and when His Majesty recovers, they shall deliver them.

§9' (i 34'–37') They will remove for the deity angry feelings about Mezzulla. Should His Majesty offer the one ox and 46 sheep in the style of Hattusa? Have you, (O deity), likewise approved? Let the extispicy be favorable: *nipašuri*, *šintaḫi*, *tanani*; the tapeworm blister "arrives"; ten intestinal coils. Result: favorable. (The offering) has already been given.

§10' (i 38'–43') They have rectified the transgressions that were identified by oracle in regard to the deity. If you, O deity, will not in any way push further beyond this evil illness of His Majesty while they are going for the seer, bringing the priest from Ashtata, and proceeding to put the cultic regulations of the deity in order, then let the lot oracle be favorable. The lot oracle was favorable three times.

§11' (i 44'–48') Because they brought the people of Ashtata and interrogated them about the cultic regulations of the deity, they said: "When a deity is angry with a person, he becomes ill. And while they communicate with the deity through an oracle, while they get him or her (the deity's image?) on its way, and while the patient recovers, they incinerate birds before the deity."

(gap)

48'. SIG$_5$-*ri A-NA* DINGIR^{LIM}-*ma-wa pí-ra-an pa-ra-a* MUŠEN.ḪI.A IZI-*an-zi*

---

§12'

ii

1'. […]

2'. [… *ka-r*]*u-ú* SUM-*an*

---

§13'

3'. [o o o *A-N*]*A*? DINGIR^{LIM} x x x ⸢^{URU}⸣*U*-⸢*ri*⸣-*ki-na* ⸢*ka-ru-ú*⸣ *ú-i-e-er*

---

§14'

4'. [o o] x x ⸢*na*⸣-*aš* EGIR-*pa* ^{URU}*Aš-ta-ta pa-a-an-za nu ka-ru-ú IŠ-PUR*

---

§15'.

5'. [*nu-kán I-N*]*A* É.⸢DINGIR^{LIM}⸣ *A-NA* DINGIR^{LIM} *ši-ip-pa-an-du-wa-an-zi*

6'. [*ti-an-zi*] ⸢*nu*⸣ ^{LÚ}⸢AZU⸣ ^{MUNUS}ŠU.GI-*ya* SIxSÁ-*at*

---

§16'

7'. [o o]-⸢*ya*?-*kán*?⸣ *A-NA* ^{d}*Iš-ḫa-ra* BAL-*an-zi* DUMU.MUNUS ^{MUNUS}*NAP-ṬAR-TI*

8'. [*i-ya-a*]*t-ta-ri IŠ-TU* ^{MUNUS}ŠU.GI SIG$_5$ *IŠ-TU* ^{LÚ}AZU ^{LÚ}MUŠEN.DÙ-*ya* NU.SIG$_5$

---

§17'

9'. [*nu-kán A-N*]*A* ⸢^{d}*Iš-ḫa-ra*⸣ BAL-*an-zi* ^{f}DINGIR.MEŠ.IR-*ma i-ya-at-ta-ri*

10'. [o o] x-*ni* MU-*ti ú-iz-zi na-an a-pa-a-aš ši-ip-pa-an-ti*

11'. [o o]-⸢*ni Ú*⸣-*UL ú-iz-zi na-an* ^{m}*A-ki-ya-aš* BAL-*i*

12'. [o o o]-*ir nu* ^{f}DINGIR.MEŠ.IR *IŠ-TU* ^{MUNUS}ŠU.GI ^{LÚ}MUŠEN.DÙ-*ya* NU.SIG$_5$ *pa-ra-a na-a-wi*$_5$ *a-ri-ya-a*[*t-ta-ri*]

---

§18'

13'. [$^{d?}$ o o]-x-*iš ku-it* SIxSÁ-*at nu* ^{d}UTU^{ŠI} *ku-it A-NA* SISKUR EGIR-*an Ú-UL*

14'. [*ti-ya-an ḫar-t*]*a*? *nu a-pa-a-at* [*i*]-*ya-at nu a-píd-da še-er ŠA* ^{d}UTU^{ŠI} *za-an-ki-la-tar*

15'. [*ER-ir*? *ŠA* ^{d}UTU^{ŠI}-*y*]*a za-an-ki-*⸢*la*⸣-*tar ma-aḫ-ḫa-an* SIxSÁ-*at na-at ka-ru-ú* SUM-*an*

§12' (ii 1'–2') *(too fragmentary for translation)*

§13' (ii 3') [... to] the deity ... they have already sent to the city of Urikina.

§14' (ii 4') [...] She (the deity) is going back to Ashtata. He (His Majesty?) has already written.

§15' (ii 5'–6') [They will begin] to make offerings to the deity in the temple. The seer and the Old Woman were chosen(?) by oracle.

§16' (ii 7'–8') [...] they will make offering to Ishhara. Should the daughter of a secondary wife go? (Inquiry by) the Old Woman: favorable; by the seer and the augur: unfavorable.

§17' (ii 9'–12') They will make offering [to] Ishhara. Massannauzzi is on her way. [...] will come (this) year, and she will offer it. [...] will not come, and Akiya will offer it. [...] Massanauzzi('s participation was inquired into) by the Old Woman and the augur: unfavorable. She has not yet gotten here.

* * *

§18' (ii 13'–20') Because [... (a deity)] was identified by oracle and His Majesty [had] not concerned himself with (his/her) ritual, he has now done that. Therefore [they investigated] the compensation due from His Majesty, and as His Majesty's compensation was determined by oracle, it has already been paid. [...] a number of *zaḫ* and a *dammara*-man were indicated by oracle [as of concern to] the deity, and an imprecation by Ankalliya and an imprecation by the *dammara*-man were (also) indicated. [Then they proceeded] to carry them forth from the temple. [...] If (you), O deity, are angry about precisely these

16'. [o o o o o *A-N*]*A*? DINGIR^{LIM} *za-ḫa-an-zi* ^{LÚ}*dam-ma-ra-a-aš-ša* SIxSÁ-*at* EME ^{m}*An-kal-li-ya* EME ^{MUNUS}*dam-ma-ra-ya* SIxSÁ-*at*
17'. [*na-aš pa-a*]-⸢*ir*?⸣ *IŠ*⸣-*TU* É.DINGIR^{LIM} *pa-ra-a pé-e-te-er*
18'. [o o o o o o o] x ⸢*ma*⸣-*a-an* DINGIR^{LUM} *ke-e-da-aš-pát wa-aš-ku-i-e-eš še-er* TUKU.TUKU-*an-za*
19'. [*ma-a-an-ma* DINGIR^{LUM}] ⸢*UL ku*⸣-*it-ki* TUKU.TUKU-*an-za nu* MUŠEN.ḪI.A SIG$_5$-*an-te-eš*
20'. [o o] x x x ⸢*IŠ*⸣-*TU* ⸢^{MUNUS}ŠU.GI KIN⸣ 3-*ŠÚ* ^{erasure} SIG$_5$

---

§19'

21'. *nu-kán IŠ-TU* ^{MUNUS}ENSI *ŠA* x [o o o o o] ⸢^{MUNUS}*dam*⸣-*ma-ra*-⸢*a*⸣-[o o o o] x x x x x [...]
22'. MUNUS ^{URU}*Iš-ki-ya-wa-za* NÍG.BA.ḪI.A x [...] x [...]
23'. *nu-wa-ra-at A-NA* SISKUR *ŠA* ^{d}UTU^{ŠI} [...]
24'. ŠÀ É.DINGIR^{LIM}-*ya-wa-kán an-tu-uḫ-šu-u*[*š* ...]
25'. *I-NA* ^{URU}*Ma-ra-aš-ša-an-ti-ya-wa*!-*za ku*-⸢*wa*⸣-*p*[*í*(-) ...]
26'. ^{f}*Ta-a-ti-wa-aš-ti-in-na* ^{MUNUS}*dam-ma-ra*[-*a-an* ...]
27'. UD.KAM-*ti-li ma-al-iš-kán-zi* ^{f}*Pa-az-z*[*a-* ...]
28'. *pa-ra-a tar*-⸢*nu*⸣-*ma-aš me-ḫur wa-aš-ta-nu-ir nu-w*[*a*(-) ...]
29'. *Ú-UL i-ya-at-ta-at* MUNUS.DINGIR^{LIM}-*ya-wa* ^{m}*Ku*-x[- ...]
30'. *nu ke-e-da-aš wa-aš-ku-i-e-eš* EGIR-*an-da* x [o] x [...]
31'. *zi-la-aš-ma TE*⸢^{MEŠ}⸣ *pu-u-ra-mi-im-ma* SIG$_5$ *IŠ-TU* ^{L}[^{Ú}AZU *IŠ-TU* ^{LÚ}MUŠEN.DÙ-*ya* (NU).SIG$_5$]
32'. ⸢*IŠ*⸣-*TU* ^{MUNUS}ŠU.GI KIN 3-*ŠÚ* SIG$_5$ *nu-kán* ŠÀ É.DINGIR^{LIM} [...]
33'. *nu* ^{m}*An-ta-ra-wa-aš pé-en-ni-iš-ta na-aš ka-ru*-⸢*ú*⸣ [...]
34'. *za*-⸢*an*⸣-*ki-la-tar-ri*$^{ḪI.A}$-*ya* SUM-*eš-ta mu-ke-eš-šar-ra* EGIR-*pa* [... *pa-it*?]
35'. *nu-za-kán mu-ke-eš-šar IŠ-TU ṬUP-PÍ me-na-aḫ-ḫa-an-ta a*-⸢*ú*⸣[-*e-er*]

---

§20'

36'. x ⸢$^{LÚ?\ erasure}$⸣ *dam-ma-ra-a-aš ku-iš* SIxSÁ-*at nu* LÚ.MEŠ *ku-e-da-ni* x [...]
37'. *a-pa-a-aš-ša a-pí-ya a-ri*-⸢*eš*⸣-*kat-ta-ri I-NA* UD.EZEN-*ma* [...]

---

§21'

38'. ^{d}UTU^{ŠI} *ku-it* GIG-*an-za pa-ra-a ta-ma-aš-ta na-an* ⸢*ma-a-an*⸣ [GIG-*an-za* o o o o -*l*]*i-i*
39'. *pa-ra-a ta-ma-aš-ki-iz-zi* < ... > NU.SIG$_5$-*at na-aš* GAM *a-ri*-⸢*i*⸣[-*e-er* ...]

transgressions, [or if] (you), O deity, are not at all angry, (let the lot oracles be favorable). The auguries were favorable. (Checked) by the Old Woman: lot oracle favorable three times.

§19' (ii 21'–35') Then [it was determined] by means of a female dream interpreter: "[...] a *dammara*-woman [...] a woman of the city of Iskiya [will ...] gifts [...], and [they will take(?)] them for the ritual of His Majesty. The persons in the temple [...] And when in the city of Marassantiya [...] Tatiwašti the *dammara*-woman [...] they grind daily. The woman Pazza[... and ...] desecrated the occasion of ritual release, and [...] did not go. And the 'Woman of the Deity' [...] following these transgressions [...]." Prognostication by means of *puramma*-extispicies: favorable; by means [of the seer and the augur: (un)favorable]; by means of the Old Woman: lot oracle favorable three times. Then in the temple [...] Then Antarwa drove away, and he [had] already [...] He paid the compensation and [performed(?)] the evocation rite. They scrutinized the evocation rite by means of a tablet.

§20' (ii 36'–37') About the *dammara*-man who was indicated by oracle: The one to whom the men will [...] will at that point be investigated through repeated oracle consultations. But on the day of the ritual [...]

§21' (ii 38'–41') In respect to the fact that the illness has beaten down His Majesty—if [the illness] will continue [...] to beat him down < ... > It was unfavorable. They continued to investigate them [...] and as many deities as were in the temple in the city of Zithara—absolutely all of them were identified by oracle (as responsible for the illness of His Majesty).

40'. *nu-kán A-NA* ^{URU}*Zi-it-ḫa-ra ma-ši-i-e-eš* DINGIR.MEŠ ŠÀ ⸢É⸣[.DINGIR^{LIM} *na-at ḫ*]*u-u-ma-an-du-uš-pát*
41'. SIxSÁ-*an-ta-at*

---

§22'
42'. *na-aš* GAM *a-ri-i-e-er nu-uš-ma-aš ŠA* ^{f}*Am-ma-ra-li* EME *pí-ra-an* SIxSÁ-*at*
43'. *IŠ-TU* ^{LÚ}AZU-*ya-at ki-iš-ša-an* SIxSÁ-*at A-NA* ^{d}UTU^{ŠI}-*wa-ra-at-kán*
44'. *ma-al-ḫa-aš-šal-la-ḫi-ti a-re-eš-kán-ta-ri*

---

§23'
45'. ^{d}*Za-wa-al-li-i-iš ku-it ŠA* ^{URU}*Zi-it-ḫa-ra A-NA* GIG ^{d}UTU^{ŠI} *še-er* TUKU.TUKU-*at-ti* SIxSÁ-*at*
46'. *nu-kán* $^{MUNUS.MEŠ}$*dam-ma-ra-an-za I-NA* ^{URU}*Zi-it-ḫa-ra pa-ra-a ne-an-zi*
47'. *nu pa-a-an-zi* EME.MEŠ EGIR-*pa a-ni-ya-an-*⸢*zi*⸣ É.DINGIR^{LIM}-⸢*ya*⸣ *pár-ku-nu-wa-an-zi*
48'. *za-an-ki-la-tar*$^{ḪI.A}$-*ya ku-e ŠA* ^{d}UTU^{ŠI} *ŠA* ^{m}*An-ta-ra-wa-*[*y*]*a* SIxSÁ-*at*
49'. *na-at pí-an-zi ḫal-lu-wa-ir-ra ku-i-e-eš na-aš PA-NI* DINGIR^{LIM} ⸢*za-ḫa*⸣[-*an-zi*]
50'. *ku-it-ma-an-ma a-pu-u-uš I-NA* ^{URU}*Zi-it-ḫa-ra* ^{d}UTU^{ŠI}-*ma ka-a-š*[*a*? …]
51'. *I-NA* UD.3.KAM *ḫa-a-li-iš-kat-ta-ri nam-ma-kán* DINGIR^{LUM} *ša-ra-a ú-da-an*[-*z*]*i*
52'. *nu A-NA* DINGIR.MEŠ *Ù A-NA* ^{d}UTU^{ŠI} *a-ni-ú-úr* GIM-*an na-at QA-TAM-MA a-ni-*[*y*]*a-an-zi*
53'. *nam-ma* ^{d}UTU^{ŠI} *ša-ak-nu-wa-an-ta-aš A-NA* ^{GIŠ}BANŠUR<.ḪI.A> *pár-ku-wa-ya-aš-ša*
54'. *A-NA* ^{GIŠ}BANŠUR.ḪI.A *erasure* EGIR-*an ḫi-ni-ik-zi* ^{d}UTU^{ŠI}-*ma-kán*
55'. ^{URU}KÙ.BABBAR-*aš i-wa-ar ar-ḫa-ya-an a-pa-ši-la ši-ip-pa-an-ti* KI.MIN *TE*^{MEŠ} SIG$_5$-*ru*
56'. *ni ši zi a-ri* 10 *TE-RA-A-NU* SIG$_5$

---

§24'
57'. DINGIR^{LIM} ^{URU}***Aḫ-ḫi-ya-wa***-*kán ku-iš* DINGIR^{LUM} ^{URU}*La-az-pa-ya* DINGIR^{LUM} NÍ.TE^{NI}-*ya A-NA* ^{d}UTU^{ŠI}
58'. *tar-nu-ma-an-zi* SIxSÁ-*an-ta-at nu* DINGIR^{LUM} *ŠA* NÍ.TE LUGAL GIM-*an ú-da-an-zi*
59'. *a-pu-u-*⸢*uš*⸣-*ša ú-da-an-zi nu a-pé-e-da-aš* GIM-*an a-ni-ú-úr I-NA* UD.3.KAM <*a-ni-ya-an-zi*>

§22' (ii 42'–44') They continued to investigate them, and the imprecation by the woman Ammarali was singled out by oracle. It was also established through the seer as follows: "They (the gods) will be questioned by oracle whether the performance of offerings is required from His Majesty."

§23' (ii 45'–56') In respect to the fact that concerning the illness of His Majesty, the Zawalli-deity of Zithara was established by oracle as being angry—they dispatched the *dammara*-women to Zithara and they proceeded to make amends for the imprecations and to purify the temple. And should they pay the compensation that was indicated by oracle for His Majesty and for Antarwa? Should they scourge before the deity those who quarreled violently? But while they are in Zithara, His Majesty has already been bowing down in obeisance for three days. Furthermore, should they bring the deity up here and perform a rite in the manner appropriate for the gods and for His Majesty? Then should His Majesty do obeisance to both the polluted and the purified offering tables? Should His Majesty himself make the offering in the style of Hattusa? Ditto. Let the extispicy be favorable: *nipašuri*, *šintaḫi*; the tapeworm blister "arrives"; ten intestinal coils. Result: favorable.

§24' (ii 57'–64') In respect to the fact that the freeing of the deity of **Ahhiyawa**, the deity of Lazpa (Lesbos), and the personal deity (of His Majesty) was indicated by oracle as incumbent upon His Majesty—when they bring the personal deity of the King, should they bring them (the other deities) too? And as <they perform> the rite for them over the course of three days, is it likewise mandated for three days for the deity of **Ahhiyawa** and the deity of Lazpa? And as His Majesty has done obeisance to the polluted and purified offering tables

60'. *A-NA* DINGIR^{LIM} ^{URU}***Aḫ-ḫi-ya-wa-a***-*ya-kán* DINGIR^{LUM} ^{URU}*La-az-pa-ya* UD.3.KAM *QA-TAM-MA-pát*

61'. *du-uk-ki-iš-zi A-NA* ^{GIŠ}BANŠUR.ḪI.A *ša-ak-nu-wa-an-da-aš-ma pár-ku-ya-aš-ša*

62'. *ma-aḫ-ḫa-an* ^{d}UTU^{ŠI} EGIR-*an UŠ-KE-EN* ^{URU}KÙ.BABBAR-*ša-ša-kán i-wa-ar*

63'. *ma-aḫ-ḫa-an ši-ip-pa-an-ta-ir a-pé-e-da-aš-ša QA-TAM-MA-pát i-ya-zi*

64'. SISKUR-*ma IŠ-TU* DINGIR^{LIM} *a-ri-ya-an-zi* KI.MIN *nu TE*^{MEŠ} SIG$_5$-*ru ni ši ta ke* 10 ^{ŠÀ}*NIR* SIG$_5$

---

§25'

65'. ^{d}UTU^{ŠI} *ku-it* GIG-*an-za pa-ra-a ta-ma-aš-ki-iz-zi nu-uš-ša-an ma-a-an*

66'. *ke-e-da-ni A-NA* GIG ^{d}UTU^{ŠI} ^{d}*Za-wa-al-li-i-iš* ^{URU}*An-ku-wa-ya*

67'. *pa-ra-a a-ra-an-za na-aš-kán A-NA* ^{d}UTU^{ŠI} *ma-al-ḫa-šal-la-ḫi-ti a-re-eš-kat-ta-ri*

68'. *nu TE*^{MEŠ} NU.SIG$_5$-*du ke-iš ne-an-za* NU.SIG$_5$

---

§26'

69'. *nu ŠA* ^{URU}*An-ku-wa-ya* ^{d}*Za-wa-al-li-i-in ú-te-er na-an ši-ip-pa-an-te-er*

---

§27'

70'. *nu* DINGIR^{LUM} *ša-ku-wa-aš-šar-ra-an A-NA* EN-*ŠU* EGIR-*pa pí-i-e-er* ^{er}DINGIR^{LUM}-*ma*^{er}-*kán*

71'. *ku-iš ar-ḫa šar-ru-ma*[*-an-z*]*i* SIxSÁ-*at na-aš I-NA* ^{URU}*Zi-it-ḫa-ra*

72'. *pé-e-du-ma-an-z*[*i* SIxSÁ-*at* o$^{?}$] x-*aš-ši* ⸢*A*-NA**⸣ É.ŠÀ *ŠA* ^{LÚ}*ḫa-an-ta-*⸢*an-ti*⸣*-ya-li-kán*

72'b. [… ^{LÚ}*ḫa-an-ta-an-ti*$^{?}$]-*ya-al-li* ⸢*ke*⸣-*e-da-ni* EGIR-*an* ⸢^{d}⸣UTU^{ŠI} *a-*⸢*ú*$^{?}$*-e-er*⸣

iii

1. *A-NA* […] x x x [*k*]*u-it* GAM-*an ḫa-ma-an-kán-zi*

2. *na-at* […] x-*an*

---

§28'

3. *AŠ-ŠUM* ^{LÚ}SANG[*A-UT-T*]*I-ma-aš-ši* ^{m}*Ar-ma-ta-al-li-in a-ri-iš-kir*

4. *na-aš Ú-U*[*L* S]IxSÁ-*at ŠA* DINGIR^{LIM}-*ya-kán ku-it ša-ak-nu-wa-an-da-aš pár-ku-i-ya-aš-ša*

5. *A-NA* ^{GIŠ}B[AN]ŠUR.ḪI.A *ta-ma-iš ši-ip-pa-an-da-aš ma-aḫ-ḫa-an-ma* ^{d}UTU^{ŠI}

6. *ḫa-at-tu-liš*-zi nu-kán ú-iz-zi* ^{URU}KÙ.BABBAR-*aš i-wa-ar a-pa-ši-la* BAL-*an-ti*

and they have sacrificed in the style of Hattusa, should he do precisely the same for them? They investigate the offering by oracle. Ditto. Let the extispicy be favorable: *nipašuri*, *šintaḫi*, *tanani*, *keldi*; ten intestinal coils. Result: favorable.

§25' (ii 65'–68') In respect to the fact that the illness continues to beat His Majesty down—if the Zawalli-deity of the city of Ankuwa is established by oracle (as responsible) for this illness of His Majesty, should he be questioned by oracle whether the performance of offerings is required from His Majesty? Let the extispicy be unfavorable: the *keldi* is turned: unfavorable.

§26' (ii 69') They brought the Zawalli-deity of Ankuwa here and made offerings to him.

§27' (ii 70'–iii 2) They returned the deity intact to his custodian. But the deity who was designated by oracle for division and for transportation to Zithara, for him to the inner chamber of the *ḫantantiyali*-man […] behind that [*ḫantanti*]*yali*-man […] His Majesty […] to […] because they tied down […]

§28' (iii 3–7) Concerning the function as his priest, they investigated Armatalli, and he was not indicated by oracle. Because another person made the offerings to the polluted and the purified offering tables of the deity, when His Majesty recovers, then he himself will proceed and make offering in the style of Hattusa. The priest is not yet finished.

7. ^{LÚ}SANGA *na-a-wi*$_5$ *zi-en-na-an-za*

---

§29'

8. *ki-i ku-it* $^{\text{DINGIR.MEŠ}}$*Za-wa-al-li-ya-aš ši-ip-pa-an-za-kán-zi pa-ra-a-ma<-za> Ú-UL ma-le-eš-ki-zi*
9. *nu ma-a-an* ^{m}PÉŠ.TUR-*aš ku-it-ki PA-NI* DINGIR^{LIM} EME-*an ar-ḫa tar-na-an ḫar-zi*
10. *nu* IGI-*zi TE*^{MEŠ} NU.SIG$_5$-*du* EGIR-*zi-ma* SIG$_5$-*ru* IGI-*zi TE*^{MEŠ} *ni ši* ZAG-*za* RA^{IṢ} NU.⸢SIG$_5$⸣ ^{erasure}
11. EGIR-*zi TE*^{MEŠ} *ni ši ta ke* 12 ^{ŠÀ}*TIR* SIG$_5$

---

§30'

12. *ŠA* ^{m}PÉŠ.TUR-*wa ku-it* EME *A-NA PA-NI* DINGIR^{LIM} *ar-ḫa tar-nu-ma-an-zi* SIxSÁ-*at*
13. *nu pár-na-al-li-iš ku-iš* ^{d}*Za-wa-al-li-i-iš ŠA* ^{d}UTU^{ŠI} ^{m}PÉŠ.TUR-*aš ku-in*
14. ^{URU}*Ar-za-u-wa ḫar-ta nu a-pé-e-da-ni pí-ra-an* EME-*an ar-ḫa tar-na-an ḫar-zi*
15. IGI-*zi TE*^{MEŠ} NU.SIG$_5$-*du* <EGIR-*zi-ma* SIG$_5$-*ru* IGI-*zi TE*^{MEŠ}> *ni* GAM *še-er-ma-aš-ši a-dam-ta-ḫi-iš* ZAG-*za an-ša-an* NU.SIG$_5$
16. EGIR-*zi TE*^{MEŠ} *ni ši ta* GÙB-*la-za* RA^{IṢ} *zi* GAR-*ri* 12 ^{ŠÀ}*TIR* SIG$_5$ ^{erasure}

---

§31'

17. *nu* GAM *a-ri-iš-kir nu-za-kán ḫur-ta-uš me-eq-qa-uš tar-na-aš na-at IŠ-TU ṬUP-PÍ a-ni-i-ir*
18. *zi-la-aš-ma kal-la-re-*⸢*eš*⸣*-kat-ta-ri nu* DINGIR^{LUM}-*ma-aš-ši al-wa-an-za-aḫ-ḫa-an-za a-pa-a-aš-ša*
19. *al-wa-an-za-aḫ-ḫa-an-za nu ki-iš-ša-an a-ri-i-*⸢*e*⸣*-er* ^{m}PÉŠ.TUR-*aš-wa I-NA* ^{URU}*Ku-wa-a-*⸢*ni*⸣
20. *a-pa-ši-la pa-iz-zi Ú-NU-UT* LUGAL-*ya pé-e-da-an-zi na-at šu-up-pa-ya-za ḫar-kán-zi*
21. ^{m}PÉŠ.TUR-*aš-ma* ^{m}*Za-pár-ti-*ŠEŠ-*ša tu-u-wa-az a-ra-an-ta-ri Ú-NU-UT* ^{f}NÍG.GA.KÙ.SIG$_{17}$-*ya*
22. *ḫar-ga-an-zi nu* DINGIR.MEŠ ^{f}*Zu-wa-ḫal-la-ti-iš* ^{f}*Ma-bi-li-iš-ša a-ni-ya-an-zi*
23. EGIR-*an-*⸢*da*⸣*-ma Ú-NU-UT* LUGAL *a-ni-ya-an-zi nam-ma ar-ḫa da-a-li-ya-an-zi*
24. *ku-it-ma-an-kán* ^{m}PÉŠ.TUR-*aš* ^{m}*Za-pár-ti-*ŠEŠ-*ša IŠ-TU* SISKUR *a-ra-an-zi*

§29' (iii 8–11) In regard to the fact that they have been making offerings to the Zawalli-deities, but he does not approve—if Mashuiluwa has loosed some imprecation before a deity, then let the first extispicy be unfavorable and the second favorable. First extispicy: *nipašuri*, *šintaḫi* striped to the right: unfavorable. Second extispicy: *nipašuri*, *šintaḫi*, *tanani*, *keldi*; twelve intestinal coils: favorable.

§30' (iii 12–16) In respect to the fact that Mashuiluwa's loosing of an imprecation before a deity has been established by oracle—has Mashuiluwa loosed the imprecation before the domestic deity of His Majesty that he has in his possession in Arzawa? Let the first extispicy be unfavorable <and the second favorable. First extispicy>: *nipašuri* below; on top of it *adamtaḫiš* smeared to the right. Result: unfavorable. Second extispicy: *nipašuri*, *šintaḫi*, *tanani*, striped to the left; the tapeworm blister is in place; twelve intestinal coils. Result: favorable.

§31' (iii 17–28) They continued the investigation. He (Mashuiluwa) had loosed many imprecations, and they recorded them on a tablet. The prognostication is repeatedly unfavorable. Now the deity is bewitched in regard to him (His Majesty), and he himself is bewitched. They researched with the following result: "Mashuiluwa will himself go to the city of Kuwalana." Should they take the furnishings of the King (there) and handle them in a pure manner? Should Mashuiluwa and Zaparti-negna stand by while they handle the furnishings of NÍG.GA.KÙ.SIG$_{17}$? Should Zuwahallati and Mabili worship the gods and thereafter treat the furnishings of the King? Should they then lure away (the deities)? Until Mashuiluwa and Zaparti-negna arrive with (the materials for) the ritual and they perform the *mantalliya*-ritual with His Majesty in the style of Hattusa and of Arzawa, should they proceed to worship the deity of His Majesty a second time? Should they turn the deity over to His Majesty there? Should he divide him there? Ditto. Let the extispicy be favorable: *nipašuri*, *šintaḫi*, *keldi*; the ... is *allaiti* on the right. Result: favorable.

25. *ku-it-ma-an-ma-aš* SISKUR *ma-an-tal-li-ya* ^{URU}KÙ.BABBAR-*aš* ^{URU}*Ar-za-wa-aš-ša i-wa-ar*

26. *IT-TI* ⸢^{d}UTU^{ŠI}⸣ *i-ya-an nu ú-wa-an-zi* DINGIR^{LUM} ^{d}UTU^{ŠI}*-ya da-a-an* EGIR-*pa a-ni-ya-an-zi*

27. *A-NA* ^{d}UTU$^{⸢ŠI⸣}$*-ya-kán* ⸢DINGIR⸣^{LUM} *a-pí-ya tar-na-an-zi ar-ḫa-ya-za-an-kán a-pí-ya šar-ri-ya-z*[*i*]

28. KI.MIN *nu TE*^{MEŠ} SIG$_5$-*ru ni ši ke* KI.LÚ-*ti-iš-kán* ZAG-*ni al-la-i-ti* SIG$_5$

---

§32'

29. *nu pa-i-u-e-ni ki-iš-ša-an-ma i-ya-u-*⸢*e*⸣*-ni I-NA* ^{URU}*Ku-wa-la-na* UN-*aš pa-iz-zi*

30. *ku-e*$^{!}$*-kán ŠA* DINGIR^{LIM} *a-ni-ú-ri kat-ta da-a-i nu-kán* DINGIR^{LUM} MÁŠ.GAL IZI-*ya iš-tar-na ar-ḫa*

31. *pé-e-da-an-zi nam-ma-*[*a*]*n a-ni-*⸢*ya*⸣*-an-za* ^{m}*Maš-ḫu-u-i-lu-wa-ma* ^{m}*Za-pár-ti-*ŠEŠ-*ša*

32. *Ú-NU-UT* ^{f}⸢NÍG.GA⸣.KÙ.SIG$_{17}$ *tu-u-wa-az ḫar-kán-zi nu* DINGIR^{LUM} *pé-di-ši pár-ku-nu-wa-an-za*

33. *nam-ma-an MA-ḪAR* ^{d}UTU^{ŠI} *ú-da-an-zi* ^{d}UTU^{ŠI}*-ya ka-a a-ni-ya-an-zi A-NA* ^{d}UTU^{ŠI}*-ya-*⸢*kán*⸣

34. *e-ni ut-tar* DÙ-*zi* MÁŠ.GAL-*ya-aš-*⸢*ši*⸣ *še-er ap-*⸢*pa-an-zi*⸣ *nam-ma-aš-ši* DINGIR^{LUM} *še-er ḫal-za-a-i*

35. *nam-ma ar-ḫa da-a-li-ya-zi ku-it-ma-a*[*n-kán* UN]*-aš IŠ-TU* EZEN *a-ri ku-it-ma-an-za*

36. [EZEN] ⸢*ma*⸣*-al-*⸢*tal-li*⸣*-ya* ^{URU}KÙ.BABBAR-*aš* ^{URU}*Ar-*⸢*za-u*⸣*-wa-aš-š*[*a i-wa*]*-*⸢*ar*⸣ ^{d}UTU^{ŠI} DÙ-*zi*

37. [*nu* DINGIR]^{LUM} $^{d!}$UTU[^{ŠI}*-y*]*a* EGIR-*pa a-ni-ya-an-zi* ^{d}UTU^{Š}[^{I}- …] x-*ya* x *ŠA* ^{m}PÉŠ.⸢TUR⸣ *erasure*

38. […] x ⸢*A*$^{!}$*-NA* ^{d}UTU^{ŠI}⸣*-kán* x […]*-ša*$^{?}$*-a-an ḫar-ti*

39. […] x

…

§33'

40'. […] x […]

---

§34'

41'. […] x x x […]

42'. [… -*z*]*i*$^{?}$ ⸢*ma*⸣*-a-an ki-nu-u*[*n* …]

43'. [… -*z*]*i*$^{?}$ *nu TE*$^{M<EŠ>}$ ⸢SIG$_5$⸣-*ru* x […]

44'. […] x-*ma* […] 10 *TE-RA-NU* ⸢SIG$_5$⸣

---

§32' (iii 29–39) We will continue and do as follows: a man will go to Kuwalana. Whatever ritual (materials) he takes down (there)—they will carry a male goat off between fires (for) the deity and then worship him. Mashuiluwa and Zaparti-negna will hold the furnishings of NÍG.GA.KÙ.SIG_{17} from afar and the deity will be purified in place. Furthermore, they will take him before His Majesty and treat His Majesty there. (The chief officiant) will do this to His Majesty: they will hold the male goat over him and he will call to the deity for him, and furthermore they will lure (the deity) away. Until [the person] arrives with (the materials for) the ritual, and His Majesty performs the *maltalliya*-[ritual] in the style of Hattusa and of Arzawa, should they subsequently treat the deity and His Majesty? His Majesty [...] of Mashuiluwa [...] to His Majesty [...] you have [...]

§33' (iii 40') *(too fragmentary for translation)*

§34' (iii 41'–44') [...] if now [...] Let the extispicy be favorable: [...]; ten intestinal coils. Result: favorable.

§35’

45’. [… *-a*]*n-na* x [o o] UD.ḪI.A*-aš* x-[*m*]*a*?*-kán* […]
46’. [… *ma-a-a*]*n-za* DINGIR^{LIM} ^{d}U[TU$^{ŠI?}$] *ma-la-an ḫar-ti nu TE*^{MEŠ} IGI[*-zi* SIG$_5$*-ru*]
47’. […] ŠU^{TI} ZAG*-aš* 12 ⌜*TE*⌝*-RA-A-NU* SIG$_5$

---

§36’

48’. [… AL]AM ^{d}LAMMA *an-da pé-e-da-an na-at na-w*[*i*$_5$! …]
49’. […].MEŠ *an-da ša-li-ki-iš-kir ki-nu-na-at-kán A*!?[*-NA* …]
50’. [*ma-aḫ-ḫa-an* … *pí*]*-an-zi na-at A-NA* DINGIR^{LIM} *QA-TAM-MA pí-an-zi*

---

§37’

51’. […] x *ku-it I-NA* ^{URU}*A-ru-uš-na* x […]
52’. […] x*-at nu-wa* MUNUS.LUGAL *ku-it*(-)[…]
53’. […] x *Ú-UL ku-it pé-e-te-er* […]
54’. [… *-y*]*a*?*-an-na*
…

§38’

56’. […] x x […]
57’. […] x […]
58’. […] x x [… .Ḫ]I.A […]
59’. […] x x x […]

---

§39’

60’. […] x x x x x*-ya-aš-ša* ⌜SIxSÁ*-at*⌝
61’. […] x É.DINGIR^{LIM}-⌜*ŠU-NU*⌝ TUKU.TUKU*-at-ti* SIxSÁ*-ta-at*
62’. […] *TE*^{MEŠ}

---

§40’

63’. […] x x-⌜*ta*⌝ *erasure* ⌜*ta*⌝ *zi-la*-⌜*aš*?⌝ x x
64’. […] x ⌜*A-NA*⌝ [AL]AM*-ŠU-ya še-er* SIxSÁ*-at nam-ma*! ⌜*kar*?*-di*<*-mi*>*-ya-an-zi*⌝
65’. […] *erasure* x*-ta-na-aš*
66’. […] *erasure*

---

§41’

67’. [… *-š*]*a* SIxSÁ*-at na-aš* GAM *IŠ-TU* ^{LÚ}AZU *a-ri-i-e-er*
68’. […] x SIxSÁ*-at* É*-SÚ ku-it A-NA* ^{f}*Ta-wa-an-na-an-na*
69’. […] x ⌜*am*⌝*-mu-uk-ma-wa* ḪA.LA.ḪI.A *te-ep-nu-ir*

§35’ (iii 45’–47’) […] days … [… If] you, O deity of His Majesty, have approved, then [let] the first extispicy [be favorable]: […]; ‘hand’ of the right; twelve intestinal coils: favorable.

§36’ (iii 48’–50’) [… the] image of the Protective Deity is carried in there, and not yet […] it […] they intruded, and now shall they give it to the deity just as they gave it [to …]?

§37’ (iii 51’–54’) […] because in the city of Arusna […] … “And because the Queen […], because they did not carry off […].”

§38’ (iii 56’–59’) *(too fragmentary for translation)*

§39’ (iii 60’–62’) […] was established by oracle […] was identified as angry in their temples […] extispicy […]

§40’ (iii 63’–66’) […] prognostication(?) […] was determined by oracle on top of his image. Are they still angry? …

§41’ (iii 67’–70’) […] was identified by oracle, and they continued the inquiry by means of the seer. […] was identified. Because for Tawananna her house(hold) […] “They reduced my portions.” […]; ten intestinal coils. Result: favorable.

70’. […]-*ta* 10 *TE-RA-A-NU* SIG$_5$

---

§42’

71’. [… *ku-it* … *A-NA*] ^{d}UTU^{ŠI} *me-mi-an tar-na-*⸢*i* SISKUR⸣-*ya A-NA* ŠEŠ LUGAL ⸢SUM-*ir*⸣

72’. [… -*y*]*a-zi* SISKUR-*ma* 1 GU$_4$ 44 UDU-*ya* SIxSÁ-*at*

73’. [… S]UM-*ir mu-ke-eš-šar-ra-aš-ši ka-ru-ú ti-i-e-er* ^{erasure}

---

§43’

74’. [… *ku-it* DINGIR$^{LUM?}$ ^{f}*Ta-wa-na-a*]*n-na-aš* x x SIxSÁ-*at na-aš IŠ-TU* É.GAL^{LIM} GAM *u-i-ya-u-wa-aš me-mi-ya-ni*

75’. [… SUD].ḪI.A KÙ.SIG$_{17}$-*ya* x x ⸢SIxSÁ-*at*⸣

---

§44’

76’. [… *ŠA* ^{N}]^{A4}*ḫé-kur* ^{d}LAMMA *me-*⸢*na*⸣[-*aḫ-ḫa-an-t*]*a*$^{?}$ *u-i-ya-at nu-za-kán me-mi-an* ⸢*tar-na*⸣-*i*

77’. […] x *an-da pa-iz-zi nu-*⸢*za*⸣ [o o -*w*]*a*$^{?}$-*ar* DÙ-*zi mu-ki-iš*[-*šar-r*]*a*$^{?}$

78’. [*ti-ya-an-zi*$^{?}$ …]-*a* SUD.ḪI.A KÙ.SIG$_{17}$-*ya-aš-ši*-[*kán*$^{?}$] ⸢*i*⸣-*ya-an-zi* KI.⸢MIN⸣ […]

79’. […] x 10 ^{ŠÀ}*TIR* SIG$_5$ *n*[*a*$^{?}$- …] x-⸢*ya-mu*⸣ x […]

80’. [… *a-ri*]-*i-e-er* ^{KUŠ}E.SI[R$^{?}$ …]

---

§45’

81’. [… -*m*]*a*$^{?}$-*at-kán* […]

82’. […] x […]

…

§46’

iv

1. ^{d}U ^{URU}*Šaḫ*[-*pí-na ku-it* SIxSÁ-*at n*]*a-aš*$^{!}$-*kán* É.DINGIR^{LIM}-*ŠU-NU* SIxSÁ-*at*

2. *nu an-tu-uḫ-š*[*u-un an-da*$^{?}$] *u-i-e-er*

---

§47’

3. ^{d}U NIR.GÁL *ku-it IT-TI* ^{d}UTU^{ŠI} SIxSÁ-*at nu* ⸢*ka*⸣-*ru-ú ku-i-e-eš* ^{erasure}

4. *wa-aš-ku-i-e-eš ŠA* MUN *ŠA* ^{GIŠ}*wa-zi-pa-ni-ti ḫu*^{er}-*im-pa-aš nam-ma-ya* ⸢*ku*⸣-*i-e-eš*

5. *wa*[-*aš-ku*]-*i-e-eš IŠ-TU ṬUP-PÍ a-ni-ya-an-te-eš* NU.SIG$_5$ *zi-la-aš-ma* SIG$_5$

§42' (iii 71'–73') [Because ...] loosed an utterance [against] His Majesty, they have given the offering to the brother of the King. [...] he will [...] The offering was determined by oracle as one ox and 44 sheep. [...] they gave, and they have already established the evocation rite.

§43' (iii 74'–75') [Because the deity of(?) Tawananna] was identified by oracle, [... she turned(?)] to the matter of bringing her down from the palace [... Attraction rites(?)] and gold were determined by oracle.

§44' (iii 76'–80') [...] sent the Protective Deity of the Rock Sanctuary [to ...] And (s)he will release the matter for him/herself. [...] will go in and perform [...] And [they will establish(?)] an evocation rite. They will perform attraction rites and (fabricate objects of) gold. Ditto. [...]; ten intestinal coils. Result: favorable. They investigated. Shoes(??) [...]

§45' (iii 81'–82') *(too fragmentary for translation)*

§46' (iv 1–2) [In respect to the fact that] the Storm-God of the city of Sahpina [was identified by oracle], and in particular in their temple, they sent a person [into (it)].

§47' (iv 3–6) In respect to the fact that the Powerful Storm-God was identified by oracle in connection with His Majesty—the transgressions that were about salt and about the roof beams(?), the transgressions that further were written upon a tablet. Result: unfavorable. Prognostication: favorable.

6. *vacat*

---

§48'

7. *ḫu-u-n[i-i]n-ku-wa-an-zi ku-it A-NA* ^{d}UTU^{ŠI} *IŠ-TU TE*$^{M<EŠ>}$ *a-re-eš-kán-zi*

8. *nu Ú-UL* SIxSÁ-*ri nu* DINGIR^{LUM} *pí-ra-an ti-ya-an-na* SIxSÁ-*at* GAM-*ma a-ri-i-e-er-ma*

9. *nu* ^{d}IŠKUR NIR.GÁL ^{d}IŠKUR ^{URU}*Ḫa-la-ab* ^{URU}KÙ.BABBAR-*ti* ^{d}IŠKUR ^{URU}*Ḫi-iš-ša-aš-*⸢*ša*⸣*-pa-ya*

10. SIxSÁ-*an-ta-at zi-la-aš-ma* SIG$_5$ *na-a-wi*$_5$ *a-ri-ya-an*

11. *erasure*

---

§49'

12. [*ḫu*]*-u-ni-in-ku-wa-an-zi ku-it TE*^{MEŠ} *pu-ra-am-me-ma* NU.SIG$_5$-*ta*

13. [*nu-k*]*án* ^{d}LAMMA ^{URU}*Ta-ú-ri-iš-ša pí-ra-an ti-ya-an-na* SIxSÁ-*at*

14. [o] x *ú-e-ḫi-ir nu-uš-ma-aš* NÍ.TE-*ŠU-NU ḫur-li-uš-ša*

15. [*ḫa-mi*$^{?}$*-i*]*n-kán-te-eš*$_{17}$ *na-aš* ⸢EGIR⸣-*pa* SIG$_5$-*aḫ-*<*ḫi*>-⸢*ir*⸣ *zi-la-aš-ma* SIG$_5$-*an-za*

---

§49'a *empty paragraph*

---

§50'

16. [o o o (MUNUS.)LU]GAL *ku-it še-er* ^{d}U ^{URU}⸢*Šaḫ*⸣*-pí-na* ⸢*ŠA*⸣ ^{URU}*Ka-ga-pa*

17. [TUKU.TUKU-*at-ti*$^{?}$] *a-re-e-er na-aš-kán* É.DINGIR^{LIM}-⸢*ŠU*⸣ SIxSÁ-*at nu* UN-*aš*

18. [o o o o o o -*š/t*]*a*$^{?}$*-an* ⸢*ka*⸣*-ru-ú a-ri-ya-at*

---

§51'.

19. [o o o o o o o *ku-i*]*t* SIxSÁ-*at nu-kán A-NA* SISKUR É.GAL^{LIM} *ku-it*

20. [o o o o o o SIxSÁ-*at*] *nu* DINGIR^{LIM} *a-píd-da-an še-er* SIxSÁ-*at*

21. [o o o o o o o o o] x-*ša-wa-kán* ŠÀ É.DINGIR^{LIM} *ku-wa-pí-ik-ki*

22. [o o o o o o o o o *Ú-U*]*L-ma*^{er} *li-in-ik-ta nam-ma-wa ḫur-za-ta*

23. [o o o o o o o o o *Ú-U*]*L* ⸢*ER*$^{!?}$⸣*-ta ma-a-an-wa u-ni me-mi-ya-an*

24. [o o o o o o o o o *pí-r*]*a-an Ú-UL* SIG$_5$-*aḫ-ḫi-ir ŠA* NÍG.KASKAL^{NI}-⸢*ya*⸣

25. [o o o o o o o o o o -*p*]*í-wa pé-eš-ki-ir ki-nu-un-ma-wa Ú-*⸢*UL* SUM-*ir*⸣

26. [o o o o o o o o o o] x x *zi-la-aš* SIG$_5$-*at*

---

§48' (iv 7–11) In respect to the fact that by means of extispicy they are investigating the beating on behalf of His Majesty—(it) is not established by oracle. An appearance before the deity has been established by oracle. They continued the investigation, and the Powerful Storm-God, the Storm-God of Aleppo in Hattusa, and the Storm-God of the city of Hissassapa have been identified. Prognostication: favorable. Not yet investigated.

§49' (iv 12–15) In respect to the fact that the *puramimma*-extispicy about the beating was unfavorable—an appearance before the Protective Deity of the city of Taurissa has been established by oracle. They turned [away(?)] and they are paralyzed(?) in their bodies and their uvulas(?). They set them in order once more. The prognostication is favorable.

§50' (iv 16–18) In respect to the fact that they investigated [the anger of] the Storm-God of Sahpina sojourning in the city of Kagapa in regard to [the King/Queen], his temple was singled out by oracle. Then a person already investigated [...]

§51' (iv 19–26) [In respect to the fact that ...] was identified by oracle and that [... was identified] concerning the ritual of the palace—a deity was established in regard to this: "[...] somewhere/somehow in the temple [...] did not swear, but cursed [...] did not investigate(?). If this matter before [...] they have not rectified, and the travel provisions [...] they have customarily been giving, but now they have not given." [...] The prognostication was favorable.

§52'

27. […] ⸢*nu PA-NI*⸣ DINGIR^{LIM} *ḫur-ti-aš*

28. *MA-ME-T*[*Ú* …] ⸢SISKUR$^{?}$⸣.MEŠ DÙ-*zi-pát nu* MUŠEN *ḪUR-RI* SIG$_5$

---

§53'

29. *ER-ar-ma ku-i*[*t* …] x *pé-eš-ta*

---

§54'

30. *A-NA* ^{d}U ^{URU}*Šaḫ*[*-pí-na* …] x *pa-a-ir*

31. ^{d}UTU$^{\check{S}I}$ *aš-ta-ni-y*[*a-i* …] x-*ir*

32. EGIR-*an-pát ti-ya*[*-at* …] x

---

§55'

33. *nu* ^{LÚ}AZU *aš-ta*[*-ni-ya-i* …]

34. *na-aš A-NA* EZEN […]

---

§56'

35. *A-BI* ^{d}UTU$^{\check{S}I}$ *ku-i*[*t* …]

36. *an-da ša-li-i*[*k-ta*$^{?}$ …]

37. x x-⸢*un*$^{?}$⸣ x […]

…

left edge

§57'

1. *MA-ME-T*[*Ú* … *ŠA* ^{d}UT]U$^{\check{S}I}$ *Ú-U*[*L* …]

---

§58'

2. *nu-uš*[(-) …] x x […]

---

§59'

3. *nu MA-ME-TÚ ku-iš ŠA* MUNUS.L[UGAL$^{?}$ …]

4. *A-NA* ^{d}UTU ^{URU}TÚL-*na ga-an*[*-ga-da-a-iz-zi*$^{?}$ …]

5. *ka-a-ri-wa-ri-wa-ar ne*-x […]

---

§60'

6. *MA-ME-TI*$^{ḪI.A}$*-za ku-wa-pí* ^{d}UTU$^{\check{S}I}$ DÙ-*zi* ⸢*nu*$^{?}$*-za*$^{?}$ *ki*⸣-x x x x *A-NA* ⸢$^{URU?}$⸣x x […]

7. *nu A-NA* ^{d}UTU$^{\check{S}I}$ *aš-ta-ni-ya-u-wa-ar Ú-UL* SIxSÁ-*at A-NA* IBILA-*ya Ú-UL* SIxSÁ-*at* x […]

§52' (iv 27–28) […] and the curses and oaths before the deity […] Should they indeed perform [the offerings(?)]? The *ḪURRI*-bird oracle was favorable.

§53' (iv 29) Because the inquiry […] he gave.

§54' (iv 30–32) They went […] to the Storm-God of Sahpina […] His Majesty … […] they […] he took responsibility […]

§55' (iv 33–34) The seer … […] and to the festival he […]

§56' (iv 35–37) Because the father of His Majesty […] intruded […]

§57' (left edge 1) The oath [… of] His Majesty(?) not(?) […]

§58' (left edge 2) And them […]

§59' (left edge 3–5) And the oath which of the Queen(?) […] (s)he reconciles(?) for the Sun-Goddess of the city of Arinna. Early in the morning […]

§60' (left edge 6–8) When His Majesty performs the oaths, then … […] And the *aštaniya*-act was not indicated by oracle for His Majesty, nor was it indicated for his heir […] Should he perform oaths concerning the father of His Majesty and the grandfather of His Majesty during the offering ceremony? Unfavorable(?). […]

8. *ŠA A-BI* ᵈUTU^{ŠI}*-ya-za-kán Ù ŠA A-BI A-BI* ᵈUTU^{ŠI} *MA-ME-TI*$^{HI.A}$ ŠÀ SISKUR.MEŠ DÙ-*zi* NU[.SIG$_5$ …]

colophon

[…] x *ŠA* ᵐ*Ḫi-mu*-DINGIR^{LIM} *a*[*k*$^?$- …]

Colophon: [...] of Himuili [...]

COMMENTARY

The king on whose behalf this oracle enquiry was conducted is not named in the text, but he can be identified as Mursili II, on the basis of references to three persons who are known from other texts to have been connected with him: his daughter Massannauzzi (§17') (represented logographically in the text as DINGIR.MEŠ.IR and called Matanazi in a letter of Ramesses II), his stepmother Tawananna (§§41', 43'), and his vassal Mashuiluwa, king of Mira (§§29'–32'). The last of these had rebelled against Mursili around the middle of his reign (ca. 1310 or later) and was deposed and replaced on the vassal throne by his nephew Kupanta-Kurunta.

The purpose of the oracle enquiry was to establish the cause of an illness from which the king suffered. This very likely was the affliction, reported in a ritual text, which suddenly came upon the king during a thunderstorm and resulted in his (at least partial) loss of speech. Many inquiries were conducted throughout the land of Hatti to determine which deity or deities were responsible for the affliction, and the reasons for divine wrath. In the west, Mashuiluwa had come under suspicion for his alleged impious utterances before the gods. The rituals prescribed here include summoning the god of Ahhiyawa and the god of Lazpa, and determining the appropriate ritual to be used for them. We do not know which particular gods of Ahhiyawa and Lazpa were fetched. Presumably they were called upon because they had specific qualities, as healing deities and so on, which made them suitable for the purpose. In any case, the inclusion of an Ahhiyawan deity in the efforts to cure the Hittite king suggests that peaceful relations had now been established between Ahhiyawa and Hatti, in the wake of the Hittite campaigns in the west against Ahhiyawan-supported Hittite rebel states in Mursili's early regnal years.

AHT 21

ORACLE REPORT (CTH 570.2)

KUB 22.56

obv.

§1'

1'. x […]

---

§2'

2'. x x […]

3'. […]

---

§3'

4'. *e-ni* ⌈*ku-it*⌉ 2-*ša*$^{?}$ […]

5'. […]

---

§4'

6'. x x ⌈*ku-it*⌉ *an-da a-ra*[*-an-zi*$^{?}$ …]

7'. x […]

---

§5'

8'. *nu-*⌈*kán*⌉ DIŠ KUR.KUR ^{URU}*Ḫat-ti* ^{GIŠ}TUKUL x […]

9'. […]

---

§6'

10'. *e-ni-pát* <*ku-it*> 2-*ša*$^{?}$ *nu* ŠE *a-uš-*⌈*zi*⌉ EGIR-⌈*pa-an*⌉-x [… DINGIR^{LUM} ŠE$^{?}$]

11'. ⌈*uš*⌉*-ki-ši nu* ŠE-*rù* x

12'. ŠE

---

§7'

13'. [o o-*i*]*š*$^{?}$*-ša* EGIR-⌈*pa*⌉ [*ka-ru-wa-r*]*i*$^{?}$*-wa-ar* x x TE$^{?}$ x […]

14'. […] x

---

§§1'–4' (obv. 1'–7') *(too fragmentary for translation)*

§5' (obv. 8'–9') Will the arms [of ... come(?)] against the lands of Hatti? [...]

§6' (obv. 10'–12') <In respect> to the fact that two ..., will it (Hatti?) experience prosperity? Hereafter, do you, [O deity], foresee [prosperity]? (If so), let it (the extispicy) be favorable. Result: favorable.

§7' (obv. 13'–14') [...] back, in the morning(?), ... [...]

§8'

15'. [*nu*$^{?}$] GIM-*an* ^{KUR}⸢*Kar*$^{?}$-*ki*$^{?}$⸣-*y*[*a* o o o] GIM-*an* ^{KUR}***Aḫ-ḫi-ya-wa***-x […]

16'. [o -*z*]*i*$^{?}$ DIŠ KUR.KUR x [o] x [o o] x ^{GIŠ}TUKUL ZAG-*aš* BIR$^{?}$ x UG[U$^{?}$ …]

17'. […] x […]

---

§9'

18'. [o ^{URU}]*Ḫat-ti* x [o] x ⸢DÙ$^{?}$⸣-*zi nu* DIŠ x x-*aš-ma-aš* ŠE-*rù* […]

19'. [o o] ^{GIŠ}TUKUL DU$_{8}$-*an-za* ⸢ZÉ *ḫi*⸣-*li*$_{8}$ GÙB-*li* RA$^{!IṢ!}$ *zu*-⸢*lu-ul*$^{!}$⸣[-*ki-iš* BABBAR]

---

§10'

20'. [*a-pé*$^{?}$]-⸢*e*$^{?}$⸣-*ez-za UL* ⸢DÙ-*zi*⸣ KUR.KUR ^{URU}*Ḫat*-⸢*ti*⸣ *e-ni-ša-an* x x […] x

21'. [o o -*z*]*i* ŠE-*rù ni* ⸢*ši*$^{?}$⸣ KAxU-*i* KASKAL.ḪI.A-*aš* ZAG-*aš ḫi-ri-du-kir*-⸢*ri*⸣-*da*

---

§11'

22'. [o o] x-*an-zi-ma* KUR.KUR ^{URU}*Ḫat-ti a-pé-za* TI-*zi* ŠE-*rù*

23'. GISKIM *a-kir-ḫi-ya-aš*

---

§12'

24'. [o o o ^{GI}]$^{\text{Š?}}$TUKUL$^{?}$ ^{URU}*Ḫat-ti* UGU ⸢BAL$^{?}$⸣-*zi* KI.MIN ŠE-*rù*

25'. ZÉ ⸢*ḫi*⸣-*li*$_{8}$

---

§13'

26'. [o o o o] x x x x-*ma*$^{?}$ ⸢*ku-it*⸣-*ki* KI.MIN ŠE-*rù ni* ⸢ZAG$^{?}$⸣-*aš* ⸢*tu*⸣-*da-me-da*

27'. [o o o -*e*]*n*$^{?}$ *uš-ki-zi* KASKAL.ḪI.A *ḫi-ri-du-kir-ri-da* GÙB-*li* RA^{I}[^{Ṣ}] x x x

---

§14'

28'. [o o o] x-*ma ku-wa-pí-ik-ki pa-iz-z*[*i* K]I.MIN ŠE-*rù ni* ⸢ZAG$^{?}$⸣-*aš*

29'. […] x ^{GIŠ}TUKUL x x x x […]

---

§15'

30'. [… -*z*]*i* ⸢*ku-it*⸣ *pa-ra*-⸢*a*⸣ […]

31'. […] NE […]

---

§8' (obv. 15'–17') [And] if the land of Karkiya(?) […] (or) if **Ahhiyawa** […], to the lands […] The 'weapon' of the right (and?) the kidney(?) upon(?) […]

§9' (obv. 18'–19') Will Hatti do/make […]? … Let it be favorable: the 'weapon' is detached; the gall bladder is *ḫilipšiman* and striped to the left; the *zulukiš* is white.

§10' (obv. 20'–21') Will it not do/make (it) [from there(?)] and the lands of Hatti thus […]? Let it be favorable: *nipašuri, šintaḫi*; 'roads' at the 'mouth'; that of the right is *ḫiridukirrida.*

§11' (obv. 22'–23') Will […] and the lands of Hatti thrive because of that? Let it be favorable. The omen is *akirḫiya.*

§12' (obv. 24'–25') Will the arms of Hatti prevail? Ditto. Let it be favorable: the gall bladder is *ḫilipšiman.*

§13' (obv. 26'–27') Will […] in any respect? Ditto. Let it be favorable: *nipašuri* of the right(?) is *tudameda*; […] faces; the 'roads' are *ḫiridukirrida* and striped on the left […]

§14' (obv. 28'–29') Will […] go anywhere? Ditto. Let it be favorable: *nipašuri* of the right […]; 'weapon' […]

§15' (obv. 30'–31') […] because forth […]

§16’

32’. [o o o o] x KUR.KUR ^{URU}*Ḫa*[*t-ti* …]-*ti*$^{?}$-x

33’. […] *tu*-⸢*da*⸣-*me-d*[*a* …] x

34’. […] x […]

rev.

§17’

1’. […]

---

§18’

2’. […] x *tar* x […]

3’. […] x […]

4’. […] x […]

---

§19’

5’. [*A-N*]*A* KUR.KUR ⸢^{URU}⸣*Ḫat-ti* ^{GIŠ}TUKUL ⸢IGI$^{!}$-*zi*$^{!}$⸣ SIG$_5$$^{!}$-*rù* EGIR-*pa-an-pát* NU.ŠE-*du ni* ⸢*ši*$^{?}$ *ke*⸣

6’. ZÉ *ḫi-li*$_8$

---

§20’

7’. ⸢*ú*⸣-*wa-an-zi ke-da-ni* É^{TI} NU.ŠE-*du ni* NU.GÁL

---

§21’

8’. *pa-ra-a ḫa-me*-⸢*eš*⸣-*ḫi* NU.ŠE-*du ni* GÙB-*za ši-ma* NU.GÁL

---

§22’

9’. KUR.KUR ^{URU}*Ḫat-ti* AN.ZA TAG-*an e-da-ni-pát* ^{LÚ}KÚR DIŠ KUR.KUR NU.ŠE-*du*

10’. INIM BAL *da*-x x x *ni ši UL* KAR$^{?}$-*at* ZAG-*za* <^{GIŠ}TUKUL> RA^{IṢ} *zul*-⸢*kiš* BABBAR⸣

---

§23’

11’. ^{GIŠ}ŠÚ.A *ú-wa*-⸢*i*⸣ *pé*-⸢*da*⸣-*i* NU.ŠE-*du zul*-⸢*kiš*⸣ BABBAR

---

§24’

12’. <<⸢*zul-kiš*⸣ BABBAR>> *ku-iš* ^{GIŠ}⸢TUKUL⸣ KUR.KUR ^{URU}⸢*Ḫat*⸣-*ti* KAR$^{!}$-*zi* NU.ŠE-*du*

13’. [^{GIŠ}TUKUL$^{?}$] DU$_8$-*an-za* ZAG-*za* RA^{IṢ}

---

§16’ (obv. 32’–34’) […] lands of Hatti […] *tudameda* […]

(gap)

§§17’–18’ (rev. 1’–4’) *(too fragmentary for translation)*

§19’ (rev. 5’–6’) Will armed force (come) [against] the lands of Hatti? Let the first (extispicy) be favorable, the second however unfavorable: *nipašuri, šintaḫi, keldi*; the gall bladder is *ḫilipšiman*.

§20’ (rev. 7’) Will they come to that house? Let it be unfavorable: *nipašuri* absent.

§21’ (rev. 8’) In the coming spring? Let it be unfavorable: *nipašuri* on the left, but *šintaḫi* absent.

§22’ (rev. 9’–10’) Will the lands of Hatti be affected(?) by …? To that particular enemy, to (his?) lands? Let it be unfavorable: … *nipašuri* and *šintaḫi* not found; <the ‘weapon’> striped on the right; the *zulkiš* is white.

§23’ (rev. 11’) Will the throne carry off woe? Let it be unfavorable: the *zulkiš* is white.

§24’ (rev. 12’–13’) Which arms will find the lands of Hatti? Let it be unfavorable: [the ‘weapon’] is detached and striped on the right.

§25’

14’. ^{GIŠ}ŠÚ.A NU.ŠE-⸢*du*⸣ *zul-kiš* BABBAR

---

§26’

15’. URU$^{\textit{LUM}}$ *ka*?-⸢*a*?⸣[-*aš*] *ŠA* x x x *a-uš-zi* NU.ŠE-*du*

16’. *ši A*-⸢*ŠAR*?⸣ *tar-na-aš* NU.ŠE

---

§27’

17’. ⸢^{URU}⸣TÚL-*na-aš*?*er* *a-uš*-⸢*zi*⸣ NU.ŠE-*du* ŠE

---

§28’

18’. ^{URU}*Ka-tap-pa-aš a-uš-z*[*i*] NU.ŠE-*du* ŠE

---

§29’

19’. ^{URU}*Ḫu-piš-ša-na-aš a*-⸢*uš-zi*⸣ NU.ŠE-*du* x-*aš* ^{GIŠ}TUKUL ⸢KI⸣-*aš* DU$_8$-*an-z*[*a* …]

---

§30’

20’. ALAM *zi*?-*da*? ŠE-*rù* ⸢É.DINGIR⸣$^{\textit{LIM}}$ x x ZAG!-*za* ZÉ *ḫi-li*$_8$ SAG.ME […]

---

§31’

21’. ALAM NU.ŠE-*du ni* ZAG ⸢*pé*⸣-*še-et*

---

§32’

22’. ^{GIŠ}ŠÚ.A *pa-a-u-w*[*a-a*]*š* NU.ŠE-*du ni* ⸢*ši*? *ta*? KAxU-*i* GÙB⸣-*za ar-ḫa-an* […]

23’. GÙB-*aš* ZAG-*aš* <<ZAG-*aš*>> *ar-ḫa pé-še*!-*et*!

---

§33’

24’. x x -*na-aš* URU.DIDLI.ḪI.A-x x URU x x […]

25’. ⁝KASKAL EN!? DINGIR$^{\textit{LIM}}$ ⁝ x-*lil*? *nu* ⸢KUR?⸣.ḪI.A *maḫ*?[- …]

26’. *e*!?-*ni*!? INIM É.DINGIR$^{\textit{LIM}}$ INIM!? *ŠA* x […]

27’. [o] x x x x *ir šar*

---

§34’

28’. […] x ŠE?-*rù* NU.ŠE-*d*[*u*] *TE*^{MEŠ} ŠE x […]

---

§25' (rev. 14') The throne? The *zulkiš* is white.

§26' (rev. 15'–16') Will this(?) city experience ...? Let it be unfavorable: *šintaḫi*; place of(?) *tarna*. Result: unfavorable.

§27' (rev. 17') Will the city of Arinna experience (it)? Let it be unfavorable. Result: favorable.

§28' (rev. 18') Will the city of Katappa experience (it)? Let it be unfavorable. Result: favorable.

§29' (rev. 19') Will the city of Hupisna experience (it)? Let it be unfavorable: the 'weapon' of ... is detached at the base(?). [...]

§30' (rev. 20') Is the divine image ... ? Let it be favorable: the temple ...; on the right the gall bladder is *ḫilipšiman*; the SAG.ME [...]

§31' (rev. 21') The divine image? Let it be favorable: *nipašuri* displaced to the right.

§32' (rev. 22'–23') The 'throne of departure'? Let it be unfavorable: *nipašuri, šintaḫi, tanani*; at the 'mouth', away to the left [...], those on the left and right severely displaced.

§33' (rev. 24'–27') The cities of [...] ... the journey of the caretaker(?) of the deity ... [...] this matter of the temple and the matter(?) of [...] ...

§34' (rev. 28') [...] Let it be favorable, (then) unfavorable. The extispicy was favorable [...]

§35’

29’. […] x x [… *n*]*i* NU.GÁL

§35' (rev. 29') […] *nipašuri* absent.

Commentary

The passages in these oracular reports (AhT 21–24) referring to Ahhiyawa are too fragmentary or too brief for comment. The earliest of them, AhT 22, probably to be dated to the reign of the first Tudhaliya, late-fifteenth century, makes reference to an unnamed enemy ruler of Ahhiya (§25), almost certainly the Attarissiya attested in the Indictment of Madduwatta (AhT 3). As we have noted, "Ahhiya" is the older form of "Ahhiyawa," and is attested only here and in the Madduwatta text.

AhT 22

Oracle Report (CTH 571.2)

KBo 16.97 + KBo 40.48

obv.

§1

1. *IŠ-TU* MUŠEN *ar-ḫa* ⸢*a-ri-iš*⸣*-ki-i*[*z-zi* o o] x *ku-wa-pí* ⸢*ku*⸣*-un-ni-eš-zi*
2. *nu* ^{d}UTU^{ŠI} *ú-ki-la wa-al-a*[*ḫ*]*-mi* EGIR-*ŠU*

---

§2

3. *ŠA* ^{erasure} ^{URU}*I-ya-ga-nu-e-na* GU$_4$.ḪI.A UDU[.ḪI.A] ^{m}*Mu-u-wa-at-ta-al-li-iš*
4. *wa-al-aḫ-zi* NU.SI[G$_5$]

---

§3

5. ^{URU}*Ka-ma-am-ma-kán ú-e-tum-ma-an-zi pa-ra-a* ⸢*ḫu-da*⸣*-a-ak na-i-wa-ni*
6. [*n*]*u a-pa-a-at* SIG$_5$*-in* EGIR-*ŠU*

---

§4

7. x x-*wa-an da-pí-ya-an ar-nu-ma-*[*a*]*n-zi* SIG$_5$

---

§5

8. [*ku-i*]*t-ma-an* LUGAL MUNUS.LUGAL ^{URU}*Ḫa-*⸢*at*⸣*-tu-ši še-er* SIG$_5$

---

§6

9. [*ku-i*]*t-ma-an a-ra-aḫ-za* ^{URU}*Zi-it-ḫ*[*a-r*]*a* EGIR-*ŠU*

---

§7

10. *ma-a-an* ^{m}*Ma-la-*LÚ*-iš Ú-UL ku-i*[*t-k*]*i ú-e-mi-ya-at na-at kat-ta-an ar-ḫa*
11. *ki-*⸢*it*⸣*-ta-ru ma-a-an wa-aš-túl-ma* [*ku-i*]*t-ki ki-ša-ri*
12. *nu* ^{UZU}NÍG.GIG.ḪI.A *kal-la-re-eš-du* NU.SIG$_5$

---

§1 (obv. 1–2) He is carrying out a remedial investigation by bird-oracle. When will it be auspicious? Should I, My Majesty, myself strike? Result: deferred.

§2 (obv. 3–4) Should Muwattalli attack the herds and flocks of the city of Iyaganuena? Result: unfavorable.

§3 (obv. 5–6) Should we send immediately to fortify the city of Kammamma? And is that favorable? Result: deferred.

§4 (obv. 7) Concerning the transport of all the ... Result: favorable.

§5 (obv. 8) While the King and Queen are up in Hattusa? Result: favorable.

§6 (obv. 9) While (they are) abroad, in the city of Zithara? Result: deferred.

§7 (obv. 10–12) If Mala-ziti has not found anything, then let it be set aside. But if some offense occurs, then let the liver oracle be unfavorable. Result: unfavorable.

§8

13. *ma-a-an* DINGIR.GE$_6$ ^{URU}*Ša-mu-u-ḫa ki-iš-ša-a*[*n*] *me-mi-iš-ki-iz-zi* MUNUS.LUGAL-*wa*

14. ^{URU}*Ša-mu-u-ḫa ú-id-du nu-wa* S[U.MEŠ] *a-pé-e-ez ki-ša-ri* NU.SIG$_5$

---

§9

15. *ku-it-ma-an* [SÍSKU]R.MEŠ *ši-pa-an-tah*[^{aḫ}-*ḫi* DINGI]R.MEŠ$^{!}$-*ya-az iš-ša-aḫ-ḫi* EGIR-*ŠU*

---

§10

16. *BE-LU*^{MEŠ} ^{URU}*Iš-ḫu-u-*⸢*pí-it*⸣*-ta wa-al-ḫa-a*[*n-zi*] EGIR-*ŠU*

---

§11

17. *ŠA* ^{URU}*Ti-ḫu-ra-aš-ši-ši* GU$_4$.ḪI.A UDU.ḪI.A [*wa-a*]*l-ḫa-an-zi* EGIR-*ŠU*

---

§12

18. *ŠA* ^{d}LAMMA SÍSKUR.MEŠ *ḫu-u-ma-an-da ka-a* ⸢*i*⸣-[*y*]*a-mi* SIG$_5$

---

§13

19. *ŠA* ^{URU}*Ta-an-ku-uš-na* SIG$_5$

---

§14

20. *ŠA* ^{URU}*Li-še-ep-ra* NU.SIG$_5$

---

§15

21. *ŠA* ^{URU}*Ta-az-zi-ša* ^{URU}*Ti-ik-ku-ku-wa* NU.SIG$_5$

---

§16

22. *ŠA BE-LU*$^{\text{MEŠ-}TIM}$ [EGIR-*ŠU*/(NU).SIG$_5$]

---

§17

23. *ŠA* KUR ^{URU}*Iš-ḫu-u-pí-it-ta* [EGIR-*ŠU*/(NU).SIG$_5$]

---

§18

24. [*ke*]-⸢*e*⸣-*el* URU-*aš* [EGIR-*ŠU*/(NU).SIG$_5$]

---

§19

25. *ŠA* KUR ⸢^{URU}⸣[*Ka*]-⸢*ḫa*⸣-*mi-iš-ša* [EGIR-*ŠU*/(NU).SIG$_5$]

---

§8 (obv. 13–14) If the Deity of the Night of the city of Samuha is speaking as follows: "Let the Queen come to Samuha so that the extispicies take place there," (should we indeed arrange for that)? Result: unfavorable.

§9 (obv. 15) While I perform the offerings, should I also worship the gods? Result: deferred.

§10 (obv. 16) Should the noblemen attack the city of Ishupitta? Result: deferred.

§11 (obv. 17) Should they attack the herds and flocks of the city of Tihurassisi? Result: deferred.

§12 (obv. 18) Should I perform all of the rituals of the Protective Deity here? Result: favorable.

§13 (obv. 19) Of the city of Tankusna? Result: favorable.

§14 (obv. 20) Of the city of Lisepra? Result: unfavorable.

§15 (obv. 21) Of the cities of Tazzisa and Tikkukuwa? Result: unfavorable.

§16 (obv. 22) Of the noblemen? [Result …]

§17 (obv. 23) Of the land of Ishupitta? [Result …]

§18 (obv. 24) Of this city? [Result …]

§19 (obv. 25) Of the land of Kahamissa? [Result …]

§20

26. *ḫa-an-te-ez-zi pal-ši ma-⸢aḫ-ḫa-an⸣* [… *ši-pa-an-da-aḫ-ḫu-un*]

27. *ki-nu-un QA-TAM-MA ši-pa-an-taḫ*^{aḫ}*-ḫi ú*$^{?}$[- … EGIR-*ŠU*/(NU).SIG$_5$]

---

§21

28. *ke-e-da-ni-pát* KASKAL-*ši pa-i-mi* ^{URU}*Ka-am-ma-ma i*-x [… *ni-pa-šu-u-ri-iš*]

29. ⸢*ši*⸣*-in-ta-ḫi-iš* ⸢*ke*⸣*-el-di-iš úr-ni-ir-ni du-wa-an-y*[*a* … EGIR-*ŠU*/(NU). SIG$_5$]

---

§22

30. *A-NA* ^{d}U ^{URU}*Ku-li-ú-i-iš-na ku-it* SÍSKUR ^{m}*Du-ud-du*(-)[o] x [o] x […]

31. *gul-aš-ki-iz-zi ni-pa-šu-u-ri-iš* ZAG-*az* GÙB-*la-az uk-tu-u-ri-iš-š*[*a*]

32. *ši-in-ta-ḫi-iš ke-el-ti-iš* ^{GIŠ}ŠÚ.A-*ḫi* GÙB-*la-an úr-ni-ir-ni-iš*

33. GÙB-*la-az wa-al-ḫa-an-za* NU.SIG$_5$

---

§23

34. *ŠA* SÍSKUR *mar-ša-i-ya-aš ni-pa-šu-u-ri-iš ši-in-ta-ḫi-iš ke-el-ti-iš a-ḫar-ri-an-za*

35. *u-ur-ki-iš úr-ni-ir-ni-iš* ZAG-*az a-*⸢*an-ša*⸣*-an-za* EGIR-*ŠU*

---

§24

36. *A-NA* ^{d}IŠKUR *ḫar-ši-ḫar-ši-ya-aš* ⸢*ṬUP*⸣*-PÍ-aš mu-*⸢*ke-eš*⸣*-šar ni-pa-šu-u-ri-iš*

37. *ši-in-ta-ḫi-iš ta-na-ni-iš* ⸢*ke-el*⸣*-ti-iš u-ur-ki-iš* KASKAL-*iš* SIG$_5$

---

§25

38. *ŠA* ^{LÚ}KÚR LÚ ^{URU}***Aḫ-ḫi-ya*** *ni-pa-šu-u-ri-iš ši-in-ta-ḫi-iš ta-na-ni-iš*

39. *ke-el-ti-iš u-ur-ki-iš zi-*⸢*za*⸣*-ḫi-iš* SIG$_5$

---

§26

40. *nu an-ze-el-ma ni-pa-šu-u-ri-iš ši-in-ta-ḫi-iš u-ur-ki-iš zi-za-ḫi-*⸢*iš*⸣ SIG$_5$

---

§27

41. *ŠA* KASKAL *IŠ-TU* [o *ni-pa*]*-šu-u-ri-iš ši-in-ta-ḫi-iš* ZAG-*az* GÙB-*la-az-zi-ya*

42. *ke-el-ti-*⸢*iš*⸣ [*úr-nir-ni-i*]*š* ZAG-*az* GÙB-*la-zi-ya ti-it-ti-an-za* SIG$_5$

---

§20 (obv. 26–27) Should I now offer [...] as [I offered ...] the first time? [Result ...]

§21 (obv. 28–29) Particularly this time should I proceed [to ...] Kammamma? [*nipašuri*], *šintaḫi*, *keldi* (are present); 'finger' (is present); and hither [... Result ...]

§22 (obv. 30–33) Which rituals should Duddu[...] write up for the Storm-God of the city of Kuliwisna? *nipašuri* firm on the right and left, *šintaḫi*, *keldi*; 'throne' unfavorable, 'finger' striped on the left. Result: unfavorable.

§23 (obv. 34–35) Concerning the ritual to counteract falsehood(?): *nipašuri*, *šintaḫi*; *keldi* is *aḫarriyant*; (parasite) track and 'finger' are smeared on the right. Result: deferred.

§24 (obv. 36–37) Concerning an evocation rite by the book (lit. 'of the tablet') for the Storm-God of Lightning: *nipašuri*, *šintaḫi*, *tanani*, *keldi*; (parasite) track, 'road.' Result: favorable.

§25 (obv. 38–39) Concerning the enemy ruler[107] of **Ahhiya**: *nipašuri*, *šintaḫi*, *tanani*, *keldi*; (parasite) track, tapeworm blister. Result: favorable.

§26 (obv. 40) Concerning us: *nipašuri*, *šintaḫi*; (parasite) track, tapeworm blister. Result: favorable.

§27 (obv. 41–42) Concerning the road/journey from [...]: *nipašuri* and *šintaḫi* on the right and left. Result: favorable.

107. The word LÚ literally means 'man,' but here, as in other contexts, it clearly refers to a leader or ruler of some kind.

rev.

§28

1. *ma-a-an a-ra-aḫ-zé-na-aš ku-it-ki* ÉRIN.MEŠ *ar-nu-wa-la-aš i-da-a-lu i-ya-az-zi*
2. ^{UZU}NÍG.GIG.ḪI.A-*kán ir-ḫa-a-aš-ša* SIG$_5$-*an-ta* ^{erasure} *ša-a-ki-ya-az-zi-ya-at*
3. ⌈*ša*⌉-*ra-a ar-ta-ri* SIG$_5$

---

§29

4. *A-WA-AT* ^{m}*I-ya-šal-la ni-pa-a-šu-u-ri-iš ši-in-ta-ḫi-iš ta-na-ni-iš*
5. *ke-el-ti-iš-kán* GÙB-*la-aš iš-ši-i* ^{UZU}ZÉ ZAG-*az ni-ni-in-kán*
6. *u-ur-ki-iš* NU.SIG$_5$

---

§30

7. ⌈*i*⌉-*ni ŠA* ^{URU}*Iš-ga-az-zu-wa ut-tar ma-aḫ-ḫa-an me-mi-ir nu* ^{d}UTU^{ŠI} *ú-ki-la*
8. *pa-i-mi nu a-pa-a-at* SIG$_5$-*in ni-pa-a-šu-u-ri-iš* ZAG-*aš* GAL GÙB-*la-aš-ma* TUR
9. *ši-in-ta-ḫi-iš* 2 *ta-na-a-ni-iš na-aš-ta* GÙB-*la-aš iš-ši-i an-da*
10. *šu-ú-*^{er}*ri-i-iš*^{er}*A-NA* ^{UZU}ZÉ *a-ta-ni-ti ki-it-ta-ri* KASKAL *A-NA úr-ni-ir-ni-ma-aš-ša-an*
11. ZAG-*aš la-at-ti-iš* GÙB-*la-az-zi-*⌈*ya*⌉ *wa-al-ḫa-an* EGIR-*ŠU*

---

§31

12. *ma-a-an* ^{d}*IŠTAR* ^{URU}*Ni-nu-u-wa* KIR$_4$ *ḫa-at-ta-an-ti ud-da-ni-i še-er kar-tim-mi-ya-u-an-za*
13. *ni-pa-šu-u-ri-iš* ZAG *IK-ŠU-UD ke-el-di-iš úr-ni-ir-ni-*⌈*iš* GÙB-*la-az*⌉ [*wa-al-ḫ*]*a-an-za*
14. *a-an-ša-an-na* GÙB-*la-az zi-za-ḫi-iš ŠA* ^{UZ}[^{U} … EGIR-*ŠU*/(NU).SIG$_5$]

---

§32

15. *nu* DINGIR.GE$_6$ ^{URU}*Ša-mu-u-ḫa-ma kar-tim-mi-ya-u*[*-wa-an-za ni-pa-šu-u-ri-iš* …]
16. ^{UZU}ZÉ ZAG-*az ni-ni-in-kán* ⌈*ŠA* $^{\mathrm{d?}}$⌉[U ^{GIŠ}TUKUL *úr-ni-ir-ni-iš*$^{?}$]
17. GÙB-*la-az wa-al-ḫa-an-za zi*[*-za-ḫi-iš* EGIR-*ŠU*/(NU).SIG$_5$]

---

§33

18. *nu* DINGIR.GE$_6$ ^{URU}*La-aḫ-ḫu-ra-ma k*[*ar-tim-mi-ya-u-wa-an-za ni-pa-šu-u-ri-iš*]

§28 (rev. 1–3) Concerning whether any foreign troops will mistreat the civilian captives: liver and edge favorable. It will persist because of (this) sign.

§29 (rev. 4–6) Concerning the matter of Iyasalla: *nipašuri*, *šintaḫi*, *tanani*, *keldi* favorable at the 'mouth'; gall bladder detached on the right, (parasite) track. Result: unfavorable.

§30 (rev. 7–11) As they have discussed this matter of the city of Isgazzuwa—should I, My Majesty, myself go, and would that be auspicious? Right *nipašuri* large but left one small, *šintaḫi*, two *tanani* favorable at the 'mouth'; fibrinous deposit lies on the gall bladder at the *atanita* as a 'road,' on 'finger' right thickening is striped on the left. Result: deferred.

§31 (rev. 12–14) Concerning whether Shaushga of Nineveh is angry about the matter of the priestess with the (ritually) mutilated nose: *nipašuri* touches the edge; *keldi* and 'finger' [striped(?)] on the left and smeared on the left; tapeworm blister on [… Result: …]

§32 (rev. 15–17) Is the Deity of the Night of Samuha angry? [*nipašuri*]; gall bladder detached on the right, ['weapon of the Storm-God,' 'finger'(?)] striped on the left, [tapeworm blister. Result: …]

§33 (rev. 18–22) Is the Deity of the Night of the city of Lahhurma [angry? *nipašuri*] firm above <the right>, *šintaḫi* […]; gall bladder loose on the right

19. ^{er}*uk-tu-u-ri-iš-ma*^{er} <ZAG-*aš*> *še-er ši-in-t*[*a-ḫi-iš* …] x […]
20. [^{UZ}]^{U}ZÉ ZAG-*az la-a-*⸢*an-za*⸣ […] *nu*? […]
21. [KASKAL *ú*]*r-nir-ni*<*-iš*>*-kán* ⸢ZAG?⸣[*-az wa-al-ḫa-an-za*? …] GÙB-*la-aš*
22. *la-at-ti-iš*! *zi-za-ḫi-iš* [EGIR-*ŠU*/(NU).SIG$_5$]

---

§34
23. *ŠA* ^{d}*IŠTAR* ^{URU}*Ni-i-nu-wa ni-pa-šu-u-ri-i*[*š* …] x GÙB-⸢*la*⸣*-aš-ma*
24. *ar-ḫa-ya-an ši-in-ta-ḫi-iš* ^{GIŠ}TUKUL *k*[*e-el-di-iš*? …] x GÙB-*la-az*
25. *ŠA* ^{d}LAMMA GÙB-*la-aš* ^{GIŠ}TUKUL KASKAL-*iš zi-za-ḫ*[*i-iš* EGIR-*ŠU*/(NU).SIG$_5$]

---

§35
26. ^{d}*IŠTAR* ^{URU}*Ḫa-at-ta-ri-na ni-pa-šu-u-ri-iš* x x [… *uk-t*]*u-u-ri-*⸢*iš-ma*⸣ ZAG-*aš še-er*
27. *ši-in-ta-ḫi-iš A-NA úr-ni-ir-ni-ma-aš-ša-an* [… EGIR-*ŠU*/(NU).SIG$_5$]

---

§36
28. *ŠA* AMA-*ŠU* ^{d}*IŠTAR ni-pa-a-šu-u-ri-iš* x […] GÙB-*la-aš-ma-aš-ši*
29. *ši-in-ta-ḫi-iš* KÁ.GAL-*kán ḫa-at-ta-an* x [… GÙ]B-*la-aš la-at-ti-i*[*š* EGIR-*ŠU*/(NU).SIG$_5$]

---

§37
30. *nu ŠA A-BI-ŠU-ma* ^{d}*IŠTAR ke-el-di-iš-pát a-ḫa*[*r-ri-ya-an-za t*]*a-ma-i-i*[*š*]
31. *ša-ga-a-iš* NU.GÁL EGIR-*ŠU*

---

§38
32. *nu ta-ma-i-iš* ^{er}*ku-iš-ki*^{er} ^{d}*IŠTAR* SIG$_5$

---

§39
33. *I-*[*N*]*A* ^{URU}*Ša-pí-nu-wa* ^{GIŠ}DAG-*ti kat-ta-an ti-i-ya-an-na ni*[*-pa-šu-u-ri-i*]*š a-ḫar-ri-ya-an-za*
34. *ši-in-ta-ḫi-iš ta-na-ni-iš ŠA* ^{d}U ^{GIŠ}TUKUL KASKAL *úr-ni*[*r-ni-i*]*š* GÙB-*la-az wa-al-ḫa-an-za*
35. 14 ^{ŠÀ}*TI-RA-NU* SIG$_5$

---

§40
36. *nu ša-ma-a-na-aš kat-ta-an Ú-UL-ma ku-it-ma-an ti-an-z*[*i*?] *ni-pa-šu-u-ri-iš-pát*

[…], ['road'], 'finger' [striped(?) on the right(?)], left thickening, tapeworm blister. [Result: …]

§34 (rev. 23–25) (Is it a matter) concerning Shaushga of Nineveh? *nipašuri*, […], the left off to the side, *šintaḫi*; 'weapon' (and?) *keldi* […] on the left, left 'weapon of the Protective Deity,' 'road,' tapeworm blister. [Result: …]

§35 (rev. 26–27) (Concerning) Shaushga of the city of Hattarina? *nipašuri* firm […], *šintaḫi* above the right; […] of the 'finger.' [Result: …]

§36 (rev. 28–29) (Concerning) the Shaushga of his mother (viz., of His Majesty)? *nipašuri*, […] its left *šintaḫi* […]; 'city gate' hollowed out, [… left] thickening. [Result: …]

§37 (rev. 30–31) Or (concerning) the Shaushga of his father? In particular, the *keldi* is *aḫarriyant*; no other sign present. Result: deferred.

§38 (rev. 32) Or (concerning) some other Shaushga? Result: favorable.

§39 (rev. 33–35) Concerning standing next to the throne in the city of Sapinuwa: the *nipašuri* is *aḫarriyant*, *šintaḫi*, *tanani*; 'weapon of the Storm-God,' 'road,' 'finger' striped to the left; fourteen intestinal coils. Result: favorable.

§40 (rev. 36–37) As long as (nothing) is set next to the foundations? Definitely *nipašuri*; above, 'finger' striped on the left. Result: deferred.

37. *úr-ni-ir-ni-iš-ša še-er* GÙB-*la-az wa-al-ḫa-an-za* [EG]IR-*ŠU*

---

§41

38. *ŠA* URU*Ši-ip-pa ku-it* SÍSKUR *na-at ma-aḫ-ḫa-an IŠ-T*[*U* dUT]U*ŠI* *ḫa-an-da-a-it-ta-ri*

39. *na-at QA-TAM-MA i-ya-mi ni-pa-šu-u-ri-i ki-ri-ḫi-i*[*š* ZA]G-*az ši-in-ta-ḫi-iš* EGIR-*ŠU*

---

§42

40. *A-NA BE-LU*MEŠ *ḫa-at-ra-a-mi nu* KASKAL LÚ.MEŠNÍ.ZU *w*[*a-a*]*l-ḫa-an-ni-iš-kán-zi ši-ya-an-da*

---

§43

41. KASKAL LÚNÍ.ZU *ši-in-ta-ḫi-iš ke-el-ti-iš-*[*š*]*a*? EGIR-*ŠU*

---

§44

42. *IŠ-TU* DINGIR*LIM* *ku-it Ú-UL ḫa-an-da-a-it-ta-ri* [*n*]*u ma-a-an A-NA* ALAM *še-er ši-in-ta-ḫi-iš-pát* EGIR-*ŠU*

---

§45

43. *A-NA* MUNUS.LUGAL *wa-aš-ši-ya-az* SIG_5

---

§46

44. *nu A-NA* MUNUS.LUGAL *Ú-UL-ma ku-it-ki i-en-zi ni-pa-šu-u-ri-iš ši-in-ta-ḫi-iš ke-el-ti-iš*

45. *úr-nir-ni-iš* ZAG-*az* GÙB-*la-az ti-it-ti-an*[*-za* G]AR-*aš-ša-an A-NA* GAR *še-er* SIG_5

---

§47

46. *ŠA* URU*Zi-it-ḫa-ra ku-i-e-eš* EZEN.ḪI.A ⸢*nu*⸣ *ki-nu-un i-ya-mi ši-in-ta-ḫi-iš*

47. UZUZÉ *er an-da uš-ki-iz-zi er u-ur-ki-iš* 2 KASK[AL *n*]*a-at-kán ḫa-an-da-a-an-te-eš*

48. *úr-nir-ni-iš* ZAG-*az wa-al-ḫa-an-za zi-za-ḫ*[*i-i*]*š* EGIR-*ŠU*

---

§48

49. *nu-za ku-wa-pí-ma* DINGIR.MEŠ *i-ya-mi nu a-pí-ya* DIN[GIR].GE_6 *nu* 3 *ni-pa-šu-u-ri-iš nu* ZAG-*aš še-er*

§41 (rev. 38–39) Which image (is appropriate) for the city of Sippa, and should I treat it as the deity specifies? *kiriḫi* on the *nipašuri*, *šintaḫi* on the right. Result: deferred.

§42 (rev. 40) Should I write to the noblemen so that they keep attacking the route used by the (enemy) scouts? (The matter) is pressing.

§43 (rev. 41) Concerning the route of the scouts: *šintaḫi* and *keldi*. Result: deferred.

§44 (rev. 42) Concerning that which is not specified by the deity, if it has to do with the image: Definitely *šintaḫi*. Result: deferred.

§45 (rev. 43) Concerning medicine for the Queen. Result: favorable.

§46 (rev. 44–45) And should nothing be done for the Queen? *nipašuri*, *šintaḫi*, *keldi*; 'finger' in place on the right and left; emplacement upon emplacement. Result: favorable.

§47 (rev. 46–48) Which are the festivals of Zithara, and should I celebrate (them) now? *šintaḫi* facing gall bladder; (parasite) track, two 'roads'—and they are parallel, 'finger' striped on the right, tapeworm blister. Result: deferred.

§48 (rev. 49–51) And where should I worship the deities, and is the Deity of the Night there? Three *nipašuri*s—that on the right has turned above; 'road,' 'finger' striped on back, but *puḫunuḫiman* on the left. Result: favorable.

50. *wa-aḫ-nu-an ḫar-zi* KASKAL *úr-nir-ni-iš* EGIR *w*[*a-al-ḫ*]*a-an-za* GÙB-*la-az-ma pu-ḫu-nu-ḫi-ma-an*
51. SIG$_5$

---

§49
52. *nu ka-a-ma* ⸢^{UZU}⸣[NÍG.G]IG.ḪI.A-*kán* ^{LÚ}*ḫa-a-aš*$^?$[-o o o o]-*ra*

---

§50
53. [o] ⸢*iš*⸣ x x [o o o] x [o o] x x [o o] x-*ta*

---

§51
54. [*Š*]*A* ^{d}*L*[*a*$^?$- …] x

---

§52
55. [*Š*]*A*$^?$ É.DINGIR$^{\textit{LI}}$[$^{\textit{M}}$ … *ni-pa-šu-u-ri-i*]*š pí-iš-ši-ya-at ši-in-ta-ḫi-iš*
56. [*nu Š*]*A* ^{d}*IŠTAR* ^{GIŠ}TU[KUL …] x-*a-an* KASKAL NU.SIG$_5$

---

§53
57. [*Š*]*A* ^{LÚ}KÚR ^{d}UTU$^{\textit{ŠI}}$ *Ú-U*[*L* …] EGIR-*ŠU*

---

§54
left edge
1a. *A-WA-AT A-I-YA-LE-E ni-pa-šu-u-ri-iš ir-ki-pé-el-l*[*i-i*]*š*
2a. ^{UZU}ZÉ *ták-ša-an ḫar-zi* EGIR-*ŠU*

---

§55
3a. *ŠA* ^{m}*Túl-pí-*^{d}U *wa-aš-ši-ya-aš ši-in-ta-ḫi-iš ŠA* ^{d}GÌR-*aš-ša-an* [*I-N*]*A* ^{GIŠ}ŠÚ.A
4a. *pít-tu-li-ya-aš ki-it-ta-ri úr-nir-ni-iš pu-ḫu-nu-u-ḫi-ma-a*[*n z*]*i* EGIR-*ŠU*

---

§56
1b. *ŠA* ^{LÚ}KÚR *ši-i*[*n-t*]*a-ḫi-iš ta-na-ni-iš a-ga-ta-ḫi-iš* NU.SIG$_5$
2b. *ta-pa-aš-ša-az* ⸢*úr*⸣*-nir-ni-iš* SAG.DU-⸢*SÚ*⸣ *še-er ar-ḫa da-an-za* NU.SIG$_5$
3b. *A-NA* SAG.DU MUNUS.LUGAL *úr-nir-ni-iš-kán* SAG.DU-*SÚ še-er ar-ḫa da-an-za* NU.SIG$_5$
4b. *ŠA* MUNUS.LUGAL *mu-un-na-*<*an-za*$^?$> DINGIR.GE$_6$ *ni-pa-šu-u-ri-iš ši-in-ta-ḫi-iš*
5b. KASKAL-*iš ne-e-a-an-za* EGIR-*ŠU*

---

§49 (rev. 52) And here? The liver ...

§§50–51 *(too fragmentary for translation)*

§52 (rev. 55–56) Concerning the [...] of the temple: [... *nipašuri*] displaced, *šintaḫi*; and the 'weapon of Shaushga' [...], 'road.' Result: unfavorable.

§53 (rev. 57) Should His Majesty not [... the ...] of the enemy? [...] Result: deferred.

§54 (left edge 1a–2a) Concerning the matter of the stag: *nipašuri* is *irkipelli* and holds the gall bladder together. Result: deferred.

§55 (left edge 3a–4a) Concerning the medicine of Tulpi-Teshshup: *šintaḫi*; a constriction lies upon the 'throne of Sumuqan,' 'finger' is *puḫunima*, tapeworm blister. Result: deferred.

§56 (left edge 1b–5b) Concerning (the matter) of the enemy: *šintaḫi*, *tanani*; *agataḫi*. Result: unfavorable.

Because of fever? 'Finger' displaced above its head. Result: unfavorable.

Concerning the person of the Queen: 'finger' displaced above its head. Result: unfavorable.

Concerning the concealed(?) Deity of the Night of the Queen: *nipašuri*, *šintaḫi*; 'road' turned. Result: deferred.

AhT 23

Oracle Report (CTH 572.1)

KUB 18.58 + KUB 6.7

ii

§1'

1'. […] LUGAL ^{KUR}***Aḫ-ḫi-ya***[***-(u)-wa*** …]

2'. […] *da-pí* ZI ME-*aš* […]

3'. [2-*Ú* …] x IGI.LÁ PAB-*mar* […]

4'. [3-*ŠÚ* … LUGAL$^{?}$] ^{LÚ}KÚR KASKAL ^{LÚ}KÚR ME[-*a*]*š* […] x-*te*$^{?}$-*li* GAR-*ri*

---

§2'

5'. […]⸢*A*⸣-*NA* ^{d}UTU$^{!ŠI}$ x […]

6'. […]-*tar da-pí* Z[I …]

7'. […] x KASKAL LUGAL ME-*aš* x x x […]-⸢*a*$^{?}$⸣ GAR-*ri*

---

§3'

8'. […] x-*ma* x x x […]

9'. […] x-*an*(-)x […]

iii

§4'

1'. […] x […]

---

§5'

2'. ⸢DINGIR^{LUM}⸣-*mu* ZÁḪ *ke-da-ni* MU-*ti u*[*š*$^{!}$-*ki-ši* NU.SIG$_5$-*du* / SIG$_5$-*ru*]

3'. DINGIR.MAḪ GUB-*iš* PAB-*mar* ÚŠ-*ya* ME-*aš* ⸢*nu-kán A*⸣-[*NA* … SUM]

4'. 2-*Ú* ^{d}UTU AN GUB-*iš pár-na-aš a-aš-šu* ME-*aš* ⸢*A*⸣[-*NA* … SUM]

5'. 3-*ŠÚ* DINGIR^{LUM}-*za* x-x-*ar-ḫa kar-pí-in* ME-*aš nu-kán* [… SUM]

---

§6'

6'. *nu-mu* DINGIR^{LUM} ZÁḪ AŠ MU.2.KAM-*ma uš-ki-ši* NU.SIG$_5$-*d*[*u*]

7'. GIG TUR PAB-*mar* ÚŠ-*ya* ME-*aš nu-kán A*-⸢*NA* GIG GAL$^{?}$⸣ [SUM]

8'. 2-*Ú* ^{d}UTU GUB *A-DÁM-MA* IGI.LÁ ME-*aš pa-i* S[UM]

§1' (ii 1'–4') Will the King of **Ahhiyawa** […]? […] took the intact soul, [and … Second (oracle): … took] observation and protection, [and … Third (oracle): …] took [the king(?)] of the enemy and the campaign of the enemy, and they are set by […]

§2'. (ii 5'–7') […] to His Majesty […]? [… took] the intact soul, [and … Second: …] took […] and the campaign of the king, and they are set by […]

§3' (ii 8'–9') *(too fragmentary for translation)*

(gap)

§4' (iii 1') *(too fragmentary for translation)*

§5' (iii 2'–5') Do you, O deity, [foresee] destruction for me during this year? [(If so), let it (the oracle result) be (un)favorable.] The birth-deity arose, took protection and death, and [gave (them) to …] Second: The Sun-God of Heaven arose, took the good fortune of the household, [and gave (it)] to […] Third: The deity took the … anger, and [gave (it) to …]

§6' (iii 6'–8') Do you, O deity, foresee destruction for me during the second year? Let it be unfavorable. The minor illness took protection and death, and [gave] (them) to the severe(?) illness. Second: The Sun-God arose, took blood and observation, and [gave] (them) to the congregation.

---

§7'

9'. *nu-mu* DINGIR^{LUM} ZÁḪ AŠ MU.3.KAM-*ma uš-ki-ši* NU.SIG$_5$-*du*

10'. LUGAL ZAG-*tar da-pí* ZI *A-DÁM-MA* EGIR-*pa* ^{GIŠ}DAG

11'. 2-*Ú* SIG$_5$-*za* ZALAG.GA ME-*aš* DINGIR.MAḪ SUM

---

§8'

12'. *nu-mu* DINGIR^{LUM} ZÁḪ AŠ MU.4.KAM *uš-ki-ši* NU.SIG$_5$-*du*

13'. SIG$_5$-*za* MU *A-DÁM-MA* ME-*aš na-at pa-i* SUM

14'. 2-*Ú pa-za* ZAG-*tar* ME-*aš nu-kán da-pí* ZI-*ni*

---

§9'

15'. *nu-mu* DINGIR^{LUM} ZÁḪ AŠ MU.5.KAM-*ma uš-ki-ši* SIG$_5$-*r*[*u*]

16'. SIG$_5$-*za* DINGIR.MAḪ IGI.LÁ ^{d}NAM *mi-nu-mar* ME-*aš nu-kán* ^{d}*Gul-še-eš*

17'. 2-*Ú* DINGIR.MEŠ GUB-*ir A-DÁM-MA* ME-*ir*$^{!}$ *pa-i* SUM

---

§10'

18'. *nu-mu* DINGIR^{LUM} ZÁḪ AŠ MU.6.KAM *u-uš-ki-ši* SIG$_5$-⸢*ru*⸣

19'. DINGIR^{LUM} *da-pí* ZI *mi-nu-mar mu-keš-šar* ME-*aš nu-kán* UN-*aš*

20'. 2-*Ú* ^{GIŠ}DAG GUB *da-pí* ZI LUGAL ZAG-*tar* ME-*aš* DINGIR.MEŠ SUM$^{!}$

---

§11'

21'. *nu-mu* DINGIR^{LUM} ZÁḪ AŠ MU.7.KAM *uš-ki-ši* NU.SIG$_5$-*du*

22'. [S]IG$_5$ GUB-*iš* MU SILIM TI ME-*aš* DINGIR.MAḪ SUM

23'. [2]-⸢*Ú*⸣ DINGIR^{LUM} *da-pí* ZI SILIM ME-*aš pa-i* SUM

---

§12'

24'. [*nu-mu*] DINGIR^{LUM} ZÁḪ AŠ MU.8.KAM *uš-ki-ši* ⸢SIG$_5$$^{?}$-*ru*$^{?}$⸣

25'. [o o o] GUB-*iš* PAB-*mar* MU.ḪI.A ME-*aš nu-kán* x x ⸢*da*⸣-*pí* ZI-*n*[*i* SUM]

---

§13'

26'. […] P[AB$^{?}$-*m*]*ar* MU.ḪI.A ME-*aš*$^{!}$ *n*[*u-ká*]*n* ^{d}*Gul-še-eš*[108]

27'. [*nu-mu* DINGIR^{LUM} ZÁḪ AŠ M]U.9.KAM-*ma uš-ki*[-*ši*] x-*mi* NU.SIG$_5$-*du*

28'. [2-*Ú* …] x IGI.ḪI.A SAG.DU-*i wa-aš-du-li* GAR-*r*[*i*]

---

108. The scribe apparently forgot to write the question before he began to record his observations.

§7' (iii 9'–11') Do you, O deity, foresee destruction for me during the third year? Let it be unfavorable. The king (took) rightness, the intact soul, and blood, (and gave them) back to the throne. Second: Favor took brightness, and gave (it) to the birth-deity.

§8' (iii 12'–14') Do you, O deity, foresee destruction for me during the fourth year? Let it be unfavorable. Favor took the year and blood, and gave them to the congregation. Second: The congregation took rightness, and (gave it) to the intact soul.

§9' (iii 15'–17') Do you, O deity, foresee destruction for me during the fifth year? Let it be favorable. Favor took the birth-deity, observation, fate, and placation, and (gave them to) the Fate-deities. Second: The deities arose, took blood, and gave (it) to the congregation.

§10' (iii 18'–20') Do you, O deity, foresee destruction for me during the sixth year? Let it be favorable. The deity took the intact soul, placation, and evocation, and (gave them) to the population. Second: The throne arose, took the intact soul, the king, and rightness, and gave (them) to the deities.

§11' (iii 21'–23') Do you, O deity, foresee destruction for me during the seventh year? Let it be unfavorable. Favor arose, took the year, well-being, and life, and gave (them) to the birth-deity. [Second:] The deity took the intact soul and well-being, and gave (them) to the congregation.

§12' (iii 24'–25') Do you, O deity, foresee destruction [for me] during the eighth year? Let it be favorable(?). [...] arose, took protection and the years, and [gave] (them) to the intact soul.

§13' (iii 26'–28') [Do you, O deity,] foresee [destruction for me during] the ninth year? Let it be unfavorable. ... [...] took protection(?) and the years, and (gave them) to the Fate-deities. [Second: ... (took) ...] and the eyes, and they are set by the head and the offense.

---

§14’
29’. […] x-⸢*ru*⸣ TA GIG GAL ḪUL-*za iš-tar-*⸢*na*⸣ *ar-ḫa ú-it*
30’. [… GI]G TUR 2-*Ú* DINGIR.MAḪ GUB-*iš* PAB-*mar* TI
31’. [… -*a*]*n* 3-*ŠÚ* DINGIR^{LUM} *da-pí* ZI MU.ḪI.A ME-*aš*

---

§15’
32’. [… *IŠ-T*]*U* ^{KUR}*Ḫat-ti* GAM-*an pít-ti-ya-mi*
33’. […]-⸢*i*⸣ *A-NA* MU.ḪI.A *še-er*
34’. […] x *ne-ya-ši* SIG$_5$-*ru*
35’. […] x x LUGAL IGI.LÁ LUGAL ME-*aš na-at pa-an-qa-u-i* ⸢SUM⸣
36’. [2-*Ú* …] x *ḫur-na-in* SILIM ME-*aš nu-kán* DINGIR.MEŠ$^{!?}$
37’. [3-*ŠÚ* … *mi*]-*nu-mar* ME-*aš* ŠÀ ŠE^{er}

---

§16’.
38’. […]-*mi* DINGIR^{LUM}-⸢*ma*?-*za*⸣ *UL* ME-*ti*
39’. […] x-⸢*mar*?⸣ SUM-⸢*an*?⸣ *ḫar-zi*
40’. […] x x ⸓*šal-ta-li-in*

---

§17’
41’. […] x *an-da ḫul-ḫu-li-ya-mi*
42’. [… -*a*]*š*? DINGIR^{LUM} [o] x *ar-ḫa a-ar*$^{!}$-*ti*$^{!}$
43’. [… -*m*]*ar* DINGIR[$^{LUM?}$ o o] x-*mar*
44’. [… *pa*]-*an-qa-u-i*
45’. [… S]UM

---

§18’
46’. […] ⸢^{É}⸣*ši-nap-ši* […]
47’. […] x-*za-ká*[*n*? …]
iv
§19’
1’. *traces*

---

§20’
2’. […]-*ul* ZÁḪ […]
3’. […] x ME-*aš nu-kán* DINGIR-*ni* [… SUM]

---

§21’
4’. [… *a*]*r-ḫa* SIG$_5$-*in iš-pár-za-i* SIG$_5$-⸢*ru*⸣

§14' (iii 29'–31') Has […] escaped from the severe illness and the evil? […] minor [illness]. Second: The birth-deity arose, (took) protection and life, [and …] Third: The deity took the intact soul and the years.

§15' (iii 32'–37') Will I flee […] down [from] Hatti? […] upon the years […] will you turn? Let it be favorable. […] took […] of the king, observation, and the king, and gave them to the congregation. [Second: …] took […] the curse and well-being, and (gave them) to the deities(?).

§16' (iii 38'–40') Will I […]? Will you, O deity, not take for yourself? […] has given […] *šaltalin*.

§17' (iii 41'–45') Will I fight in […]? Will you, O deity, step(?) away […]? […] the deity […] gave to the congregation.

§18' (iii 46'–47') […] *šinapši*-building […]

(gap)

§19' (iv 1') *(too fragmentary for translation)*

§20' (iv 2'–3') […] destruction […]? […] took […], and [gave] (it) to the deity.

§21' (iv 4'–6') Will […] escape successfully [from …]? Let it be favorable. […] took placation, observation, and … of the household. [Second: …]

5'. [… *-a*]*š mi-nu-mar* IGI.LÁ *pár-na-aš* x*-a-iš* ME*-aš*
6'. [2-*Ú* …] x ME*-aš na-*⸢*at*⸣*-kán kar-pí* GAR*-ri*

---

§22'
7'. [*nu-mu* MU.ḪI.A$^{?}$] GÍD.DA
8'. […] x ḪUL*-ya* ME*-aš* DINGIR.MEŠ*-aš*
8'a. [SUM]

---

§23'
9'. [o] x *ku$^{?}$-iš* ZÁḪ SUR$_7$ x x x x x x MU ZÁḪ
10'. [A]Š ^{KUR}*Kar-an-du*<*ni-aš*> ZAG*-tar* DINGIR.MEŠ*-aš mi-nu-mar* ⸢*a-aš-šu*⸣ ME*-aš kar-pí* GAR*-ri*
11'. ⸢2⸣-*Ú* DINGIR^{LUM} *da-pí* ZI MU ÚŠ ME*-aš* ⸢*nu-kán an-da* SUD⸣.LIŠ

---

§24'[109]
12'. [o] x x IB$^{?}$ ZIG$^{?}$ x-x*-an* ⸢*ku$^{?}$-iš$^{?}$*⸣ SUM *ta*[- o o o o] x
13'. […] x KUR *i-wa-*⸢*ar*⸣ x*-pí$^{?}$* BAL⸢*-mar*⸣ […] *ku-wa-pí* x x
14'. […] x*-ma* 𒑱*nu-pát-za-ma* 𒑱*nu-mu$^{?}$-za$^{?}$* ⸢ME⸣[*-aš*] ⸢*na$^{?}$-at$^{?}$*⸣ *da*<*-pí*> ZI
15'. [DINGIR^{LUM} … *A-NA*] LUGAL $^{LÚ!}$KÚR$^{!}$ ḪUL *uš-ki-ši nu* ⸢GISKIM⸣.MEŠ ^{d}UTU UN*-an* < … >

---

§25'
16'. [… *Š*]*A$^{?}$* LUGAL ḪUL-⸢*ya*⸣ SIxSÁ*-at* x*-i a-pa-at$^{!}$*
17'. […] x*-tar* IZI ME*-aš nu-kán* ^{d}⸢*Gul*⸣*-še da-pí* ZI
18'. [… *-a*]*t$^{?}$*

---

§26'
19'. [… *t*]*a-ma-i* NU.SIG$_5$*-du*
20'. [… *-k*]*án kar-pí* GAR*-ri* NU.SIG$_5$

---

§27'
21'. […] x *ar-ḫa* ⸢*ki-kiš*⸣*-ta-ri*
22'. [… *n*]*e šal-li wa-aš-túl* PAB*-mar*
23'. […]
24'. […]

---

§28'
25'. […] x x GAR-⸢*ri*⸣

109. Much of this paragraph appears to have been erased.

took […], and it is set by the anger.

§22’ (iv 7’–8’) [Will I enjoy] long [years? …] took […] and evil, and [gave] (them) to the deities.

§23’ (iv 9’–11’) […] whatever destruction … in Babylonia. The rightness took the placation of the deities and the good, and they are set by the anger. Second: The deity took the intact soul, the year, and death, and (gave them) to SUD.LIŠ.

§24’ (iv 12’–15’) … took, and (gave) them to the intact soul. Do you, [O deity], foresee evil for the king of the enemy? Will the Sun-God <give?> omens to the population?

§25’ (iv 16’–18’) […] and the evil of the king were determined by oracle … […] took fire, and (gave it) to the fate-deities and the intact soul.

§26’ (iv 19’–20’) […] Let it be unfavorable. […] is set by the anger. Result: unfavorable.

§27’ (iv 21’–24’) Will […] be transformed? […] great offense and protection […]

§28’ (iv 25’) […] is set [by …]

AhT 24

Oracle Report (CTH 572.2)

KBo 48.22

1'. [… ^{KU}]^{R}***Aḫ-ḫi-ya-w*[*a*** …]
2'. […] x x LÚ.MEŠ ***Aḫ-ḫ*[*i-ya-wa*** …]
3'. [… *da-p*]*í* ZI TI$^{!}$-*tar*$^{!}$ ME-*aš* […]
4'. […] ZAG-*tar* MÈ GU_4? […]
5'. *traces*

[… land of] **Ahhiyawa** […] people of **Ahhiyawa** […] took [the intact] soul and life, [and …] rightness, battle, oxen(?) […]

AHT 25

LETTER (CTH 581*)

KBo 18.135

obv.

§1’

1’. […] ⸢*iš*$^{?}$⸣ […]
2’. […]-*e-zi k*[*a*$^{?}$- …]
3’. [… *n*]*am-ma pa*[- …]
4’. [… -*d*]*u*$^{?}$ *e-ep*[(-) …]

---

§2’

5’. [… -*a*]*n*$^{?}$-*mu Ú-UL z*[*i*- …]
6’. […] x.MEŠ *ku-i-e-eš ḫa*[- …]
7’. [… *k*]*a*$^{?}$-*a-aš-ma-an-na-aš A*-⸢*NA*⸣ […]
8’. […] x *tar-nu-um-me-ni nu A-NA* ^{d}[…]
9’. [… *nu-mu* … *ki-iš-ša-an TÀ*]*Š-PUR I-NA* ^{KUR}***Aḫ-ḫi-ya-u-wa-wa*** *pa-a-u-*
-wa[*-an-zi* …]
10’. [… *nu-ut-ta* … *ki-i*]*š-ša-an ḫa-at-ra-a-nu-un* EGIR-*an*[*-ma-wa-ra-an*$^{?}$ …]
11’. […] *na-aš-ma-wa-ra-an-mu ar-ḫa up-pí* […]
12’. [… *na-aš-ma*]*-wa-ra-an-za-an I-NA* É-*KA an-da* [*e-ep*$^{?}$ …]
13’. […] x-*aš-ši a-píd-da-an* EGIR-*an-da ki-iš*[*-ša-an TÀŠ-PUR* …]
14’. […] ⸢*a*⸣-*pí-ya-pát*$^{!}$ *e-eš-du ma-a-an-w*[*a* …]
15’. [… *a-pa*]*-a-at* ⸢*ša*⸣-*a-ki tu-el-wa-za* […]
16’. […]-⸢*el*$^{?}$⸣ [*pé*$^{?}$⸣-⸢*e*$^{?}$⸣-*da-an-zi nu-w*[*a*(-) …]
17’. […]

---

§3’

18’. [… *ú*/*pé-e-d*]*a*$^{?}$-*aš nu*[(-) …]
19’. […] x TUKU.TUK[U- …]
20’. […] x-*ir* […]

rev.

§4’

1’. […] x […] x *pí*$^{?}$ […]

§1' (obv. 1'–4') *(too fragmentary for translation)*

§2' (obv. 5'–17') […] not (to?) me […] those which […] now for us to […] we will set free. And to […] You wrote to me [… as follows]: "To go to **Ahhiyawa** [… " And] I wrote as follows […] to you: "[… him] back, or send him off to me [… , or detain(?)] him for yourself in your house […]" Thereupon [you wrote] back as follows concerning him(?): "[…] let him be there. If […] know that! Your […] they will transport(?), and […]"

§3' (obv. 18'–20') [… he brought/took(?)], and […] angry […] they […]

(gap)

§4' (rev. 1'–7') […] those of […] you say: "Not […] He was human." Then him […] oracular inquiry […] back not […] I will give. And even now,

2'. […] x *a-pu-u-uš ŠA* x […]
3'. […] *me-ma-at-ti*$^{!}$ *Ú-UL-wa*[(-) …]
4'. […] x UN-*aš e-eš-ta na-an* […]
5'. [… *-a*]*t*$^{?}$*-ta a-ri-ya-še-eš-šar* […]
6'. [… *-š/t*]*a-az-ma* EGIR-*pa Ú-UL* […]
7'. [… *p*]*í*$^{?}$*-iḫ-ḫi nu ki-nu-un-pát ku-it-ma-an* […]

---

§5'
8'. […]-⸢*ma*$^{?}$⸣ *nu-wa* ^{GIŠ}MÁ.ḪI.A *ú-e-er nu-*⸢*wa*⸣*-aš*[- …]

while […]

§5’ (rev. 8’) […] “Then the ships came, and [… ”]

COMMENTARY

This text mentions a journey to Ahhiyawa, but is otherwise too fragmentary for analysis.

AHT 26

VOTIVE PRAYER OF PUDUHEPA(?) (WIFE OF HATTUSILI III) (CTH 590)

The Hittite king and queen might make promises of future gifts to a deity should that god or goddess assist in the resolution of some pressing problem. Here the queen employs this strategy to secure divine intervention against the ever-troublesome Piyamaradu.

KUB 56.15

ii

§1’

1. [*A-N*]*A* ^{d}UTU^{Š}[^{I} …]
2. [*nu*] *A-NA* $^{ḪUR.S}$[^{AG} … 1 GU$_4$ 8 UDU *am-ba-aš-ši*?]
3. 1 GU$_4$ 8 UDU *ke-e*[*l-di-ya pí-iḫ-ḫi*]

---

§2’

4. *A-NA* ^{d}U ^{d}*Ḫé-bat* ^{URU}x […]
5. *ku-i-e-eš ku-i-e-eš* DINGIR.MEŠ […]
6. *pa-ra-a ti-ya-mi*

---

§3’

7. *ma-a-an-na-mu* ^{d}DÌM.NUN.ME x [… *Ú-UL e-ep-zi* …]
8. *A-NA* x.ḪI.A *ša-ri-wa-mu-kán* x […]
9. *nu A-NA* DINGIR^{LIM} ⸢GAŠAN⸣-*YA* 1 GU$_4$ 8 UDU *a*[*m-ba-aš-ši*]
10. 1 GU$_4$ 8 UDU *ke-el-di-ya pí-iḫ-ḫi* […]
11. *ku-it AŠ-RU IŠ-*⸢*TU*⸣ Ì *šu-un-ni-y*[*a-an* …]
12. [*nu*] *A-NA* DINGIR^{LIM} ⸢GAŠAN⸣-*YA ku-un-ga-an* x x [… ALAM KÙ.SIG$_{17}$]
13. [KI.LÁ.BI] ⸢1 *MA*⸣-*NA* DÙ-*mi na-an IŠ-TU* Ì.DÙG[.GA *iš-ki-mi*?]
14. [*na-an t*]*e*?-*eḫ-ḫi na-an A-NA* DINGIR^{LIM} *pí-iḫ-ḫi*

---

§1' (ii 1–3) [On behalf of] His Majesty [I will ... , and I will give] to Mount [... one ox and eight sheep as a burnt offering] and one ox and eight sheep for well-being.

§2' (ii 4–6) For Teshshup and Hebat of (the town of) [... , and for] whatever deities [...], I will step forward.

§3' (ii 7–14) And if the goddess Mamma [does not seize me ...], then I will give to the goddess, My Lady, one ox and eight sheep [as a burnt offering] and one ox and eight sheep for well-being. [...] which location is sown with sesame(?) is secured for the goddess, My Lady. [...] I will make [an image of gold(?)], one mina [in weight, anoint(?)] it with fine oil, take [it], and give it to the goddess.

§4'

15. [*nu* MUNUS.LUGAL *ku-wa*]*-pí* AŠ ^{URU}*Iz-zi-ya A-NA* A.AB.BA *p*[*a*$^{?}$*-it*$^{?}$ ...]

16. [o o o o o] x *nu-za-kán* MUNUS.LUGAL *A-NA* A.AB.BA ⸢*kiš-an*⸣ [*IK*- -*RU-UB*]

17. [o o o o o o] *ma-a-an-wa* A.AB.BA EN-*YA A-NA* DINGIR.⸢MEŠ⸣ [*iš-tar-na*$^{?}$ ...]

18. [o o o o o o] x-*a-ši* ^{m}*Pí-ya-ma-ra-du-un-mu-kán* [...]

19. [o o o o o o-*i*]*t-ti UL-aš-mu-kán iš-pár-za-zi* [...]

20. [o o o o o o o] x *ku-it* SISKUR *pí-iš-kán-zi* [...]

21. [o o o o o o o] ⸢*A-NA*⸣ SISKUR A<.AB>.BA$^{!}$ *ku-it ḫa-an-ta-a-an n*[*e*$^{?}$- ...]

22. [o o o o o o o o] x x-⸢*wi*$_{5}$⸣ *A-NA* DINGIR.MEŠ-*ya-kán ku-e-da-aš* [...]

23. [o o o o o o o o] x ⸢TI⸣-*an e-eš-ta* ⸢*nu*⸣ *a-pé-e-da-n*[*i* ...]

24. [o o o o o o o o]-*an-da-aš* NINDA.GUR$_{4}$.RA *ma-*⸢*al-la*⸣*-a-i*

---

§5'

25. [o o o o o o o o ^{URU}*K*]*um-*⸢*ma*⸣*-an-ni ma-a-an* ^{m}*Pí-ya-ma-ra*[*-du-un*]

26. [o o o o o o o o o] x x *IŠ-TU E-DÁ-TI e-ep-t*[*i*]

27. [...] x A x KÙ.SIG$_{17}$ MUŠEN KÙ.SIG$_{17}$ *E-DA-N*[*U* KÙ.SIG$_{17}$]

28. [...] ⸢^{m}⸣*Pí-ya-ma-ra-du-uš-ša-at-k*[*án* ...]

29. [...]-⸢*a*$^{?}$⸣-*i*

---

§6'

30. [... *k*]*u-e-da-ni-pát* INIM-*ni š*[*e-er* ...]

31. [... *a*]-⸢*pé*⸣*-e-da-ni* KÙ.SIG$_{17}$ [...]

§4' (ii 15–24) [When the Queen went] to (the town of) Izziya, to the Sea, […] then the Queen [made a vow] to the Sea as follows: "[…] If you, the Sea, My Lord, [… among] the gods, and you […] Piyamaradu to me so that he does not elude my grasp, […] which offering they will give […] which is prepared for the Ritual of the Sea(!)." […] to/for the gods whom […] it was living, and to/for that one […] he will grind the […] thick loaves of bread.

§5' (ii 25–29) […] (the town of) Kummanni. If you seize Piyamaradu alone(?), [… I will give you(?) a … of gold], a bird of gold, and a (symbol of) a unit of time [of gold]. Piyamaradu [will …] it/them […]

§6' (ii 30–31) […] on which precise matter […] gold to/for that one […]

COMMENTARY

There is no reference to Ahhiyawa in what survives of this document, probably to be identified as one of the votive texts of Puduhepa, chief consort of Hattusili III. But its references to Piyamaradu, who had been supported by the Ahhiyawan king in his anti-Hittite enterprises, indicates the Hittite regime's continuing concern over his activities and its repeated failure to run him to ground or keep him out of Hittite territory, either by military force or by appeals to the Ahhiyawan king for his cooperation. Puduhepa as chief priestess of the Hittite realm now sought divine assistance in the task, with promises of rich rewards to the deities addressed if her prayers were answered.

One final comment about Piyamaradu: His name is linked with events associated with the reigns of Muwattalli II, Hattusili III, and Tudhaliya IV. Given that Muwattalli's reign ended ca. 1272 and Tudhaliya's began ca. 1237, Piyamaradu's career as an anti-Hittite activitist in the west must have covered at least three and a half decades. The longevity of his career is extraordinary enough in itself. But even more extraordinary is the fact he could for so long have so successfully defied Hittite authority, resisting all efforts by his adversaries to run him to ground—and perhaps ending his days peacefully in an island haven provided by his Ahhiyawan supporters, whose interests he had served so well.

AHT 27A–B

LETTERS FROM THE HITTITE COURT TO AMMURAPI OF UGARIT

Each of this pair of letters sent by the Hittite Great King and one of his highest officials to the vassal king of Ugarit deals basically with the same group of topics, concluding with the unacceptable delay of a shipment of (copper) ingots from Ugarit to (Ah)hiyawans currently present in the land of Lukka.[110] The identity of the recipient dates this correspondence to the last decades of the existence of both Hatti and Ugarit, making it likely that the unnamed "My/His Majesty" here was Suppiluliuma II, the final known ruler of the Anatolian Hittite state.

110. I must express my thanks to Professor F. Malbran-Labat, who provided me with a full transliteration of these texts in advance of their primary publication. The bulk of the texts are already presented in transliteration and translation in Lackenbacher and Malbran-Labat 2005a, 2005b.

AhT 27A

Letter from Suppiluliuma II to Ammurapi, king of Ugarit

RS 94.2530

obv.

§1

1. *um-ma* ⸢^{d}UTU-*ši*⸣-*ma*
2. *a-na* ^{m}*Am-mu-ra-pí-i-ma qí-bi-ma*

---

§2

3. *a-nu-um-ma it-ti* ^{d}UTU-*ši*
4. *gab-bu dan-níš šu-ul-mu*

---

§3

5. *um-ma-a a-na* ^{m}*Am-mu-ra-pí-i-ma*
6. $^{\mathrm{NA_4}}$ZA.GÌN *ša a-na* LUGAL *tu-še-bi-la*
7. LUGAL *i-na pa-an* $^{\mathrm{NA_4}}$ZA.GÌN-*ka ḫa-di dan-níš*
8. *ù at-ta* $^{\mathrm{NA_4}}$ZA.GÌN SIG$_5$ *bu-ʾ-i*
9. *ki-i* $^{\mathrm{NA_4}}$ZA.GÌN *i-ḫad-da-ak-ku*
10. *a-na* ^{d}UTU-*ši šu-bi-la*

---

§4

11. *ù* LUGAL *A-mur-ri it-ti* ^{d}UTU-*ši a-ši-ib*
12. *aš-šum šùl-mi-ka ù* É$^{?}$-*ka ša a-na* ^{d}UTU-*ši*
13. *ta-am-ḫu-ru* ^{d}UTU-*ši i-na* UGU *di-ni-ka*
14. *a-za-az* LUGAL *A-mur-ri aš-šum di-ni-ka*
15. *a-ṣa-ab-ba-su-ú-ma ki ša ul-te-ri-su-ka*
16. *at-ta-ma te-še-em-mi*

---

§5

17. *ù* DUMU-*ka ša a-na* UGU-*ḫi* ⸢^{d}UTU⸣-*ši*
18. *taš-pu-ra ši-ki-in šùl-mi-šu*
19. *ša i-ba-áš-šu-ú ki-i* SIG$_5$-*iš*

§1 (obv. 1–2) Thus says His Majesty: Say to Ammurapi:

§2 (obv. 3–4) Now everything is very well with My Majesty.

§3 (obv. 5–10) Say to Ammurapi: The King (of Carchemish) is very happy with your lapis lazuli that you sent to him. Now search out good lapis lazuli like the lapis lazuli he is pleased (to have received from) you, and send it to My Majesty.

§4 (obv. 11–16) The King of Amurru is staying with My Majesty. Concerning your prosperity and your household(?) about which you appealed to My Majesty—I will preside over your legal dispute. I will summon the King of Amurru in regard to your case. You will hear how I will arrange (matters for?) you.

§5 (obv. 17–rev. 26) Concerning your son whom you sent to My Majesty—after I had taken those measures necessary for his well-being, I have sent him to

20. *ki-ma al-ta-ka-an-šu ù a-na* UGU-*ka*
21. *al-tap-ra-áš-*⸢*šu*⸣
rev.
22. *ù at-ta i-na pa-an ša-at-t*[*i*]
23. *a-na* UGU-*ḫi* ^{d}UTU-*ši al*[*-ka*]
24. *ù šum-ma a-ma-tu*$_4$ *mi-im-ma* ⸢*i-ka*⸣*-la-ka*
25. *ḫa-an-tiš* DUMU *a-na* UGU-*ḫi* ^{d}UTU-*ši*
26. *šu-up-ra*

---

§6
27. ⸢^{d}UTU⸣-*ši ul ú-ra-ad-da-ma il-la-nu-uš-šú*
28. *a-na ru-qí ul ú-maš-ša-ar-šu*
29. *a-na da-ar* U$_4$.MEŠ *it-ti* ^{d}UTU-*ši lu a-ši-ib*

---

§7
30. *aš-šum* ^{LÚ}ÉRIN.MEŠ *il-ki ša a-na* $^{\langle d\rangle}$UTU-*ši ta-am-ḫu-ru*
31. *i-na* KASKAL *an-ni-ti* ^{m}*Ša-ta-al-li ul áš-pu-ra-ma-ku*
32. *e-nin-na iq-ta-bu-ú-ni*
33. *um-ma-a* **LÚ *Ḫi-ya-a-ú*** *i*[*-na* KUR] *Lu-uk-ka-a*
34. *a-ši-ib ù* PAD.MEŠ-*šu ya-nu*
35. *a-ki a-ma-ti an-ni-ti ya-nu na-ṭù*
36. *la ta-qa-ab-ba-a*
37. ^{GIŠ}MÁ.MEŠ *a-na* ^{m}*Ša-ta-al-li i-din-ma*
38. PAD.MEŠ *a-na* **LÚ.MEŠ *Ḫi-a-ú-wi-i*** *lil-qu-ú*
39. AŠ KASKAL *ša-ni-ti* ^{d}UTU-*ši ul ú-ra-da-ma*
40. ^{LÚ}ÉRIN.MEŠ *il-ki a-na* UGU-*ḫi-ka*
41. *ul i-ša-ap-pa-ar*
42. *ṭup-pí ri-ki-il-ti*
43. *ša* ^{d}UTU-*ši il-ṭu-ra-ak-ku*
44. *ma-am-ma ri-ki-il-ta-ka ul-li-iš*
45. *ul ú-ša-an-na*

you. As for you, at the beginning of the year come to My Majesty, and if some matter holds you back, send (your) son immediately to My Majesty.

§6 (rev. 27–29) My Majesty will not again allow him (to travel) far alone(?). He shall stay with My Majesty forever.

§7 (rev. 30–41) Concerning those owing a service obligation about whom you have appealed to My Majesty—on this occasion have I not sent Satalli to you? Now I have been told that the **(Ah)hiyawan** is tarrying in [the land] of Lukka, but that there are no (copper) ingots for him. In this matter don't tell me that there is no appropriate action. Give ships to Satalli, so that he may take the ingots to the **(Ah)hiyawans**. On a second occasion My Majesty will not again send to you persons owing a service obligation.

AhT 27B

Letter from Penti-Sharruma, a Hittite official, to Ammurapi, king of Ugarit

RS 94.2523

obv.

§1

1. *um-ma* ^{m}*Pi-in-di-*^{d}LUGAL*-ma*
2. ^{LÚ}*tup-pi-nu-ra ḫu-bu-ur-ti-nu-ra*
3. LÚ.GAL-*ú* DUGUD *ša* KUR *Ḫa-at-ti*
4. *a-na* ^{m}*Am-mu-ra-pí-i* LUGAL KUR *Ú-ga-ri-it*
5. ŠEŠ.DÙG.GA-*ya qí-bi-ma*

---

§2

6. *a-nu-um-ma it-ti* ^{d}UTU-*ši gab-bu*
7. *dan-níš šu-ul-mu*
8. *it-ti-ya šu-ul-mu*
9. *ù at-ta* ŠEŠ-*ú-a šu-lum-ka*
10. *šu-up-ra*

---

§3

11. *um-ma a-na* ^{m}*Am-mu-ra-pí-i-ma*
12. $^{\mathrm{NA_4}}$ZA.GÌN *ša a-na* ^{d}UTU-*ši tu-še-bi-la*
13. ^{d}UTU-*ši i-na pa-ni ḫa-di dan-níš*
14. *a-ma-ta an-ni-ta tu-ud-da-mi-iq*
15. *da-an-ni-iš*
16. *aš-šum* $^{\mathrm{NA_4}}$ZA.GÌN *a-na* ^{d}UTU-*ši tu-še-bi-la*
17. *i-na pa-an* ^{d}UTU-*ši tu-uk-ta-bi-ta-an-ni*
18. *ù a-na ya-ši* $^{\mathrm{NA_4}}$ZA.GÌN *am-mi-ni*
19. *la tu-še-bi-la*
20. *i-na* ŠÀ-*bi-ka-a e-te-li*

lower edge

21. *e-nin-na* ⸢*ki-i*⸣ $^{\mathrm{NA_4}}$ZA.GÌN
22. *ib-tá-aq-qú-um-ma*

§1 (obv. 1–5) Thus says Penti-Sharruma, the Chief Scribe and ..., weighty nobleman of Ḫatti: Say to Ammurapi, King of Ugarit, my beloved brother:

§2 (obv. 6–10) Now everything is very well with His Majesty, and it is well with me. May you, my beloved brother, send me news that you are well.

§3 (obv. 11–rev. 25) Say to Ammurapi: His Majesty is very happy with the lapis lazuli that you sent to him. You did very well in this matter. Because of the lapis lazuli that you sent you have accrued honor in the eyes of His Majesty. But why have you not sent lapis lazuli to me? Have I lost your affections? Now, when you have (next) alloted and sent lapis lazuli to His Majesty, likewise send good lapis lazuli to me personally.

23. *a-na* ^{d}UTU-*ši tu-še-bi-la*

rev.

24. *a-na ya-ši a-kán-na-ma* ^{NA_4}ZA.GÌN ⸢SIG$_5$⸣

25. *a-na ra-ma-ni šu-bi-la*

---

§4

26. *ù aš-šum šùl-mi-ka ù* É$^{?}$-*ka*

27. *ša a-na* ^{d}UTU-*ši taq-bu-ú*

28. *e-nin-na* LUGAL *A-mur-ri it-ti* ^{d}UTU-*ši a-ši-ib*

29. *a-na* ^{d}UTU-*ši a-na-ku a-qa-bi-ma*

30. *aš-šum* É$^{?}$-*ka ù šùl-mi-ka* LUGAL *A-mur-ri*

31. *i-ṣa-ab-ba-at-ma ul-te-ri-su-ka*

---

§5

32. *ù pa-an ša-at-ti* DUMU-*ka šu-up-ra-am-ma*

33. *it-ti* ^{d}UTU-*ši lu-ši-ib*

---

§6

34. *ù* ^{LÚ}ÉRIN.MEŠ *il-ki ša ta-am-*⸢*ta-na*⸣-*ḫa-ru*

35. *i-na* 1-*et* KASKAL *an-ni-ti* ^{m}*Ša-ta-al-li*

36. *tu-še-er-si-ma* PAD.MEŠ *a-na* **LÚ *Ḫi-ya-ú-wi-i***

37. *a-na* KUR *Lu-uk-ka-a li-il-qé*

38. ⸢^{d}UTU⸣-*ši ul ú-ra-ad-*⸢*da*⸣-*ma*

39. [^{LÚ}ÉRIN.MEŠ] *il-ki a-na* UGU-*ḫi-ka*

40. [*ul*] *i-šap-pa-ra*

41. [*ṭup-pi*] *ri-ki-il-ti ša* ^{d}UTU-*ši*

42. [*e-p*]*u-ša-ak-ku*

43. ⸢*an-ni*⸣-*tu-um-ma ri-ki-il-ta-ka*

upper edge

44. *ma-am-ma ri-li-il-ta*

45. *ul ú-ša-áš-na*

§4 (rev. 26–31) Concerning your well-being and your household(?) about which you spoke to His Majesty—the King of Amurru is presently staying with His Majesty. I will speak to His Majesty and he will summon the King of Amurru concerning your household(?) and your well-being, and he(!) will arrange (matters for) you.

§5 (rev. 32–33) At the beginning of the year send me your son so that he may stay with His Majesty.

§6 (rev. 34–U.E. 45) In respect to those owing a service obligation about whom you have been appealing—on the first occasion you ... Satalli. Let him take (copper) ingots to the **(Ah)hiyawan**; he shall take (them) to the land of Lukka. His Majesty will [not] again send you [persons] owing a service obligation. Regarding the treaty [tablet] that His Majesty made for you—no one will alter this treaty of yours.

COMMENTARY

These documents are parallel letters found among the recently unearthed archives of the "house of Urtenu" in Ras Shamra (Ugarit). One was written by a Hittite king, almost certainly Suppiluliuma II, the last king before the fall of the empire, the other by a high official in the Hittite court called Penti-Sharruma. The addressee of both letters is Ammurapi, the last king of Ugarit. The letters deal with a range of matters, including a request to Ammurapi for a consignment of lapis lazuli, of similar quality to that which he had previously dispatched to the Hittite viceroy in Carchemish. And both letters end with a rebuke. Ammurapi is taken to task for his failure to ship to the "Hiyawa-men" in Lukka a cargo of what is designated by the logogram PAD.MEŠ in the letters. Hiyawa is an aphaeresized[111] form of the name Ahhiyawa—our last known reference to Ahhiyawa

111. "Aphaeresis" designates the loss of a letter or syllable from the beginning of a word.

in Late Bronze Age sources. Previously translated as "food rations" (thus Lackenbacher and Malbran-Labat 2005), PAD.MEŠ is more likely to have referred to metal ingots (thus Singer 2006: 255–58). They were to be dispatched to the Ahhiyawans who were at that time in the land of Lukka, in southwestern Anatolia.

The ingots were perhaps made of copper and tin, like those found in the Late Bronze Age Uluburun shipwreck off the coast of Lycia, part of Lukka territory. If so, they must have been sent to the Ahhiyawans to enable them to manufacture their own bronze weapons. Alternatively, the ingots were made of precious metals, silver and gold, and were intended as payment to the Ahhiyawans for services rendered or about to be rendered. In either case, it is likely that the Hittite king had hired these Hiyawa-men as mercenaries. In any event, the dispatch of the cargo of metal to them by way of ship from Ugarit to the coast of Lukka was clearly a matter of urgency.

By this time, the Ahhiyawan kingdom referred to in earlier Hittite texts had lost its Anatolian territories. The Hiyawa-men were no doubt private groups of Ahhiyawan/Mycenaean adventurers who remained on the Anatolian mainland in the wake of the loss of Ahhiyawan sovereignty in the region or came there in the wake of growing upheavals in the Greek world. They now made their living as freebooters or as mercenaries in a foreign king's hire. Suppiluliuma may have used them as a local defense force in the west during his campaigns to Lukka and other lands in the region (as recorded in the so-called Südburg inscription in Hattusa). They may also have had a seagoing capacity, their ships perhaps joining the naval forces assembled by Suppiluliuma for his sea battles off the coast of Alasiya (Cyprus) and his engagements with his enemies on Alasiyan soil (see Bryce 2005: 332–33).

AHT 28

INSCRIPTION OF WARIKA, KING OF (AH)HIYAWA

This monumental text of Warika was discovered in 1997, certainly having long previously strayed from its original context, in the village of Çineköy, thirty kilometers south of Adana. Inscribed upon a statue base in the form of a chariot pulled by a pair of bulls, the composition, like those of Karatepe, is bilingual—Phoenician and Luwian written in Anatolian hieroglyphs. Only the latter version has been treated here. The subject and patron of the inscription also appears in several Neo-Assyrian cuneiform tablets of the reigns of Tiglath-pileser III and Sargon II as Urikki, king of Que (Tekoğlu and Lemaire 2000: 1003).

Çineköy

§1 [EGO-*mi*] ⸢*Wa/i*⸣+*ra/i*-⸢*i*⸣[-*ka-s*]*á* [o o o o o (INFANS)*ni*]-*mu-wa/i-za*--*sa* [*Mu-ka*]-*sa-sa* || | INFANS.NEPOS-*si-sà* | ***Hi-ya-wa/i*[-*ni*]-*sá*[URBS]** | REX-*ti*-⸢*sa*⸣ | (DEUS)⸢TONITRUS⸣-*hu-t*[*a-sa* SERVUS-*ta*$_4$-*sa* (DEUS) SOL-*mi-sa* CAPUT-*ti-i-sa*]

§2 [*á-wa/i-mu*] *Wa/i-ra/i-i-ka-sá* "[TER]RA" *la-tara/i-ha* [***Hi-ya-wa/i*--*na*(URBS)**]

§3 [*ARHA-ha-wa/i la+ra/i+a-nú-ha* ***Hi*]-*ya*-⸢*wa/i*⸣-*za*(URBS)** TERRA+*LA*+*LA-za* || | (DEUS)TONITRUS-*hu-ta-ti* | *á-mi-ya-ti-ha* | *tá-ti-ya-ti* | DEUS-*na*<-*ti*>

§4 | *wa/i-ta* (EQUUS.ANIMAL)*sù-na* (EQUUS)*sù-wa/i* | SUPER+*ra/i-ta* | *i-zi-ya-ha*

§5 EXER[CITUS-*la/i/u-za-ha*] || EXERCITUS[-*la/i/u-ni*] | SUPER+*ra/i-ta* | *i-z*[*i*]-*ya-h*[*a*]

§6 | REL-*p*[*a*]-*wa/i-mu*-⸢*u*⸣ | *Su+ra/i-wa/i-ni-sa*(URBS) | REX-*ti-sa* | *Su+ra/i-wa/i-za-ha*(URBS) | DOMUS-*na-za* | *ta-ni-ma-za* | *tá*[-*ti-na* MATER-*na-ha*] || | *i-zi-ya-si*

§7 | ***Hi-ya-wa/i-sa-ha-wa/i*(URBS)** | *Su+ra/i*-⸢*ya*⸣-*sa-ha*(URBS) | "UNUS"--*za* | DOMUS-*na-za* | *i-zi-ya-si*

§8 REL-*pa-wa/i* || *274<-*ta*>-*li-ha* (CASTRUM)*ha+ra/i-na-sà* [PUGNUS-*la/i/u-mi-tà-ya-sà*]

§9 [AEDIFICARE-*MI-ha-ha-wa/i*] | ORIENS-*mi-ya-ti* | ⸢*la*⸣-*ya*$^!$-*ni* 8 || OCCI-DENS-*mi-ti-ha* <VERSUS-*na/i*> 7 CASTRUM-*za*

§10 | REL-*pa-wa/i* ("LOCUS")pi_x(*ba*$^?$)-*tà-za* | *za-ya* "FLUMEN"-*sa pa+ra/i-ni-wa/i-i* || | MAGNUS+*ra/i* *180+*311-*za* | *á-sa-tá*

§11 || *wa/i-a* | *á-mu* | *á-mi-ya-ti* COR-*na-ti* || ("TERRA")*ta-sà*-REL-+*ra/i* REL$^?$ || | *i*$^?$-*zi*$^?$-*ya*-x(-)*á*$^?$-*wa/i* URBS-*MI*$^?$-*ni-zi* SOLIUM$^?$ […] ||

§12 | [… OMNIS-*MI-ma*$^?$]-⸢*ya*⸣ *ARHA* (BONUS)*u-sa-nu-mi-na*

§1 I am Warika, son of […], descendant of Mukasa, **(Ah)hiyawan** king, [servant of] the Storm-God, [man of the Storm-God].

§2 [I], Warika, extended [(the territory of) the city of **(Ah)hiyawa**],

§3 [and made prosper] the **(Ah)hiyawan** plain through the help of the Storm-God and my paternal gods.

§4 I added horse to horse;

§5 I added army to army.

§6 Indeed, the Assyrian king and all the Assyrian dynasty became (like) a father and mother to me,

§7 and **(Ah)hiyawa** and Assyria became a single house.

§8 Indeed, I smashed [powerful] fortresses,

§9 [and I built] fortresses—eight to the east and seven <to> the west.

§10 Indeed, these places were … for the palace of the River (Land).

§11 And I, by myself, […] in the land … towns […]

§12 [… all] extremely good things.

Commentary

Warika (Awariku), the subject of this inscription, is well known from Assyrian texts of the second half of the eighth century as Urikki, king of Que. In Luwian texts, he is also attested in the famous Karatepe Luwian-Phoenician bilingual inscription, authored by one of his subordinate rulers, a man called Azatiwata (see Çambel 1999, Hawkins 2000: 45–68). In the Luwian version of the Karatepe inscription, Warika's kingdom is called Adanawa (its inhabitants are called the Danunians in the Phoenician version). But in the Luwian version of the

Çineköy inscription, Warika calls his kingdom Hiyawa. The kingdom was located in southeastern Anatolia, in the region called Cilicia Tracheia/Aspera ("Rough Cilicia") in Classical sources, and extended over much of the territory covered by the Late Bronze Age country Kizzuwatna. We do not know why Warika's kingdom was called Adanawa in one Luwian text and Hiyawa in another. But we have noted that Hiyawa is simply an aphaeresized form of Ahhiyawa, and it is possible that the name reflects a migration of populations of Ahhiyawan/Mycenaean origin from western Anatolia or the Aegean world to Cilicia at the beginning of the Iron Age. If the commonly assumed link between the Hittite name Ahhiyawa and the Greek Achaia is valid, then the migration theory would appear to tie in with the claim by the Greek historian Herodotus (7.91) that the Cilicians were originally known as Hypachaians ("sub-Achaians").

In his titulary, Warika identifies himself as a descendant of Mukasa. So too in the Karatepe bilingual he is said to belong to the house of Muk(a)sa. In the Phoenician version of both inscriptions, the name is represented as MPŠ. The precise correspondence between Muksas/MPŠ in these inscriptions and Moxus/Mopsus in Classical texts has led scholars to link Warika's ancestor with the legendary Greek seer and city-founder Mopsus. An emigrant from western Anatolia to Cilicia, according to Greek tradition, Mopsus is associated with the foundation of a number of cities in southern Anatolia. It is at all events possible that the name by which Warika calls his kingdom in the Çineköy inscription indicates that Adanawa's ruling dynasty was founded by the leader of a Greek colonizing group. The Semitic name for the kingdom, Que/Qaue/Quwe, may have been derived from Hiyawa. The name Adanawa was a long-established one in the region, extending back at least to the Hittite Old Kingdom, when the land then called Adaniya was involved in a rebellion against the king Ammuna (mid-sixteenth century) and later became part of the kingdom of Kizzuwatna. In the Iron Age, the use of the name Adana(wa) may have been confined to the kingdom's capital. That is but one possible explanation of the apparently alternative names for Warika's kingdom in the Luwian texts.

Warika notes in his inscription his close links with the Assyrian king and the Assyrian royal dynasty in general. Tekoğlu and Lemaire (2000: 1004) suggest that his relationship with Assyria at this time was one of alliance or partnership, in which the Assyrian king exercised the role of protector/suzerain, and probably had a treaty with him. Such a partnership, they believe, was essential to the success of Warika's long reign, which began ca. 738 in the reign of the Assyrian king Tiglath-pileser III and extended over three decades into the reign of Sargon II.

Epilogue

Mycenaean–Hittite Interconnections in the Late Bronze Age Revisited

In tracing the history of Mycenaean-Hittite interconnections in the Late Bronze Age, we must assume, at least for the sake of argument, that we are correct in identifying Ahhiyawa with the Mycenaean Greeks, as set forth in the introduction to this volume. If we do not, there is no point to this exercise, for there is no other reference in the Hittite records to any entity that could be the Mycenaean Greeks. We would not be able to discuss the history of their interactions except through the material artifacts, of which there are relatively few, as we shall see below. If, however, we are agreed that the Hittite references to Ahhiyawa are references to the Mycenaean Greeks, then we can discuss the textual evidence as well as the archaeological evidence for their interactions over the centuries. This we will do for the remainder of this essay.

The history of relations between Ahhiyawa and the Hittites over time can be determined by discussing the facts that can be retrieved from the texts once they have been put into tentative chronological order, as we have already done in the introduction (see again Table 1), and then both comparing and augmenting those with the archaeological data that we possess. We will not here completely restate the comments that have already been made above after each individual text, nor shall we go over again the numerous arguments and debates that have been made in the past about many of them, but rather we will here pull out some of the salient facts and link them to the archaeological data. In so doing, we are able to trace not only the overall history of Mycenaean-Hittite relations over the course of the Late Bronze Age, but also parts of the careers of individuals such as the rascally Piyamaradu and the wily Attarissiya, as well as a portion of the history of individual places such as Millawanda/Milawata (Miletus) and Wilusa (probably Troy and/or the Troad).

Overall, the archaeological and textual evidence clearly demonstrates that there were well-established connections between the Aegean and western Anatolia during the late-fifteenth through the thirteenth centuries B.C.E., as we shall see below. Connections between the Aegean and inland Anatolia, however, are much less well attested during this same period of time and so it remains a matter of debate as to just how much direct contact there was between the Hittites and the Mycenaeans. All of this material has been much discussed in the past (see, e.g., all with many additional references, Bryce 1989a, 1989b, 1998, 2003b; Mee 1978, 1998; Güterbock 1983, 1984, 1986; Mellink 1983; Mountjoy 1998; Cline 1991a, 1991b, 1994, 1998, 2008, 2010; Kelder 2004–2005, 2005, 2010b), but bears reexamination in light of the new transliterations, translations, and commentaries presented above.

Of the Ahhiyawa texts as a whole, seven date to the late-fifteenth–early-fourteenth century B.C.E. (one example), the fourteenth century, or the fourteenth–thirteenth centuries B.C.E. (in order: **AhT 22, 3, 1A, 1B, 20, 12**, and **9**). Another thirteen date to specific periods during the thirteenth century B.C.E. (**AhT 7, 6, 4, 8, 15, 26, 18, 14, 11, 5, 2, 27A**, and **27B**), in addition to which are nine more that also date to the thirteenth century B.C.E. but cannot be more closely dated (**AhT 10, 13, 16, 17, 19, 21, 23, 24**, and **25**); this makes a total of twenty-two texts that date to this century. One final text dates to the eighth century B.C.E. (**AhT 28**), long after Ahhiyawa proper had ceased to exist. It seems fairly clear that we have a period of tentative initial contact during the late-fifteenth and the fourteenth centuries B.C.E., then a period of intense involvement and interaction during the thirteenth century B.C.E., followed by a cessation of contact in the twelfth century B.C.E. (probably attributable to the destruction of one or both kingdoms/areas).

It is more difficult to say whether the archaeological data corroborate the textual data, for the extant remains are relatively few. For instance, the only study done of Hittite objects found in the Bronze Age Aegean remains that of Cline (1991a; see also 1994). Only a dozen objects in the Bronze Age Aegean are even potentially Hittite in origin, and these are scattered far and wide both in time and location, from Middle Minoan I–II to Late Helladic IIIC (i.e., from ca. 2000–1150 B.C.E.) and from mainland Greece to Rhodes. They include cylinder seals, seal impressions, and bullae; a sphinx statuette; a silver stag rhyton; and a silver "Smiting God" statuette (Cline 1991b; see now also the brief discussion by Kelder 2010b: 98).

As Cline states (1991a: 140), these possible Hittite objects constitute only one percent of all of the Orientalia imported from Egypt and the Near East during these centuries. They cannot be used in any way during a discussion of Mycenaean-Hittite interactions except insofar as the total lack of such objects speaks against any sustained importation of identifiable Hittite objects into the Late Bronze Age Aegean. This, of course, does not mean that such trade never existed, because even a lively trade in perishable or 'invisible' goods such as textiles, horses, slaves, and raw materials such as tin and silver would not leave identifiable traces in the archaeological record (see not only the discussion in Cline 1994: 70–74, but also Bryce 1989b: 13–14; 2003b: 60–62; Mee 1998: 141; Kelder 2004–2005: 52; 2010b: 58–59).

An indication that trade may well have been in such perishable goods can be perhaps seen in the Mycenaean artifacts that have been found in Anatolia, mostly on the western and southern coasts. These were first catalogued in detail by Mee in 1978 and then updated by him twenty years later (Mee 1998). The most recent itemizations have been done by Kelder (2004–2005; 2010b: 121–36, 140), but one should note that there are differences and discrepancies in the dating of the reported objects, including between Kelder's own publications, with no explanation given. Apart from a few Mycenaean-style tombs, and possible architecture such as houses and kilns found at sites like Miletus (Kelder 2010b: 52), which was under Mycenaean control for a period during the Late Bronze Age, the objects most commonly found are Mycenaean closed vessels, such as stirrup jars, which were usually used to transport liquid commodities including wine, olive oil, and perfume.

Interestingly, such vessels are comparatively common on the western coast where, as the texts show, the Ahhiyawans were active (see now also Kelder 2010b: 62). However, they are almost nonexistent in the inland regions of central Anatolia. If the Hittites were importing such liquid items from the Mycenaeans, they were clearly decanting the liquids from the breakable ceramic vessels and placing them into other, unbreakable, containers such as leather pouches or bags before the arduous trip up through the mountain passes and into central Anatolia (Cline 1994: 71; Bryce 2003b: 61; Kelder 2010b: 59). It is also possible that the Hittites were not importing anything from the Mycenaeans and that there was an embargo in place, as has been suggested elsewhere (Cline 1991b; 1994: 71–74; see further consideration in Bryce 2003b and Kelder 2010b); this will be brought up again below.

According to the extant evidence, Mycenaean involvement in western Anatolia, and probable interaction with the Hittites, had apparently begun by the reign of Tudhaliya I/II, sometime before the Assuwa Rebellion in the late-fifteenth–early-fourteenth century B.C.E. The Annals of Tudhaliya describe Assuwa as a confederacy of twenty-two cities and areas in western Anatolia, including Taruisa and Wilusiya (Wilusa in other texts), that is, the region, and probably the city, of Troy (KUB 23.2 ii 13–39, iii 9–10). This coalition rebelled against the Hittites in the late fifteenth century B.C.E., forcing Tudhaliya to send an army and quash the revolt. Mycenaean involvement in the rebellion is circumstantially indicated by a bronze sword of either Mycenaean manufacture or Mycenaean influence that was discovered in 1991 at Hattusa, the capital city of the Hittites. On the sword is an inscription written in Akkadian that states: "As Tudhaliya the Great King shattered the Assuwan country, he dedicated these swords to the Storm-God, his lord" (see full discussion in Cline 1996; 1997, with earlier references).

Mycenaean involvement in the rebellion may also be circumstantially indicated in a much later Ahhiyawa text (**AhT 6**). This is a translation into Hittite of a letter sent by the king of Ahhiyawa to a Hittite king, probably Muwattalli II, in the early- to mid-thirteenth century B.C.E., and which is at least partly concerned with much earlier events. The letter, which until recently was thought to be have been sent *by* Muwattalli but is now identified as one of the few to have been dispatched by an Ahhiyawan king (see Latacz 2004: 243–44), is concerned primarily with the ownership of a group of islands lying off Anatolia's Aegean coast that had formerly belonged to the king of Ahhiyawa, but that had apparently been seized by the Hittites.

Within the letter, after the greeting from the king of Ahhiyawa in the first line, we are told (in the reconstructed text) that, sometime in the past, a Hittite king named Tudhaliya (undoubtedly I/II) had defeated the king of Assuwa and subjugated him. The letter is damaged and incomplete, but it now seems, based on the new transliteration and translation by Beckman and the commentary by Bryce presented above, that a diplomatic marriage had taken place between the current Ahhiyawan king's "great-grandfather" and an Assuwan princess at a time prior to the Assuwan rebellion and that the islands were transferred by the Assuwan king to the bridegroom as part of the dowry. The Hittites claimed that Tudhaliya's victory over Assuwa had given them possession of Assuwa's offshore territories but, according to the letter's author, the victory had only taken place after these territories had already been presented to Ahhiyawa. Now the Ahhiyawan king was seeking to reaffirm his claim to the islands through diplomatic means.

The new translation of this letter does not necessarily indicate that the Mycenaeans were actually drawn into the Assuwa Rebellion or that it was an example of an earlier or pre-Trojan War, as previous translations had potentially suggested (see Cline 1996; 1997; cited in Kelder 2004–2005: 65 and 2010b: 25), but the inscribed sword found at Hattusa does imply some sort of involvement nevertheless. At the very least, it is clear that the Mycenaeans were present on the western coast of Anatolia by the late-fifteenth–early-fourteenth century B.C.E. and interacting diplomatically with the Assuwans and, quite likely, the Hittites as well.

In terms of archaeological remains from this same time period, that is, Late Helladic (LH) II remains in Bronze Age Aegean terms, apart from the inscribed sword found at Hattusa, Mycenaean artifacts from this period have only been found at Miletus (where they are preceded by Minoan remains) and Clazomenae on the Anatolian mainland (see, e.g., Mee 1998: 137; Kelder 2004–2005:

72–73; 2010b: 54–55, 131–32). Mee says simply, "If there were Mycenaeans in the eastern Aegean at this time, they remain elusive" (Mee 1998: 137).

We now come to the earliest of the Ahhiyawa texts (**AhT 22**), which is one that has just been redated and is now thought to be from the reign of Tudhaliya I/II in the late-fifteenth–early-fourteen century B.C.E. This, an oracle report, mentions a man named Attarissiya of/from Ahhiya (the older and shorter form of Ahhiyawa). We will meet Attarissiya again almost immediately, in the next—and one of the most famous—Ahhiyawa texts, but here he is simply referred to as "the enemy ruler of Ahhiya."

The next text is **AhT 3,** the so-called Indictment of Madduwatta, which is among the most-commonly cited in discussions of interactions between the Hittites and the Mycenaeans. Dating to the early-fourteenth century B.C.E., during the reign of Arnuwanda I, but referring frequently to events that happened earlier in the time of Tudhaliya I/II, the text is concerned with "the duplicitous activities of a Hittite vassal [Madduwatta] in western Anatolia," as stated above in the introduction to this text (see also Bryce 1986; summations in Hawkins 1998: 25; Kelder 2005b: 139–40; 2010b: 23–25; Collins 2007: 44–45, in addition to the references given in the Sources section below). In the part that concerns us, we are told that Madduwatta had been attacked by Attarissiya, described as a ruler of Ahhiya, and had been rescued by Tudhaliya, who then set Madduwatta up as a vassal ruler. Attarissiya then attacked Madduwatta a second time, forcing Tudhaliya to come to Madduwatta's rescue once again.

As noted above, we do not know much about Attarissiya, apart from the fact that he was a Mycenaean apparently fighting on the Anatolian mainland during the late-fifteenth–early-fourteenth century B.C.E. He also seems to have taken part in naval raids on Alasiya (Cyprus), perhaps in coordination with his former rival Madduwatta, as mentioned in this text; these would be the earliest such raids of which we know and indicate that Attarissiya and the Ahhiyawans had access to some sort of navy, which is not too surprising.

The next two texts that might document contacts between the Mycenaeans and the Hittites are related: the Ten-Year Annals (**AhT 1A**) and the slightly later and more detailed Extensive Annals (**AhT 1B**) of Mursili II. We know that these date to the late-fourteenth century B.C.E. (or possibly the early-thirteenth century B.C.E., in the case of the Extensive Annals), since Mursili came to the throne in ca. 1322 B.C.E. The mentions of Ahhiyawa are found in the discussions of the events from years 3–4, a time when Mursili and the Hittite army were present in western Anatolia, primarily putting down a number of rebellions and conquering the kingdom of Arzawa.

One of the areas that had rebelled against the Hittites was the Land of Millawanda (Milawata), which was located on the western coast of Anatolia and which would—several hundred years later—become the territory of the Classical city Miletus. According to the Extensive Annals, Millawanda had switched its allegiance from the Hittites to the king of Ahhiyawa and so had to be brought back under Hittite control. Two Hittite commanders, named Gulla and Malaziti, and their forces, acting on the orders of Mursili II, captured the city, only to have it return to Ahhiyawan control within a few decades (for which see below, **AhT 4**).

We are told in these Annals that a man called Uhha-ziti, the king of Arzawa, whose capital city Apasa later became the Classical city of Ephesus, had also allied himself with the Ahhiyawan king. These particular texts make it clear that the king of Ahhiyawa was personally interested in what was happening in western Anatolia at this time and that he was willing to ally himself with local rulers at the expense of good relations with the Hittites. And when Uhha-ziti's forces were defeated by Mursili, Uhha-ziti himself "went across the sea to the islands and remained there," as the text records. It is generally thought that these islands lay just off the Aegean coast and belonged to the territory controlled by the king of Ahhiyawa, as pointed out above. A number of other Arzawan refugees fled with Uhha-ziti to these Ahhiyawan islands, including his own sons Piyama-Kurunta and Tapalazunawali (see also Hawkins 1998: 14; Collins 2007: 50).

It is perhaps not surprising, then, to find that LH IIIA1 pottery dating to the early-fourteenth century B.C.E. has been found at both Miletus (Millawanda/Milawata) and Ephesus (Apasa), as well as at Liman Tepe, Panaztepe, Torbali, and Troy (Cline 1996: 147–48; Mee 1978: 127, 134–35, 146; 1998: 138; Mountjoy 1998: 35–36; Kelder 2004–2005: 56, 58–59, 67–68, 72–74, and Table 1; 2010b: 54–55, 121–22, 127–29, 131–32). There is also the intriguing fragment of a Hittite bowl, found at Hattusa in a late-fifteenth or fourteenth century B.C.E. context, incised with a picture of a probable Mycenaean warrior "in full battle array, complete with plumed and horned helmet" (Cline 1996: 147; Kelder 2010b: 40, ill. 1; cf. previously Cline 1994: 121 no. C.1, with earlier references).

Eventually, according to these Annals of Mursili, after Uhha-ziti died while in exile on these islands, the Mycenaeans seem to have settled matters with the Hittites, even going so far as to turn over the royal prince Piyama-Kurunta and other Arzawan refugees to the Hittites, after Mursili sent a formal delegation by ship to the Ahhiyawan king. If Mursili had indeed completely conquered the land of Arzawa and was now in control of much of western Anatolia, as the texts seem to indicate, it would make sense that the Mycenaeans correctly realized that it was time to come to terms with the Hittites and establish friendly relations (perhaps once again).

Another text from the time of Mursili II, probably to be dated a few years before 1310 B.C.E., during the middle of Mursili's reign, based upon the people named in the tablet, is an oracle report (**AhT 20**). The Hittite king had become ill and the "god of Ahhiyawa," among other deities, including that of Lazpa

(Lesbos), was summoned. No doubt this was merely a statue of the god, but the very fact that it was brought to the Hittite king implies good relations between the Hittites and the Mycenaeans at this time.

Two other texts may come from the reign of Mursili II (or from those of the kings ruling immediately after him): a prayer text (**AhT 12**) and a letter sent from a Hittite king probably to a king of Ahhiyawa (**AhT 9**). As the dating and authorship are not completely certain, these texts can only be dated generally to the late-fourteenth–mid-thirteenth century B.C.E.

The first of these two texts (**AhT 12**) is very fragmentary but contains the extremely interesting news that someone, generally assumed to be a Hittite queen, had been banished ("dispatched") to "the Land of Ahhiyawa, beside the sea." As discussed above, in the commentary following the text, even if this text does record the banishment of a former queen, it is unclear which one it was, for there are three possible candidates, either Suppiluliuma's first or second wife or Mursili's second wife, depending upon who was the author of the text. What is important here, though, is the fact that the person in question was sent to Ahhiyawa, an act that could only have been done with the complete agreement of, and through prior arrangement with, the king of Ahhiyawa.

The second of these two texts perhaps to be dated to the reign of Mursili II is a fragmentary letter sent from a Hittite king probably to a king of Ahhiyawa (**AhT 9**). It is clearly one of a series of letters and responses being sent back and forth between the two rulers, who might have regarded each other as equals at this point, if the phrase "we the brothers" is being deliberately used to refer to the writer and the addressee, as pointed out above. Beyond that speculation, we cannot venture much farther.

In looking at the archaeological evidence from this time period, it is clear that trade and contacts were taking place more freely by the mid-fourteenth–early-thirteenth century B.C.E., that is, during the LH IIIA2 and LH IIIA2-B1 periods, perhaps because of the more cordial relations between the Mycenaeans and the Hittites at the time. According to Mee, there were Mycenaean settlements "on most of the eastern Aegean islands" at this time and Mycenaean IIIA2 and IIIA2–B pottery has been found at more than a dozen different sites on the coast of western Anatolia (e.g., Akbuk, Cerkes Sultaniye, Clazomenae, Dereköy, Düver, Ephesus, Erythrae, Gavurtepe, Kuşadası, Liman Tepe, Müsgebi, Mylasa, Panaztepe, Old Smyrna, Tire-Ahmetler, and Troy), as well as LH IIIA2–B vessels at Maşat in central Anatolia (Mee 1978: 128, 132–33, 137–43, 146; 1998: 138; Mountjoy 1998: 35–36; Kelder 2004–2005: 54–60, 62–63, 68, 71, and Table 1; 2010b: 54–55, 121–22, 124–28, 130–36). Mountjoy (1998) sees this time period, and this region, as the "Interface" between the Mycenaeans and the Hittites, which they undoubtedly were.

Mee also reports that in "the late fourteenth or early thirteenth century, Miletus was fortified.... the evenly spaced bastions recall Hittite rather than Mycenaean defensive architecture" (Mee 1998: 139). He also notes that Miletus was destroyed by fire late in the LH IIIA2 period, which corresponds with the attack on Millawanda by the Hittites in the third year of Mursili II's reign, that is, ca. 1319 B.C.E., as described above; the Hittites would then have been responsible for the subsequent construction of the new fortifications just noted (Mee 1978: 135; 1998: 142 and n. 80; see also Mellink 1983: 139; Hawkins 1998: 14; Kelder 2004–2005: 74, with additional earlier references; 2010b: 26–27).

The archaeological evidence thus corroborates the details derived from the Ahhiyawa texts regarding Mycenaean influence and/or activity at Millawanda (Miletus), Apasa (Ephesus), and the islands off the Anatolian coast during the fourteenth and early-thirteenth century B.C.E., and probably also the fact that Miletus was see-sawing between Hittite and Mycenaean influence and/or occupation during this same period. The cessation of Mycenaean pottery at Ephesus after the LH IIIA2 period may also be a corroboration that the kingdom of Arzawa, with its capital Apasa (Ephesus), had been conquered by Mursili II and the Hittites (see also Kelder 2004–2005: 78; 2010b: 27 and n. 74 on Miletus, 55–56 on Ephesus).

In sum, after looking at the first seven Ahhiyawa texts, chronologically speaking, as well as the references in a slightly later text (**AhT 6**), in addition to the relevant archaeological evidence, we can say fairly confidently that there were Mycenaeans active on the Anatolian mainland probably during the late-fifteenth and certainly during the fourteenth and early-thirteenth centuries B.C.E. The relations between the Hittites and the Mycenaeans during this period seem to have had a rocky start, as the Mycenaeans established themselves in Millawanda (Miletus) and elsewhere, but then evolved into a more peaceful relationship once the Hittites took over control of what had been the lands of Arzawa.

Moving now into the early- and mid-thirteenth century, and beginning during what was probably the reign of Muwattalli II, we find that the relationship between the Hittites and the Mycenaeans had apparently taken a turn for the worse. A letter (**AhT 7**) sent by Manapa-Tarhunta, king of the Seha River Land (part of the Arzawa Lands), to an unnamed Hittite king does not actually name Ahhiyawa, but much of the letter is taken up with the activities of a "renegade Hittite" named Piyamaradu, whom we meet here for the first time but will take up with again in a moment when discussing the "Tawagalawa Letter" (**AhT 4**).

According to the letter, Piyamaradu had just defeated Manapa-Tarhunta and forced him to acknowledge Piyamaradu's son-in-law Atpa as his superior. At some point, perhaps already at this time or soon thereafter, Atpa was also the ruler of Milawata (Miletus), which was "under the overlordship of the king of Ahhiyawa," as described above, which makes this letter relevant to our discussions. It is thought by many scholars that Piyamaradu was probably acting on behalf of, or in collusion with, the Ahhiyawans in an attempt to undermine Hittite authority in western Anatolia once again.

A second letter (**AhT 6**), this one now thought to have been sent by a king of Ahhiyawa to a ing of Hatti (probably Muwattalli II), is one of the few remaining texts that traveled in that direction. This is the text that has been partly discussed already, for it is the one that mentions the Assuwa Confederacy and its rebellion during the time of Tudhaliya I/II. Apart from the importance of the text for the details about the possible interactions between the Ahhiyawans, Assuwa, and the Hittites in that earlier period, the fact that this letter is written in Hittite is extremely important.

As mentioned above, recent research (see the papers forthcoming in the volume edited by Teffeteller) suggests that this letter is a translation into Hittite of a message sent to the Hittite king by his peer, the king of Ahhiyawa. It is unlikely that the Ahhiyawan king spoke, or wrote, Hittite himself, but it is unclear whether this means that there were scribes—either Mycenaean or Hittite—at either the Ahhiyawan or the Hittite court who were sufficiently fluent in both Mycenaean Greek and Hittite so as to translate a text from one language to another. It may have been translated by a bilingual scribe (or pair of scribes) at some intermediate point in between the two areas, such as at Miletus on the western coast (see also the earlier, but related, discussion concerning possible Anatolian scribes in Mycenaean Greece in Bryce 1999). If it is a translation of a letter originally sent from Mycenae, for instance, in the heartland of Ahhiyawa, then it is a real mystery as to why no return correspondence—not simply from the Hittites but also from the Egyptians, Mittanni, Kassites, Assyrians, Cypriots, and Canaanites—has yet been found anywhere at Mycenae, or at any other Mycenaean or Minoan sites for that matter. It may simply be a matter of not yet having found the "Foreign Archives" at these Aegean sites, but it may be something else entirely (see Cline 2010 and forthcoming, for a more detailed discussion of this problem).

Piyamaradu appears once again in the next Ahhiyawa text (**AhT 4**). This is a letter sent by a king of Hatti (probably Hattusili III) to a king of Ahhiyawa during the mid-thirteenth century B.C.E. and is actually only the last of what were once three full tablets. It is known as the "Tawagalawa Letter." In the letter, Hattusili addresses the Ahhiyawan king as a "Great King" and as "brother." This speaks volumes about their relationship, for whether cordial or not and whether or not Hattusili was deliberately trying to flatter the Ahhiyawan king (see discussion in Bryce 2003b: 65–68), the use of such terms was reserved for kings at a specific level who were considered peers, that is, the kings of Hatti, Egypt, Babylon, Mittanni, Assyria, and apparently Ahhiyawa.

Despite its modern name, the letter is more concerned with the continuing hostile activities of Piyamaradu than it is with the man named Tawagalawa. Tawagalawa, however, is of great interest to us, for we are told that he is the brother of the Ahhiyawan king. He is also, interestingly, said to have been acquainted with, and even ridden ("mounted the chariot") with Tapala-Tarhunta, the personal charioteer of the Hittite king himself. According to this text, Tawagalawa is present in person in western Anatolia, where he had been sent to gather, and bring back to Ahhiyawan territory, various individuals who were rebelling against the Hittites.

Included among these is Piyamaradu, who had continued to raid Hittite vassal lands in western Anatolia, and who had now been granted asylum/refuge in Ahhiyawan territory. As Bryce points out above in his commentary on the text, "Piyamaradu was seen as the fomenter and leader of the anti-Hittite movements in the west and was the chief target of the Hittites' western campaign on this and probably other occasions." We are told that Piyamaradu had fled first to Millawanda, where his son-in-law Atpa was in charge and which was now Ahhiyawan territory. He then continued on, via ship, probably to one of the islands just off the western coast that was controlled by Ahhiyawa (see also brief discussions by Hawkins 1998: 25–26; Kelder 2005a: 153, 156**;** 2005b: 141–42, citing Bryce 1989a; Kelder 2010b: 27–30; Collins 2007: 63–64, in addition to the other references listed in the Sources section below).

Since it is clear from the letter that Ahhiyawa was actively supporting anti-Hittite activities in western Anatolia (Collins 2007: 53), it seems likely that relations between the two powers continued to be icy during this period. This is corroborated by a reference in the letter to a dispute between the Hittites and Ahhiyawa over the region of Wilusa in northwestern Anatolia (usually identified as Troy and/or the Troad). It is not clear whether there was an outright battle or merely a diplomatic dispute, but it is the only reference we have to direct conflict between the two powers. Although the letter makes clear that the incident had happened sometime earlier, it is not certain whether it was simply earlier in Hattusili's reign or if it took place during the earlier reign of his brother, Muwattalli II. However, given the thirteenth-century B.C.E. date of the letter, the discussion is particularly interesting in light of the later Greek legends concerning the Trojan War and Mycenaean activity in the Troad region at this approximate time (i.e., ca. 1250 B.C.E.).

Whether relations were icy or not, "Great Kings" were still expected to include greeting gifts to their peers when sending a message. It is not surprising, therefore, that the next Ahhiyawa text (**AhT 8**), which is a letter sent to a king of Hatti (probably Hattusili III) during the mid-thirteenth century B.C.E., is concerned with a gift that was to be given to the Ahhiyawan king. In the end, it was decided to send a silver rhyton and a gold rhyton that had been taken from a gift that was supposed to be sent by the Hittite king to an Egyptian pharaoh, quite possibly Ramesses II. (Note that previous readings of this text had implied that the rhyta had been taken from a gift received *from* the Egyptian pharaoh, which would have then made this one of the earliest recorded instances of "regifting").

The next text (**AhT 15**) may also have been sent by Hattusili III, for it is a fragmentary letter sent by a Hittite king to another Great King during the thirteenth century B.C.E., and refers to a previous letter that he had written to the king of Egypt. Within the letter are also references to Piyamaradu, once again, and to the Hittite king's contacts with the king of Ahhiyawa, but it is so fragmentary that we cannot be clear whether the events under discussion were contemporary or had happened earlier nor whether the relations between the Hittites and the Mycenaeans at this time were peaceful or hostile.

Although there is no actual mention of Ahhiyawa in the next text (**AhT 26**), which may be classified as a votive prayer probably to be attributed to Puduhepa, the wife of Hattusili III, during the mid-thirteenth century B.C.E., Piyamaradu is mentioned yet again and so we may include it in our discussions here. Since the Hittites have failed, through both military activities and diplomacy, to curtail Piyamaradu's activities against them, Puduhepa is now apparently seeking divine assistance in the matter, in her role as the chief priestess, promising offerings and objects of gold if Piyamaradu is seized and brought to her. It seems that her efforts were in vain, as Piyamaradu appears in one more text, from the later reign of Tudhaliya IV (see below).

The final text perhaps to be dated to the reign of Hattusili III (or, less likely, to his successor, Tudhaliya IV) is a "boundary" list (**AhT 18**) dating to the mid- to late-thirteenth century B.C.E. The inclusion of Ahhiyawa in the fragmentary text, which was probably a listing of the kingdoms (and their boundaries) in western and southern Anatolia, indicates that Ahhiyawa was probably still in control of—that is, exercised sovereignty over—territory on the western coast, but gives no indication of the nature of the relationship between Hatti and Ahhiyawa at that time.

It makes sense, then, to find that LH IIIB1 and IIIB2 pottery, dating to the thirteenth century B.C.E., has been found at Miletus in both the city itself and the tombs, and that most of the Mycenaean pottery found there was locally produced rather than imported (Mee 1998: 139; see previously Mee 1978: 133). This would seem to indicate that there were Mycenaeans living at Miletus during this period, which would not be at odds in the least with the textual evidence just discussed (Mee 1978: 149). There is also specific LH IIIB1 pottery at Bayraklı, Besik Tepe, Beyesultan, Beylerbey, Çerkes, Çine-Tepecik, Clazomenae, Dereköy, Düver, Müsgebi, Panaztepe, Telmessos, Torbali, and Troy, all on the western coast or just inland, and, although there is a decrease from the previous period, many of the same sites plus a few others have LH IIIB2 pottery as well, including Besik Tepe, Clazomenae, Dereköy, Düver, Müsgebi, Sardis, Telmessos, and Troy (Mee 1978: 124, 146; Kelder 2004–2005: 58, 60, 62–63, 71, 74, 79, and Table 1; 2010b: 123, 140; Günel and Herbordt 2010).

There are other Ahhiyawa texts that date to the thirteenth century B.C.E. but that cannot be assigned to any particular reign or even more closely during this century (**AhT 10, 13, 16, 17, 19, 21, 23, 24,** and **25**). Most are too fragmentary to make any sort of comment about, though one (**AhT 19**) does mention a copper vessel of Ahhiyawan type or manufacture, which is one of the few objects of Mycenaean manufacture or influence that can documented as having come into Hittite hands (apart from the inscribed bronze sword from two hundred years earlier).

However, Ahhiyawa appears in a number of texts that can be dated specifically to the reign of Tudhaliya IV, in the mid- to late-thirteenth century B.C.E. During this period, Ahhiyawa's decline and demotion from the list of Great Powers can be traced. In a letter (**AhT 14**) from the king of Hatti (probably Tudhaliya IV), mention is made of Urhi-Teshshup (Mursili III), who had once been king but who had been deposed by Hattusili III long before. Urhi-Teshshup had sought support from a number of powerful foreign kings, including the king of Ahhiyawa. He found temporary exile in Egypt during the reign of Ramesses II (Collins 2007: 60), but at what point this took place is uncertain, since the chronology of the events following his overthrow is unclear. Here it is simply reported that the king of Ahhiyawa did not come to the aid of Urhi-Teshshup; neither did the other king mentioned in the text.

In a subsequent royal edict (**AhT 11**), which he issued in the late-thirteenth century B.C.E., Tudhaliya IV documented offenses of the Seha River Land in western Anatolia. Among these were a rebellion led by a man named Tarhuna-radu, who was encouraged and supported in this endeavor by the king of Ahhiyawa. Tudhaliya crushed the rebellion and, it is thought, began the gradual process of ending Ahhiyawan presence and interference in western Anatolia by capturing Milawata/Millawanda (Miletus). It used to be thought, following the original translation by Sommer, that the mention of Ahhiyawa in this text implied that the king of Ahhiyawa had himself been present on the Anatolian mainland (see brief discussion in Cline 1996: 146–47, with references), but subsequent translations—including that given above—now show that the mention is much more mundane and that Tarhuna-radu was simply "relying upon" the king of Ahhiyawa (cf. also Hawkins 1998: 20).

Although the next document (**AhT 5**) does not mention Ahhiyawa by name, it is concerned with Milawata/Millawanda (Miletus), as well as with Piyamaradu once more, and the land of Wilusa yet again (cf. Hawkins 1998: 19, 28). This is a letter sent during the late-thirteenth century B.C.E. by a king of Hatti (probably Tudhaliya IV) to a western Anatolian ruler, probably Tarkasnawa, king of Mira in the Arzawa Lands (see now Günel and Herbordt 2010 for a recent publication of a Hittite bulla with his name on it found at the site of Çine-Tepecik, in the same context as Mycenaean IIIB1 pottery). Known as the "Milawata Letter," this text makes it clear that Milawata no longer belonged to the Ahhiyawan king but was now under Hittite control (cf. Bryce 1985). How this happened is not spelled out in the text, but it is obvious that Ahhiyawa's influence in western Anatolia had waned, if not ceased entirely, by this point. Kelder sees the "Hittite architectural features in the city wall of Late Bronze Age Miletus, Hittite grave gifts, ... [and] a possible representation of a Hittite god or even king on a locally made (Mycenaean) krater" as all dating to this period, after Miletus had come back under Hittite control (Kelder 2005a: 153; citing Niemeier 1998: 42 and 2002: 298).

We are also told in this text (**AhT 5**), though it may or may not be relevant, that a king of Wilusa named Walmu, who had been driven from his land by rebels, was to be reinstated, probably as a "military vassal" (*kulawaniš*), after Tarkasnawa had handed him back to Tudhaliya. This probably indicates that Hittite aid to this kingdom, which had been ongoing since the days of Muwattalli II when a treaty was signed with Alaksandu, the ruler of Wilusa, in the early- to mid-thirteenth century B.C.E., was still continuing. Finally, we are also given clues in the text that Piyamaradu was still alive and active to a certain extent. He must have been reasonably advanced in age by this point, since the references to him come from texts dated to the reigns of Muwattalli II, Hattusili III, and Tudhaliya IV, covering a period of at least thirty-five years.

The final indication that Mycenaean influence on the western coast of Anatolia, and indeed perhaps in the entire Eastern Mediterranean, had fallen by the wayside and that relations between the Hittites and the Mycenaeans had essentially ended, may be found in a treaty signed between Tudhaliya IV and his brother-in-law/nephew Shaushga-muwa, the vassal king of Amurru (located in northern Syria) in the late-thirteenth century B.C.E. (**AhT 2**; for the most recent discussion of this text, see now Devecchi 2010). Ahhiyawa is mentioned twice in the document. One occurrence appears just after the description of an embargo being set up against Assyria, which was an enemy of the Hittites at the time. According to the translation given above it reads, "[You shall not allow(?)] any ship [of] Ahhiyawa to go to him (that is, the king of Assyria) [...]" A very similar translation just published by Devecchi (2010: 254) begins "Do n[ot allo]w any ship [of Ahh]iyawa to go to him!" These two versions, which are quite comparable to the original translation published by Sommer so long ago, seem much more likely than the translation suggested by Steiner (1989), who restores "warships" instead of ships of Ahhiyawa. His suggestion has not been met with enthusiasm by other scholars (see now especially Devecchi 2010: 251–54 and previously, among others, Lehmann 1991: 111 n. 11; Niemeier 1998: 25 n. 8).

The reference to Ahhiyawa here has usually been seen as part of the embargo being set up against Assyria. Some scholars have seen the embargo as being extended to include Ahhiyawa as well, thereby helping to explain the lack of Mycenaean objects in central Anatolia and of Hittite objects in the Bronze Age Aegean (see, e.g., Cline 1991, 1191b; 1994; brief discussions in Mee 1998: 143; Bryce 2003b; Kelder 2010b: 31–32, 59). However, Bryce (2010: 50) has recently suggested that it could have been cargoes of mercenaries, rather than merchandise, unloaded from Mycenaean ships that were to be stopped from traveling to Assyria in that time of war.

The second mention of Ahhiyawa in this text occurs a few lines earlier, in a list of Great Kings with whom Tudhaliya considered himself to be equal, where the king of Ahhiyawa was included and then erased. Much has been made of this erasure by scholars, including the fact that this entire tablet appears to be a rough draft. But the conclusion held by all is that Ahhiyawa, which had been one of the Great Powers, apparently no longer held that status at this time in history, perhaps in part because Milawata/Millawanda (Miletus) and the Ahhiyawan footholds on the western coast of Anatolia had been lost to the Hittites.

The final texts which can be documented chronologically appear somewhat as footnotes to the above history of Mycenaean-Hittite interactions. Two (**AhT 27A** and **B**) are letters sent from Suppiluliuma II and Penti-Sharruma, a Hittite official, to Ammurapi, king of Ugarit, in the late-thirteenth century B.C.E. These, recently found at Ugarit and still essentially unpublished outside of the current volume, contain the first references to Ahhiyawa found in a different language, that is, Akkadian rather than Hittite (see especially Singer 2006: 255–58, with references). Among other matters, both of the letters mention men from (Ah)Hiyawa waiting in the land of Lukka, in southwestern Anatolia; these men are thought to have been freebooters or mercenaries, rather than representatives of the Ahhiyawan king (Bryce 2010).

The archaeological remains appear to corroborate the fact that contact between Mycenaeans and Hittites essentially ceased after the mid- to late-thirteenth century B.C.E., for little LH IIIB2 pottery has been found, and LH IIIC pottery only occurs sporadically, including a few sherds or vessels at Çine-Tepecik, Clazomenae, Domuztepe, Larisa, Miletus, Pitane, Sardis, and Troy on the western coast, a larger number of sherds at various sites in Cilicia, including Tarsus, on the southeastern coast of Anatolia, and a stirrup jar at Fraktin in central Anatolia (which undoubtedly arrived via Cilicia), in twelfth-century B.C.E. contexts (Mee 1978: 124 n. 5, 125–26, 128, 131–32, 147, 150; Kelder 2004–2005: 54–58, 60–61, 74, 79, and Table 1; 2010b: 123, 125, 127, 129–31, 133–35; Günel and Herbordt 2010).

The last Ahhiyawa text (**AhT 28**) dates from several centuries later, during the Neo-Assyrian period in the mid- to late-eighth century B.C.E., in a bilingual inscription set up by a king named Warika. He refers to his kingdom in the region of Cilicia as Hiyawa. It is most likely that this inscription represents the situation as it appeared during the Iron Age, after surviving descendants of the Mycenaeans had perhaps migrated to the area of Cilicia following the collapse of the Late Bronze Age world. Given the finds of LH IIIC pottery concentrated in the region of Cilicia, as just mentioned, such a scenario is not hard to imagine (cf. Mee 1978: 150; Kelder 2004–2005: 71).

Conclusions

It is now possible to put together a succinct, yet comprehensive, view of Mycenaean-Hittite relations during the Late Bronze Age, according to both the archaeological evidence and the Ahhiyawa texts, as spelled out above (cf. also Kelder 2005a: 154).

In terms of correlations between the reigns of the Hittite kings to which the Ahhiyawa texts date and the ceramic periods of the Late Bronze Age Aegean (see Mountjoy 1998: 46, Table 1), the time of Tudhaliya I/II, during the late-fifteenth–early-fourteenth century B.C.E., falls within the LH II period. At this time, both Ahhiyawa and the Hittites were apparently involved in the Assuwa Rebellion, with the Mycenaeans aiding the Assuwans and the Hittites suppressing the rebellion. We also have the first mention of Ahhiya and the enemy ruler Attarissiya. Archaeological evidence includes the inscribed bronze sword found at Hattusa and Mycenaean pottery from Miletus and Clazomenae.

The reigns of Arnuwanda I through Mursili II (early-fourteenth century B.C.E.–ca. 1295 B.C.E.) fall within the LH IIIA1 and IIIA2 periods. During the time of Arnuwanda I, we have textual mentions of Attarissiya's attacks on the Hittite vassal Madduwatta. Miletus goes back and forth between Hittite and Mycenaean control, according to the Annals of Mursili II, at the same time as the Mycenaeans get involved in the affairs of the Land of Arzawa and the city of Apasa, and a man named Uhha-ziti, with Mycenaean IIIA1 pottery found at both of these sites. Towards the end of this period, during the third year of Mursili II's reign, the Hittites attacked Milawata/Millawanda, which is confirmed by a destruction level at Miletus dating to the late LH IIIA2 period, and apparently conquered the Land of Arzawa, which may be reflected in the lack of Mycenaean pottery at Ephesus after this time. Overall, relations between the Mycenaeans and the Hittites during this period seem to have begun as hostile and become peaceful over the course of the fourteenth century B.C.E., with occasional flare-ups. The high point of Mycenaean activity on the western coast is during the LH IIIA2 period, at which time Mycenaean pottery is found at more than a dozen sites in this region.

Muwattalli II, Urhi-Teshshup, Hattusili III, and Tudhaliya IV (ca. 1295–1209 B.C.E.) all ruled during what was the LH IIIB period in the Aegean. During this time, covering most of the thirteenth century B.C.E., relations between the Mycenaeans and the Hittites seem to have worsened once again, in large part because of Mycenaean involvement in the rebellious activities of Piyamaradu, a "renegade Hittite subject." Ahhiyawa appears to have controlled islands off the coast of Anatolia, as well as still being involved at Miletus, where quantities of LH IIIB pottery have been found, much of it locally produced. Additional LH IIIB pottery is found at a few other sites, but importation or local production had dropped off by the LH IIIB2 period. By the time of Hattusili III, Ahhiyawa was regarded as a Great Power and its king was addressed as a "Great King" and as "brother." But soon thereafter, during Tudhaliya IV's reign, after Tudhaliya had recaptured Miletus (Milawata/Millawanda) ca. 1220 B.C.E. while crushing a rebellion in the Seha River Land that had been encouraged by the Mycenaeans, Ahhiyawa was deleted from a text listing the other Great Powers and was banned from contact with Assyria. Clearly relations between the Mycenaeans and the Hittites were at a lower point than they had ever been before; as it turned out, both were in an irreversible decline.

In the reigns of Arnuwanda III and Suppiluliuma II (ca. 1209 B.C.E. onward), which occurred during the equivalent of the early LH IIIC period in the twelfth century B.C.E., Mycenaean IIIC pottery is found primarily in Cilicia and there are no mentions of Ahhiyawa in Hittite texts. Relations come to an end altogether soon thereafter, when both the Mycenaean and the Hittite civilizations collapse in the decades after 1200 B.C.E.

In sum, when comparing and contrasting the extant archaeological data with the available textual data, we may quote a recent article by Bryce, who states "there is some irony in the fact that the kingdom which had the closest political dealings with the Mycenaean world [i.e., the Hittite kingdom] has, in comparison with a number of its contemporaries, left so little trace in the archaeological record of any form of contact with this world" (Bryce 2003b: 72). However, although few indications exist for contact between the Mycenaeans and the Hittites in inland Anatolia or for the Mycenaean importation of Hittite objects to mainland Greece or elsewhere in the Bronze Age Aegean, there were clearly contacts between the Mycenaeans and the Hittites, attested both textually and artifactually, on the western coast of Anatolia, as has long been known (Cline 1994: 68–74, with previous references). It remains to be determined whether such contacts, ebbing and flowing over the centuries, also resulted in the similarities seen in Hittite and Mycenaean fortification architecture; hypothesized Hittite influences on Greek epic dialect; possible links between certain works of Greek literature and earlier Hittite compositions, such as Hesiod's *Theogony* and the Hittite-adapted Hurrian *Epic of Kumarbi*; and the Greek mythical traditions regarding the western Anatolian origins of the Atreid dynasty at Mycenae and the building of Tiryns' walls by giants from Lycia (see, e.g., Cline 1994: 69; 1997; West 1997; Burkert 1998).

Sources

AhT 1A (CTH 61.I). Ten-Year Annals of Mursili II, Years 3–4. **Texts:** A. KBo 3.4 + KUB 23.125. B. KBo 16.1 + KUB 31.137 + KBo 16.2 (+) KBo 44.239 (+) KBo 44.2. C. KUB 19.38 (+) KUB 14.21. **Date:** Late-fourteenth century B.C.E. **Editions:** Götze 1933: 38–75; Grélois 1988. **Translations:** del Monte 1993: 62–67; Beal in Hallo and Younger 2000: 85–86; Minneck in Chavalas 2006: 253–59. **Discussions:** Sommer 1932: 310–13; Cancik 1976: 102–51; Heinhold-Krahmer 1977: *passim*; van Seters 1983: 108–11; Haas 2006: 78–83.

AhT 1B (CTH 61.II). Extensive Annals of Mursili II, Years 3–4. **Texts:** A. KUB 14.15 + KBo 16.104. B. KUB 14.16. C. KBo 16.5 + KUB 19.40. D. KBo 12.37. **Date:** Late-fourteenth–early-thirteenth century B.C.E. **Editions:** Götze 1933: 36–75. **Translations:** del Monte 1993: 77–82. **Discussions:** Sommer 1932: 307–9; del Monte 1974: 360–61; Cancik 1976: 102–51; Heinhold-Krahmer 1977: *passim*; van Seters 1983: 108–11; Haas 2006: 78–83.

AhT 2 (CTH 105). Treaty between Tudhaliya IV of Hatti and Shaushga-muwa, king of Amurru. **Texts:** A. 93/w (+) KUB 23.1 + KUB 31.43 (+) KUB 23.37 (+) 720/v (+) 670/v. B. 1198/u + 1436/u + 69/821 + KUB 8.82. **Date:** Late-thirteenth century B.C.E. **Editions:** Szemerényi 1945; Kühne and Otten 1971. **Translations:** Beckman 1999: 103–7; Singer in Hallo and Younger 2000: 98–100. **Discussions:** Götze 1929; Sommer 1932: 320–27; Ranoszek 1950; Zaccagnini 1988; Steiner 1989; Singer 1991a: 172–73; Klengel 1992: 173; 1995; Altman 1998; 2004: 440–60; Devecchi 2010.

AhT 3 (CTH 147). Indictment of Madduwatta. Reign of Arnuwanda I. **Text:** KUB 14.1 + KBo 19.38. **Date:** Late-fifteenth–early-fourteenth century B.C.E. **Edition:** Götze 1928. **Translation:** Beckman 1999: 153–60. **Discussions:** Sommer 1932: 329–49; Otten 1969; Heinhold-Krahmer

1977: 260–75; Güterbock 1983: 133–35; Hoffmann 1984; Schachermeyr 1986: 141–61; Bryce 1986.

AhT 4 (CTH 181). Letter from a king of Hatti (probably Hattusili III) to a king of Ahhiyawa—the "Tawagalawa Letter." **Text:** KUB 14.3. **Date:** Mid-thirteenth century B.C.E. **Editions:** Forrer 1929: 95–232; Sommer 1932: 2–194; Hoffner 2009: no. 101. **Translations:** Garstang and Gurney 1959: 111–14 (extracts); Miller in Janowski and Wilhelm 2006: 240–47. **Discussions:** Heinhold-Krahmer 1983; 1986; 2002; 2010; Güterbock 1990; Gurney 2002; Bryce 2003a: 199–212.

AhT 5 (CTH 182). Letter from a king of Hatti (probably Tudhaliya IV) to a western Anatolian ruler (Tarkasnawa, king of Mira?)—the "Milawata Letter." **Text:** KUB 19.55 + KUB 48.90. **Date:** Late-thirteenth century B.C.E. **Editions:** Forrer 1926: 233–61; Sommer 1932: 198–240; Hoffner 2009: no. 102. **Translation:** Garstang and Gurney 1959: 114–15. **Discussions:** Hoffner 1982; Bryce 1985; 1998: 339–42.

AhT 6 (CTH 183). Letter from a king of Ahhiyawa to a king of Hatti (probably Muwattalli II). **Text:** KUB 26.91. **Date:** Early- to mid-thirteenth century B.C.E. **Editions:** Sommer 1932: 268–70; Hagenbuchner 1989: no. 219; Hoffner 2009: no. 99. **Discussions:** de Martino 1996: 30–33; Taracha 2001; Freu 2004: 293–99; Latacz 2004: 243–44; Melchert forthcoming.

AhT 7 (CTH 191). Letter from Manapa-Tarḫunta of the Seha River Land to a king of Hatti (probably Muwattalli II). **Date:** Early-thirteenth century B.C.E. **Text:** KUB 19.5 + KBo 19.79. **Editions:** Houwink ten Cate 1983/84: 38–64; Hoffner 2009: no. 100. **Discussion:** Singer 2008.

AhT 8 (CTH 209.12). Letter from a Hittite official to a king of Hatti (Hattusili III?). **Text:** KBo 2.11. **Date:** Mid-thirteenth century B.C.E. **Editions:** Sommer 1932: 242–48; Hagenbuchner 1989: no. 302.

AhT 9 (CTH 209.16). Letter from a king of Hatti(?) (perhaps Mursili II or Hattusili III) to a king of Ahhiyawa(?). **Text:** KUB 23.95. **Date:** Mid-fourteenth–thirteenth century B.C.E. **Editions:** Sommer 1932: 262–65; Hagenbuchner 1989: no. 217.

AhT 10 (CTH 209.17). Letter. **Text:** KUB 23.98. **Date:** Thirteenth century B.C.E. **Editions:** Sommer 1932: 266–67; Hagenbuchner 1989: no. 218.

AhT 11 (CTH 211.4). Offenses of the Seha River Land (royal edict of Tudhaliya IV?). **Text:** KUB 23.13. **Date:** Late-thirteenth century B.C.E. **Editions**: Sommer 1932: 314–18; Güterbock 1992. **Discussions:** Heinhold-Krahmer 1977: 249–52; Easton 1985: 194; Hawkins 1998: 20.

AhT 12 (CTH 214.12.A). Prayer of Mursili II/Muwattalli II/Urhi-Teshshup(?). **Text:** KUB 14.2. **Date:** Late-fourteenth–mid-thirteenth century B.C.E. **Edition:** Sommer 1932: 298-306. **Discussion:** Houwink ten Cate 1994: 251-52.

AhT 13 (CTH 214.12.B). Memorandum(?). **Text:** KUB 21.34. **Date:** Thirteenth century B.C.E. **Editions:** Sommer 1932: 250–52; Hagenbuchner 1989: no. 173.

AhT 14 (CTH 214.12.C). Extract from a letter(?) from a king of Hatti(?) (Tudhaliya IV?) concerning Urhi-Teshshup. **Text:** KBo 16.22. **Date:** Mid- to late-thirteenth century B.C.E. **Edition:** Güterbock 1936: 321–26.

AhT 15 (CTH 214.12.D). Letter from a king of Hatti (Hattusili III?) to another Great King. **Text:** KUB 26.76. **Date:** Thirteenth century B.C.E. **Discussion:** Mouton 2007: no. 8.

AhT 16 (CTH 214.12.E). Fragment. **Text:** KBo 19.83. **Date:** Thirteenth century B.C.E.

AhT 17 (CTH 214.12.F). Fragment. **Text:** KUB 31.30. **Date:** Late-thirteenth century B.C.E.

AhT 18 (CTH 214.16). "Boundary" list(?). Reign of Hattusili III or Tudhaliya IV(?). **Text:** KUB 31.29. **Date:** Mid- to late-thirteenth century B.C.E. **Edition:** Sommer 1932: 328. **Discussion:** Heinhold-Krahmer 2007a.

AhT 19 (CTH 243.6). Inventory. **Text:** KBo 18.181. **Date:** Thirteenth century B.C.E. **Editions:** Košak 1982: 118–26; Siegelová 1986: 363–77. **Discussion:** Heinhold-Krahmer 2007b: 200.

AhT 20 (CTH 570.1). Oracle report. **Text:** KUB 5.6 + KUB 18.54 + KBo 53.103 (+) KUB 50.123. **Date:** Late-fourteenth–early-thirteenth century B.C.E. **Partial edition:** Sommer 1932: 275–94. **Discussions:** Ünal 1974: 1, 168–70; van den Hout 1998: 3–6, 21–24; Beal 2002: 24–27; Jasink 2004; Haas 2008: 68–75.

AhT 21 (CTH 570.2). Oracle report. **Text:** KUB 22.56. **Date:** Thirteenth century B.C.E. **Partial edition:** Sommer 1932: 296–97.

AhT 22 (CTH 571.2). Oracle report. **Text:** KBo 16.97 + KBo 40.48. **Date:** Late-fifteenth–early-fourteenth century B.C.E., reign of Tudhaliya I/II(?). **Edition:** Schoul 1994a. **Discussions:** de Martino 1992; Klinger 1998: 104–11; 2010: 163–65; van den Hout 2001: 426.

AhT 23 (CTH 572.1). Oracle report. **Text:** KUB 18.58 + KUB 6.7. **Date:** Late-thirteenth century B.C.E.

AhT 24 (CTH 572.2). Oracle report. **Text:** KBo 48.22. **Date:** Thirteenth century B.C.E.

AhT 25 (CTH 581*). Letter. **Text:** KBo 18.135. **Date:** Thirteenth century B.C.E. **Edition:** Hagenbuchner 1989: no. 171.

AhT 26 (CTH 590). Votive prayer of Puduhepa(?) (wife of Hattusili III). **Text:** KUB 56.15. **Date:** Mid-thirteenth century B.C.E. **Edition:** de Roos 2007: 240–43. **Discussions:** Heinhold-Krahmer 2007b: 195; 2010: 203.

AhT 27A. Letter from Suppiluliuma II to Ammurapi, king of Ugarit. **Text:** RS 94.2530 (unpublished). **Date:** Late-thirteenth century B.C.E. **Language:** Akkadian. **Partial transliteration:** Lackenbacher and Malbran-Labat 2005a. **Discussion:** Singer 2006.

AhT 27B. Letter from Penti-Sharruma, a Hittite official, to Ammurapi, king of Ugarit. **Text:** RS 94.2523 (unpublished). **Date:** Late-thirteenth century B.C.E. **Language:** Akkadian. **Partial transliteration:** Lackenbacher and Malbran-Labat 2005a, 2005b. **Discussion:** Singer 2006.

AhT 28. Inscription of Warika, king of (Ah)hiyawa. **Text:** ÇINEKÖY. **Date:** Mid-late eighth century B.C.E. **Language:** Hieroglyphic Luwian. **Edition:** Tekoğlu and Lemaire 2000. **Discussion:** Forlanini 2005: 111–14; Lanfranchi 2009.

Bibliography

Altman, A. 1998. "On Some Assertions in the 'Historical Prologue' of the Šaušgamuwa Vassal Treaty and Their Assumed Legal Meaning." Pages 99–107 in *XXXIVème Rencontre Assyriologique Internationale. Kongreye Sunulan Bildirler*. Edited by H. Erkanal, V. Donbaz, and A. Uğuroğlu. Ankara: Türk Tarih Kurumu.

———. 2004. *The Historical Prologue of the Hittite Vassal Treaties*. Ramat-Gan: Bar-Ilan University Press.

Beal, R. 2002. "Gleanings from Hittite Oracle Questions on Religion, Society, Psychology and Decision Making." Pages 11–37 in *Silva Anatolica: Festschrift für Maciej Popko*. Edited by P. Taracha. Warsaw: Agade.

Beckman, G. 1999. *Hittite Diplomatic Texts*. 2nd ed. Atlanta: Scholars Press.

———. forthcoming. "*Aḫḫijawa* und kein Ende: The Battle over Mycenaeans in Anatolia." In the proceedings of the workshop "Mycenaeans and Anatolians in the Late Bronze Age" held in Montreal, Quebec, January 4-5, 2006. Edited by A. Teffeteller. Oxford: Oxford University Press.

Bryce, T. 1985. "A Reinterpretation of the Milawata Letter in the Light of the New Join Piece." *AnSt* 35:13–23.

———. 1986. "Madduwatta and Hittite Policy in Western Anatolia." *Historia* 35:1–12.

———. 1989a. "Ahhiyawans and Mycenaeans—An Anatolian Viewpoint." *OJA* 8:257–310.

———. 1989b. "The Nature of Mycenaean Involvement in Western Anatolia." *Historia* 38:1–21.

———. 1999. "Anatolian Scribes in Mycenaean Greece." *Historia* 48:257–64.

———. 2003a. *Letters of the Great Kings of the Ancient Near East. The Royal Correspondence of the Late Bronze Age*. London: Routledge.

———. 2003b. "Relations between Hatti and Ahhiyawa in the Last Decades of the Bronze Age." Pages 59–72 in *Hittite Studies in Honor of Harry A. Hoffner Jr.* Edited by G. Beckman, R. Beal, and G. McMahon. Winona Lake, Ind.: Eisenbrauns.

———. 2005. *The Kingdom of the Hittites*. New (Revised) Edition. Oxford: Clarendon.

———. 2010. "The Hittite Deal with the Ḫiyawa-Men." Pages 47–53 in *Pax Hethitica: Studies on the Hittites and their Neighbours in Honour of Itamar Singer*. Edited by Y. Cohen, A. Gilan, and J. Miller. Wiesbaden: Harrassowitz.

———. 2011. "Ahhiyawa." Pages 10–11 in *The Routledge Handbook of the Peoples and Places of Ancient Western Asia: From the Early Bronze Age to the Fall of the*

Persian Empire. London: Routledge.
Burkert, W. 1998. *The Orientalizing Revolution: Near Eastern Influence on Greek Culture in the Early Archaic Age*. Cambridge, Mass.: Harvard University Press.
Çambel, H. 1999. *Corpus of Hieroglyphic Luwian Inscriptions*, vol. 2: *Karatepe-Aslantaş*. Berlin: de Gruyter.
Cancik, H. 1976. *Grundzüge der hethitischen und alttestamentlichen Geschichtsschreibung*. Wiesbaden: Harrassowitz.
Chavalas, M., ed. 2006. *The Ancient Near East: Historical Sources in Translation*. Oxford: Blackwell.
Cline, E. H. 1991a. "A Possible Hittite Embargo Against the Mycenaeans." *Historia* 40:1–9.
———. 1991b. "Hittite Objects in the Bronze Age Aegean." *AnSt* 41:133–43.
———. 1994. *Sailing the Wine-Dark Sea: International Trade and the Late Bronze Age Aegean*. Oxford: BAR International Series 591.
———. 1996. "Assuwa and the Achaeans: the 'Mycenaean' Sword at Hattusas and Its Possible Implications." *BSA* 91:137–51.
———. 1997. "Achilles in Anatolia: Myth, History, and the Aššuwa Rebellion." Pages 189–210 in *Crossing Boundaries and Linking Horizons: Studies in Honor of Michael Astour on His 80th Birthday*. Edited by G. D. Young, M. W. Chavalas, and R. E. Averbeck. Bethesda, M.D.: CDL.
———. 1998. "Amenhotep III, the Aegean and Anatolia." Pages 236–50 in *Amenhotep III: Perspectives on his Reign*. Edited by D. O'Connor and E. H. Cline. Ann Arbor: University of Michigan Press.
———. 2008. "Troy as a 'Contested Periphery': Archaeological Perspectives on Cross-Cultural and Cross-Disciplinary Interactions Concerning Bronze Age Anatolia." Pages 11–19 in *Anatolian Interfaces: Hittites, Greeks and Their Neighbors. Proceedings of an International Conference on Cross-Cultural Interaction, September 17–19, 2004, Emory University, Atlanta, GA*. Edited by B. J. Collins, M. R. Bachvarova, and I. C. Rutherford. Oxford: Oxbow.
———. 2010. "Bronze Age Interactions between the Aegean and the Eastern Mediterranean Revisited: Mainstream, Margin, or Periphery?" Pages 161–80 in *Archaic State Interaction: The Eastern Mediterranean in the Bronze Age*. Edited by W. Parkinson and M. Galaty. Santa Fe, N.M.: School for Advanced Research.
———. in press. "A Trout in the Milk: The Case of the Missing Ahhiyawa Letters." In the proceedings of the workshop Mycenaeans and Anatolians in the Late Bronze Age held in Montreal, Quebec, January 4–5, 2006. Edited by A. Teffeteller.
Collins, B. J. 2007. *The Hittites and Their World*. Atlanta: Society of Biblical Literature.
del Monte, G. 1974. "Mašḫuiluwa, König von Mira." *Or* 43:355–68.
de Martino, S. 1992. "Personaggi e riferimenti storici nel testo oracolaire ittito KBo XVI 97." *SMEA* 29:33–46
———. 1996. *L'Anatolia occidentale nel medio regno ittita*. Florence: Vantaggio.
de Roos, J. 2007. *Hittite Votive Texts*. Leiden: Nederlands Instituut voor het Nabije Oosten.
del Monte, G. 1993. *L'annalistica ittita*. Brescia: Paideia.
Devecchi, E. "Amurru between Hatti, Assyria, and Ahhiyawa. Discussing a Recent Hypothesis." *ZA* 100:242–56.

Easton, D. 1985. "Has the Trojan War Been Found?" *Antiquity* 59:188–96.
Fischer, R. 2010. *Die Aḫḫijawa-Frage*. Wiesbaden: Harrassowitz.
Forlanini, M. 2005. "Un peuple, plusieurs noms. Le problème des ethniques au Proche Orient ancien. Cas connus, cas à découvrir." Pages 111–19 in *Ethnicity in Ancient Mesopotamia: Papers Read at the 48th Rencontre Assyriologique Internationale*. Edited by W. H. van Soldt. Leiden: Nederlands Instituut voor het Nabije Oosten.
Forrer, E. 1924a. "Vorhomerische Griechen in den Keilschrifttexten von Boghazköi." *MDOG* 83:1–22.
———. 1924b. "Die Griechen in den Boghazköi-Texten." *OLZ* 1924:113–18.
———. 1926. *Die Boghazköi-Texte in Umschrift, II*. Leipzig: Hinrichs.
———. 1929a. *Forschungen* I/2. Berlin: Selbstverlag.
———. 1929b. "Für die Griechen in den Boghazköi-Inschriften." *Kleinasiatische Forschungen* 1: 252–72.
Freu, J. 2004. "Les îles de la mer Égée, Lazpa, le pays d'Aḫḫiyawa et les Hittites." *Res Antiquae* 1: 275–323.
Friedrich, J. 1927. "Werden in den hethitischen Keilschrifttexten die Griechen erwähnt?" *Kleinasiatische Forschungen* 1: 87–107.
Garstang, J., and O. R. Gurney. 1959. *The Geography of the Hittite Empire*. London: British School of Archaeology at Ankara.
Götze, A. 1927a. "Zur Geographie des Hethiterreiches." *Kleinasiatische Forschungen* 1: 108–14.
———. 1927b. "Zur Chronologie der Hethiterkönige." *Kleinasiatische Forschungen* 1:115–19.
———. 1927c. "Randnoten zu Forrers 'Forschungen.'" *Kleinasiatische Forschungen* 1:125–36.
———. 1928. *Madduwattaš*. Leipzig: Hinrichs.
———. 1929. "Zur Schlacht von Qadeš." *OLZ* 832–38.
———. 1933. *Die Annalen des Muršiliš*. Leipzig: Hinrichs.
Grélois, J.-P. 1988. "Les annales décennales de Mursili II (CTH 61, I)." *Hethitica* 9: 17–145.
Günel, S., and S. Herbordt. 2010. "Ein hethitischer Siegelabdruck aus Çine-Tepecik." *AA* 2010/1:1–11.
Gurney, O. R. 1997. "The Annals of Hattusili III." *AnSt* 47:127–39.
———. 2002. "The Authorship of the Tawagalawa Letter." Pages 133–41 in *Silva Anatolica: Anatolian Studies Presented to Maciej Popko on the Occasion of His 65th Birthday*. Edited by P. Taracha. Warsaw: Agade.
Güterbock, H. G. 1936. "Neue Aḫḫijavā-Texte." *ZA* 43:321–27.
———. 1983. "The Hittites and the Aegean World: 1. The Ahhiyawa Problem Reconsidered." *AJA* 87:133–38.
———. 1984. "Hittites and Akhaeans: A New Look." *PAPS* 128:114–22.
———. 1986. "Troy in Hittite Texts? Wilusa, Ahhiyawa, and Hittite History." Pages 33–44 in *Troy and the Trojan War*. Edited by M. J. Mellink. Bryn Mawr.
———. 1990. "Wer war Tawagalawa?" *Or* 59:157–65.
———. 1992. "A New Look at One Aḫḫiyawa Text." Pages 235–43 in *Hittite and Other Anatolian and Near Eastern Studies in Honour of Sedat Alp*. Edited by H. Otten, E. Akurgal, H. Ertem, and A. Süel. Ankara: Türk Tarih Kurumu.

Haas, V. 2006. *Die hethitische Literatur*. Berlin: de Gruyter.

———. 2008. *Hethitische Orakel, Vorzeichen und Abwehrstrategien*. Berlin: de Gruyter.

Hagenbuchner, A. 1989. *Die Korrespondenz der Hethiter*. Heidelberg: Winter.

Hallo, W. W., and K. L. Younger, eds. 2000. *The Context of Scripture II: Monumental Inscriptions from the Biblical World*. Leiden: Brill.

Hawkins, J. D. 1998. "Tarkasnawa, King of Mira, 'Tarkondemos,' Boğazköy Sealings and Karabel." *AnSt* 48:1–31.

———. 2000. *Corpus of Hieroglyphic Luwian Inscriptions, Volume I. Inscriptions of the Iron Age*. Berlin: de Gruyter.

Heinhold-Krahmer, S. 1977. *Arzawa. Untersuchungen zu seiner Geschichte nach den hethitischen Quellen*. THeth 8. Heidelberg: Winter.

———. 1983. "Untersuchungen zu Piyamaradu I." *Or* 52:81–87.

———. 1986. "Untersuchungen zu Piyamaradu II." *Or* 55:47–62.

———. 2002. "Zur Erwähnung Šaḫurunuwas im 'Tawagalawa-Brief.'" Pages 359–75 in *Anatolia Antica: Studi in memoria di Fiorella Imparati*. Edited by S. de Martino and F. P. Daddi. Florence: LoGisma.

———. 2007a. "Anmerkungen zur Aḫḫiyawa-Urkunde KUB 31.29 (Bo 5316/AU XVIII)." Pages 315–26 in *Festschrift in Honor of Belkıs Dinçol and Ali Dinçol*. Edited by M. Doğan-Alparslan and H. Peker. Istanbul: Ege.

———. 2007b. "Zu diplomatischen Kontakten zwischen dem Hethiterreich und dem Land Aḫḫiyawa." Pages 191–207 in *Keimelion: Elitenbildung und elitärer Konsum von der mykensichen Palastzeit bis zur homerischen Epoche*. Edited by E. Alram-Stern and G. Nightingale. Vienna: Österreichische Akademie der Wissenschaften.

———. 2010. "Zur Datierungsgeschichte des 'Tawagalawa-Briefes' und zur problematischen Rolle des Fragments KBo 16.35 als Datierungshilfe." Pages 191–213 in *Pax Hethitica: Studies on the Hittites and their Neighbours in Honour of Itamar Singer*, edited by Y. Cohen, A. Gilan, and J. Miller. Wiesbaden: Harrassowitz.

Hoffner, H. A., Jr. 1982. "The Milawata Letter Augmented and Reinterpreted." *AfO Beiheft* 19:130–37

———. 2009. *Letters from the Hittite Kingdom*. WAW 15. Atlanta: Society of Biblical Literature.

Hope Simpson, R. 2003. "The Dodecanese and the Ahhiyawa Question." *BSA* 98:203–37.

Hout, Th. van den 1998. *The Purity of Kingship: An Edition of CTH 569 and Related Hittite Oracle Inquiries of Tutḫaliya IV*. Leiden: Brill.

———. 2001. "Bemerkungen zu älteren hethitischen Orakeltexten." Pages 423–40 in *Kulturgeschichten. Altorientalische Studien für Volkert Haas zum 65. Geburtstag*. Edited by T. Richter, D. Prechel, and J. Klinger. Saarbrücken: Saarbrücker Verlag.

Houwink ten Cate, P. H. J. 1974. "The Early and Late Phases of Urhi-Tesub's Career." Pages 123–50 in *Anatolian Studies Presented to H. G. Güterbock on the Occasion of His 65th Birthday*. Edited by K. Bittel, P. H. J. Houwink ten Cate, and E. Reiner. Istanbul: Nederlands Historisch-Archaeologisch Instituut in Het Nabije Oosten.

———. 1983/1984. "Sidelights on the Aḫḫiyawa Question from Hittite Vassal and Royal Correspondence." *JEOL* 28:33–79.

———. 1994. "Urhi-Tessub Revisited." *BiOr* 51:233–59.

Hrozný, B. 1929. "Hethiter und Griechen." *Archiv Orientální* 1:323–43.

Huxley, G. L. 1960. *Achaeans and Hittites*. Oxford: Vincent-Baxter.
Janowski, B., and G. Wilhelm, eds. 2006. *Briefe*. TUAT, NF 3. Gütersloh: Gütersloher Verlag.
Jasink, A. M. 2004. "Influenze reciproche fra area egea e area anatolica: l'aspetto del culto." Pages 401–32 in *Antiquus Oriens: Mélanges offerts au Professeur René Lebrun*. Edited by M. Mazoyer and O. Casabonne. Paris: L'Harmattan.
Kelder, J. M. 2004–2005. "Mycenaeans in Western Anatolia." *Talanta* 36–37:49–88.
———. 2005a. "The Chariots of Ahhiyawa." *Dacia, Revue d'Archéologie et d'Histoire Ancienne* 48–49 (2004–2005):151–60.
———. 2005b. "Greece during the Late Bronze Age." *JEOL* 39:131–79.
———. 2008. "A Great King at Mycenae. An Argument for the *Wanax* as Great King and the *Lawagetas* as Vassal Ruler." *Palamedes* 3:49–74.
———. 2010a. Review of Fischer, *Die Ahhijawa-Frage*. *Bryn Mawr Classical Review* 2010.10.32. Online: http://bmcr.brynmawr.edu/2010/2010-10-32.html.
———. 2010b. *The Kingdom of Mycenae: A Great Kingdom in the Late Bronze Age Aegean*. Bethesda, MD: CDL.
Klengel, H. 1992. *Syria: 3000 to 300 B.C.: A Handbook of Political History*. Berlin: Akademie.
———. 1995. "Historischer Kommentar zum Šaušgamuwa-Vertrag." Pages 159–72 in *Studio Historiae Ardens. Ancient Near Eastern Studies Presented to Philo H. J. Houwink ten Cate on the Occasion of His 65th Birthday*. Edited by Th. P. J. van den Hout and J. de Roos. Leiden: Nederlands Instituut voor het Nabije Oosten.
Klinger, J. 1998. "Zur Historizität einiger hethitischer Omina." *AoF* 25: 104–11.
———. 2010. "Der Kult der Ištar von Šamuḫa in mittelhethitischer Zeit." Pages 153–67 in *Investigationes Anatolicae: Gedenkschrift für Erich Neu*. Edited by J. Klinger, E. Rieken, and C. Rüster. Wiesbaden: Harrassowitz.
Košak, S. 1982. *Hittite Inventory Texts (CTH 241–250)*. Heidelberg: Winter.
Kretschmer, P. 1924. "Alakšanduš, König von Viluša." *Glotta* 13: 205–13.
———. 1935. "Alaksandus *ʾAlexandros*." *Glotta* 24: 203–51.
———. 1936. "Nochmals die Hypachäer und Alaksandus." *Glotta* 24: 203–51, 273.
Kühne, C., and H. Otten. 1971. *Der Šaušgamuwa-Vertrag*. Wiesbaden: Harrassowitz.
Lackenbacher, S., and F. Malbran-Labat. 2005a. "Ugarit et les Hittites dans les archives de la 'Maison d'Urtenu.'" *SMEA* 47:227–40.
———. 2005b. "Penti-Šarruma (suite)." *NABU* 2005/90.
Lanfranchi, G. 2009. "A Happy Son of the King of Assyria: Warikas and the Çineköy Bilingual (Cilicia)." Pages 127–50 in *Of God(s), Trees, Kings, and Scholars: Neo-Assyrian and Related Studies in Honour of Simo Parpola*. Edited by M. Luukko, S. Svärd, and R. Mattila. Helsinki: Finnish Oriental Society.
Latacz, J. 2004. *Troy and Homer: Towards a Solution of an Old Mystery*. Oxford: Oxford University Press.
Lehmann, G. A. 1991. "Die 'politisch-historischen' Beziehungen der Ägäis-Welt des 15.–13. Jh.s v. Chr. Zu Ägypten und Vorderasien: Einige Hinweise." Pages 105–26 in *Zweihundert Jahre Homer-Forschung: Rückblick und Ausblick, Colloquium Rauricum 2*. Edited by J. Latacz. Stuttgart: Teubner.
Luckenbill, D. D. 1911. "A Possible Occurrence of the Name Alexander in the Boghaz-Keui Tablets." *Classical Philology* 6:85–86.

Mee, C. 1978. "Aegean Trade and Settlement in Anatolia in the Second Millennium B.C." *AnSt* 28:121–55.

———. 1998. "Anatolia and the Aegean in the Late Bronze Age." Pages 137–48 in *The Aegean and the Orient in the Second Millennium. Proceedings of the 50th Anniversary Symposium, Cincinnati, 18–20 April 1997*. Edited by E. H. Cline and D. Harris-Cline. Aegaeum 18. Liège: Université de Liège.

Melchert, H. C. forthcoming. "Mycenaean and Hittite Diplomatic Correspondence: Fact and Fiction." In the proceedings of the workshop *Mycenaeans and Anatolians in the Late Bronze Age* held in Montreal, Quebec, January 4–5, 2006. Edited by A. Teffeteller.

Mellink, M. J. 1983. "The Hittites and the Aegean World: Part 2. Archaeological Comments on Ahhiyawa-Achaians in Western Anatolia." *AJA* 87:138–41.

Mountjoy, P. A. 1998. "The East Aegean-West Anatolian Interface in the Late Bronze Age." *AnSt* 48:33–67.

Mouton, A. 2007. *Rêves hittites: Contribution à une histoire et une anthropologie du rêve en Anatolie ancienne*. Leiden: Brill.

Niemeier, W.-D. 1998. "The Mycenaeans in Western Anatolia and the Problem of the Origins of the Sea Peoples." Pages 17–65 in *Mediterranean Peoples in Transition: Thirteenth to Early Tenth Centuries BCE*. Edited by S. Gitin *et al*. Jerusalem: Israel Exploration Society.

———. 1999. "Mycenaeans and Hittites in War in Western Asia Minor." Pages 141–55 in *Polemos: le contexte guerrier en Égée à l'âge du bronze*. Edited by R. Laffineur. Aegaeum 19. Liège: Université de Liège.

———. 2002. "Hattusa und Ahhijawa im Konflikt um Millawanda/Milet." Pages 294–99 in *Die Hethiter und ihr Reich; das Volk der 1000 Götter*. Edited by H. Willinghofer and U. Hasekamp. Stuttgart: Theiss.

Page, D. L. 1959. *History and the Homeric Iliad*. Berkeley and Los Angeles: University of California Press.

Ranoszek, R. 1950. "A propos de KUB XXIII 1." *ArOr* 18:236–42.

Schachermeyr, F. 1935. *Hethiter und Achäer*. MAOG 9.1–2. Leipzig: Harrassowitz.

Schuol, M. 1994a. "Die Terminologie des hethitischen SU-Orakels. Eine Untersuchung auf der Grundlage des mittelhethitischen Textes KBo XVI 97 unter vergleichender Berücksichtigung akkadischer Orakeltexte und Lebermodelle, I." *AoF* 21: 73–124.

———. 1994b. "Die Terminologie des hethitischen SU-Orakels. Eine Untersuchung auf der Grundlage des mittelhethitischen Textes KBo XVI 97 unter vergleichender Berücksichtigung akkadischer Orakeltexte und Lebermodelle, II." *AoF* 21:247–304.

Siegelová, J. 1986. *Hethitische Verwaltungspraxis im Lichte der Wirtschafts- und Inventardokumente*. Prague: Národní Muzeum.

Singer, I. 1983. "Western Anatolia in the Thirteenth Century B.C. according to the Hittite Sources." *AnSt* 33:205–17.

———. 1991a. "A Concise History of Amurru." Pages 135–95 in S. Izre'el, *Amurru Akkadian*. Atlanta: Scholars Press.

———. 1991b. "The 'Land of Amurru' and the 'Lands of Amurru' in the Šaušgamuwa Treaty." *Iraq* 53:69–74.

———. 2006. "Ships Bound for Lukka: A New Interpretation of the Companion Letters RS 94.2530 and RS 94.2523." *AoF* 33:242–62.

———. 2008. "Purple-Dyers in Lazpa." Pages 21–43 in *Anatolian Interfaces: Hittites, Greeks and their Neighbors: Proceedings of an International Conference on Cross-Cultural Interaction, September 17–19, 2004, Emory University, Atlanta, GA*. Edited by B. J. Collins, M. Bachvarova, and I. Rutherford. Oxford: Oxbow.

Sommer, F. 1932. *Die Aḫḫijavā-Urkunden*. Munich: Verlag der Bayerischen Akademie der Wissenschaften.

———. 1937. "Aḫḫijawā und kein Ende?" *Indogermanische Forschungen* 55: 169–297.

Starke, F. 1997. "Troia im Kontext des historisch-politischen und sprachlichen Umfeldes Kleinasiens im 2. Jahrtausend." *Studia Troica* 7: 447–87.

Steiner, G. 1964. "Die Ahhijawa-Frage heute." *Saeculum* 15:365–92.

———. 1989. "'Schiffe von Aḫḫiyawa' oder 'Kriegsschiffe' von Amurru im Šauškamuwa-Vertrag?" *UF* 21:393–411.

———. 2007. "The Case of Wilusa and Ahhiyawa." *BiOr* 64/5–6: 590–611.

Szemerényi, O. 1945. "Vertrag des Hethiterkönigs Tudhalija IV. mit Ištarmuwa von Amurru (KUB XXIII 1)." *OrAnt* 9:113–29.

Taracha, P. 2001. "Mycenaeans, Ahhiyawa and Hittite Imperial Policy in the West: A Note on KUB 26.91." Pages 417–22 in *Kulturgeschichten. Altorientalische Studien für Volkert Haas zum 65. Geburtstag*. Edited by T. Richter, D. Prechel, and J. Klinger. Saarbrücken: Saarbrücker Verlag.

Tekoğlu, R., and A. Lemaire. 2000. "La bilingue royale louvito-phénicienne de Çineköy." *CRAIBL*:961–1007.

Ünal, A. 1974. *Ḫattušili III*. Heidelberg: Winter.

van Seters, J. 1983. *In Search of History: Historiography in the Ancient World and the Origins of Biblical History*. New Haven: Yale University Press.

West, M.L. 1997. *The East Face of Helicon: West Asiatic Elements in Greek Poetry and Myth*. Oxford: Clarendon.

Zaccagnini, C. 1988. "A Note on Hittite International Relations at the Time of Tuthaliya IV." Pages 295–99 in *Studi de storia e di filologia anatolica dedicati à Giovanni Pugliese Carratelli*. Edited by F. Imparati. Florence: ELITE.

INDICES

1. DEITIES

Alalu, **2**, §20'
Allatum, **2**, §20'
Ammizadu, **2**, §20'
Ammunki, **2**, §20'
Antu, **2**, §20'
Anu, **2**, §20'
Apandu, **2**, §20'
Askasepa, **2**, §20'
Birth-deities, **23**, §§5', 7', 9', 11', 14'
Deity of the Night, **22**, §48
    of Lahhurama, **22**, §33
    of Samuha, **22**, §§8, 32
Ea, **2**, §20'
Enlil, **2**, §20'
Ereshkigal, **2**, §20'
Fate-deities, **23**, §§9', 13', 25'''
Hatagga of Ankuwa, **2**, §20'
Hebat, **26**, §2'
Huwassanna of Hupisna, **2**, §20'
Ishara, **20**, §§16', 17'
Kuniyawani of Landa, **2**, §20'
Kurunta. *See* Tutelary Deity
La[…, **22**, §51
Lady of Landa, **2**, §20'
Mamma, **26**, §3'
Mezzulla, **1A**, §§13', 15', 17', 18', 21', 24', 27'
mercenary deities, **2**, §20'
mountain-dweller deities, **2**, §20'
Munki, **2**, §20'
Napsara, **2**, §20'
Nara, **2**, §20'
Ninlil, **2**, §20'
Shaushga, **22**, §38
    of the Father (of His Majesty?), **22**, §37
    of the Field, **1B**, §4'
    of Hattarina, **2**, §20'; **22**, §35
    of the Mother (of His Majesty?), **22**, §36
    of Nineveh, **22**, §§31, 34
Sun-Goddess of Arinna, **1A**, §§13', 15', 17', 18', 21', 24', 27'; **1B**, §4'; 2, §1; **11**, §1; **20**, §59'
Storm-God, **1A**, §16'; **4**, §3; **5**, §6'; **6**, §3; **7**, §4; **26**, §2'; **28**, §§1, 3
    of Aleppo, **20**, §48'
    of the Army, **1B**, §4'; **2**, §20'
    August, **1B**, §4'
    of Hatti, **1B**, §4'
    of Hissassapa, **2**, §20'; **20**, §48'
    of Kuliwisna, **22**, §22
    of Lightning, **22**, §24
    pishaishaphi, **8**, §1'
    Powerful, **1A**, §§13', 15', 17', 18', 21', 24', 27'; **1B**, §§4', 5'; **20**, §§47', 48'
    of Sahpina, **20**, §§46', 50', 54'
    of Heaven, **5**, §2
Teshshup. *See* Storm-God
Tuhusi, **2**, §20'
Tutelary Deity, **20**, §§36', 44'; **22**, §12

Tutelary Deity, *cont'd*
of Hatti, **1B**, §4'
of Taurissa, **20**, §13
War-God of Arziya, **2**, §20'
of Ellaya, **2**, §20'
Zawalli(ya), **20**, §§23', 25', 26', 29', 30'

2. PERSONS

Agapurusiya, **5**, §6'
Akiya, **20**, §17'
Ammarali, **20**, §22'
Ammurapi, **27A**, §§1, 3; **27B**, §3
Anani-piya, **14**
Ankalliya, **20**, §18'
Antahita, **3**, §23'
Antarawa, **20**, §§19', 23'
Apallu, **19**, §8'
Armatalli, **20**, §28'
Arnuwanda II, **1A**, §12
Atta, **19**, §6'
Attarissiya, **3**, §§1, 2, 3, 4, 7, 12, 36'
Atpa, **4**, §§5, 6; **7**, §4
Awayanassa, **4**, §5
Aziru, **2**, §3
Gulla, **1B**, §1'
Hattusili III, **2**, §§1, 5
Himuili, **20**, colophon
Huha, **7**, §4
Iyasalla, **22**, §29
Kagamuna, **6**, §3
Kassu, **7**, §§3, 4
Kisnapili, **3**, §§12, 13, 14
Kulana-ziti, **5**, §§7', 9'
Kupanta-Kurunta, **3**, §§6, 8, 9, 10, 16, 17, 21', 27'; **4**, §4
Kurunta, **4**, §5
Lahurzi, **4**, §2
Mala-ziti, **1B**, §1'; **22**, §7
Manapa-Tarhunta, **1A**, §§26', 27'; **1B**, §§11', 14'; **7**, §1
Mabili, **20**, §31'
Marasa, **3**, §28'
Masanuzzi, Massannauzi, **2**, §7; **20**, §17'
Mashuiluwa, **1A**, §27'; **1B**, §§2', 5', 12', 14'; **20**, §§29', 30', 31', 32'
Masturi, **2**, §§7, 8
Madduwatta, **3**, passim
Mazlauwa, **3**, §23'
Mizzulla, **20**, §§3', 5', 6', 7', 9'
Mukasa, **28**, §1
Muksu, **3**, §33'
Mulliyara, **3**, §§29', 31', 32', 36'
Mursili II, **2**, §§1, 3
Muwattalli, **22**, §2
Muwattalli II, **2**, §§4, 5, 7, 8
Muwatti, **1B**, §12'
Muwa-walwi, **1B**, §§11', 14'; **11**, §2
NÍG.GA.KÙ.SIG_{17}, **20**, §§31', 32'
Niwalla, **3**, §§30', 31'
Partahulla, **3**, §§14, 18
Benteshina, **2**, §5
Penti-Sharruma, **27B**, §1
Piseni, **3**, §§10, 11, 32'
Piyama-Kurunta, **1A**, §§17', 25'; **1B**, §§2', 10'
Piyamaradu, **4**, §§4, 5, 8, 13; **5**, §6'; **7**, §4; **15**, §1'; **26**, §§4', 5'
Puskurunuwa, **3**, §11
Sahuranuwa, **4**, §10a
Satalli, **27A**, §7; **27B**, §6
Shapili, **2**, §§4, 5
Sharri-Kushuh, **1B**, §§5', 8', 9'
Shaushga-muwa, **2**, §§2, 6, 7, 8
Siggauna, **7**, §4
Sippa-ziti, **14**
Suppiluliuma I, **2**, §3
Talmi-Teshshup, **14**
Tapala-Tarhunta, **4**, §8
Tapalazunawali, **1A**, §§20', 21', 22'
Tabarna, **11**, §2
Tarhuna-radu, **11**, §1
Targasnalli, **1A**, §27'; **1B**, §14'

Tatiwasti, **20**, §19'
Tawagalawa, **4**, §§1, 5, 8
Tawananna, **20**, §§41', 43'
Tulpi-Teshshup, **22**, §55
Tudhaliya I, **2**, §1; **6**, §3
Tudhaliya IV, **2**, §1; **11**, §1
Uhha-ziti. **1A**, §§12, 16', 17', 18', 20', 22', 23', 25'; 1A, §§1', 2', 5', 10', 11
Urhi-Teshshup (Mursili III), **2**, §8; **14**
Walmu, **5**, §7'
Warika, **28**, §§1, 2
Zaparti-negna, **20**, §§31', 32'
Zidanza, **3**, §12
Zuwa, **3**, §28'
Zuwahallati, **20**, §31'
Ah[... , **3**, §11
Ku[..., **20**, §19'
Pazza[..., **20**, §19'
Sa[..., **8**, §6'
Duddu[..., **22**, §22
Us[..., **3**, §33'
...]-ili, **4**, §10a
...]nizzi, **8**, §6'
...]-nu, **19**, §3

3. Cities
(not including those appearing in divine epithets)

Ankuwa, **20**, §§25', 26'
Anzili, **1B**, §4'
Apasa, **1A**, §17'; **1B**, §5'
Appawiya, **1B**, §14'
Arinna, 5, §9'; **11**, §1; **21**, §27'
Arsani, **1B**, §12'
Arusna, **20**, §37'
Ashtata, **20**, §§3', 5', 6', 7', 10', 11', 14'
Attarimma, **1A**, §12; **1B**, §§8', 10'; **4**, §1. *See also* Countries
Atriya, **4**, §4; **5**, §§4, 9'
Aura, **1B**, §§5', 14'
Awarna, **5**, §9'
Carchemish, **1B**, §§5', 9'; **15**, §1'
Dalauwa, **3**, §§13, 14, 15
Dasmaha, **1A**, §13'
Hallawa, **14**
Hapanuwa, **1B**, §§2', 12'
Hattusa, **1A**, §§18', 24', 25', 26', 27'; **1B**, §§1', 2', 3', 4', 9', 10'; **8**, §4'; **9**, §1'; **20**, §§9', 23', 24', 28', 31', 32', 48'; **22**, §5
Hinduwa, **3**, §§13, 14
Hupissana, **21**, §29'
Huwarsana, Hursana, **1A**, §12; **1B**, §§8', 10'
Impa, **1B**, §§2', 5', 12'
Ishupitta, **1A**, §15'; **22**, §§10, 17
Isgazzuwa, **22**, §30
Iskiya, **20**, §19'
Iyaganuena, **22**, §2
Iyalanda, Iyalanti, **4**, §§2, 4. *See also* Countries
Izziya, **26**, §4'
Kagapa, **20**, §50'
Kamamma, **22**, §§3, 21
Kar(a)kisa, **1B**, §11'; **3**, §35'
Kummanni, **26**, §5'
Kussuriya, **14**
Kutappa, **21**, §28'
Kuwalana, **20**, §32'
Kuzastarina, **1B**, §4'
Lipa, **1A**, §25'
Lisepra, **22**, §14
Maharmahaya, **3**, §33'
Marassantiya, **20**, §19'
Millawanda, Milawata **1B**, §1'; **4**, §§4, 5, 12; **6**, §4'. *See also* Countries
Palhuissa, **1A**, §§15', 16'; **1B**, §4'
Peshura, **1A**, §15'
Piggaya, **3**, §36'
Pina, **5**, §9'
Pitassa. *See* Countries
Puranda, **1A**, §§18', 20', 21', 22', 24'; **1B**,

4. Countries, Districts, Peoples (Hatti not included)

Zumanti, **3**, §24'
Zumarri, **3**, §§24', 29'

5. Mountains

Arinnanda, **1A**, §§18', 19'; **1B**, §§8', 9', 10'
Hariyati, **3**, §4
Lawasa, **1A**, §17'
Lebanon, **2**, §20'
Pisaisa, **2**, §20'
Sarissiya, **2**, §20'
Zippasla, **3**, §§4, 5, 8

6. Rivers

Astarpa, **1A**, §§17', 19'; **1B**, §10'
Seha, **1A**, §§26', 27'**;** **1B**, §§11', 14'; **11**, §1
Sehriya, **1B**, §5'; **2**, §7
Siyanta**,** **3**, §§21', 22'

7. Texts Translated

KBo 2.11, **8**
KBo 3.4, **1A**
KBo 12.37, **1B**
KBo 16.1, **1A**
KBo 16.2, **1A**
KBo 16.5, **1B**
KBo 16.22, **14**
KBo 16.97, **22**
KBo 16.104, **1B**
KBo 18.135, **25**
KBo 18.181, **19**
KBo 19.38, **3**
KBo 19.79, **7**
KBo 19.83, **16**
KBo 40.48, **22**
KBo 44.2, **1A**
KBo 44.239, **1A**
KBo 48.22, **24**
KBo 50.123, **20**
KBo 53.103, **20**

KUB 5.6, **20**
KUB 6.7, **23**
KUB 8.82, **2**
KUB 14.1, **3**
KUB 14.2, **12**
KUB 14.3, **4**
KUB 14.15, **1B**
KUB 14.16, **1B**
KUB 14.21, **1A**
KUB 18.54, **20**
KUB 18.58, **23**
KUB 19.5, **7**
KUB 19.38, **1A**
KUB 19.40, **1B**
KUB 19.55, **5**
KUB 21.34, **13**
KUB 22.56, **21**
KUB 23.1, **2**
KUB 23.13, **11**
KUB 23.37, **2**
KUB 23.95, **9**
KUB 23.98, **10**
KUB 23.125, **1A**
KUB 26.76, **15**
KUB 26.91, **6**
KUB 31.29, **18**
KUB 31.30, **17**

Lightning Source UK Ltd.
Milton Keynes UK
UKOW04f1856070216

267905UK00001B/175/P

9 781589 83268